# The Best of
# ROUND THE HORNE

# The Best of
# ROUND THE HORNE

Barry Took with Mat Coward

# B◻XTREE

First published 2000 by Boxtree
an imprint of Macmillan Publishers Ltd
25 Eccleston Place, London SW1W 9NF
Basingstoke and Oxford

www.macmillan.co.uk

Associated companies throughout the world

ISBN 0 7522 1809 3

1 3 5 7 9 8 6 4 2

A CIP catalogue record for this book is available from
the British Library.

Typeset by SX Composing DTP, Rayleigh, Essex
Printed in Great Britain by Mackays of Chatham plc, Chatham, Kent

# CONTENTS

# FOREWORD

It's amazing for me to think, looking back, that on a cold November day in 1964 when Marty Feldman and I were asked by the BBC to write a series for Kenneth Horne and Co to replace *Beyond Our Ken*, we refused. We had other irons in the fire at that time and it seemed at first like a poisoned chalice. After all, *Beyond Our Ken* (which I had co-written for the first forty-one episodes with Eric Merriman) was a success, and we thought that it was possible that we would be unable to match it in style or popularity.

With all the benefits that hindsight grants it is preposterous to compare the two Kenneth Horne series. *Beyond Our Ken* was funny enough and had successful running characters, the various writers involved had come up with good material and many of the outrageous puns are remembered with affection today. *Round the Horne* however, as this collection of scripts shows, had infinitely more going for it and, dare I say, a philosophy.

It was topical, of course. It was not designed for long life nor was a long shelf life expected of it. Marty and I wrote it for the week it was to be broadcast, conscious that only a delayed repeat, the following week, could be relied upon. My memory might be at fault but I seem to recall that the original script fee plus the extra repeat fees brought us in a total of £250–£300 per episode, which we shared. Not to be sneezed at but not earth shattering, as our joint fees were much greater for television.

So, offered the job, we politely declined and, as I have described elsewhere, went back from our meeting with the BBC Light Entertainment people and over lunch in my London flat talked ourselves into doing it.

At the time I was thirty-six years old and Marty was thirty-one. We'd had a fair bit of success already in our four years of writing as a team and we were, without being conscious of it, at or nearing our writing peak. I remember that lunch vividly. Marty was a vegetarian and my wife, Lyn, thoughtfully prepared dishes he could eat. Over the tomato soup, cheese omelettes and salad we started inventing characters and sketches until by about 2.30 p.m. we'd put together what clearly could be a workable script.

One idea I remember concerned the private lives of the great and good and we took David Attenborough, even in the mid-1960s a prominent and popular broadcaster, as our model. In the sketch Mrs. Attenborough described the things David brought back from his travels: a tribe of pygmies living in the airing cupboard, Eskimos in the deep freeze, and so on. Some years later I showed the sketch to Jane and David Attenborough, who by then had become good friends. They didn't find it at all funny.

Armed with our lunchtime quota of ideas we went back to the BBC and after some discussion agreed to write six episodes 'to see how it went' and, if it 'went' well, would write the remainder of the proposed series: sixteen programmes.

The new Horne series at that time – late 1964 – was tentatively called *It's Ken Again*. We duly wrote a script, had a read through with the cast and plunged into the rewrites required for the first of the new series, which I had persuaded all concerned to call *Round the Horne*.

The philosophy of *Round the Horne* was a simple one. It was based on the belief that the listener was a sensible person with a mind of his or her own, who understood a great deal about the world and its workings, human behaviour good and bad, and had a desire to be entertained on an intelligent level.

As writers, Marty Feldman and I had always tried to write down-market material in an up-market way; that is to say, earthy but full of insight. We didn't write jokes as much as comments on human aspirations (viz: Gruntfuttock's grandiose dreams against the reality of his inability to realize them). We never shied away from vulgarity, feeling that most people have a streak of vulgarity in them that has as much validity as intellect, and people bright enough to know this loved what we wrote. They didn't need to do the 'working out in the margin' of what we tried to do but understood, perhaps unconsciously, what we were on about.

Marty and I talked endlessly about life, art, humour, passion, and the nature of existence. We absorbed what the '60s had to offer and coughed it up in thirty-minute segments: the episodes of *Round the Horne*. Our friendship lasted from the time we met in 1955 until Marty's death in 1982. For ten years we wrote radio, television and movie scripts at an astonishing rate. Marty bored easily; I became impatient. These two elements combined to make us write literally as fast as we thought.

In my mind and in subsequent discussions, I saw Kenneth Horne as the maypole around which the fantastic creations woven by the script for the brilliant cast would dance. The maypole idea did in fact give us a shape and purpose to aim for. It becomes apparent as you read the scripts that although Kenneth Horne is, theoretically, overwhelmed by the rest of the cast he is central to everything that happens from first to last. Naturally, many other ideas, theories and brainwaves came under discussion, but we never lost sight of that majestic figure of Kenneth Horne as master of the revels. His natural authority made this possible and the esteem and affection in which he was held by cast, singers, musicians, writers and production team, made the whole thing throb with life. The affection was mutual, by the way, as Horne had a wonderful knack of liking (almost) everybody, and if they had a sense of humour they would become friends, for life.

Any successful show must be peopled by individuals with special talent but who can blend selflessly into the group. That was certainly the case with *Round the Horne* and largely accounts for its success at the time of the original recordings and its cult status subsequently.

Let me give you an example of its staying power and quote from a letter sent to me in May 1999 from Mr. Clive Neil Robinson of Sheerness:

> It must have been about six years ago I bought my first 'RTH' tape, I suppose the reason I had not bought one previously was I thought it might come across very dated like listening to 'ITMA'. I have always been interested in comedy, being 37 years old I just missed out on being the right sort of age to have heard it first time. Kenneth Williams was always one of my 'fave' performers, and I became intrigued about 'RTH' after reading his diaries.
>
> So after I had listened to the first cassette I was bowled over by not only the consistently high quality of the material but by the premier cast. The only thing I knew about Hugh was that he was in a children's programme 'Pardon My Genie' when I was young, that Betty had done film work, Bill was the air raid warden (why did he get so little to do apart from Seamus?), and I vaguely knew that Kenneth Horne had been in 'Much Binding', and to my surprise BT and MF as writers, I had grown up with you as being 'Mr. Points of View'. The writing on 'RTH' is not just entendre, it's far more intelligent than that.
>
> I must have listened to these tapes so many times now but to know them is to love them and familiarity certainly brings no contempt, when Hugh says 'Oh look parky flooring, bona' or Kenneth W says 'Do you want me to lay on a turkey!' I just crease up. My favourite sketch to date is the one which starts with KH saying 'I'm an old Negro trumpeter, and I dare say it comes as a surprise to my wife!' – inspired!, then there's the recurring 'take that, take that, and that . . . oh no thanks I've already got one', which slays me every time.

Clive Robinson is not unique. I have had many letters over the years in similar vein, and these letters plus strong sales of the audio cassettes are the principal reasons for Boxtree publishing this collection of scripts. What is here is not the manicured version but the scripts 'warts and all' with the cuts that were made, for time or taste reasons, by the producer. John Simmonds, who produced all but one episode of *Round the Horne* (of which more later) had a keen eye for what was and what was not allowable and he shared our view that in the permissive atmosphere of the mid-1960s, taste – *BBC* taste – could be stretched to include hitherto taboo subjects and ideas. Thus Julian and Sandy were born and flourished and today people ask 'How did you get away with it?'

Read the scripts and wonder no more. When read the material is not even remotely filthy nor does it nudge and wink in the way that, for instance, the camp character in *Are You Being Served?* does. There the emphasis is on homosexual sex. With Julian and Sandy it's about a relationship as sound and as long-lasting as that of any heterosexual couple. The more interesting aspect of Julian and Sandy is their affectionate relationship with the absolutely straight Kenneth Horne. The introduction of Gordon as a bit of rough trade was a joke within a joke, as are the occasional moments when the dominant Sandy talks about the subordinate Julian's past misadventures. 'You traitor,' says Julian.

It was a facet of Marty Feldman's character that he became bored easily and in fact we both became rather tired of the inevitability of these popular characters and wrote them out of the script to be recorded on 6 February 1967. Producer and cast were outraged and, with a sigh of 'Oh well, as you like it,' we hurriedly wrote them back in and they stayed, firm favourites with listeners, until the very last programme.

When Marty left the show in 1967 I wrote the Julian and Sandy spots alone – with the exception of two episodes when, in a bit of a *quid pro quo*, I co-wrote with Marty something he was engaged in and in return he co-wrote the camp couple with me.

Rather than spell out all the changes and developments in this foreword we have used footnotes which, when read in conjunction with the scripts will, I hope, add explanation and historical detail, and enhance your enjoyment.

Good comedy is characterized by the energy of the performers. Victoria Wood, a slave to the notion of rhythm, brings enormous energy to her writing and when scripting for Julie Walters, Celia Imrie and others has the ideal tools to achieve her aims. Eddie Izzard, supremely laid back, is actually bursting with energy, much of it directed at giving the illusion that none is being expended.

With *Round the Horne* the energy of Kenneth Williams is apparent as is that of Betty Marsden in many of her characters, and Bill Pertwee in his. Hugh Paddick, on the other hand, used his energy in more subtle ways, discreetly helping his companions to a total greater than the sum of its parts. As Julian, as ageing juvenile 'Binkie' Huckaback, he brings reality to what otherwise could be farce and the humour gains from his reading of the part.

One of Bill Pertwee's skills was being able to impersonate well-known comedians and actors, so that he could give colour and style to even a small role. His contribution was not as large as that of others but was extremely valuable. When he was dropped (for reasons of economy and not ability) in the last series he was missed rather in a way that the loss of a front tooth is not catastrophic but it radically changes the appearance of the smile. His Seamus Android (based on a popular Irish entertainer of the day, Eamonn Andrews) was a joy and, once established, was a useful addition to the 'regulars' in the show.

Betty Marsden gave everything she did drive and style. She understood perfectly what was required and brought intelligence and feeling to the various roles we saddled her with. As J. Peasmold Gruntfuttock's consort, Buttercup, she was totally vulgar; as Trilby in a parody of the Victorian novel of that name she was as demure a heroine as one could have wished for. Whatever we gave her she tackled full out, an ability which gladdens the heart of any scriptwriter.

Married to a successful anaesthetist and living in style in a large house in Hampstead, and later, when widowed, in a canal barge moored on the Thames, she brought originality and flair to both her private and professional life. She died, in July 1998, while drinking and laughing with friends – an end which, had she contemplated it, she would have relished.

So much has been written and spoken about Kenneth Williams that I'm hard put to know what to say about him. That he was a comic genius there is no doubt. But he was also an intellectual, or rather he saw himself as an intellectual, and was certainly literate, well-read and intelligent. He could write elegantly, as his books of anecdotes show, and he contributed regularly to *Radio Times* and *Punch*. The volume of his collected correspondence makes fascinating reading, and the annotated diaries reveal a rather vain, irascible man living through deep and often devastating traumas about his work, his sexuality and his life.

As an actor his range was tremendous: Shakespeare, Shaw, Anouilh, the *Carry On* films, *Jackanory*, *Will o' the Wisp* (a charming animated series in which Kenneth played all the parts of the strange creatures who inhabited a mysterious wood), *Just a Minute* where his simulated rages reached epic proportions, *Hancock's Half Hour*, *International Cabaret*, *Round the Horne*; he gave each one something special. It was a delight to write for him, and although we never became soul mates I cherish the memory of our friendship, which was long-standing and based on mutual respect.

He had one ritual to psych himself up for the recording. He had used it on *Beyond Our Ken*, and here, to my surprise, four years later he was doing it on *Round the Horne*. It consisted of telling four jokes in a set order, all rather rude and, to be frank, not terribly funny except one, which he delivered in the voices of an old man and a supercilious doctor. I found it extremely funny and in fact often include it in my after-dinner speeches. It goes as follows:

> An old man goes to the doctor. He says, 'Doctor, I was having a pee and my dick came off in my hand. But I didn't throw it away, I put

it in my tobacco pouch and brought it round to see if you could sew it back on.' So, the doctor takes the tobacco pouch, looks into it and says, 'This isn't a penis. This is two ounces of Old Holborn Ready Rubbed Shag.' The old man says, 'Oh, Gawd! I've smoked my cock.'

Having heard Williams deliver that joke (the others aren't worth repeating) a hundred times it's sort of stuck with me and I cannot forget it, even if I want to. The joy of it was, of course, hearing Kenneth Williams' inimitable delivery.

It goes without saying that a successful comedy show is more than a bunch of actors standing round a microphone cracking jokes, although that could describe many *un*successful shows. The making of a good radio or television show is like completing a jigsaw puzzle. If all the pieces fit the picture emerges, and all those bits of sky turn out to be valuable too.

Let's look at what is required.

Well, first, the script. It should be literate, sayable – a crucial point, and it's a fact that many scripts which read amusingly don't stand up to scrutiny when the lines are spoken aloud.

The cast must have between them a wide range of voices. This is particularly important in a radio comedy such as *The Goon Show* or *Hancock's Half Hour*, *I'm Sorry I'll Read That Again* or *The Hitchhiker's Guide to the Galaxy*.

*Hancock's Half Hour* is a particularly good example of 'voice casting'. Hancock always the same, Sid James likewise but a voice of a totally different timbre and a style of performance quite different from Hancock. Bill Kerr Australian, Kenneth Williams endlessly versatile. The combination was dynamite. With *Round the Horne* it was similar, although more versatility was required from the supporting cast. Horne, the centre of gravity as it were, never attempted nor was asked to be anyone but himself, and Douglas Smith the announcer, although given extremely silly things to do, was always at bottom the urbane BBC announcer.

Let us suppose, then, that script and cast are good and fit easily together. What now needs to be added? In a dramatic formula there is a need for sound effects. These give the audience the information they need to know where and when things are happening. It is not necessary for an actor to say, 'My word, it's cold out here in central Russia.' The sound of blustery wind and the distant howl of a wolf sets the scene well and if dialogue is added to that – e.g. 'It's getting colder, General Bonaparte, and Moscow is still a hundred miles away' – you know the date and the situation. Sound effects (printed F/X) help dialogue and must be indicated in the script.

Music is also important for creating a mood or acting as punctuation. If there is singing in the show then accompaniment for the singer is necessary and the band thus employed can be called up for those music links that are required. Taped music or CDs can also be used, but ideally a mixture of standard recordings and original music from a studio-based orchestra is the best option.

Today, budget restrictions make these costly extras almost unusable and I think it is a shame that what helped to make the *Goons*, *Round the Horne*, and *I'm Sorry I'll Read That Again* so eminently listenable, many years after the original recordings, is not available to contemporary comedy series.

The mixture, then, should be a variety of sounds both vocal and musical, and above all it should be designed to give pleasure to the listener.

In *Round the Horne* all these elements were in place but at first, as with most new things, the result was not always perfect. The early scripts are too long and the necessary cuts made the humour on the remaining pages somewhat uneven. The cast too was not entirely happy with what they were given to say, or sure of their new characters, but these faults were noted and fixed. By programme four or five in the first series most of the dross had gone and for the next forty-plus programmes there was little to complain about. (Except the *double entendres*, of course!)

Having mentioned the *double entendres*, let me say here for the first time in print, and with my hand on my heart, that Marty and I were not aware of everything into which the audience read a double meaning. Let me give one example. The script which caused most offence contained a monologue delivered by Kenneth Horne. It was in a programme in the first series and was broadcast at Easter 1965. Reading it here in this book will give you the opportunity to become a 'do it yourself' censor. What would you cut?

I guess the offence in this story of the man who invented the crumpet lies in describing him as a 'master baker', which could have been misheard as 'masturbator'. That was *not* our intention. The other possible offence came in saying that he 'designed a triangular crumpet for the YWCA'. That does sound rude but again I must plead 'not guilty' as we had written YMCA, whose logo was, and for all I know still is, triangular – or at least has a triangle incorporated in it. The masculine to feminine gender was changed during rehearsal. The rest of the item is fairly innocuous, mildly vulgar but quite amusing. The crumpet appeared in the one show that John Simmonds did not produce. Had he been at the helm he would most likely have cut the offending words. But he was ill and his sub didn't like to tamper with a script which was not really his concern.

There is no doubt that if you are seeking *double entendres* almost anything can be made to fit the bill. More interesting than smut, however, is the number of literary references that crop up in the scripts. Not only the full-blown parodies, such as our version of *The Picture of Dorian Gray*, but incidentally. 'The story so far' is a literary device; 'the answers to last week's questions' is another, and as you will read, the scripts are dotted with other references that give *Round the Horne* its special quality.

I've written about Kenneth Williams' foibles, but what of Kenneth Horne's? One remains in my mind. Horne would never admit to knowing of the game Monopoly. As far as he was concerned, it did not exist and I wondered why, until it occurred to me that at one time he had been a director of Chad Valley Toys, a fierce rival to the manufacturer of Monopoly, Waddingtons.

Probably the most emotional person connected with *Round the Horne* was the producer, John Simmonds. Generally speaking it was hidden under a dour exterior but it showed clearly in his occasional moods of 'Black Dog', a phrase coined by Winston Churchill to describe deep depression. In these moods Simmonds could find nothing amusing in the script he was reading and would phone to say, 'Sorry, boys, this week it isn't funny.' Now, deep down most scriptwriters believe that nothing they write is funny but that luck has caused people to laugh at the writing. Our first reaction to John Simmonds on one of his Black Dog days was to rush to our copy of the script and re-read it, dreading to find that, no, it *wasn't* funny.

On one occasion, we read and were puzzled. Not only was it no less funny than the previous week's effort but in places, in our judgement, it was funnier. We phoned John back and asked him what specifically he found 'unfunny'. His reply was that he found none of it funny and particularly the sketch about the two elderly Shakespearean actors who had turned up to do Kenneth Horne's housework. 'They're so sad,' said Simmonds. 'Can't you make them chorus boys?' So we did. We rewrote the sketch and the people who arrived to do Horne's housework *were* chorus boys. And so, gentle reader, Julian and Sandy were born.

Generally, it must be said, we thought out our characters fairly thoroughly before we wrote them into a script. The exception was J. Peasmold Gruntfuttock who kept popping up in our minds and so into the scripts in various guises. Gruntfuttock was Marty's favourite character and years later, when he was in Hollywood, he'd write to me signing himself Gruntfuttock. I suppose he was to Marty what Eccles became to Spike Milligan – a sort of *alter ego*. My own favourites were Dame Celia Molestrangler and ageing juvenile Binkie Huckaback. I loved writing the Coward-esque pastiches and I revelled in the wonderful performances of Hugh Paddick and Betty Marsden, their timing immaculate and the togetherness they engendered in the characters quite remarkable in such an otherwise noisy and robust show. But then, noisy shows need quiet moments.

In the early days of *Round the Horne*, audience research documents show a very divided audience, with many complaints about the noise from a 'studio claque'. Actually, the only reason they laughed was because they were relieved that their adored performers were back in action and, give or take a no-no, the things they were asked to say were funny. With the coming of the 'set piece' characters, Julian and Sandy, Rambling Syd Rumpo, Charles and Fiona, Chou En Ginsberg and the rest, all was well and the audience both in the studio and at home were delighted.

Here are some audience reactions to the first and second programmes to be aired, according to the Audience Research Department, 23 March 1965. One listener commented:

> I felt the tone of the whole show was vulgar and in trying to be with-it, it lost something of the pleasantly ironic effect that Kenneth Horne usually has without achieving any satirical purpose.

And, says the report,

> A large minority who were not so unfavourably disposed, complained that the 'moronic behaviour' of the audience was so annoying and distracting that it came near to ruining the show for them: the 'guffaws', immoderate laughter and near pandemonium killed some of the jokes stone dead for the listener and made it seem worse than it was.

And,

> A small group objected to the 'crudity' of the show and the suggestiveness put into the words by the artists' intonations: 'if this was not meant to be smut, the cast grossly misinterpreted the script.'

On the other hand, many felt

> It was a slick, fast-moving show that appealed to the whole family ('from great-grandad to the children').

And the report sums up the audience reaction by saying:

> Many were delighted to have Kenneth Horne back ('so suave and urbane with a wink in his voice') with the same team who appeared to work together so harmoniously and with such enthusiasm as if they were enjoying the show as much as the audience.

Which was indeed the case.

As you can see by those remarks, we hadn't hit our stride yet, but we changed things, rewrote, invented new characters and dropped what clearly was not working, and time and confidence that we were on the right lines paid dividends.

The BBC hierarchy were divided in their reaction to the programme. Some of the more stuffy thought it was in deplorable taste and not the sort of thing that the BBC should be disseminating. Others saw its merits and its appeal to a younger audience. That, curiously, is what has kept *Round the Horne* alive for all these years. It is constantly being discovered by a new generation. Because its themes are universal its appeal is universal and it thrives because what it has to say chimes with what people feel needs to be said.

Where *The Goon Show* and *I'm Sorry I'll Read That Again* appealed to the anarchist in us, *Round the Horne* appealed to the reasonable, rational side of our temperament with humour that was basically good-natured but not afraid to offend. More than anything, *Round the Horne* laughed at itself and mocked its own inadequacies.

In one sketch, the rear end of a pantomime horse has been blown through the roof.

HORNE: This looks like the work of a maniac.

PERTWEE: What does?

HORNE: This script.

Then there are the Kenneth Williams 'Nobody loves me' or 'I'm not being serviced' outbursts – all, as you will read, carefully scripted.

But, that said, it was a joy to be part of the team that created *Round the Horne*. I was involved with the show at a time of my life when I was very happy and I think that some of that happiness overflowed into the scripts.

At the start of a new century, a new millennium, it's interesting to look back at the twentieth century and think of the good things it produced. Radio was certainly one of them, and through many fine programmes it left an indelible mark on culture of the time. I am proud that I was there, then, with *Round the Horne*.

BARRY TOOK
July 1999

Editor's note: text cut from the original scripts, which was not recorded, is shown between square brackets.

# SERIES 1
# PROGRAMME 1

*FIRST BROADCAST* – Sunday 7 March 1965

## INTRODUCTION

Much of the now familiar comic style of the show that early versions of the script still call *It's Ken Again!* is already in place in this first episode. The opening joke – 'a recital of old Japanese folk songs given by some old Japanese folk' – has an unmistakably Hornean flavour (though in fact it was cut from the show, presumably for reasons of space).

None of the major recurring characters have yet arrived, unless you count Spasm and his reminiscing mistress, but we do have the spoofs, the absurd names, 'the story so far', numerous catchphrases, Williams' complaints and 'improvisations', and 'the answers to last week's quiz'.

Some of Took and Feldman's obsessions are also on view, as in the reference to Edgar Allan Poe, one of their favourite writers, and a slightly tasteless joke about the comedian Jimmy Clitheroe, who was a midget. Barry and Marty seem to have had it in a bit for poor old Jimmy, perhaps seeing his long-running and hugely popular radio sitcom, *The Clitheroe Kid* (1958–72), as the kind of dated, 'ee-bah-gum' comedy to which they represented a younger, hipper alternative. (A couple of decades later, comedians of the Comic Strip generation felt much the same way about *Terry and June*.)

It's obvious from the start that this is a very different kind of show to its more traditional predecessor *Beyond Our Ken* which, while funny enough in its way and in its time, lacked the élan, the ambition, and the sheer inventiveness of even this first, comparatively unsophisticated *RTH* script.

BILL: (Announcer voice) Here are details of some of tonight's programmes. [Later this evening there will be a recital of old Japanese folk songs given by some old Japanese folk.]

BETTY: At 8.25 a navvy will be talking about 'Top of the Picks'.

HUGH: Immediately following this, the BBC extends an invitation to *Come Dancing* with Lord Boothby[1]. Er – I'm sorry – I'll read that again. With Lord Boothby in the studio tonight will be a panel consisting of Richard Burton, Wilfred Lawson and Jimmy Edwards[2] in this week's edition of *Does the Team Drink*.

KEN W: And finally, for those of you interested in Flower Arrangement, A.G. Street will be reading an extract from *Lady Chatterley's Lover*[3].

DOUGLAS: But meanwhile, for those of you who are more easily pleased – it's *Round the Horne*.

*Orchestra: Music up and then under announcement . . .*

DOUGLAS: As this is the first programme of a new series – here is the story so far. In the last episode, as you may remember, we left winsome, curvaceous Kenneth Williams held captive in Lisle Street by the mysterious Chinese gynaecologist, Hugh Paddick, and his sinister bodyguard, gnarled, grizzled Betty Marsden. Inch by inch the ceiling is descending while a drink-crazed crocodile, played by the Fraser Hayes

Four in a skin, snaps at a rope which holds him suspended above a vat of tepid chicken fat (played by Bill Pertwee).

*(Clears throat and starts to read)* 'Suddenly the door creaked open and silhouetted in the doorway stood a ghastly apparition; a nightmare creature of hideous aspect. It shuffled forward and spoke . . .'

KENNETH: My name is Kenneth Horne.

*Orchestra: Music*

KENNETH: Hello and welcome to *Round the Horne*.

*(Applause)*

You have just been listening to *An evening with Douglas Smith*. Now, as this is the first programme, you won't have heard last week's. The script, as you may have gathered, is by Edgar Allen Poe, who, as you know, wrote such masterpieces of horror as *The Tell-Tale Heart*, *The Pit and the Pendulum* and *Compact*[4]. [There will, of course, be other changes, for one thing,] We shall not hesitate to make outspoken political comment.

BILL: (Shouts) Disraeli had warts!

HUGH: (Shouts) Gladstone wears a wig!

KEN W: (Shouts) Bonar Law's got hairy ears!

KENNETH: Yes. That's just a taste of what's in store. [We shan't pull our punches on this show. We shall not be

---

1. A Conservative politician and noted orator.
2. Respectively, two actors and a comedian, noted for their alcohol intake. *Does the Team Think* was a radio panel game.
3. The 1928 novel by D.H. Lawrence was banned as obscene in the UK, until a famous trial in 1960. A.G. Street was a radio pundit.
4. A bi-weekly BBC TV soap, running from 1962–5, concerned with a women's magazine. Not, in point of fact, written by Mr Poe.

afraid of topical satire. If necessary we shall name names.

HUGH: *(Shouts)* Yeti Rosenkrantz.

BETTY: *(Shouts)* The Reverend Willis Peasemold!

KEN W: *(Shouts)* Prinny Cattermole and Doctor Jacques Von Armpit!

KENNETH: These are just four of the names we shall name.] None shall escape the lash of our scorn. We shall not be afraid to tell you the truth, even if it concerns the highest in the land . . .

KEN W: *(Shouts)* Princess Margaret is married to Antony Armstrong-Jones[5].

HUGH: I say – steady.

[BETTY: *(Shouts)* Mrs. Harold Wilson is living with a man at number Ten Downing Street.]

BILL: *(Shouts)* Obadiah Silt travels on the tube without paying his fare!

KENNETH: Really? How do you know?

BILL: I'm Obadiah Silt.

KENNETH: Truth with honour, that's our policy.

KEN W: – Yes, and a bit of smut.

KENNETH: Now, how does a show like this come into being? That is a question I'm frequently asked. Well, perhaps not frequently, I should have said <u>never</u>. And so, in response to listeners' intense apathy from time to time we are going to present a feature on 'The Backroom Boys of the BBC'. To those chaps who spend all their time in a small backroom in Broadcasting House, we'd like to say . . .

KEN W: Hurry up in there. There's

other people want to use it.

KENNETH: Down, Williams! Heel boy! Amazing – I swear he understands every word I say. Now of all the people [behind the scenes] who make a show like ours impossible, no group is more important than the Programme Planners. [That august body of elder statesmen whose acute grasp of up-to-the-minute public taste determines the BBC's output.] Let us eavesdrop now on one of their meetings as they voice their opinions on the sort of thing that you, the public, want to hear . . .

KEN W: *(Old old man) (Angrily)* Filth! Tripe! Unsavoury muck!

[BETTY: *(Char)* Well, it's fresh from the canteen, Sir Arnold.

HUGH: Call these poached eggs, woman?

BETTY: No, Sir Clive – it's tea.

KEN W: Oh well, it's wet and warm. *(Tasting sounds)* Well, it's wet . . . are you sure it's not poached eggs?

BILL: *(Chairman)* Elevenses can wait, gentlemen. We have vital issues to consider at this meeting. *(Raps on table)*] Gentlemen – we are facing a crisis. We in radio must win back the audiences that we lost to the talkies.

CAST: *(Ad lib)* They'll never catch on! Talking pictures are a nine-days wonder –

HUGH: It's just a flash in the pan . . .

[KEN W: I still think it's poached eggs.]

BILL: Let us face facts, gentlemen. We must cut down on expenses. Economize. As you know, we've already made a start. *Five to Ten* has been cut down. It's now going to be

---

5. The two were indeed married, in 1960 – and divorced in 1978.

*Two and a Half Minutes to Ten* – and to cut expenses even further, we're using an unfrocked vicar. Sir Clive, what measures have you taken in Light Entertainment?

HUGH: Well, we've cut the budget of *Movie-Go-Round* by fifty per-cent. It's now going to be called *Movie Go Halfway Round* – [and to save even more money, we're only broadcasting excerpts from silent pictures. Then there's *Grand Hotel*, with Reginald Leopold and the Palm Court Orchestra. In future, this will be a live broadcast from the saloon bar of the Dog and Duck. And we're hoping against hope that there'll be someone in there who can play the piano. How about the Discussion and Quiz Programmes, Sir Arnold?

KEN W: We've considerably reduced the running costs of *Round Britain Quiz*. It's now *Round Balls Pond Road*.]

BILL: Very good, very good. What about Children's Programmes? [Can't we make some slashes there? After all, the little perishers don't pay for their licences, do they?]

KEN W: We've taken off most of the children's programmes. In fact we made a small profit when we demolished Toytown. We sold Larry the Lamb at three and six a pound . . . And Peter Brough[6]'s been very helpful. You remember that dummy he had – that lovable little wooden rascal . . . what was his name? Eamonn Andrews. Yes, well he's been chopped up and Mr. Brough's hawking him around as matches. [And not only that, but we've managed to sell his clothes to Jimmy Clitheroe.]

BILL: Capital, capital. I have one or two other schemes for cutting corners. We could telescope some of the shows together. [The Dales[7] can move in with the Archers. Walter Gabriel can help out in the garage, while in return Mrs. Dale can take her turn mucking out the pigsty. Other suggestions for combining shows are] *Have a Go While You Work. Lift Up Your Housewives Choice* – [and *Two Way French*[8] *for Six Form Favourites at Bedtime.*

HUGH: That brings us to Kenneth Horne.

KEN W: An expensive show – big cast – orchestra – vocal group – can't we put Kenneth Williams on short time – can't Betty Marsden take in washing? Goodness me – they ought to help out a little.

HUGH: P'raps Hugh Paddick – or whatever he calls himself nowadays – p'raps he could do a turn as Commissionaire? And Bill Pertwee – can't we get him on something constructive – making artificial flowers or something?

BILL: And Kenneth Horne himself – goodness me – a man of his age. He's old enough to work for his keep. Can't we cut their salaries?

HUGH: We could, if we paid them. No. There's only one thing we can do – we can save on the script.

KEN W: How?

HUGH: Pay the scriptwriters so much a laugh – and then – get rotten writers in.

---

6. A radio ventriloquist. His dummy was called Archie Andrews.
7. *Mrs Dale's Diary* was a long-running radio serial.
8. This gag, conflating the titles of a number of radio series for suggestive effect, was cut – and if Barry says he doesn't know why, he's lying!

CAST: *(Ad lib)* Brilliant! Wonderful! Marvellous!]

BILL: Well, all these economy measures should save the BBC a lot of money. [We have our duty, gentlemen – we are a public trust – and by making these economies unselfishly and ruthlessly,] We may soon be able to put into effect the plan that I know is nearest to all our hearts – we can vote ourselves a substantial increase in our salaries.

CAST: *(Ad lib)* Hear, hear, etc.

*Orchestra: Brief music link*

[KENNETH: And so was born *Round the Horne*. And for this, I'd like to say a heartfelt thank you to the Programme Planners who unfortunately cannot be with us today as they are still on their yachts in Bermuda.

*Orchestra: Intro (à la Webster Booth)*

DOUGLAS: *(Over intro)* And now – the *Kenneth Horne Song Book* – the haunting voice of Kenneth Horne – as opposed to his singing voice.

*Music up, with Kenneth Horne singing*

*(Applause)*

KENNETH: According to the experts, ballads are on the way back – but another very popular type of number is the 'odd noise' type; you know, like 'Right Said Fred'[9]. Both these facets are combined in my first song in this series, which I call 'As you wander down love's highway how about it', and in this I'm backed by my group the Here-to-Fours.

*Kenneth & Orchestra: Song*

*Verse:*
Love is a wonderful thing so they say
It's thrilling all men will agree
When into one's life comes the girl of one's dream
And that's jus' what's happened to me.

*Chorus:*
Every time I see Edna La Planche
I go . . . (tacit)

HUGH: *(Bell)*

BETTY: *(Shriek)*

BILL: *(Cork)*

KEN W: *(Calico)*

When we're together she gives me carte blanche
With her . . .

HUGH: *(Bell)*

BETTY: *(Shriek)*

BILL: *(Cork)*

KEN W: *(Calico)*

Her cooking's superb, you should sample her sole
And I can't keep my hands off her toad in the hole
I eat it for breakfast and dinner and lanche
Then go . . .

HUGH: *(Bell)*

BETTY: *(Shriek)*

BILL: *(Cork)*

KEN W: *(Calico)*

*(Applause)]*

*Orchestra: Timp Roll*

DOUGLAS: *(Over roll)* Now we come to the section of the show we call 'Trends'.

---

9. A 1962 chart hit for comedian Bernard Cribbins.

*Orchestra: Music up into brief theme music – fading behind*

KENNETH: It's a feature specially for the younger crowd – the jet set, the trendy, with-it pace-setters, the few who are switched on, as opposed to many who by now will have switched off.

KEN W: *(Shouts)* Bonar Law's got hairy ears!

KENNETH: Oh dear. Give him something to say and he milks it to death!

[KEN W: And droopy lobes. His lobes droop.

KENNETH: Don't improvise, Williams.]

KEN W: And a mole on his hip, shaped like an artichoke!

KENNETH: Stop it, Williams!

[KEN W: *(Screams)* I'm an iconoclast. Whatever that means. I will be heard. Like a globe artichoke, I tell you.

*Pause*

KENNETH: Have you finished?

KEN W: Yes.

HUGH: *(Mutters)* Gladstone wears a wig.

KENNETH: Now you've started him off.] Now where was I? What new trends are there on the fashion scene?

BETTY: Bosoms are back!

KENNETH: I'm very pleased to hear it. Welcome back bosoms. It's good to have you around again.

BETTY: And waists are back where they belong.

KENNETH: Oh, and where's that?

BETTY: Round the knee. This year Jacques Fath[10] is very keen on plastic hip-length waders with cuban heels.

KEN W: *(Old man)* Well, if he's so keen on them, let him wear them hisself. You couldn't get me into a pair. They're downright <u>effinimate</u>.

KENNETH: Thank you, Norman Hartnell[11] – and good luck with your new series of *Doctor Who*.

BETTY: So – to re-cap. This year the new fashion trends are backs out, hips in, thighs out, knees up – and that's what it's all about.

CAST: *(Sing)* Oh Hokey Cokey! – etc. Knees bend, knees bend, Rah! Rah! Rah!

KENNETH: That was the Male Voice Choir of the Hellfire and Damnation Tabernacle of Aberystwyth.

Now on to Travel Trends – where are people going for their holidays this year? Well, if you want to get away from it all, and you want to put your feet up and relax – why not spend a couple of weeks in the Urals?

KEN W: Are you still there?

KENNETH: [It's a desolate region with nothing to comment it – quite frankly, it's not everyone's idea of a holiday, but you'll find plenty to amuse yourself with, if you're young, energetic and stark raving mad.]

Then there's a package holiday in Jugoslavia – a walking tour – it lasts five days, or three if you run.

[Nearer home, there's Holland. Now many people think that Holland is flat

---

10. A clothes designer.
11. Norman Hartnell was the Queen's dress designer; William Hartnell was the first actor to play the lead in *Doctor Who*.

and boring and dull, but personally I've always found that it is.]

But here's one that's becoming increasingly popular with English tourists. 'Three weeks in a Spanish Jail'.

But for the more adventurous, what about this novel way of getting to Moscow? 'Fly U.2[12] – the airline that gets you there, and gets you back eventually when they can find a spy to exchange you for'.

Oh, there's no end to the vista that opens before the modern traveller. [You'll see strange, exotic customs, and mingle with people whose way of life is very different from your own.] But always remember the three cardinal 'Don'ts' of foreign travel. Don't drive on the left, don't tip more than fifteen per cent, and finally – don't wash your feet in it.

DOUGLAS: Now, what's new in Art? This week at the Codpiece Gallery, there's an exhibition of Pop Art by an exciting new artist, Toulouse Rickett.

KENNETH: Mr. Rickett – I must say I was intrigued, not to mention appalled, by some of these paintings. This one, for instance – er – what is it?

KEN W: *(Petulant)* How can I define it? [You people, you're all the same. Come in here meddling and asking questions, poking your nose into what doesn't concern you, and stuffing my pockets with your bourgeois money.] It's a montage, if you must know, composed of *objets trouvés*.

KENNETH: I gathered that, but where exactly did you *trouvé* that particular *objet*?

KEN W: You mean this hinged wooden seat? Actually it comes from the Gents Wash and Brush Up in Paddington. I've created a collage using it as a centrepiece, against a background of motor bike parts, raspberry jam and a final demand for the rates. I call it 'Prelude to a down payment on a gas cooker'.

[KENNETH: Why?

KEN W: I've just paid a tenner for it.]

KENNETH: And these three pictures?

KEN W: Ah yes – my triptych, I knew you'd like these – they express the chaos of man's environment, his inability to communicate, and his eternal quest for the immutable and the unknowable – you can have it for three quid. I've been working in a new and exciting medium – fruit salts.

KENNETH: No thank you, I er . . .

KEN W: But there's thirty bob's worth of fruit salts there alone.

KENNETH: Yes, I realise that but . . .

KEN W: Fifteen bob, there, I can't say fairer than that can I? . . .

KENNETH: No, really, I just don't care for . . .

KEN W: My goodness me, you don't have to look at them. You can scrape the fruit salts off with a breadknife and use 'em. Tone you up they will . . . looks as though you need it. Make a new man of you. Five bob.

KENNETH: No.

KEN W: *(Whining)* Lend me sixpence for a cup of tea?

KENNETH: No.

---

12. An American U-2 spy plane, piloted by Gary Powers, was shot down over Soviet airspace in 1960.

*Small pause*

KEN W: Would you like to meet a nice girl? I know a . . .

KENNETH: No. I'm sorry.

KEN W: Fascist pig! Philistine! Capitalist hyena! Reactionary Imperialist! *(Shouts)* You've got a red nose! *(Shouts)* You're bald! Go home Yank! Oh. He's gone. *(Small pause)* Oh, it's so dispiriting. How can a sensitive artist like me survive in this money-grabbing world!

*Orchestra: Sting chord*

KENNETH: Recently I had the pleasure – quite recently – last Thursday it was, to meet the man [who actually wrote the song I sang earlier in the programme, and since it's our policy to encourage young, talented plagiarists,] I've invited him along tonight to talk about his work. Ladies and Gentlemen – Lemuel Ghast[13]. Mr. Ghast, I believe you've just completed yet another musical based on one of Charles Dickens' books.

HUGH: *(Lemuel) (East End lisp)* Yes, Mr. Horne, I've been working on it for some minutes now and it's almost complete. It's based on Dickens' well-loved classic *Sketches by Boz*. I'll just sing you a snatch of the theme song. *(Sings – to the tune of 'Out of Nowhere')* Sketches by Boz from out of nowhere.

KENNETH: Forgive my criticism, but that tune sounds rather familiar.

HUGH: Ah yes, but that is possibly because it is. All my tunes are. For instance, dig this. *(Sings – to the tune of 'God Save the Queen')* I'm Martin Chuzzlewit, old Martin Chuzzlewit, that's who I am – or let me lay this on you, baby. *(To the tune of 'Because')* Bleak House you come to me with naught save love – [And then I sat down and nicked *(Sings to tune of 'Baby Doll')* You called me Edwin Drood a year ago – yes, you did, yes you did.]

KENNETH: But you've used everybody else's tunes. Isn't that stealing?

HUGH: Aha – [you're a fly one, Mr. Horne. No, I prefer to say I've been influenced by some of the great composers.

KENNETH: But it's still plagiarism, isn't it?

HUGH: Yes,] but I prefer to say I've been influenced. But between ourselves, Dickens is on the wane. I mean, he's been done to death. I'm planning at the moment to do a musical on another book. *The Old Testament*. You may have read it.

KENNETH: No, but I saw the film.

HUGH: Tawdry and mundane to my mind in comparison with the masterpiece I'm planning. I've already approached Harry Secombe . . .

KENNETH: For what part?

HUGH: The twelve tribes of Israel. And wait till you see the act. [The sets we're going to use will be completely revolutionary.] The main piece represents the whole world. Sean Kenny[14] has promised to make it for us in six days.

[KENNETH: And the songs? I suppose they'll be in your own imitable style?

---

13. The name is a play on Lionel Bart, whose Dickensian musical *Oliver!* opened in London in 1960.
14. An innovative theatrical set designer.

HUGH: Of course. The climax of the musical comes when the Children of Israel cross the Red Sea – I'm – er getting real children by the way. I toyed with the idea of jockeys, but they come out more expensive – and then, of course, they have to be Hebrew jockeys – which of course entails beards and that class of thing. The result would be, I'm afraid, more like *Snow White and the Seven Dwarfs*, which would make a farce of the whole enterprise.]

KENNETH: [Yes, it often does.] But this song you were telling me about, the theme song.

HUGH: Oh yes, that. Well, it comes as they finally flee from Pharaoh and have their first taste of freedom, they sing, what will definitely be the hit of the show – *(Sings)* Everything's Coming Up Moses for you and for me!

*Orchestra: Music*

BETTY: So much for this week's edition of 'Trends'. [We hope you've enjoyed this session of off-beat, with-it trendsetters.] Next week we'll bring you some more fab people talking, gear people raving, drunk people mumbling and rude people gesturing. And so, goodbye to those of you who are with-it, and to those of you without it . . .

HUGH: Just send a stamped addressed envelope and we'll tell you where to get it.

*Orchestra: Music link*

*(Applause)*

[KENNETH: Is conversation killing the Art of Television? These days it seems that all we get on television is talk, talk, talk. Every time I switch on the set, there's somebody jabbering at somebody else – David Frost talking to Bernard Levin, Kenneth Wolstenholme talking to Danny Blanchflower, Richard Dimbleby talking to Robin Day, Muriel Young talking to Pussy Cat Willum. Frankly, it's all beyond me, especially Muriel Young talking to Pussy Cat Willum.

KEN W: *(Shouts)* Ollie Beak's got hairy ears!

KENNETH: Be that as it may, we thought that we would like to find out what sort of television programmes other countries have to put up with. This week, we're going to look at German television[15]. First – the facts!

BILL: 2.5 of the average German watches 8.5 hours television per week. What the other 7.5 of him does we haven't found out, nor do we care.

BETTY: You would if you were married to him. 7.5 of him coming reeling home at 3.6 o'clock in the morning reeking of beer.

BILL: There are two channels on German television, one of which is commercial, and one of which isn't.

KENNETH: These are some of the commercials that the average German watches on his television set –

*Orchestra: Commercial-type music*

BETTY: *(German accent)* We swam and picnicked together by a waterfall – and then we goose-stepped together through the Black Forest, then we tunnelled under the Berlin Wall, then we wrestled in mud together in the Reeperbahn, then he took me in his arms and to complete the pleasure he gave me a liverwurst.

---

15. This rather over-long sketch was cut, but most of it was used in series 1, programme 7, and is printed there. The section which follows was not re-used.

*Orchestra: Chord. Brass flare*

BILL: *(German accent) (Cheery)* Eat Schmidt's Sauerkraut, the sauerkraut with the less fattening centre. Run down to the corner shop and buy some now. *(Abrupt change of tone)* That is an order!

HUGH: *(German)* Drink a pinta schnappsa day.

*Orchestra: Chord*

KENNETH: Don't just say Braun – say Eva!

*Orchestra: Chord*

KEN W: You're never alone with a Frankfurter.

*Orchestra: Punctuating chord*

KENNETH: And now back to the studio for the second part of that gemütlich quiz show – Double Your Pfennigs!

*Orchestra: 'Deutschland über Alles' played in* Double Your Money *style on organ etc.]*

KENNETH: Here now to sing a number from their new LP – *Music to Clip Your Toenails By* – are the Fraser Hayes Four.

*Fraser Hayes & Orchestra: 'Stay with the Happy People'*

*(Applause)*

KENNETH: Thank you the Fraser Hayes Four, and get well soon.

[KEN W: *(Screams)* The Fraser Hayes Four have got eight hairy ears.]

DOUGLAS: Ladies and gentlemen, *The Clissold Saga.*

*F/X: Cracked old gramophone record: Surface noises under as Betty sings*

BETTY: *(Sings)*
I've fallen in love with love

For love is always new,
I fell in love with love, my love
When I fell in love with you . . .

*Hold under*

KENNETH: This week marks the ninetieth birthday of a grand old lady . . . Lady Beatrice Counterblast – known to generations of theatre lovers, cinema lovers, and in fact lovers of all kinds as Ben Clissold. Under that name she rose from humble beginnings to the dazzling heights of stardom in a career that spanned seventy-five years, and almost as many husbands. And so as a humble tribute to this very great star, we intend to present a radio biography. Last week I went down to Chattering Parva, her country home, where she lives in utter seclusion, served only by her faithful man-servant [and her gardener. I can't describe my feelings of excitement and awe as I walked up the drive towards the great house . . .]

*Fade and fade up . . .*

*F/X: Footsteps on gravel*

*Wind howling: Rook cawing.*

*Doorbell chimes. Rattle of chains and bolts & then:*

*Huge door creaks open.*

KENNETH: Good evening, my man.

KEN W: *(Spasm) (The manservant)* 'Oo be you? Be you man or be you ghastly manifestation?

KENNETH: I be Kenneth Horne – who be you?

KEN W: I be Spasm. Go back to London young master afore 'tis too late – this place be accursed. *(Small pause)* Have ee come to exorcise this mad nun of Chattering Parva?

KENNETH: No – I've come to interview Lady Counterblast. We're doing her life story on the BBC.

KEN W: They'd broadcast any filth these days.

KENNETH: We won't be doing anything like that.

KEN W: Well, there won't be much to say then. Through there.

KENNETH: Thank you.

KEN W: We all be doomed, etc.

*F/X: Footsteps on marble floor*

*F/X: Knock on door*

BETTY: Come in.

*F/X: Door opens*

BETTY: Who are you?

KENNETH: I'm Kenneth Horne. I've come to talk to you about doing your life story.

BETTY: Come and sit by me on the sofa dear boy and tell me what you want to know.

KENNETH: Well, according to your biographer, Hesketh Podmore, you've been married many times –

BETTY: Yes. Many times. Many, many times. Many, many, many, many *(Ad lib)*.

KENNETH: Tell me about your first husband – Lord Randolph, the Marquis of Tranby.

BETTY: Well, it was in the year 1891 that I first met him. [Ah, London in the Nineties.] The Old Cafe Royal, [plush, gilt, chandeliers. The cream of London's Vie Bohème] – Wilde, Whistler, Beardsley, the Incomparable Max –

[KENNETH: Yes, I remember him. Wonderful man *(Sings)* Why does everybody call me bighead?[16] *(Spoken)* A good idea, son. Yes.

BETTY: Max Beerbohm. Yes, they were all there. Oh, the elegance, the witty conversation, the gaiety of it all . . . imagine the effect it had on a young girl, up from the country for the first time . . .

KENNETH: I see – good *fin de siècle* – eh?]

*Orchestra: Music up*

*F/X: Cafe Society Atmosphere: Clink of glasses etc.*

KENNETH: *(Whistler)* Waiter?

BILL: *(Waiter)* Yes, Mr. Whistler?

KENNETH: Another absinthe frappé for me – oh, and a tumbler of neat gin for Mother here. She's been sitting for me all day.

BILL: Very good, sir.

BETTY: *(Very young: Approaching)* Excuse me – but aren't you James McNeill Whistler, the famous painter and celebrated wit whose epigrams scorch whoever they touch? [The great Dandy and Bohemian whose eccentricities are the talk of artistic circles?] Surely you must be he?

BILL: *(Gruff voice)* No dearie, I'm his mum. That's Jim there, with the monocle.

BETTY: Forgive me. [I'm overcome with embarrassment.] You see, I've only just arrived from the country. I wish to become an actress.

---

16. The first line of Max Bygraves' signature tune. He was, and remains, a very popular entertainer.

KENNETH: Then I must introduce you to Oscar Wilde. See, that's him over there – the big, fleshy man – looks like Peter Finch.[17] Oh Oscar –

HUGH: *(Wilde) (Coming on)* Ah, my dear Whistler – I've just been polishing up an epigram. Perhaps you'd like to hear it?

KENNETH: Not particularly.

HUGH: What's got four wheels and flies all round?

KENNETH: I don't know. What's got four wheels and flies all round?

HUGH: A corporation dustcart.

KENNETH: Capital! I shall dine out on that for a week.

HUGH: That shows the kind of places you eat at.

BETTY: *(Breaks into peals of laughter)*

HUGH: I'm very taken with this young lady here. What is she?

KENNETH: A pushover I should think.

BETTY: I'm an actress, sir. Could you perhaps find a part for me in one of your plays?

HUGH: This is a stroke of luck. Last night at the theatre, Mrs. Sibyl Nosegay, playing the part of Lady Windermere, slipped and fell on her fan –

BETTY: But surely that is one of the biggest parts in the West End.

HUGH: Oh, I never listen to gossip, ducky. Do you think you could play Lady Windermere?

BETTY: I don't know – I've only ever played Maria Marten in the Red Barn.

HUGH: Well, it's much the same, dear – just camped up with some posh chat and a few jokes. You can start

rehearsing this afternoon . . .

*Orchestra: Music under . . .*

BETTY: *(Old)* And that's how it was – I was an immediate success. After that, London was at my feet – I played in *A Woman of No Importance*, *Candida* and *The Second Mrs. Tanqueray*.

KENNETH: What happened? Did the first Mrs. Tanqueray fall on her fan too?

BETTY: Every night admirers flocked around me – I was the toast of London, but I was only interested in one man – at a time, of course. Night after night I was intrigued by a small bent figure who sat alone in a stage box ogling me.

KENNETH: Who was he?

BETTY: Nobody seemed to know. Some said he was of Royal Blood, a prince perhaps – [others whispered that he was an eccentric millionaire,] while yet others thought he might just be an old tramp who crept in there for a kip. But one night, I was in my dressing room, changing after the performance, when there came a knock on my door.

*F/X: Knock on door*

BILL: *(Doorman)* Miss Clissold – there's a gentleman to see you – says he's the Marquis of Tranby, but he looks more like the Dog and Duck.

BETTY: *(Young)* Show him in.

KEN W: *(Very, very old)* Forgive my intrusion my dear, but I am your unknown admirer. I've ogled you from afar, and now I'd like to ogle you from close to. My dear, may I just . . .

BETTY: *(Squeals)* Oh, Marquis! What are you doing?

---

17. Peter Finch played Oscar Wilde in a film of his life story.

KEN W: Just an old man's whim. Miss Clissold, would you like to make me the happiest man in the world . . .

BETTY: What? Here?

KEN W: I'm proposing marriage. I have little to offer you, just my estates in Ireland, a coal mine or two in Wales and several million pounds in hard cash.

BETTY: What does it matter as long as we have each other?

KEN W: Then you'll say yes?

BETTY: Frequently.

*Orchestra: Music up: 'Wedding March' – down and fade under . . .*

KENNETH: What a romantic story. And so you were married.

BETTY: *(Old)* Yes. And it was idyllic – a dream come true. We never had a single quarrel, right up until the time he died.

KENNETH: It sounds like it must have been an ideal marriage.

BETTY: It was. The happiest four hours of my life.

*Orchestra: Chord*

KENNETH: What a heart-warming load of old rubbish that was. Next week we continue the saga of one of the world's best-loved, or should I say most-often-loved women with Episode Seven of the Bea Clissold story – the censor has cut the intervening six. But for the moment, it's goodnight from us all in the studio – but before I go, I'd like to give you the answers to last week's quiz. The answer to question one was – three and a half inches. The answer to question two was, of course, Lionel Bart or a pork pie. Not many of you got that. The other answers were – a pound of tripe, Charlie Drake, Alma Cogan's mother, Attila the Hun, Sheffield Wednesday, Maria Monk[18] and four times a night. Well, that's all there is from us – except to announce the details of our new competition – listeners are invited to complete this limerick –

The Bishop of Bagshot was narked,

When a pretty young barmaid
    remarked . . .

Postcards please to Kenneth Horne, c/o BBC, London. To the sender of the best postcard goes this week's prize – an unexpurgated, unretouched, glossy art study of Kenneth Williams' epiglottis. Adults only. Well, that's it and this is Kenneth Horne, the voice of them all, saying . . .

KEN W: Kenneth Horne's got hairy knees.

*Orchestra: Music*

DOUGLAS: That was *Round the Horne*, starring Kenneth Horne, with Kenneth Williams, Hugh Paddick, Betty Marsden and Bill Pertwee. On the musical side you heard the Fraser Hayes Four, and Paul Fenoulhet and the Hornblowers, with incidental music composed by Edwin Braden. The mixture was prepared by Barry Took and Marty Feldman, who should be taken three times a day and shaken, and the whole ghastly witches' brew was stirred up by John Simmonds, who ought to be ashamed of himself.

ALL: Shame – Shame – Resign, etc.

*Orchestra: Music up and out*

*(Applause)*

*Orchestra: Play out*

---

18. Author of *Awful Disclosures of the Hotel Dieu Nunnery of Montreal*, a book which caused a major scandal in Canadian Roman Catholic circles in 1836.

# SERIES 1
# PROGRAMME 5

*FIRST BROADCAST* – Sunday 4 April 1965

## INTRODUCTION

It's hard to imagine life, let alone *Round the Horne*, before Julian and Sandy, but in fact this is only their second appearance (their first in this book) – and they are already fully realized characters. It's worth remembering that male homosexuality was not legalized in Britain until 1967; I don't think it's putting too much weight on the shoulders of a mere radio sketch show to suggest that social historians in the future will speculate about the effect this cheeky, lovable, camp pair had on twentieth-century social attitudes. Perhaps one day the Marine Commando Club, Paddington, will be declared a World Heritage Site?

Meanwhile, J. Peasmold Gruntfuttock makes his disgusting debut (his name was always spelt Peasmold in the scripts, but has been mis-spelt Peasemold ever since, possibly in order to keep one step ahead of the authorities). It's an amusing piece, but I think it's fair to say that Gruntfuttock at this stage has yet to reveal his full glorious awfulness – although you will notice that he is already fixated on Judith Chalmers, a broadcaster who has had the good fortune to be used as a punch line (or punchbag) by comedians during four separate decades. Four so far, that is.

Wilfred Pickles is mentioned in this episode, and not for the last time – he and his radio quiz show *Have a Go!*, which ran from the 1940s into the '70s, seem to have invited Took and Feldman's scorn. Pickles, a Yorkshireman, is also remembered as the first person with a non-'BBC' accent to read the BBC news, in 1941.

The sending-up of stiff-upper-lip British films, which is to become a favourite *RTH* sport, begins with the Noel Coward-like *Brief Interlude*. Charles and Fiona, however, do not appear by name until the eighth show.

DOUGLAS: Here are details of some of tonight's programmes.

[BILL: At eight o'clock, the lesser-spotted giraffe will be in the studio discussing and showing you film of the mating habits of Armand and Michaela Denis[1].]

HUGH: At nine o'clock you can hear a dramatised serial of the *Fall of the House of Usher*. Tonight's episode is entitled – 'Usher, Usher, all fall down'.

KEN W: And [finally] at 10.30 on BBC3, the Israeli Little Theatre Group are presenting their dance and mime company – The Yiddisher Mummers.

DOUGLAS: Meanwhile, for those of you more easily pleased, here's thirty minutes of star-studded rubbish as Kenneth Horne takes you – *Round the Horne*.

*Orchestra: Sig. tune*

DOUGLAS: The story so far – husky, strapping Betty Marsden is madly in love with sweet, ethereal Kenneth Williams, he of the bedroom eyes and bathroom mind. Together they stroll through the thick, tangled undergrowth, played by thick, tangled Hugh Paddick, in his ineffable manner – as opposed to his usual manner which is extremely effable. Pausing by the trunk of a petrified oak, played by petrified Bill Pertwee, he took her in his arms – his firm young kneecaps pressed against the madras cotton of his trousers, her mouth became a scarlet wound of anguish as she gasped out the words –

KENNETH: Good evening. My name is Kenneth Horne.

*Orchestra: Music*

KENNETH: Hello and welcome to

*Round the Horne*. That was Douglas Smith, who appeared by permission of the Foots Cray branch of the Edgar Lustgarden Fan Club and Burial Society.

[Now, here are the answers to last week's quiz. The answer to question one was an army surplus vest or a banjo. For those of you who thought it was Dusty Springfield, all I can say is you obviously weren't paying attention. Question two – a tricky one this – you remember we asked you to complete some well-known phrases – and the answers are . . . like a light . . . with the lark, and . . .] Now, it's nice to have the chance . . .

KEN W: I bet it is.

KENNETH: Quiet, Williams. [It's nice to have the chance to air one's views on various topics. And tonight I'd like to talk about a creature that has long baffled science.

KEN W: Oh, get on with it.

KENNETH: There's another creature that's long baffled science. But the one I'm referring to is the dinosaur. What happened to the dinosaur?

HUGH: Don't tell me you've lost it again.

BETTY: I hope it hasn't gone running in the road.

BILL: If people can't keep pets properly they shouldn't have 'em.

KENNETH: Now, the dinosaur lived, as we all know, many millions of years ago – at least the one I'm referring to did. His name was George. And he lived with his family in Potters Bar, near the golf course. The dinosaur's natural enemy was Neanderthal man, a sort of Mick Jagger who couldn't

---

1. A Belgian husband-and-wife team of presenters of TV wildlife programmes.

help it – a carnivorous mammal who subsisted entirely on a diet of dinosaur – dinosaur and chips – dinosaurburgers – dinosaur trotters. Of course, this diet ruined the health of the Neanderthal man and it didn't do much for the dinosaur. What with this and the Ice Age coming to Potters Bar, some of the dinosaurs decided to head south. They got as far as Bognor Regis, but none of the boarding houses would take them in. You know what they're like about pets. So in the end they just hung about the pier playing the slot machines, but Bognor Regis being what it is, they soon died of boredom. Nobody knows what happened to the other dinosaurs; some claim that they became extinct, others claim that they became transmuted into another species, but my own theory is that they're still hanging about somewhere and they'll show up when they're hungry. Oh well, I just thought I'd mention it.

And now to our feature, 'The Backroom Boys of the BBC'. This week the personnel department, where a highly skilled panel screens possible employees to make sure that the right man gets the right job . . .]

*(Fade – and fade up)*

BILL: *(Sir Arnold)* Well, I think we should have given that last chap the job. He had the right background.

HUGH: *(Sir Clive)* I don't agree. We don't want that type of person in the BBC. Look what he said –

BILL: Well, he said he was a Fellow of All Souls . . .

HUGH: Oh, is that what it was. *(Chuckles)* I thought he said he played Othello at Walsall.

BETTY: *(Lady Brink)* Well, shall we have the next one in?

BILL: Yes. And remember it is our duty to make sure that we only employ the best type of person with the right type of background, even though it is only for a menial position.

*F/X: Door opens*

BETTY: Come in, Mr. – er . . .

KEN W: *(Old man)* Gruntfuttock – Peasmold Gruntfuttock. J. Peasmold Gruntfuttock. *(Pause)* Esquire. *(Pause)* I'm not titled or anything.

BILL: That's all right, we're democratic here. Now – why did you apply for this job?

KEN W: Well, they sent me up here from the Labour. It was either this or a window dresser in the horsemeat shop. And I got turned down for that, so I come here.

HUGH: I see. Well, you couldn't have made a better choice. Now, there's a few questions we must ask you –

BETTY: Why do you want to work for the BBC?

KEN W: I want to get my hands on Judith Chalmers.

BILL: What we meant was, if we gave you a job in the BBC, what would you actually like to do . . .

KEN W: I'd like to get her in the broom cupboard and . . .

[HUGH: Mr. Gruntfuttock – would you like to tell us something about your background? Now, education –

KEN W: Private.

HUGH: I see, a private education.

KEN W: *(Viciously)* No. I mean, mind your own business.] I have the voices see. They tell me what to do. Go forth

– the voices said – go up to the BBC and get your hands on Judith Chalmers.

BETTY: I see. Now – where do you feel your special aptitude lies? What sort of post did you have in mind?

KEN W: Well, I'd like the job of Director General of Broadcasting.

HUGH: I'm terribly sorry old chap, but Sir Hugh Greene's already got it.

KEN W: Just like up the horsemeat shop. [They give the job to this Paddy 'cos he was wearing a collar. 'Go on', they says, 'Clear off', they says. So I threw a brick through their window and run off down the road.] Oh well, if the job as Director General has gone I wouldn't mind going for to be Director of the Spoken Word, or Head of Talks, or stoking the boilers; something where there's luncheon vouchers involved.

BILL: I see – and what sort of salary did you have in mind?

KEN W: Oh, about five thousand a year if I was Director of the Spoken Word, but I'll take two pounds ten a week if it's the boilers. It's all the same to me.

HUGH: Yes. A very reasonable attitude. Now, Mr. Gruntfuttock, if you wouldn't mind leaving us for a moment, I must consult with my colleagues.

KEN W: Yes, I shall hang about in the waiting room drawing on the wall till you're ready for me. [Or I might set fire to the waste paper basket. It's up to the voices really.]

F/X: Door opens and closes

BILL: Well, Lady Brink?

BETTY: Poor devil. I really do feel sorry for people like that. He's completely unstable – illiterate, aggressive and utterly stupid.

HUGH: I agree. He should be put out of the way – in a place where he can do no harm to anybody . . .

BILL: Then you think . . .?

HUGH: Yes. It's the best thing for him, poor simpleton. Let's call him in.

F/X: Door opens

HUGH: Come in, Mr. Gruntfuttock. Sorry to have kept you waiting.

[KEN W: 'Salright. I've been amusing myself. I slashed the curtains with me penknife, emptied the ink wells all over the carpet and then I ripped the telephone off its wire and threw it out the window.

BILL: Well, as long as you haven't been bored. Now,] We've come to a decision. We can't offer you the job of stoking the boilers, because, well frankly you're not up to it. But there is one job we can offer you, which seems in keeping with your personality, qualifications and temperament . . .

KEN W: Head of Channel Two?

BILL: Not quite as bad as that. No. You're going to be the new compere on Not So Much a Programme[2] . . !

Orchestra: Music

KENNETH: All the characters portrayed in that sketch were of course living or dead or Kenneth Williams. And now – Episode Five of The Clissold Saga.

Orchestra: Fanfare

---

2. Not So Much a Programme More a Way of Life was a short-lived, thrice-weekly BBC TV satire show, featuring David Frost, Eleanor Bron and Michael Crawford, amongst others; the successor to That Was The Week That Was.

KENNETH: Once again today we salute that grand old boiler Beatrice Clissold – an actress who delighted so many people a few years ago in *The Little Hut on Shaftesbury Avenue*, [before the police raided it –] but who achieved her greatest fame in Hollywood, where she was applauded for her *Cat On a Hot Tin Roof*, praised for her *Fanny by Gaslight*, and acclaimed by everyone who remembers her *Splendour in the Grass*.

Last week I went back once again to visit Lady Counterblast, as she now is, at her isolated country home at Chattering Parva . . .

*Tape: Usual effects (ending with door creaking open)*

KEN W: *(Spasm)* Ar. You be Lobby Lud and I claim the five pounds.

KENNETH: No. It's just a trick of the light. I'm Kenneth Horne.

[KEN W: Oh. Go home, young master. Go back to London. This house be accursed. Lackaday! Oh woe! Lackaday and woe! And fie an' all. Lackaday, woe and fie – and while we're on the subject, rue! Oh lackaday, woe, fie and rue –

KENNETH: Sounds like a firm of estate agents.]

KEN W: Ar, you may jest, but you haven't seen what I've seen. *(Clock chimes)* 'Tis time, 'tis the hour for the headless Abbot of Chattering Parva to manifest hisself. He comes a galloping by holding his cassock above his knees, a-looking for his head . . . *(Gasp)* Here he comes now . . .

*F/X: Running footsteps*

. . . Evening, George.

BILL: *(Cheery. Out of breath)* Evening, Mr. Spasm.

*F/X: Footsteps run off*

*Sudden crash and thud of body falling*

KEN W: Can't see where he's going. That's the worst of having no head. Now, I suppose you'll be wanting to see the mistress. Follow me . . .

KENNETH: You've been with Lady Counterblast a long while, haven't you?

[KEN W: Ar – I have. I remember many's the time I dandled her on my knee. Aye, I've dandled her on my knee many a time – till one night her husband come home unexpected.]

*F/X: Door opens*

KEN W: 'Tis the young master. *(Chuckles)* Young Master?

BETTY: Ah, Mr. Horne.

KEN W: Er – the headless abbot's back. madam. Shall I make up a bed in the spare room?

BETTY: No. The mad nun's in there. [Remember what happened last time. We had complaints from the phantom neighbours.] Alright, Spasm. You may leave us.

KEN W: We're all doomed. Doomed. I've got a touch of the dooms.

*F/X: Door closes*

[KENNETH: Is he safe?

BETTY: Don't let Spasm worry you, Mr. Horne. He may appear to be a dangerous lunatic – but in reality – he is.]

KENNETH: Well, Lady Counterblast – in the past few weeks you've told us about your early years on the stage, but I believe you made your biggest impact in films. You started in silent pictures, didn't you?

BETTY: Yes. I often appeared in Fatty Arbuckle's shorts. They were the biggest draws in Hollywood at the time. Perhaps you'd like to see some excerpts from my films. I have the projector set up here. I'll just switch on.

*F/X: Switch on: Whirring projector . . .*

BETTY: Now, this is one of the first talkies I made at Elstree Studios. I co-starred with Hamilton Grosvenor.

KENNETH: Oh yes – I remember the film. It was called *Brief Interlude*.

BETTY: Shh – it's starting . . .

*F/X: Whirring of projector*

*Railway station noises*

HUGH: *(à la Jack Hawkins)* I've put your bags on the rack.

BETTY: Thank you, darling.

HUGH: Well, this is – goodbye.

BETTY: *(A touch of the Margaret Leightons)* Yes, darling. The train leaves in five minutes. God, darling, how I hate railway stations –

HUGH: I shall always remember these last few sad, sweet, unutterably poignant moments – I suppose you'll be going back to your husband and the children in Hadley Wood.

BETTY: My place is with Roger – he needs me.

HUGH: I need you too – [oh God, darling, God, God, God!] How I need you – darling.

BETTY: Don't, darling. It makes it so much more difficult.

HUGH: I can't help myself, darling.

*(They kiss)*

[BETTY: I've got powder all over your uniform.

HUGH: It doesn't matter. Nothing matters now that you're leaving me.] Must you? Must you go . . .?

BETTY: Yes. But I shall always remember this brief meeting – these stolen moments of bittersweet madness.

*F/X: Guard's whistle. Train door closing: Hiss of steam, etc.*

BETTY: The train'll be moving soon – goodbye.

HUGH: One – last – kiss . . . try not to forget me . . .

BETTY: I won't. I won't. *(Change of tone)* Oh, and here's sixpence for your trouble, porter.

HUGH: *(Very formal)* Thank you, madam.

*Orchestra: Music*

BETTY: *(Old)* Yes, they were wonderful films we made at Elstree, but then I got an offer to go back to Hollywood. Darryl F. Poltergeist said he'd make me a star if I would just come across.

KENNETH: And did you?

BETTY: Many, many times. Many, many, many times *(etc.)*. In those days the fashion was for films based on the lives of the great. [I played Mrs. Beethoven, Mrs. Genghis Khan and Mrs. Ivan the Terrible.] Here is a scene from the one I enjoyed most, where I played Mrs. Guglielmo Marconi, wife of the famous inventor . . .

*F/X: Whirring projector: Hammering, sawing, etc.*

BETTY: *(Italian. Coming on mic)* Hey Guglielmo, I gotta da lunch.

BILL: *(Italian)* Come in, Carissima –

BETTY: All the time you working on your invention you got no time for me and the bambinos no more.

BILL: What bambinos?

BETTY: Giuseppe, Luigi, Roberto, Enrico, Maria, Marcello, Gina, Rudolfo, Claudia, Leonardo, Benjamino, Fillipo –

BILL: But darling –

BETTY: Wait a minute – I haven't finished – Anselmo, Umberto, Sophia, Benito and Seamus.

BILL: Seamus? I don't remember no Seamus.

BETTY: Seamus – you know the little one with the red hair and freckles, and the Irish accent and the – hey, you know you quite right – musta belong to Mrs. Riley up the road. Whatsa wrong with you, Guglielmo – all the time is work, work, work.

BILL: Is a my invention. I have only just finished it. Is a magnifico idea. Is going to make da name of Marconi remembered always. Look Carissima – here – on the bench.

BETTY: What? Dis little box with wires and valves inside it?

BILL: Look, it works like this – you turn dis little knob – so –

F/X: *Radio switched on – static and then . . .*

KEN W: *(Wilfred Pickles)* This week *Have a Go!* comes to you from a Sewage Farm in Chichester.

F/X: *Radio set switched off*

BETTY: It's a marvellous invention. What are you going to call it?

BILL: Spaghetti Bolognese.

Orchestra: *Link*

BETTY: *(Old)* Ah, Hollywood – what a wonderful experience. That's where I got my Oscar you know.

[F/X: *On film, door opens and closes*

BETTY: *(As Lady C)* What are you doing here?

KEN W: *(Starting quietly and working up to an insane frenzy)* Ah, you didn't expect to see me did you, me proud beauty – you thought you were too clever for me, didn't you? That's what the others thought . . .

BETTY: Others? What others?

KEN W: The postman, the vicar – yes, now you know – I may as well tell you the rest, since you'll never live to give me away. Yes. I did for them both. They laughed at me. Laughed in my face. Laughed *(Insane laugh)*.

BETTY: You're – you're mad . . .

KEN W: *(Snarls)* Don't call me mad. That's what they said. That's what they said at that place. They locked me up, but I escaped – yes – I'm cleverer than them all – I'll show them. I'll take over the world – I'll show them who's mad. No – it's no use trying that door – it's locked. Come here. *(Quietly)* I have to do this – you do understand, don't you? It won't hurt. *(Shouts)* Oh would you – come here – come back . . .

F/X: *Door opens*

HUGH: Alright, Sergeant – grab him.

*(Ad lib protesting and screaming as Ken is led off)*

F/X: *Whirring projector – then it's switched off*

KENNETH: What a remarkable piece of acting, Lady Counterblast.

BETTY: That wasn't acting. That was a home movie we took of Lord Counterblast before they took him away.

KENNETH: Well, it's always nice to have these little family mementoes.

BETTY: Yes –] I'm afraid that's all I have left of my long career.

[KENNETH: But you mentioned your Oscar before.

BETTY: Yes. There's my Oscar.] A great comfort and a great source of pleasure to me in my old age.

*F/X: Door opens*

BILL: *(Young and virile)* Oh, I didn't realise you had company, Beattie – I'll come back later when you're alone.

*F/X: Door closes*

KENNETH: Who's that muscular young man in the leopard skin bathing trunks?

BETTY: Oh him – that's my Oscar.

*Orchestra: Sketch pay-off*

KENNETH: That concludes *The Clissold Saga* – a story to warm your hearts – now here's something to turn your stomach over – here to sooth your savage breasts are the Fraser Hayes Four to sing a track from their new LP, *Issy Bonn*[3] *at Oberammergau.*

*(Applause)*

*Fraser Hayes & Orchestra: 'Day In, Day Out'*

*(Applause)*

KENNETH: Thank you the Fraser Hayes Four, and on behalf of us all, I'd just like to say a heartfelt good riddance.

Now – Trends!

*Orchestra: 'Trends' Link*

KENNETH: This is the section of the show devoted to the pacesetters, the trendy with-it crowd, those with get-up-and-go, I should do it now before we start. First, Fashion.

BETTY: Hair is being worn shoulder length this season.

KENNETH: Not by me, it isn't.

BETTY: Mary Quant has done it again . . .

KENNETH: And you want me to break the news to her mother?

BETTY: She's done something incredible in oilskin . . .

BILL: I think that's her own affair. [It's not our place to meddle.

BETTY: Of course, with the new fashions she has to have the figure to wear them – try fabulous Giovanni's new five-day diet plan.

BILL: Day one – slice of toast and a finely grated broad bean. Day two – half a fricasséed prune. Day three – one whole starch-reduced grape. Day four – take the pith of one peach and simmer it gently over a low gas. Then throw it away. Day five – summon next of kin.]

KENNETH: Medicine. What are the new trends in medicine? The question they're all asking in Harley Street is 'How can one avoid catching Trubshawe's disease?' Well, the answer is quite simple. Keep well clear of Trubshawe. But what are the <u>trendy</u> people suffering from? Well, with me in the studio tonight is Dr. Mendelssohn Privet, doctor to the stars of show business.

---

3. A comic and singer of sentimental songs, such as 'My Yiddishe Momma'.

HUGH: *(German)* Good evening – that'll be five guineas.

KENNETH: Now tell me, Doctor – you number among your patients many celebrities.

HUGH: Oh yes. I was consultant on Ringo's tonsils, I treated Bernard Levin for his inferiority complex and once I treated Janette Scott for frostbite.

KENNETH: And I believe recently you operated on all of the Rolling Stones.

HUGH: Yes. To remove moss. And then – Sandie Shaw, I've treated her often for corns. And of course I treat the animal celebrities. Pinky and Perky – a nasty case of swine fever that was. I was called in only last week when Ollie Beak got the moth. But I suppose I am best known in this field because I am actually the man who attended to Bill and Ben when they were pot-bound.

[KENNETH: But I believe that you are also world-famed in the field of psychoanalysis for your connection with Jung and Adler . . .

HUGH: Is quite right. Muriel Young[4] and Larry Adler. I treated Larry for six months for a wheezy chest before I found he'd swallowed his harmonica. Naturally, I removed the vital organ. But, as you say,] I also deal with the mind. Young Helen Shapiro, I treated him. And then I had this patient – terribly mixed up he was. He thought he was Kenneth Williams – there was nothing I could do for the poor wretch, you see it turned out he was.

KENNETH: How tragic. Well, it's been a privilege having you here, Doctor.

[HUGH: Thank you, but I must hurry away now. I have to attend to P.J. Proby[5]. He had a rather unfortunate accident. I'm afraid he'll need at least fourteen stitches.

KENNETH: Good gracious – where?

HUGH: In his trousers.]

KENNETH: Thank you, Dr. Privet. Now, since we've been doing these Trend spots, I've become more appearance conscious. [I mean, it's all teen this and teen that these days, but I thought just because I'm nearly thirty –

KEN W: Thirty? Round the neck.

KENNETH: I thought, well there's no reason to let myself go,] so I popped into one of those gents' boutiques in Chelsea to get myself some with-it accoutrements. This shop had one of those very masculine names – I can't remember – Butch, I think it was called.

*F/X: Shop doorbell*

KEN W: *(Coming on mic)* Coming, ducky. Hello – I'm Sandy and this is my friend Julian.

KENNETH: Aren't you those two actors from Rentachap male domestics?

HUGH: Yes, we're resting. We're just filling in here between jobs. Normally we do commercials. You may have seen me in that one where me and this girl scamper through the snow, then we drink hot chocolate and then whatever her pleasure is, I complete it.

KEN W: [And I'm the one in that detergent ad that keeps going into people's houses and asking housewives impertinent questions

---

4. Children's TV presenter.
5. Mid-Sixties pop star famous for splitting his trousers.

about their underwear. But we're between jobs at the moment so we're working here.] Now, what can we show you?

KENNETH: Well, I thought it was about time I sort of got with-it sartorially.

HUGH: Yes, well, let's see what we've got. [We've got some absolutely bona black leather Hardy Amies briefs embossed with pictures of Brian Epstein. Or] how about a pair of tight jeans? You've got the calves for it – hasn't he, Sandy?

KEN W: Oh, yes, he's got the calves. But what about his ankles? They're a bit on the thick side.

KENNETH: What's that got to do with it?

HUGH: Well, if you've got thick ankles, you'd never get them on. There's some nice, lime green raffia hipsters though. Do you see yourself in hipsters?

KENNETH: No. I'm more the paunchster sort. What I had in mind was a suit – something fairly conservative. Something I could wear when I go to my club.

KEN W: How about this lurex seersucker with the polka dot motif?

KENNETH: I couldn't wear that at my club.

HUGH: It's what we wear when we go to our club.

KENNETH: What club's that?

KEN W: The Marine Commando Club in Paddington.

KENNETH: Yes, but it's hardly the same as the Athenaeum.

HUGH: Oh, you are hard to please. Show him your swatch.

KEN W: Here – have a quick browse through these. See, you have your bold tartan, your herringbones, your hound's-tooth, your seersucker, and there's your Harris Tweed. Show him your Harris, Julian. He's got a very bold Harris. It's purple. With a gold fleck.

KENNETH: Yes. I rather like that.

KEN W: Right. Let's just have your measurements. I'll call them out, Julian, and you write them down. Now – chest, forty-two. Expanded – forty-two. Waist, forty-two. Hips, forty-two. Well, you're consistent, I'll say that for you. Pity the shift's gone out of fashion.

HUGH: Now to go with it, I suggest these bell-bottomed white leather trousers – the fluorescent shirt with the tab collar [– cuban-heeled knee length black boots, and a kinky little red leather hat.]

KENNETH: Don't you think that's going a bit too far?

KEN W: No, of course not – there – if you'd just like to slip into the changing room and put the stuff on, we'll wrap up your old suit.

KENNETH: Thank you.

HUGH: And put it in the incinerator.

*Orchestra: Music*

KENNETH: All that remains for me now is to give you the results of last week's limerick competition. The winning entry came from a Mr. Griffith of Little Cherrington, Warwickshire, and it goes as follows . . .

A young market gardener from Bude
Developed a cactus quite lewd
He said when it trembles
It rather resembles
Sophia Loren in the nude.

This week's opening two lines are –

Two men in a factory near Cork
Were eating their soup with a fork.

All you have to do is complete the limerick. Entries please to *Round the Horne*, c/o BBC, London, W1.

And to the sender of the best complete limerick goes this week's prize. A do-it-yourself taxidermist's kit, comprising a live gorilla, a loaded gun and three hundredweight of kapok. Well that's all for now, so cheerio – see you next week.

*Orchestra: Signature tune*

DOUGLAS: That was *Round the Horne*, starring Kenneth Horne, with Kenneth Williams, Hugh Paddick, Betty Marsden and Bill Pertwee. On the musical side you heard the Fraser Hayes Four and Paul Fenoulhet and the Hornblowers, with incidental music composed by Edwin Braden. The script was written by Barry Took and Marty Feldman and the recorded programme was produced by John Simmonds.

*Orchestra: Music up and out*

*(Applause)*

*Orchestra: Play out*

*(Applause)*

# SERIES 1
# PROGRAMME 7

*FIRST BROADCAST* – Sunday 18 April 1965

## INTRODUCTION

By now, the series is beginning to settle into its lasting shape, although some of the sketches are still a little (to coin a phrase) 'dragged out', and the changes of scene, tone and pace are not yet as smooth as they would soon become.

Julian and Sandy, and Gruntfuttock, are now regulars – if you'll pardon the singularly inappropriate expression – as is the spoof of a popular TV genre, with Kenneth Horne playing the lead role.

The writers' scheme of building the show around Horne, using him as a maypole about which the entire fandango of ludicrousness revolves, is already working beautifully. Surrounded by outrageous characters, Horne remains a slightly old-fashioned gent, who is appealingly lost in the rapidly changing world of the mid-Sixties. Despite being willing to have a go at anything, he is noticeably not 'with-it', in dress, manner or speech: 'He bugged your dig? I'm afraid I don't quite . . .'

In lesser hands, this could have been mediocre, and even tiresome, nothing more than a predictable procession of generation gap gags. Instead, for all Horne's air of baffled amiability and suit-and-tie respectability, we are constantly aware that there is more genuine naughtiness in just one of his plummy monosyllables than in an entire Swinging London full of posing phonies.

The band's newly appointed conductor, Edwin Braden ('Great hairy fool!'), plays a big part in this episode; but, what with it being a non-speaking role, and what with this being radio, he probably didn't get paid any extra for it.

DOUGLAS: Here are details of some of tonight's programmes.

[BILL: At eight-thirty this evening you will be able to hear a programme entitled 'I Was An Alcoholic' in which Malcolm Muggeridge will be talking to a tick.]

HUGH: At ten o'clock a panel of teenagers will be discussing the growing problem of delinquency among clergymen.

KEN W: Bernard Levin will be talking about how he has been a lifelong sufferer from foot-in-the-mouth disease.

DOUGLAS: Meanwhile, for those of you who are more easily pleased, here's thirty minutes of glittering codswallop as we take you *Round the Horne*.

*Orchestra: Sig. tune*

DOUGLAS: The story so far: Inspector Bill Pertwee, he of the beetling brows, and spidery legs, leant against the mantelpiece in the library at Mallory Grange and surveyed the company. His eyes darted round the room and rolled under the ottoman – played by Hugh Paddick in a yashmak. Who was the murderer? Was it the butler – balding, bow-legged old Betty Marsden? Or perhaps the lovely nubian belly dancer, Kenneth Williams. Suddenly the lights went out and he heard a sound the like of which no man had heard and lived. In an awful croak the words rasped out . . .

KENNETH: Good evening. My name is Kenneth Horne.

*Orchestra: Music*

KENNETH: Welcome to *Round the Horne*. [That was Douglas Smith, who appears by permission of the Frinton

on Sea Home for Unmarried Mothers and Bingo. I'm sorry, that should read or Bingo.] Well here to begin are the answers to last week's quiz – question one – [the sporting question – the answers were a hole in one, a hole in two, and a cigarette burn in the other. The answer to question two –] well, of course, the odd man out was Edwin Braden; the others, of course, are washable.

By the way, Edwin Braden has taken over the baton from Paul Fenoulhet on this show – we hope that in time he'll learn to use it. So for the rest of this series, Edwin will be on the podium. Now, finally the question on etiquette – the answer was in three parts – as follows: not with your fingers; you shouldn't in the bath; and yes, if you feel you really must but you get crumbs in the bed. Which attracts the birds. Well, today marks the anniversary of that eminent Victorian bird-fancier, Nemesis Fothergill – known perhaps better to ornithologists and the police as the Birdman of Potters Bar. He first achieved prominence when he discovered Trusspott's Yellow-Backed Cornpaw – which Trusspott had been looking for, for weeks. Shortly after this he was the first man to record the cry of the Lesser-Spotted Willow Warbler, so called because it had less spots than other willow warblers. This bird emitted a sound resembling, er – Chuck a chuck a chuck pee whit pee whit – which during the mating season changed to chuck a chuck a chuck, heh heh heh heh – [Well, I suppose during the mating season he'd have more to be happy about.

Encouraged by this success, Nemesis went out to record other sounds of the hedgerow – he came up with one which sounded like – Ar – Ooooh –

Ar – Ooh. At first he attributed this to a nesting wood pigeon, but on closer investigation he discovered it to be a farmer and a landgirl. Perhaps Nemesis was best known for his experiments in crossbreeding. Although being short-sighted this led to some surprising results as witness Fothergill's Lesser-Spotted Flying Fox Terrier – a species which is almost extinct – fortunately. I mean, it's a bit unnerving to find a bird scratching at the door and barking to go walkies. But certainly his most successful venture in this field was to produce a turkey with six legs, for large families who each wanted a drumstick. The experiment was a great success, but unfortunately he could never catch the blighters.]

Well, there you are – don't say I never tell you anything. And now we come to the spot in the show where we pay tribute to the Backroom Boys of the BBC. This week the Audience Research Department. The people who go from door to door finding out what you, the public, want to hear or see. Last week I went out with one of the BBC's highly trained investigators to see how it was done.

F/X: *Street noises as background*

HUGH: Well, you see Mr. Horne, we just take a typical street like this and then we go from door to door, asking questions and filling out this questionnaire. You take this side of the road, I'll take the other . . .

KENNETH: Right – I'll try this house first.

F/X: *Knock on door*

BETTY: You the sanitary?

KENNETH: No.

BETTY: The H.P.?

KENNETH: No.

BETTY: The council?

KENNETH: No.

BETTY: *(Calls)* Ned! It's the law, son!

F/X: *Door slams. Knock on Door. Door opens*

[KENNETH: Look, madam, this won't take a moment I . . .]

BETTY: *(Screams)* You're not taking my Neddie away from me. He's a good boy. Don't send him back to that place.

KENNETH: I only wanted to ask you a few questions. You see . . .

BETTY: *(Whimpering)* I meant to take the stuff back to the supermarket, honest. Those tins of salmon must have just fell off the shelf and slipped down me bloomers. I didn't realise till I got back here. I haven't been well. I've been under the doctor – I had one of me turns. Ned – tell the constable.

BILL: *(Deep. Gruff. Hysterical)* You're not taking my mummy. Don't take her away from me. What'll become of me? Who'll look after me if you lock up my mummy? I'll have to get a job.

KENNETH: Now calm yourself – I'm trying to explain, but it's very difficult to be coherent with you belabouring me about the knees with a pick-axe handle.

BETTY: Stop it, Neddie, or you'll get done for G.B.H. an' all. *(Whispers)* Constable – if I turn Queen's evidence against my Neddie, will it go easier for me? Don't let 'em send me back to that place.

KENNETH: I don't want to send anyone anywhere. I'm just conducting an enquiry on behalf of the BBC into people's viewing and listening habits.

BETTY: *(Suddenly normal)* Oh – er – yes, well we feel that there's too much violence on television.

*Orchestra: Brief music link*

*F/X: Ring on doorbell. Door opens.*

KENNETH: Good morning, Mr. . . . er

KEN W: Gruntfuttock. Peasmold Gruntfuttock. J. Peasmold Gruntfuttock – Archbishop.

KENNETH: Archbishop?

KEN W: It's a honorary title. I give it to myself. See I'm a lay preacher up the hellfire and damnation tabernacle, over the chip shop in Brixton – do you know it?

KENNETH: Yes, as a matter of fact, I do. But I thought it was a dance hall.

KEN W: Yes, it was, but it did come to pass that Philistines and their birds did cause a great unrest in the land, and verily the bogeys did descend upon them, and did smite them hip and thigh and send them forth for a carpet up Wormwood Scrubs; then they did hire the place to the Brotherhood of a Friday, being as how Sundays was Bingo. Come up and confess your sins one Friday, Brother. You hear some smashing sins up there of a Friday, after the pubs have closed.

KENNETH: Yes, I'll er – try to pop in one Friday – but what I really wanted to know is – what do you watch of an evening?

KEN W: That building across the road – with these binoculars. Oh, you should see the sin that goes on over there, Brother. Lights burning all night. People creeping about in their night attire – yea – and females in black stockings, going from bed to bed – yea verily 'tis a house of sin, Brother.

KENNETH: I'm sorry to disappoint you, but it's the General Hospital.

KEN W: Oh well – another illusion shattered.

KENNETH: Yes, very interesting [Mr. . . . er

KEN W: Gruntfuttock.]

KENNETH: [Yes, well] Could you tell me something about your viewing habits –

KEN W: Yes, I am, as you may have gathered, by vocation – a Peeping Tom. So, when any lissom young female, viz Judith Chalmers or Peggy Mount[1] comes on the screen, I shut the doors on the front of the set immediately.

KENNETH: Why do you do that?

KEN W: I like to watch through the keyhole.

*Orchestra: Music link*

[KENNETH: Well, I spent the rest of that day going from door to door asking people their preferences. Fifty-eight per cent said that they preferred the BBC, thirteen percent said they were don't knows, twenty-eight per cent said they preferred the Eamonn Andrews show to all other brands of margarine, but one per cent –

*F/X: Knock on door. Door opens*

KENNETH: Excuse me, sir – could you tell me what you like on television?

HUGH: Well, in my impartial opinion there's nothing to compare with *Coronation Street*. I watch it –

---

1. A British character actress, of imposing shape, voice and visage. Not normally, it has to be said, considered a sex symbol.

regularly – and so does my whole family – and so does everyone where I work. When I go into work in the mornings I ask all the people I meet – What's your favourite programme? And they all answer – '*Coronation Street* – Mr. Bernstein[2].'

*Orchestra: Music*

KENNETH: That's given you some idea of what the average millionaire who owns his own television company watches.] So much then for the Backroom Boys – Smith – put that hip flask of foot embrocation away and announce the next item.

DOUGLAS: Sorry, sir – it's purely medicinal. Now, Trends.

*Orchestra: 'Trends' music*

KENNETH: This is the part of the show for the Jet-Set – as opposed to people of my age – the Sopwith Camel Crowd – first, fashion.

BETTY: Bosoms are out again.

KENNETH: Well, when they come in will you tell them I called.

BETTY: Swimwear. Two-piece bathing suits are out – and everybody's wearing one-piece costumes.

KENNETH: Really? Which piece?

BILL: *(Gruff)* Well, I always wear the bottom piece. It avoids complications.

BETTY: Here's some inside news – guess who was seen in a Royal Park, wearing a one-piece woollen suit?

KENNETH: A sheep. Now here are some travel trends. A few suggestions for with-it holidays. 'Sunny Cannibal-Infested South Borneo beckons' – I've never known anybody who's come back disappointed, but then I've never known anybody who's come back. Or finally there's a fine choice of agricultural working holidays. You can go Hopping in Kent or even better, Leaping about in Leicestershire. Or if you prefer there's Blackberrying in Norfolk, Muckspreading in Shropshire or Chicken-sexing in Hampshire.

BETTY: Finally, we come to trends in entertainment. Following the trend in pirate radio stations comes news of a new development – a German pirate TV station operating from a ship somewhere off the coast of Germany called the *SS Himmler*. Here is an excerpt from a typical quiz show.

*Orchestra: Glock. Plays opening phrase of 'Deutschland über Alles'*

DOUGLAS: *(German accent)* This is Douglas Schmidt welcoming you to another session of that gemütlich quiz show *Double Your Pfennigs*. And here is your genial quizmaster – Happy Heinrich Schnitzel.

HUGH: *(Jovial German) (A sort of cross between late Vic Oliver and Himmler)* Thank you, good evening and welcome to another session of *Double Your Pfennigs*. Brunhilda – bring on the first contestant.

BETTY: *(Marlene Dietrich)* Jawohl, Herr Schnitzel. *(Goes off mic singing)* Falling in love again, never wanted to . . .

HUGH: What a girl, ha ha, always playing so hard to get. You know what her telephone number is? Ha ha. Nein nein nein. *(Silence. Shouts)* Laugh!

---

2. Sidney Bernstein, later Lord Bernstein, was a co-founder of Granada TV, which made *Coronation Street*.

*F/X: Audience laughs mechanically. Sound cut off quickly*

HUGH: Alright. We've had our little fun, now on with the show.

BETTY: Here is the first contestant. Herr Wilhelm Schtumpf.

HUGH: Well, Willie, and where are you from?

KEN W: Well, Happy Heinrich, I am from Dusseldorf.

HUGH: How about that. A big hand for Willie Schtumpf from Dusseldorf.

*F/X: Applause. It cuts off suddenly*

HUGH: I can see we're going to have a lot of fun tonight. Brunhilda – the first question.

BETTY: It's a question on music. For one hundred pfennigs – who wrote the Emperor Concerto?

KEN W: Er – the Emperor.

HUGH: Ha ha ha – no, Willie – think – who wrote the Emperor Concerto?

KEN W: I can't remember.

HUGH: *(Voice becoming more sinister)* Come, Willie, ha ha ha – you can remember if you try.

KEN W: *(Becoming nervous now)* I can't – and I have these headaches.

HUGH: *(Voice positively sinister)* For the last time – who wrote the Emperor Concerto?

KEN W: *(Shouts)* I can't think – I can't remember. How can I think with you twisting my arm.

HUGH: *(Screams)* We have ways of making you talk, you know –

KEN W: Please – please – don't shine those lights in my eyes.

[BETTY: *(Quietly)* You think he knows something, Kapitän?

HUGH: He knows but he's stubborn, just like all the rest. You have to admire his bravery though.]

BETTY: Let me talk to him. *(Huskily)* Hello, Big Boy!

KEN W: Who, me?

BETTY: I like you. When this is all over we can go away somewhere together. Look, Willie, don't be a fool, tell him what he wants to know – I know this Happy Heinrich – he'll stop at nothing to get what he wants.

KEN W: But I don't know. I can't remember.

HUGH: I have a little friend who might help to jog your memory.

BETTY: Not *(Horror)* Otto? Not that sadistic subhuman giant you keep in the cellar?

HUGH: Yes, ten minutes in the soundproof booth with Otto, I think you'll find will loosen your tongue. Well? For the last time *(Shouts)* who *(Slaps him)* wrote *(Slap)* the *(Slap)* Emperor Concerto?

KEN W: *(Screams)* Alright! Alright! Don't beat me any more. I'll tell you – just let me . . .

HUGH: Ah, just as I thought – a cyanide tablet. We're wise to that caper on *Double Your Pfennigs*.

KEN W: *(Screams and sobs)* Alright, you've beaten me, you inhuman fiend! You may have got me, but there's others – all over the world – people are arming, democracy's on the move, yes, I'll tell you, why shouldn't I? Your days are numbered, Happy Heinrich! Numbered! . . .

*Orchestra: Creep in 'Wild Blue Yonder' under and build to a pitch as*

*Ken finishes speech*

KEN W: . . . The skies are dark over Europe now but there in the West – the dawn is breaking. Uncle Sam is girding up his loins. His loins I tell you – his loins! [Freedom will prevail!] Beethoven. It was Beethoven. I knew all along. Beethoven wrote the Emperor Concerto. *(Sobs)*

*(A pause)*

HUGH: *(Back to original cheery self)* Ha ha ha – well done, Willie – and now would you like to go on for the next question?

KEN W: *(Back to normal)* No, ta – I'll stick here.

HUGH: Now will you take the money or open the Lucky Box thirteen? Remember it may contain a high-powered car – a transistor radio – or it may be the booby prize. Well? What should he do?

AUDIENCE: *(Chant)* Open the box – open the box!

KEN W: I've decided to open the box.

HUGH: What a sportsman – here's the key, now see what Frau Luck has in store for you.

*F/X: Key in lock. Door opens*

KEN W: Oh – just what I've always wanted. It's a . . .

*F/X: Huge explosion*

HUGH: *(Cheery)* Oh well – you can't win them all. The Boche has beaten us. Come back next week when there'll be three hundred pfennigs in the jackboot. Danke schön.

*Orchestra: Final chord*

KENNETH: Well, that's one contestant who won't be back next week. And now, here are the Fraser Hayes Four with a track from their new LP, *Hepzibah Menhuin Goes Latin.* Ladies and gentlemen – the Fraser Hayes Four.

*Fraser Hayes & Orchestra: The Fraser Hayes Spot:*

*'Just a Spoonful of Sugar'*

*(Applause)*

DOUGLAS: And now a tribute to one of the world's ace crime-fighters.

*Orchestra: Burke's Law theme*

BETTY: *(Husky)* It's *Horne's Law*[3]!

*Orchestra: Music up and out*

BETTY: *(Young and sexy)* Why Captain Horne – you play a mean game of strip poker. Right – I'll see you . . . What have you got?

KENNETH: Well, I've got three kings and Mr. Bun the Baker.

BETTY: I've got a full house – your turn to take something off.

KENNETH: Right – what shall it be? My galoshes or my balaclava?

BETTY: Don't tantalise me. Captain – you drive me to distraction –

KENNETH: No. You drive – I'm tired. Careful, careful – you're crushing my carnation.

*F/X: Phone rings: Phone up*

KENNETH: Captain Horne – Homicide and Cars Washed. What? What? What? [You'll have to speak up – what?] I'll be over right away.

*F/X: Phone down*

---

3. *Burke's Law* was a US TV series about a playboy police chief. It was itself something of a send-up, which didn't save it from being parodied by *RTH*.

BETTY: Something wrong?

KENNETH: No – Edwin Braden's disappeared – they suspect – murder!

BETTY: Oh well – so long as it's not bad news.

*Orchestra: Music link*

BILL: Well, Captain, what happened was this – It was during the rehearsals for *Round the Horne*. Braden went round to the pub for a quick drink and never came back.

KENNETH: But from what I've heard that's quite usual.

[BILL: Yes, but he normally gets back just before the show.

KENNETH: Normally is not a word I would use in connection with Braden.] Have you checked all his usual haunts?

BILL: Yes. We checked the Amelia Fullbright House for down and out Lascars and they say his bed hasn't been slept in – and then we tried his club – the Ginger Camel in Soho – but he hadn't tried to cash a cheque there for days –

KENNETH: Have you tried the Y.W.C.A.?

BILL: But surely he's not a member . . .

KENNETH: No, but I've often seen him hanging about outside. Now, the Ginger Camel you say?

BILL: Yes, he was friendly with a girl in the show there. Miss Exotica – does a sort of an act with a snake . . .

KENNETH: Oh good. I like animal acts. I'll pop over there and make some enquiries.

*Orchestra: Music link*

*F/X: Knock on door*

BETTY: *(French)* Entrez.

*F/X: Door opens*

KENNETH: Miss Exotica?

BETTY: Yes, zat is so. I don't recognize you – have we had the pleasure?

KENNETH: No, we haven't even met. I'm Captain Horne – police.

BETTY: *(Common as muck)* Well why didn't you say so, dearie?

KENNETH: Well, Miss Exotica . . .

BETTY: Lil.

KENNETH: Yes, well, I'm enquiring about Edwin Braden – did you know him?

BETTY: Oh yes – the Major. What about him?

KENNETH: He's disappeared.

BETTY: Good job too. I was a decent respectable girl till I met him. He's no good; he's low and deceitful and rotten and depraved and I hate his guts. Here – I hope nothing's happened to him. He may have been a rotter – but he was all man – oh Captain, you didn't know him like I did. When he'd take you in his arms and press you against him and kiss you passionately. Oh, you don't know what it was like . . .

KENNETH: No, but I'll take your word for it.

[BETTY: It was like the fourth of July and Christmas and Thanksgiving all rolled into one.

KENNETH: Really, from what I've heard of Braden, I should have thought it was more like Halloween.]

BETTY: I trusted him, but he lied to me – he said he liked my act with the snake – he said he'd get me on

*Zoo Time.* But he never – all he did was nick my snake and flog it to a handbag manufacturer. What kind of man is that, Captain? A man who would pinch my asp and run away. I'm having to do my act with a length of hosepipe now – where's the exotic Eastern mystery in a length of hosepipe? But I didn't kill him –

KENNETH: Have you any idea of who might have? Did he have any enemies?

BETTY: Well, there was Ziggy the trombone player in the Hornblowers – he hated Eddie.

KENNETH: Where could I find this Ziggy?

BETTY: He hangs out at a salt beef sandwich den near Archer Street.

*Orchestra: Music link*

HUGH: *(Cool)* Yeah, he was uncool that Braden cat, he bugged me, dig?

KENNETH: He bugged your dig? I'm afraid I don't quite . . .

HUGH: No, man, you putting me on? Like, what I mean is, he was my connection, you know – he turned me on to salt beef sandwiches – until it became an addiction, dig? You know the way it starts, you have a puff at a gherkin just for kicks and then one day you wake up in a cold sweat – you've got to have a salt beef sandwich *(Sobs)* with mustard. Now look at me, man – I got a salt beef monkey on my back! Yeah – I knew Braden – but I didn't kill him.

KENNETH: But you had a motive.

HUGH: Yeah, baby, but so did everyone. The writers of the show – they hated him – you see he was blackmailing them. He knew they were receiving stolen jokes and passing them off as their own. Yeah –

Captain – you should see the writers –

*Orchestra: Music link*

*F/X: Typewriter:*

*Knock on door: Door opens*

*Typewriter stops*

KENNETH: Are you the two writers?

HUGH: Yes – I'm Julian, and this is my friend Sandy.

KENNETH: Surely you're those two out of work actors from Rentachap?

KEN W: Yes, well we've taken up scriptwriting as a sideline – well it's not a full week's worth, is it? We sort of model ourselves on Muir and Norden –

HUGH: Yes, I'm sort of the Frank Muir.

KEN W: And I'm more the Christine Norden. But we do all types of writing. You've got to be versatile. You may have seen some of the things we've done. *The Four Just Men* – but only just. Then we wrote *Ready Steady Whoops!*

KENNETH: Why did you call it that?

KEN W: Well I hadn't intended to but as I was typing the title I broke a fingernail on the typewriter.

HUGH: Then you might have seen my *Compact.*

KENNETH: Why? Have you lost it?

KEN W: Oh, bold!

HUGH: I wrote the one where Ian Harmon come into the office and burst into tears when Mrs. Chater told him sales was going down – then Ben had this screaming row with Doug 'cos he said he'd nicked his eyebrow tweezers, [but Adrian took them over the pub and they had a couple of pink gins and they made it up. Then Alan gives in his notice and takes up ballet.] Then Gussie confesses she's Mitch's mother, so Mitch gives Elliot Morrow a good thrashing with his own stick and runs off and becomes a stoker in the merchant navy.

KENNETH: But surely Mitch is a woman?

HUGH: Oh is he? They never said. [P'raps that's why they cut the scene.

KEN W: I told him to watch the programme first, but you can't talk to him – he's very moody –

HUGH: You can talk. Moody? Look how you sulked when they rejected your idea for that series.

KEN W: Well, they said they wanted something tough and rugged with a Western background.

HUGH: Yes but really – *Frontier Coiffeur*!

KEN W: Well I've noticed in those Westerns they haven't got one decent hairdresser in Dodge City. Look at that Miss Kitty – sloppy cat – and it's a good shopping centre. Nice passing trade – do very well there.

HUGH: Quite possibly. But even so you can't call your tough rugged hero Marshal Alphonse of Mayfair.]

KENNETH: I appreciate your problems, but I'm enquiring about the mysterious disappearance of Edwin Braden.

KEN W: Oh him? Great hairy fool.

KENNETH: Yes, that fits the description I have – well, anyway we believe that he has been foully slain – all the evidence points to . . . you two – you had the means, the motive and the . . .

*F/X: Door opens*

BILL: Captain Horne! Something terrible has happened.

KENNETH: Good heavens what?

BILL: Take a grip of yourself, sir – We've found Edwin Braden.

KENNETH: Dead?

BILL: Worse . . .

*Orchestra: Chord*

BILL: Alive!

*Orchestra: Music*

BETTY: *(Husky)* Alright Captain – it's your call.

KENNETH: I'll raise you a woolly sock.

BETTY: I'll raise you a pair of nylons.

KENNETH: A Fair Isle pullover and my braces.

BETTY: You're playing for high stakes, Captain. If you win this hand it means I'm left with practically nothing on –

KENNETH: Alright then, in that case, I'll see you. That's *Horne's Law*.

*Orchestra: Music*

KENNETH: Well that's all for today, but we'll be back with another edition of *Round the Horne* next week. Before I go, here is the prize-winning entry in our limerick competition. From Mrs. H. Fisher –

Two men in a factory near Cork
Were eating their soup with a fork.
One said to his friend
Use the opposite end –
Oh look, I've invented a spork.

Here are the opening two lines of the next competition, the answer to which will be given in two weeks' time.

A cockney was pushing his barrow
Through Battersea's streets wide and narrow.

I'll repeat that. *(Does)* And to the sender of the best completed limerick goes this week's prize of a glossy nude photograph of Richard Dimbleby's knees – hmmmm – I wouldn't mind going in for that myself. Well, cheerio – see you next week.

*Orchestra: Signature tune*

DOUGLAS: That was *Round the Horne*, starring Kenneth Horne, with Kenneth Williams, Hugh Paddick, Betty Marsden and Bill Pertwee. On the musical side you heard the Fraser Hayes Four and Edwin Braden and the Hornblowers. The script was written by Barry Took and Marty Feldman and produced by John Simmonds.

*Orchestra: Music up and out*

*(Applause)*

*Orchestra: Play out*

*(Applause)*

# SERIES 1
# PROGRAMME 11

*FIRST BROADCAST* – Sunday 16 May 1965

## INTRODUCTION

In writing the introduction to this episode, I am working from Barry Took's own copy of the rehearsal script. Here I find, after an early mention of Edwin Braden, an 'X' in a circle, and next to it, in blue ink in Barry's lively handwriting, the words '*Gt Hairy fool*'. How could the writers have forgotten such a crucial line? Possibly it was included in response to a Williams ad lib during rehearsal – though one thing that emerges from comparing these scripts with the *RTH* tapes, is that there were virtually no ad libs.

This is not surprising, perhaps: weekly light entertainment shows in those days were banged out at high speed, with rehearsal in the morning, before recording a couple of hours later, for broadcast the following week. There was no time for messing around.

More significantly, by now the performers trusted the writers to get it right. The most notable thing about these scripts is that they are funny on the printed page. The same cannot be said of many other comedy shows, which (reasonably enough) work only in the medium for which they were written.

*RTH* was being scripted by a pair of talented writers, at or near the height of their powers, whose strengths were highly complementary, and who were more than capable of doing their own editing as they went along. More than that, though, it is a comedy of words, above all – of the sounds and rhythms of words, as well as of their meanings; a comedy of juxtaposition, of confusion and contrast – see this episode's 'Story so far' by way of illustration. *Round the Horne* was written and performed by word-lovers, and has been treasured by logophiles ever since. No wonder it works so well on paper.

DOUGLAS: Here are some details of this week's programmes on radio and TV.

[BILL: In *Farming Today*, a chicken will be in the studio talking about Ted Moult[1] boxing.]

HUGH: Tonight the House of Commons Amateur Operatic Society will be doing *Mr. Mikardo*.

KEN W: And finally in *Holiday Hour*, there will be a talk entitled Cicely – given by Jack Hulbert.

DOUGLAS: Meanwhile, for those of you who are more easily pleased, here's thirty minutes of whimsical muck as we take you *Round the Horne* –

*Orchestra: Music*

DOUGLAS: The story so far. Swaggering, gold-toothed buccaneer Betty Marsden, he of the barrel chest and eyes like bungholes, sat idly tying a granny knot in his granny, played by sweet lavender-smelling Bill Pertwee. Meanwhile, on the poop deck leggy, voluptuous Bolivian heiress, Kenneth Williams struggled for control of the wheel, with mad bosun Black Hugh Paddick, scourge of the Spanish Main, and none too popular in Hounslow, where, in an ivy-covered old cottage, sat his ivy-covered old mum – wringing her hands through the mangle and crooning to herself over and over again the words . . .

KENNETH: My name is Kenneth Horne.

*Orchestra: Music*

KENNETH: Hello and welcome to *Round the Horne*. That was Douglas Smith, who police believe can help them in their enquiries. He appears by permission of the Y.M.C.A. – Tel Aviv. Now the answer to last week's quiz. Question one – the collective nouns. Well, of course, it's a <u>pride</u> of lions, a <u>covey</u> of baked beans and a <u>herd</u> of Edwin Braden. Now most of you had a pride of lions – a few of you had <u>covey</u> of baked beans – but none of you had heard of Edwin Braden.

KEN W: I have – great hairy fool.

KENNETH: The answer to question two – the 'what do you do with it?' question. Well, of course, the answer is – you stuff it – with either kapok or feathers and not with sage and onion. I would have accepted 'down' but on no account 'up'.

And now we come to the section of the show where we invite minorities to air their views. This week we are honoured by a return state visit of the man who is self-appointed head of an autonomous kingdom within Great Britain – Mr. . . . er –

KEN W: Gruntfuttock. King Gruntfuttock Of Peasmoldia.

KENNETH: Which, I believe, consists of Railway Sidings Hoxton and as far up Buttermold Street as the pub?

KEN W: Yes, that is my kingdom. The Holy Peasmoldian Empire.

KENNETH: Holy?

KEN W: Yes. See, this Empire is wholly my own idea. You see, I have the voices – they speak to me, you know. They tell me things – go forth Gruntfuttock my child, they did say, go forth and claim thy rightful inheritance – and they added P.S. my child, and while you're out, get us an ounce of shag.

KENNETH: Like Joan of Arc?

---

1. An amiable farmer, who was also a radio and TV panellist.

KEN W: No, they prefer Old Hobson's Curly Cut. So I did gird up my loins, and go forth up the High Street, proclaiming myself as king.

KENNETH: And how did people respond to this?

KEN W: Very gratifying considering. One woman give me a shilling.

KENNETH: And now you claim that you're king?

KEN W: Yes, I even issue my own coinage. Here is the Peasmoldian penny piece. Notice my likeness on the front, and see what it says. Gruntfuttockius Rex Peas. Omn. Ind. Imp. D.D. Latin, you know.

KENNETH: I see. Translated that means Gruntfuttock King of all Peasmoldia. Ind. Imp.? Emperor of India?

KEN W: Yes, that's the pub in Buttermold Street.

KENNETH: What's the D.D. for?

KEN W: Drunk and Disorderly. [I have committed several other offences of a crude and highly colourful nature, but there wasn't room on the coin for them.] The lady depicted by my side is her Royal Highness, my gracious good lady wife. Queen of all Peasmoldia. She's here with me, I'll summon her worshipful majesty to come forth. Oi – Kipperfeet!

BETTY: *(Crone)* What?

KEN W: Stop scratching yourself and come and meet Mr. Horne.

BETTY: 'Allo cheeky face.

KEN W: I told you not to say that when you meet strangers. Say what I taught you, Buttercup.

BETTY: We are graciously pleased to grant you an audience.

KEN W: You may address her now – she's given you leave. We'll waive the kissing of her hand, seeing as how grubby it is.

KENNETH: Quite – now – tell me – er King – er –

KEN W: Grunt-futtock – it's hyphenated. Double barrelled, it is. My grandfather was a Grunt from the Rotherhithe Grunts, and he married an Hoxton Futtock, thus uniting two great houses.

KENNETH: Very interesting. [Now being king, I suppose you find you have little time to yourself. Do you patronize the Arts?

KEN W: Yes. We have the Royal Command Film Performance. Last year we went up the Odeon in Leicester Square and commanded them to show *I was a Teenage Call Girl Werewolf* and *Nudist Paradise*, but they refused – got very nasty about it. Threw us out.

BETTY: Yes. We were not amused. And when they showed *Lord Jim* – they wouldn't even let us in. And there's me left alone in the palace, the Royal Supper going cold, the Royal Beer going flat. What am I? I'm a drudge. My Queen Mother was right – I never should have married him –

KEN W: Your Queen Mother? That gin-swigging slagheap!

BETTY: Don't you speak about my mother like that! You pig!

KEN W: Watch it – I'll have you beheaded.

BETTY: He's always saying that, Mr. Horne. He can't, you know. It's just talk.

KEN W: I'll have you incarcerated in the Tower.

**BETTY:** We haven't got a tower.

**KEN W:** Well, I'll lock you in the coalshed then.

**BETTY:** You do, and I'll tell my brother when he gets out. You know what he's like when he's been on the meths. He'll give you a good kicking.

**KEN W:** You must forgive us, Mr. Horne – just a Royal Tiff. Don't let it leak out to Richard Dimbleby – he'd feel very let down.

**KENNETH:** No I won't.] Now, before you go – which I hope is any moment now, would you like to broadcast a message to your loyal subjects?

**KEN W:** No. Because we are all assembled here – to whit the wife and me. Anyway, we must have it away now, because Royal Duties are pressing. Besides, the Royal Horse and Cart are parked on a meter.

*F/X: Piercing whistle*

**KEN W:** Oi! Buttercup! Put your cap on, we're going.

*(Exit mumbling and arguing ad lib)*

*Orchestra: Music*

**KENNETH:** What a majestic couple they make. Oh well, I suppose they're part of life's rich tapestry. The moth-eaten part. Smith! Stop picking crumbs out of Edwin Braden's moustache and introduce the next item.

**DOUGLAS:** Certainly, sir – and now Episode Three – count them, three – of *Kenneth Horne, Master Spy*. This week 'From Russia With Love and Kind Regards to Auntie Mabel, The Twins, and All At Number Three'!

*Orchestra: Music*

**KENNETH:** It all began in the luxuriously appointed stateroom of my twin-screw, diesel-driven, private rubber duck moored in Cannes Harbour. I was relaxing after a case. [A whimsical smile danced in my eyes, slid down the bridge of my nose, trotted across my cheek and scampered into my ear.] Suddenly the phone rang.

*F/X: Phone rings*

**KENNETH:** My face became an impassive mask cut off the back of a cereal packet. I answered it. Hello, Yogi Bear speaking.

**BILL:** You can drop the disguise, Horne. This is Haverstrap here – I've got Brown-Horrocks on the extension . . .

**KENNETH:** Well, that's your problem.

**BILL:** No, Colonel Brown-Horrocks. Intelligence. He wants to speak to you –

**HUGH:** Horne?

**KENNETH:** Yes, sir.

**HUGH:** Look, Horne, something nasty's come up. I've had the P.M. on my neck all morning.

**KENNETH:** Put a poultice on it. It'll soon go down.

**HUGH:** Get back to London immediately. There's a music link leaving in two seconds. Be on it.

*Orchestra: Very brief music link: About two bars*

**KENNETH:** Blast! Missed it. I'll have to charter a private sound effect.

*F/X: Clip-clop of hooves into distance*

*Fade and fade up*

**HUGH:** Any sign of Horne, Miss Golightly?

BETTY: It's hard to see from here –

HUGH: Well, get off my lap and look out of the window.

F/X: *Clip-clop of approaching hooves*

BETTY: There's a pair of coconut shells drawing up – someone's getting off – yes, sir – it's Horne!

F/X: *Door opens*

HUGH: Aah, Horne!

KENNETH: Aah, Brown-Horrocks!

HUGH: You must be worn out after your journey. Care for a spot of lunch?

KENNETH: Yes, sir.

HUGH: Good. There's one on my lapel. Scrape it off, there's a good chap. Now to business. Since you've been away there's been an extraordinary outbreak of truth. All sorts of people in all walks of life have suddenly started telling the truth. If it spreads any further it could mean the end of the British Way of Life. Look at the newspapers.

[KENNETH: *(Reads)* 'The Daily Globe. First with the filth. All the news that is unfit to print.' Good heavens, look at these headlines. 'Famous ageing drunken film star, Lolita Frascati in London in pathetic attempt to boost her career, told our interviewer, "I hate Englishmen, I can't stand London, and I think your police are lousy."'

HUGH: And this – 'Well-known financier, Lord Trusspott, floats new share swindle. He told our City reporter, "I only hope people are mugs enough to fall for it".' You see, Horne, the whole country's upside down.] Listen to some of these recordings we took off the radio. This is the report of a society wedding by a well-known commentator.

KEN W: *(Dimbleby)* I am standing here in the freezing cold outside St. Budolph's Westminster, with an unctuous grin on my face, preparing to give you snobs at home details of yet another dreary society wedding, between Daphne, the eldest daughter of the Duke of Stukely, [that well-known drink-sodden simpleton, and the Honourable Alistair Twick, the son, he says, of that senile pantaloon, the Earl of McWhirter. And here they come now. The spotty fat bride, her face suffused with acne, clinging desperately to the arm of old blubber-lips, the chinless wonder. What an array of glittering nobodies there are here today. What a waste of anybody's time. Still, if I do it often enough, I might cop for a knighthood.

F/X: *Tape off*

[KENNETH: Good heavens!

HUGH: But that's not all – listen to this – this was taken off commercial television –

F/X: *Tape on*

BILL: I am not a doctor, I am a seedy old out of work actor dressed up in this white jacket and stethoscope in a pathetic attempt to fool you. These tablets I'm holding in my hand cost two and six a jar. They're not worth tuppence. Formula 2xc with the mystery ingredient Lustopruntophite – what is it? Epsom salts and chalk.

F/X: *Tape off*]

KENNETH: This is really alarming. What do you think is causing it?

HUGH: We don't know, but it's affecting all sorts of people – here's a transcript of a recent trial at the Old

Bailey – the prisoner pleaded guilty to disorderly behaviour in a public place, [removing certain items of attire and demanding money with menaces,] but he was dismissed because as the judge said, and I quote, 'Don't worry mate, I've often done the same thing myself, only of course, being a judge nobody dared nick me for it.'

KENNETH: Well, what do you make of it, Brown-Horrocks?

HUGH: Obviously somebody's been getting at these celebrities – brainwashing them perhaps – or a truth serum – the only link between all the victims is that they've all been patients at the same private rest home in Geneva. An establishment run by Doctor Chou En Ginsberg –

[KENNETH: Not that fiendish mastermind, whose sworn intention it is to wreak his diabolical revenge on society – that insane arch-criminal, the mention of whose very name strikes terror into the hearts of all decent people? Not him?

HUGH: No. That's his brother Norman.] We want you to get out to Geneva and stop him, [before he gets at the politicians. Once they start telling the truth we're done for. Now Horne – we've got a specially equipped car for you – through here –

KENNETH: Brown-Horrocks pressed a secret button on his trousers and a secret passage in his office swung back to reveal a hidden bookshelf – removing several volumes, he led me down a stairway till we came to a garage – before my eyes stood a huge gleaming monster –

HUGH: This is Sgt. Rackstraw – he'll show you the car –

KENNETH: Hmm – it's a Sporchini 5000 isn't it Sgt.?

BILL: Yes, sir, with certain modifications.

*F/X: Tap on glass*

BILL: Bulletproof windscreen – hub-caps with knives attached – and this is an ingenious little device – you press this button, so – and it squirts hot jam all over your pursuers – so –

*F/X: Squirt*

BILL: Raspberry as you see, sir – what happens is the seeds get in their teeth, they go mad, poking about with their tongues getting 'em out, by which time you're away. Should they persist, you press this button –

*F/X: Squirt*

BILL: See, a cloud of feathers flies out, creating a diversion and adhering to the jam.

KENNETH: Devilish.

BILL: Yes, but we're dealing with some pretty tough customers. Now there are two machine guns hidden behind the headlights – that's for use in traffic jams – if you get stuck up Oxford Street in the rush hour you'll find they clear the street in no time.

KENNETH: What's this knob here?

BILL: If your jam runs out and your feathers don't work, and the machine guns stuck, you just turn this knob and . . .

*F/X: Radio switched on*

*Grams: sig. tune Archers*

*F/X: Radio switched off*

HUGH: All right, Horne. No time to waste – better get going.

KENNETH: And with that, the interview was over. Brown Horrocks gave me a curt smile of dismissal. Then he tightened his lips, screwed up his eyes, unscrewed his ears and juggled them with great dexterity. I climbed into the driving seat of the car, did a racing change and slid into Jermyn Street. Then with a deft flick of the wheel I turned right and roared into the provision department of Fortnum & Mason where a devilled crab, disguised as Douglas Smith, waited to get me to Switzerland.] Smith! – announce me to Geneva.

DOUGLAS: Some hours later at the private nursing home of Doctor Chou En Ginsberg in Geneva.

KENNETH: Thank you, Smith. I knocked on the huge front door. It opened and standing there was the doctor's receptionist. Was this the lovely and desirable Ramona, the sultry temptress who had lured so many men to their doom in her arms? As if in answer to my unspoken thoughts she said –

BETTY: (Common) Yes. I am the lovely and desirable Ramona, the sultry temptress who has lured so many men to their doom in my arms.

KENNETH: Oh well, one more can't hurt.

F/X: Kiss

KENNETH: We clung together passionately, my mouth searched for hers, and found it exactly where I'd suspected it would be all along. Under her nose. She looked at me hungrily. I looked at her hungrily, then she spoke, her voice little more than a hoarse whisper.

BETTY: Would you like some sardines on toast?

KENNETH: Later, when we break for tea . . . [our eyes meet again, her arms twine round my neck and she pulls me roughly against her – er, Smith –]

F/X: Kiss

DOUGLAS: (Wearily) Yes, sir?

KENNETH: You know what's expected of you.

DOUGLAS: Yes, sir. [We draw a veil over what is about to transpire.] Three days later . . .

KENNETH: Three days?

DOUGLAS: [Well there's no point in rushing these things.] Three days later Master Spy Horne shambled nimbly up the stairs to Doctor Chou En Ginsberg's study.

F/X: Knock on door

KENNETH: (Chou En Ginsberg) Come in.

F/X: Door opens

KENNETH: Ah – Chou En Ginsberg! We meet at last –

KEN W: Yes, I've been hanging about here for fifteen pages. What brings you here, Horne?

KENNETH: I've tumbled a little caper.

KEN W: Yes, I know. I heard the pair of you larking about downstairs. Most delightful lady. Now, Mr. Horne – would you care for some light lefleshment? Say – a drugged drink?

KENNETH: It would be lude to lefluse.

KEN W: I will summon my concubine, Lotus Blossom.

F/X: Gong

KEN W: Ah – Lotus Blossom –

HUGH: (Gruff) Yers, guv.

KEN W: Carries her age well, doesn't she? Most gifted of all my geishas – skilled at the arts of provocative dancing – you would care to see her perform sensual song and dance telling age-old story of the love of sun-god for Chinese maiden? Lotus Blossom –

HUGH: Yers, guv?

KEN W: After two – a-one, a-two –

HUGH: *(Sings listlessly)* Oh-hokey-cokey-cokey – knees bend, knees bend, rah rah rah!

KEN W: There – does that not turn your blood to fire? No? Strange – never affects me either.

HUGH: [Well, I am a many-splendoured thing, as it happens, Mr. Horne.] Perhaps you'd care to sample one of my many other delights?

KENNETH: I'd sooner have the drugged drink.

HUGH: Suit yourself.

KEN W: Very well – bring us two goblets of the delicate sake of the Cantonese region, as drunk by generations of my honourable ancestors. Let it be of a fragrant bouquet so that as we sip we may inhale the perfume of a thousand flowers . . . [and contemplate the wonders of a solitary bamboo leaf floating upon limpid waters of still, cool, mountain lake –] *(Snide)* – oh and while you're at it, bring us a couple of pork pies.

HUGH: Yers, oh mighty mandarin – I hasten to do your bidding, cock.

KEN W: Now, Mr. Horne – what brings you here?

KENNETH: I've come to thwart your evil plan to inject everybody with your truth serum. You're mad, Doctor.

KEN W: *(Screams)* Don't call me mad – I'm not mad. *(Quietly)* Irritable first thing in the morning *(Screams)* but not mad!

*F/X: Gong*

HUGH: Two pints of sake – the drug's in the one on the left. Oh – and here's your pies.

KEN W: So, Mr. Horne – you wish to stop me? Well, life, Mr. Horne, is like a game of chess – you understand the meaning of the term stalemate?

KENNETH: Yes?

KEN W: Well do not eat pie – it is stale, mate. You are not drinking your drugged drink – what's the matter, Something wrong with it?

KENNETH: No, cheers.

KEN W: Bottoms up, Mr. Horne.

KENNETH: How little did he know that I'd switched the glasses. He drank deeply and then his face changed colour, he clutched at his throat, and then with a last effort he pulled himself up to his full height – two foot three – and towered over me. He was standing on the wardrobe – his face convulsed in anger –

KEN W: Ah, so – Mr. Horne, you may have beaten me this time, but you haven't heard the last of Doctor Chou En Ginsberg – M.A. Failed – Goodbye –

KENNETH: And with that he trod on a laugh which gave way under his feet, and he plunged headfirst into the lake. And me? Well, my job was done – but I still had some unfinished business to attend to – I went downstairs to where Ramona was waiting for me – she looked at me provocatively, her mouth a scarlet wound –

BETTY: You've come back – I knew you would.

KENNETH: Yes – and you know what I want – my sardines on toast.

*Orchestra: Music*

KENNETH: And now, here are the Fraser Hayes Four with a track from their new LP – *Albert Schweitzer at the Organ of the Tower Ballroom, Blackpool.*

*(Applause)*

*Fraser Hayes & Orchestra: 'Button Up Your Overcoat'*

*(Applause)*

DOUGLAS: And now – Trends!

*Orchestra: Music*

KENNETH: First – trends in the theatre. The nostalgia for the '30s continues. Soon to open in London's West End is yet another Noel Coward revival – *Blithe Laughter*, starring Celia Backstroke and Albert Runt. Here is an excerpt from the play.

*Grams: Old cracked record 'Room with a View'*

BETTY: Excited, Charles?

HUGH: Yes, Fiona, intoxicatedly, flutteringly, heart-thumpingly, passionately excited. And yet somehow – calm. And you, Fiona?

BETTY: Yes, I'm calm too. Resignedly, tranquilly, stoically, placidly calm. And yet – somehow – excited.

HUGH: I know.

BETTY: I know you know.

HUGH: I know you know I know.

BETTY: Yes, I know. These poignant bittersweet moments of shared happiness mean more to me than life itself. Who was it said 'Stolen fruit tastes the sweetest'?

HUGH: It was you, just now.

BETTY: Ah, that's where I heard it.

*They kiss*

HUGH: Oh Fiona – [God, Fiona –] how I adore these mad, feverish, turbulent, tempestuous moments of tremulous, simmering, volcanic, ungovernable, madcap, frenzied, delirious, euphoric bliss – you're so provocatively tantalizing, so piquantly thrilling, so – so – oh but I can't find the words –

BETTY: I know.

HUGH: I know you know.

BETTY: I know you know I know.

HUGH: Yes, I know. But I must go now, Fiona – I have my duty to do.

BETTY: Oh, Charles, you look so splendid in your uniform. Yes – go – now – before my husband comes back. He would never understand.

HUGH: And shall I see you again?

BETTY: Tomorrow morning – at the same time – and I'll have two extra pints of milk, milkman, and some cottage cheese.

*Orchestra: Music*

KENNETH: Well, I don't know about you but I, personally, found that unutterably, inexpressibly, enchantingly, heart-flutteringly nauseating. Next – trends in music – folk singers are still in – none more so than our next guest, Rambling Syd Rumpo.

KEN W: Good evening. Since I was here last, I've been a'ramblin' and a'roving and a'making a nuisance of myself all over the country, a'pickin' up of folk songs, among other things, a'vagabonding and a'gypsying hither and thither, the starry sky my ceiling, my only companion my faithful guitar and a bird called Charmian I picked up in a coffee bar – a doodle-o, a rang me down, cheerup, cheerup, lackaday, etcetera.

KENNETH: And what are you going to sing for us today?

KEN W: This is an old gypsy clothes peg peddler's lament – which is sung by old gypsy clothes peg peddlers whenever they're lamenting. It tells the story of a handsome young gypsy who goes to this door a'trying for to sell his pegs. He says 'Missus, will you a'buy of my pegs-o' – to which she replies, 'No, I will not buy of your pegs-o – clear off out of it else I'll set the dog on you.' To which he replies 'Oh all right then' and he goes. And then he sings this lament.

*(Sings with guitar accompaniment)*

Oh sibyl my roodey ooney-o
O sibyl my roodey dey
And who will truddle my thunderjug
When I am far away –
With a hippity hoppity lul fol ay
And a mickle-ay, muckle-ay, rumble-
    O!

KENNETH: Thank you Rambling Syd Rumpo – that was very moving. On behalf of all the listeners, I'd just like to say a heartfelt good riddance. [Now still on the subject of pop music – we have with us in the studio, the latest of the current crop of girl singers from Liverpool – Miss Angy Spock – and she's talking to well-known D.J. Pete Frontkettle.

BILL: Now Angy, I believe your last record got into the top ten in record-breaking time – why do you think that was?

BETTY: *(Liverpool accent)* It could be because the kids dig me or more likely it's because my manager went round the record shops and bought fifty thousand copies.

BILL: I believe your sudden rise to fame was a real fairy story.

BETTY: Oh no. You don't want to believe that. I was picked up in a fish and chip shop in Lime Street by this greasy agent, see, so anyway we went off to New Brighton and he made me . . .

BILL: Yes, thank you . . .

BETTY: A star overnight.

BILL: Yes, thank you. And now that you are a star is it going to change your way of life?

BETTY: No, I shall remain the same unspoiled . . . I've always been. Of course, it'll change my parents' life – they've always lived in dire poverty – that's near Everton, you know. Well, now that I've been lucky enough to become tops of my chosen profession, I shall be able to do little things for them –

BILL: Like what?

BETTY: Well, buy up the mortgage of their old home where they've lived all their lives – and evict 'em.

BILL: And now you've reached the pinnacle, Angy – what is your ambition?

BETTY: Well, I don't want to be thought of as just a pop singer. I want to become an all-round entertainer. Mind you, I've had experience in that line. I've been all round the fellows I know and they all agree I'm extremely entertaining.

BILL: Well, good luck, Angy and I

hope that we'll all be able to enjoy you in the near future.]

KENNETH: Now finally – trends in modern living. Well, more and more fashionable people are flocking to unfashionable areas to live. Well, I don't like to feel I'm out of the swim, so when I saw an advertisement in one of the Sunday papers which read – 'Thinking of making a move? Why not consult Bona Homes – Estate Agents', I went along to their place in Chelsea –

*F/X: Shop Bell*

*Door opens*

KENNETH: Hello – anybody there?

HUGH: Hello, I'm Julian and this is my friend Sandy.

KEN W: We're Bona Homes – that is, we're filling in here between acting engagements on the telly. We've just finished one together – you know – a soap commercial it is – where I'm dancing with this girl in yards of net – not me – her. Anyway, she's acting a bit funny towards me and I can't understand why – so then Julian comes over and whispers something in me ear – and then I have a bath.

HUGH: He took his bath lovely. Now, Mr. Horne – what can we do for you?

KENNETH: I'm looking for a small town house – somewhere in Islington I thought.

HUGH: Oh, you don't want Islington, does he, Sand?

KEN W: Oh no! Not Islington! Oh no! Definitely not. No, it's been tarted up out of all recognition – but if you're looking for something unspoilt, we've got some divine slums in Brixton. Brixton's still unspoilt, isn't it Jule?

HUGH: Oh fabe! We've got a bona slum property just come in – two up, two down, one out the back – very nice.

KENNETH: How much?

[HUGH: Nine nine five oh, O.N.O. Then there's your F. and F. on top –

KEN W: And your C. and C. – that's extra. But then you have your underfloor C.H. thrown in –

KENNETH: How much?]

KEN W: Fifteen thousand.

KENNETH: Too dear –

HUGH: Well, how much was you thinking of paying?

KENNETH: Well, I thought about ten thousand –

HUGH: Ten thousand? *(Squeals with laughter)* Did you hear that, Sand?

KEN W: *(Laughing)* Yes, but say it again, I enjoy a good laugh.

HUGH: You won't get nothing for ten thousand – unless you go further out. There's a nice conversion on the A1 near Stevenage – stands right on the main road – that's nice ennit, Sand?

KEN W: Oh fantabulosa! And it's detached as well. We can recommend that very highly – all on one level – well you don't want to go climbing stairs at your age, do you –

HUGH: No, he can't be doing with that.

KEN W: And it's very you – I can just see you living there. It's a bijou *pied à terre* really, isn't it, Sand?

HUGH: Yes. And it's very cheap, only eight thousand nine hundred. And you only have to share part of the year, but they're nice people, you'll like them. Two old Irishmen – but they're only there in the winter when they're gravelling.

**KENNETH:** Gravelling? What sort of place is it, then?

**HUGH:** Didn't we tell you? It's a workman's hut.

*Orchestra: Music*

**KENNETH:** Well, naturally I refused it. But they did in the end fix me up with what I wanted – a town house. Trouble is, the town is Dumfries. How shall I describe it – it's a sort of duplex open-plan converted slaughterhouse – still, it's near the station.

Well, that's it for this week, except to give you the results of last week's limerick competition – The winning entry came from Mr. W. A. Beecham, Bristol, and went as follows:–

Two nudists who lived in Foots Cray
Went out for a picnic one day
As one filled the kettle
He sat on a nettle
And warmed up his cold consommé.

This week's competition begins with the following two lines –

A sailor from near Portland Bill
Once married a mermaid named Lil –

I'll repeat that:

A sailor from near Portland Bill
Once married a mermaid named Lil –

All you have to do is to complete the following three lines suggesting one of the many marital difficulties they may have encountered.

Answers please on a postcard to *Round the Horne*, c/o BBC, London, W1. And to the sender of the best entry goes this week's prize – a compendium of games including a shove ha'penny board and a ha'penny

with instructions on how to shove it. See you next week.

*Orchestra: Signature tune*

**DOUGLAS:** That was *Round the Horne*, starring Kenneth Horne, with Kenneth Williams, Hugh Paddick, Betty Marsden and Bill Pertwee. On the musical side you heard the Fraser Hayes Four and Edwin Braden and the Hornblowers. The script was written by Barry Took and Marty Feldman and produced by John Simmonds.

*Orchestra: Music up and out*

*(Applause)*

*Orchestra: Play out*

(Applause)

# SERIES 1
# PROGRAMME 14

*FIRST BROADCAST* – Sunday 6 June 1965

## INTRODUCTION

This is one of the best episodes from the first series, in which many of the most popular regular characters and spots are running at full strength. Gruntfuttock is in particularly fine form as Dictator of the Free People's Republic of Peasmoldia, assisted by his charming lady wife, Buttercup – a role in which that marvellously versatile actress Betty Marsden showed how to get a lot of laughs out of only a few lines.

Parodies of the James Bond films were a more or less compulsory element in comedy shows at that time, but the inventiveness of 'Kenneth Horne, Special Agent' lifts it well above the herd. With its in-jokes and back references, it's a good example of the way in which the sum of *RTH* is greater than the parts of its hole . . . or something like that. Increasingly, *RTH* is moving away from the old format of a sketch show where each skit is a separate entity; instead, for half an hour each week, the listener enters a different universe, in which everything relates to everything else.

The way in which the performers drop in and out of character helps to achieve this. Programme 14 contains some especially choice examples of Williams' complaints to Horne ('I've got medals for acting! Medals. And a certificate for tap-dancing') and his interruptions of his own performance as Chou En Ginsberg.

None of the performers is ever reliably or consistently 'in character', because each of them has an on-going personality, for the purposes of the show, quite apart from the various roles they play.

DOUGLAS: Here are details of some of this week's programmes on BBC1.

BILL: At 9.25 on Tuesday, you'll be able to see a new programme entitled *Ladies and Gentlemen, It Is My Pleasure*, with Malcolm Muggeridge.

HUGH: On Saturday night, the BBC regret *Hot Line*.

KEN W: Later that night there'll be a direct broadcast by the new television satellite, bringing you a person-to-person interview with Sonny Liston in New York. Yes, once again, *Early Bird* catches the worm.

DOUGLAS: Meanwhile, for those of you who are more easily pleased, here's thirty minutes of depressing and cheerless nonsense as we take you *Round the Horne*.

*Orchestra: Music*

DOUGLAS: The story so far; it had been a long winter in Stalag 15. Oberleutnant Kenneth Von Williams, the Camp Commandant, he of the pure Aryan stock to which he'd just added a beef cube, stood surveying the assembled prisoners. Who was behind the attempted escape? Was it beefy, ruddy-faced Wing Commander Betty Marsden – he of the handlebar moustache and low-slung racing seat? Or was it bulldog-chinned, dog-eared Captain Hugh Paddick? He levelled his loaded revolver – played by Bill Pertwee with a load on. 'Achtung,' he barked, wagged his tail and scratched at the door to go walkies. They knew that this was it – and then suddenly in the sky they heard the low monotonous drone that they all knew so well –

KENNETH: My name is Kenneth Horne.

*Orchestra: Music*

KENNETH: That was Douglas Smith, well-known unfrocked pig breeder of no fixed abode, [who can be seen currently in the West End appearing in Pirandello's *Italian Straw Hat*, which he stole from Luigi Pirandello – a wet fishmonger of Eastcheap.] Now, the answers to last week's questions. First – complete the titles of the following horror films question. The first one was *The Creature From The Black——* The answer was, of course, 'Lagoon' and not 'And White Minstrel' as a Mr. George Mitchell of London suggested. Part Two of the horror movie question was *The Cabinet of——* Well, it was, of course, 'Doctor Caligari' and not, as one of you said, 'Harold Wilson', but nice try Mr. A.D. Home[1] of Kinross. Finally, the film classic title was *Gone With The _Wind_*, not the Christmas Club money, Mr. 2437 of Dartmoor – or even 'Gone With The Lodger', as suggested by Edwin Braden – oh, I can't help feeling there's some deep-seated personal grievance there. Well, now it's time to meet [the man who's set up his own kingdom in Hoxton. His Imperial Majesty Gruntfuttock Rex.

KEN W: No, not Rex. J. Peasmold Gruntfuttock, or as I title myself now, Fidel Gruntfuttock, Dictator of the Free People's Republic of Peasmoldia.

KENNETH: Free Peoples?

KEN W: Yes, there's just the three of us. Me, my brother-in-law, Air Vice Marshall Scarface Thrupp, and my good lady wife who has condescended to grace us with her presence. Say hello to Comrade Horne, Comrade Buttercup.

---

1. Sir Alec Douglas-Home, leader of the Conservative Party.

BETTY: Hello, Comrade cheeky-face.

KEN W: She, Mr. Horne, is the first lady of the State of Peasmoldia.

KENNETH: Sort of like Lyndon Johnson's wife – Ladybird Johnson.

KEN W: Yes, only she is known as Colorado Beetle Gruntfuttock. At least, that's what I call her.

KENNETH: Well Mr. . . . . er –

KEN W: Fidel Gruntfuttock. Or, to give me my full title – Fidel El Gruntfuttocko, Founder of the State – Father of the Republic – Liberator of the oppressed and best prices given for second-hand gents' clothing.

KENNETH: Now, I believe, you're a benevolent despot?

BETTY: Yes he is . . . he is.

KEN W: Shut up you counter-revolutionary hay bag! I can have you liquidated, you know. Yes, Mr. Horne, there's a whole new spirit abroad in Peasmoldia. Revolution is in the air. We are rumbling with it. Rumbling.

F/X: *Creep in 'Red Flag' under and build*

KEN W: Soon the free people of Peasmoldia will arise and cast off their shackles. We have nothing to lose but our chains, and so to you at home I say – bestir yourselves, and like a lion roused from his slumbers, gird up your loins. Not now, Buttercup. Fellow citizens, we march upon the Town Hall tomorrow. There will be a bloody revolution in the streets.

F/X: *Cut music dead*

KEN W: Or if wet – in the Scouts' Hut! Peasmoldia arise!

*Orchestra: Quick musical tag*

KENNETH: There they go – the revolting Gruntfuttocks – and now something even more revolting –] Douglas Smith. Stop flaunting your calves at Betty Marsden in that provocative way – make the announcement.

DOUGLAS: Yes, sir. And now, more savagely revealing than *Compact*, more breathtaking in its grandeur than *White Heather Club*[2] – more naked in its unashamed violence than Muriel Young talking to Pussy Cat Willum – we bring you *Kenneth Horne – Special Agent*.

*Orchestra: Music*

KENNETH: I was having a few drinks at my club – The Junior Army and Navy Reform and Stripperama – I'd just downed my eighth pint when I got a call to go to the Yard.

KEN W: *(Character voice)* You're wanted on the phone Mr. Horne, sir.

KENNETH: Thank you, Trusspott.

KEN W: *(Own voice)* Here, is that all I get to say? It's not much of a part – I mean, 'You're wanted on the phone Mr. Horne, sir.' I'm not going to build a career on that, am I? And I specially asked people to listen – I mean, the shame when I go home and my mum says[3], 'You didn't have much this week, son.'

KENNETH: I'm very sorry – it's just the way it came out.

KEN W: *(Whimpering and sniffling)* She says you're keeping me back. You're not letting me flower. I could have been a star today – another Sir

---

2. A TV show featuring traditional Scottish entertainment.
3. In fact, Williams' mother was almost certainly not at home, but sitting in the studio audience; she never missed a recording of *RTH*.

John Gingold – Oh where is my early promise? Where are the snows of yesteryear? *(Screams)* I've got medals for acting! Medals. And a certificate for tap-dancing.

KENNETH: Please – this is very embarrassing in public. There's people listening.

KEN W: They have a right to know. *(To audience)* It's not fair, the way they treat me on this show. When we go off on outings, they won't let me sit with the driver. *(Shouts)* I have to sit in the back with Edwin Braden – him! That great hairy fool! I've been held back – I could have been a star! A star! I could have been a somebody. There it's out now, and I'm glad!

KENNETH: Feeling better? Can we go on now?

KEN W: Yes all right. *(Into character)* You're wanted on the phone Mr. Horne, sir.

KENNETH: I hurried to the phone booth immediately.

*F/X: Phone up*

KENNETH: Hello, Marianne Faithfull speaking.

HUGH: Alright Horne, you can drop the disguise. This is Brown-Horrocks. I want you to get over here as quickly as you can. I shall be waiting for you at the bottom of the next page disguised as a footnote.

*F/X: Phone down*

KENNETH: Brown-Horrocks was rattled – I could hear it. It took a great deal to rattle Brown-Horrocks. There was no time to waste. I leapt into my 2.4 drophead Douglas Smith, and roared off . . .

DOUGLAS: *Car noises: Followed by animal roar*

KENNETH: What's the matter, Smith? Got a tiger in your tank[4]?

DOUGLAS: No, I think it's a puss in the boot.

KENNETH: No one likes a clever dick, Smith.

*Orchestra: Quick music link*

*F/X: Door opens*

HUGH: Horne!

KENNETH: Aah, Brown-Horrocks! What's afoot?

HUGH: I shall treat that feed line with the contempt it deserves, Horne. Now listen carefully, Horne, here comes the plot. Chou En Ginsberg – Japanese mastermind and underwater haberdasher – has struck again. He's set up a pirate radio station and is jamming BBC news broadcasts. Listen to this.

*F/X: Radio on*

BILL: This is the nine o'clock *(F/X beep)* and this is *(F/X beep beep)* reading it. Today in Parliament, members met in the lobby to *(F/X beep)* When the house re-assembled, George Brown rose to his feet and delivered a strong *(F/X beep)* which was greeted with cries of 'Resign' from all sides. In the following *(F/X beep)* the *(F/X beep)* for *(F/X beep)* asked if there was any truth in the rumours that *(F/X beep)* was being used to *(F/X beep)* Barbara Castle. Mr. Harold Wilson replied that he wasn't aware of any *(F/X beep)* but that he would be delighted to *(F/X long series of beeps)* Sir Alec in a public *(F/X beep)* on television.

---

4. 'Put a tiger in your tank' was an advertising slogan for petrol.

*F/X: Radio switched off*

KENNETH: Good heavens – how awful.

HUGH: Yes, but it got a few cheap laughs, didn't it? Now this pirate radio station – we have one slight clue that might give us a lead to its whereabouts. There is a Chinese junk moored on the Serpentine. It's called the *SS Ginsberg*. It's just a hunch, but there might be something in it. Get out there and stop him immediately.

KENNETH: Yes, sir. And with that, the interview was over – he glanced at me quizzically – I glanced at his quizzically – he squared his jaw, cubed his ears, divided his nose, and took away the number he first thought of. Some hours later found me on the banks of the dangerous garbage-infested waters of the Serpentine, putting on my goggles, buckling on my snorkel and dancing in my tails. [I leapt in and started to swim towards the *SS Ginsberg*. Suddenly I felt a slimy tentacle fasten itself around my ankle – it was the dreaded banana skin that was known to infest these waters. Pulling out my fruit knife I plunged it again and again into the yellow skin of my adversary until it released its hold.] Soon I was clambering aboard the junk – a knife clenched between my teeth and my teeth safely hidden in a secret compartment in my mouth. They'd never think of looking there. I crawled along the deck when suddenly a figure loomed above me. I looked up and there stood a beautiful girl – wearing more leather than an Aberdeen Angus. She spoke –

BETTY: I am Grotty Thunderghast – Chou En Ginsberg's personal bodyguard. I guard his personal body, you know. Don't try anything, Mr. Horne. I am a Black Belt sixth dan, a master of karate, an expert in jujitsu – if you make one false move I shall hit you with my handbag.

KENNETH: My cool grey eyes surveyed her – she was <u>my</u> kind of woman. She gave me a look which made my hair stand up on end. And there's not many women who can do that. I took her in my arms and held her tenderly in my double entendre – eh? Oh sorry, that's the producer's note on my script. And then, putting emphasis on certain words, she said –

BETTY: *(Husky)* Keep it clean and bright and don't overrun. *(Change of voice)* Eh? Oh it's another note from the producer.

KENNETH: We clung together in a tempestuous embrace and then – Smith.

DOUGLAS: *(Cheerfully)* Oh well, they say the onlooker sees most of the game –

KENNETH: Smith! Don't be ribald.

DOUGLAS: I'm sorry, sir. Ahem – three seconds later –

KENNETH: Three seconds?

DOUGLAS: Don't blame me, sir – I've had a producer's note too. Three seconds later, Special Agent Horne capered reluctantly up the companionway to the state room of the fiendish Chou En Ginsberg.

*F/X: Knock on door*

KEN W: Come in!

KEN W: *(Dr. Chou)* Ah, Horne – *(Small pause)* Well?

KENNETH: Well what?

KEN W: *(Snide[5])* Aren't you going to say Ah Chou – and then I can say Bless you like I did last week. Oh go on – be a sport –

KENNETH: Very well – Ah Chou! *(Pause)* Well?

KEN W: Well what?

KENNETH: Aren't you going to say Bless you?

KEN W: No, I've gone off the idea. *(Back into character)* So, Mr. Horne, you have tracked me down.

KENNETH: Yes, and I'm going to put a stop to your evil plan to undermine the BBC etc, etc., etc. as established earlier on.

KEN W: Yes, but first – let us have some entertainment. I will summon Lotus Blossom, most beautiful of all my concubines.

*F/X: Gong*

KEN W: Ah, Lotus Blossom, my little bamboo shoot, my little lychee nut –

HUGH: Yers, oh mighty warlord – oh celestial radiance – your slightest whim is my command, mate.

KEN W: Between ourselves, Mr. Horne, Lotus Blossom not all she cracked up to be. But sing, my precious flower, sing song of lonely warrior who dleams of leturn to homeland far away and sings plaintive tladitional song of yearning for place of birth. Song entitled, Hissalon Huaytoo Tia pa hiary – after me – a-one, a-two –

HUGH: *(Long way to Tipperary)* Hissalon Huaytoo tis pa Hiary, Hissalon Way to go –

KEN W: Thank you, Lotus Blossom – please keep in touch. Now, Mr. Horne – eyes down for big oriental flash finish. Yes, I'm trying to understand BBC news broadcasts.

KENNETH: But why?

KEN W: Because they would not let me be news leader on ladio for Blittish Bloadcasting Corpolation. Would not even let me lead lacing lesults – they say I too tall.

KENNETH: I'll have a word with Loy Lich if you like.

KEN W: Ah no! Too late now. Lesentment and flustlation turn my leason. Levenge shall be mine. I shall destloy BBC – and you cannot stop me.

KENNETH: Oh can't I, Ginsberg? This Douglas Smith I'm holding in my hand is timed to go off in ten seconds. Smith?

DOUGLAS: *(Wearily)* Tick tock tick tock tick tock.

KENNETH: Well, Doctor Chou En Ginsberg?

KEN W: Not that! Not that! Don't let him off. Don't let him off. Alright – I surrender.

KENNETH: And with that he ran around in ever decreasing circles and with a despairing cry disappeared through one of his own portholes. It's a good trick if you can do it. But although I foiled him that time, we in MI5 feel that we haven't heard the last of . . .

KENNETH: Doctor Chou En Ginsberg M.A. Failed. Goodbye.

*Orchestra: Music*

5. Refers to one of Williams' stock voices – the same one that would whine, 'No, stop messin' about!' in *Hancock's Half Hour.*

KENNETH: And what of the strange junk – well, here are the Fraser Hayes Four to sing some as they give you a track from their new LP *Pinky and Perky sing the Quintin Hogg[6] Songbook*.

*Fraser Hayes Four: 'It's a Lovely Day Today'*

DOUGLAS: And now – Trends.

*Orchestra: Music*

KENNETH: This is the part of the show for the trendy – the with-it – the people who are switched on, as opposed to people like me who have been cut off at the mains. First – the cinema. Here is trendy film columnist Peter Frontkettle with news from the studios.

BILL: Well-known film producer Lippy Angst is planning something really exciting when he goes on the floor at Shepperton with *Esther Waters* – playing the title role is Pandora Lust – and here she is with me now. Pandora, that's a very unusual name isn't it?

BETTY: *(Sexy)* Yes, it's not my own you know – but I felt that with the name I had, I just wasn't getting anywhere.

BILL: Then what was your real name?

BETTY: Rock Hudson, [but it turned out there already was one.

BILL: Er – yes, well passing hurriedly on – here's more news of forthcoming films. Big excitement at M.G.B. studios when it was announced that Peter Sellers <u>himself</u> had agreed not to star in their next film. Rumours have been confirmed that Tod Doppelganger is to make the Jean Harlow story and among those touted to play the coveted title role are Carroll Baker, Debbie Reynolds, and Tippie Hendren – but my own personal hunch is that the coveted title role of Jean Harlow will go to our own Jimmy Saville.]

KENNETH: Meanwhile on release there's a revival of that great British film classic of the Thirties – *The Legend of the Glass Intermezzo*, starring Celia Molestrangler and Binkie Huckaback. Here is an excerpt.

*Studio: Piano concerto ('Dream of Olwen'-type music)*

*F/X: Door opens: Piano stops*

BETTY: Oh darling Charles – you startled me coming in like that – through the French windows.

HUGH: Oh darling Fiona, I had to see you.

BETTY: I felt you would.

HUGH: I felt you felt I would.

BETTY: I felt you felt I felt you would.

HUGH: I felt that too. And yet I was uncertain. Breath-haltingly, tooth-chatteringly, nerve-twitchingly, lip-bitingly uncertain. And yet somehow – sure. And you darling, darling Fiona?

BETTY: I was sure too. And yet somehow – uncertain. Sure that I was uncertain, but certainly unsure, and yet surely, certainly unsure – with that sure certainty that comes from knowing.

HUGH: Yes I know.

BETTY: I know you know.

HUGH: I know you know I know.

BETTY: Yes I know. And yet now I no longer care.

---

6. Conservative politician, aka Lord Hailsham.

HUGH: Ah Fiona – to know – to care – or uncaring know and knowing care or not, still unknowing and caring, and knowing care not or no. Shall we ever know?

BETTY: Or knowing, care?

HUGH: Or caring, know – oh Fiona, you take a man's heart in your hands and laugh in its face – play for me Fiona – one last time – our rhapsody.

*Studio: Piano plays rhapsodic theme while Betty talks*

BETTY: One tries to forget – I don't know – so many things. Oh Charles – do you remember that gay night in Warsaw?

*Studio: Piano stops.*

HUGH: Ah Warsaw – how could I forget?

BETTY: And Budapest?

HUGH: How could I ever forget Budapest?

BETTY: And do you remember that doorway of the basement shop in the Balls Pond Road?

HUGH: Ah who could forget that time – no, I don't remember that.

BETTY: Oh well – it must have been someone else then, it was so dark.

BETTY: Oh why did you come here Charles – to torture me, to drive me mad?

HUGH: No madam, to tune the piano.

*Orchestra: Music*

KENNETH: Oh, they don't make films like that any more. They just show them on television every Sunday afternoon. And now, trends in music. Yet again we are under-privileged to have with us that doyen of folk singers, Rambling Syd Rumpo.

KEN W: Well now, dang me down a doodle oh, in the past week I've been a'rambling and a'roving amid the bosky retreats and pastoral solitude of the Cool Orang-Utan nightclub-o where I am currently appearing-o a-pulling down three grand a week with my simple homespun rubbish-o – Chirrup chirrup, and a fusset gone away-o.

KENNETH: And what are you going to sing for us this week, Rambling Syd?

KEN W: Well, I thought I'd give ee a sea shanty – it's an old Cornish lobster potters' song, [sung by the fishermen of they parts, when they go out a potting lobsters.] It tells the story of a young lobsterman who sings to his ladylove. 'For I'm going away my fair young maid – upon the salty main-o. For when the lobsters spawn and the tide flows free and the North Star guides a sailor to a haven in your arms I shall come home a'bearing ee a parrot and fine laces and perfume and a new sink tidy for what you have always craved'. And to this his ladylove answers 'Eh! What's that you said,' 'cos she weren't listening. So he sings to her 'What's the matter, you got cloth ears? I'm not saying all that again.' And he goes. And as he goes he sings this little lament.

*(Sings)*

Haul away me dangle boys
Haul away, haul away,
For I'm bound down Rio
Yo ho ho and hee hee hee
When you're outward bound and the
    wind blows free,
Free-o free-o
Early in the morning.

KENNETH: Thank you, Rambling Syd, – and sling your hook-o. Ah we shall never look upon his like again – if we play our cards right. Now, the other week [I received a phone call from the *Radio Times* asking me for a photo of myself that they could publish. Well, unfortunately the only one I have is a candid snap of me lying on a bearskin rug – with no clothes on – mind you, it was taken quite a long while ago. Let's see now – yes, must have been three months. That is, I was three months old when it was taken . . . I was sort of bald all over in those days. Anyway, I didn't think it would be suitable for the *Radio Times*, this being a family show – so I went to have a new photo taken. Actually] I popped into a new little photographer's in Chelsea. It was called the 'Studio Bona'.

F/X: *Shop bell*

KENNETH: Hello – anybody there?

HUGH: Oh hello, I'm Julian and this is my friend Sandy –

KEN W: We're filling in as photographers between acting engagements on the telly. We've just done this one where I'm all dragged up as a sultan, squatting on me cushion, all surrounded by these dolly little palones.

HUGH: Yes – and there's me stood at his side wearing a pair of great baggy trousers and full of Eastern Promise, waving me fan over him.

KEN W: Yes, he waves his fan lovely. So anyway, then this bird trolls in wiggling her hips at me – and I look at her with burning masculine desire, and then she gives me a bit of marshmallow.

HUGH: Oh it was fabe! But apart from that we've only been doing odds and ends – hither and thither you know.

KEN W: So we're filling in as photographers. Now what can we do for you?

KENNETH: Well I just wanted a portrait. Nothing too sexy. Something that brings out the roguish twinkle in my eye – and with particular emphasis on the dimple. But I leave it to you.

HUGH: Mmm – let's see now. How about if we did you like we did that chap – what's his name – big Scotch fella – takes James Bond in them films. Siobhan Connery.

KEN W: Oh yes – fabe! Shirt slashed open to the waist – flexing your deltoids, with your chest bulging – a lock of your tousled mop falling carelessly over your – mmm – I can see difficulties.

KENNETH: No. I don't think it's quite me anyway.

KEN W: Well, have a browse through some of our work here. Jule – show him your folio.

HUGH: Yes, now you have your various atmosphere photographs. There's your broody intellectual – like we done for Kathy Kirby. Then there's your dewy-eyed ingenue – like we done for Felix Aylmer. Or this is a bona one – look – not suitable for you, mind, but see her lounging on a settee in a figure-hugging Courrege trouser suit, with a collar of diamonds at her neck – we had a load of trouble getting that pose.

KENNETH: Hold on, I recognize that face.

HUGH: Course you do. It's Gladys Cooper.

KENNETH: Looks more like Henry Cooper.

KEN W: There, Jule! I told you it was.

HUGH: No wonder we had all that trouble getting him to pose like that.

KEN W: Well this one here's not <u>Lena</u> Horne – so watch it. Now, how can we express his personality best? Go on Jule – start creating. Think of something startling to do with him.

HUGH: Don't rush me. Don't rush me. [Yes – yes – yes – yes! I've got it! No, it's slipped away again.

KEN W: It does you know, Mr. Horne. It slips away from him.

HUGH: It's coming back! It's coming back!

KEN W: It's coming back, Mr. Horne.

HUGH: It's here!] Oh yes. I see him all grainy, absolutely stark and lit from the bottom. There!

KEN W: Fantabulosa! Quick – do it now – while the mood's upon you.

HUGH: Right, here we go – under the hood. Come on, Sand – give us a hand with him. Right? Ready?

*Small pause*

KEN W: Er – just one thing – I'm not telling you your own business, but should I be under the hood with you?

*Orchestra: Music*

KENNETH: In the end the photo came out like an original Armstrong – not Jones, <u>Louis</u> Armstrong. [It was a bit under-exposed, so I had to send the *Radio Times* the one of me in the nude on a bearskin rug. They're going to print it too. So next week's edition of the *Radio Times* will only be sold to genuine art connoisseurs over the age of eighteen – state profession when ordering.] Well, that's all for this week, except to announce the winner of last week's limerick competition. The winner is Mrs. Churchill of Rainham, Essex, and the winning entry is as follows:–

A monkey who lived in the zoo
Got terribly bored with the view –
It wasn't the grille
That made him feel ill
But the people who kept looking
   through.

The last limerick of our present series begins with the following two lines:

A short-sighted surgeon named Sprake
Once made a quite stupid mistake –

I'll repeat that:

A short-sighted surgeon named Sprake
Once made a quite stupid mistake –

All you have to do is to complete the limerick suggesting what mistake he might have made. Answers please, not to the B.M.A., but to *Round the Horne*, c/o BBC, London, W1. And to the sender of the best completed limerick goes this week's prize of a glossy photo of Alma Cogan, dressed as the harbour master at Looe. Cheerio. See you next week.

*Orchestra: Signature tune*

DOUGLAS: That was *Round the Horne*, starring Kenneth Horne, with Kenneth Williams, Hugh Paddick, Betty Marsden and Bill Pertwee. On the musical side you heard the Fraser Hayes Four and Edwin Braden and the Hornblowers. The script was written by Barry Took and Marty Feldman and produced by John Simmonds.

*Orchestra: Music up and out*

*(Applause)*

*Orchestra: Play out*

*(Applause)*

# SERIES 2
# PROGRAMME 1

*FIRST BROADCAST* – Sunday 13 March 1966

## INTRODUCTION

Bill Pertwee's 'Uriah Heap' interjections, in which he begs Mr. Horne to give him more to do, 'however menial', reflect the fact that alone of the performers, he did not yet have a major recurring character to call his own. He was the cast's odd-job man, filling in with bits and pieces as and when required – a crucial role in such a show, and if his contribution to the first series was not especially noticeable, that is probably a tribute to his quiet professionalism.

However, for the beginning of the second series, Took and Feldman have come up with something a bit more meaty for Bill to chew on, with the introduction of Seamus Android.

The Irish broadcaster Eamonn Andrews is best remembered today as the presenter for many years of *This Is Your Life*, but it was in another incarnation that he caught the attention of Barry and Marty. They had been guests on Andrews' Sunday night TV show, and had been amazed at what they saw as his hysterically funny inability to engage in simple chat without descending into gibberish – a fairly significant failing, one might think, for the host of a chat show. (Off camera he was charming and articulate.)

Pertwee was a skilled impressionist, and his take-off of Eamonn Andrews is at the same time both spot-on and utterly ridiculous. Seamus proved to be his only major character in *RTH*, and Bill left the programme after series 3, as a result of a BBC economy drive. He was soon to find much greater fame on television, as the air raid warden in *Dad's Army*, a performance which is still held in the highest regard by critics and viewers alike.

BETTY: (*As Clitheroe's mother. Calls*) Jimmy! Jimmy! Oh where is that little scamp?

KEN W: (*Clitheroe, coming on mic*) Here I am, mother.

BETTY: Where have you been? Your tea's nearly cold.

KEN W: Sorry, mother. I've been up the post office to collect my old age pension. Mother, I've been thinking – why can't I wear long trousers like the other boys.

BETTY: Long trousers, you little tinker – whatever for?

KEN W: Well, the hair on me legs is beginning to turn grey. After all mother, I'm nearly eighty-three. (*Whining*) Please mother, please –

BETTY: Shut your moaning cakehole and eat your tea.

KEN W: Oh, alright. What is it, mother?

BETTY: What you always have – monkey glands.

*Orchestra: Sig. tune*

BILL: Yes, the studio that gave you the Clitheroe Kid now gives you a show so heart-warming, so knee-trembling, so nose-gripping, that only the BBC would dare –

HUGH: Ladies and gentlemen – the programme that contains ninety-nine per cent of all known jokes – *Round the Horne.*

*Orchestra: Sig. tune up*

*(Applause)*

DOUGLAS: The story so far – the Japs were getting nearer. Brutal drill-pig Sergeant Hugh Paddick – a regular now for the last twenty-one years (thanks to Boggis Fruit Salts) crouched in a foxhole. Nearby a fox, played by nimble Betty Marsden in a skin, crouched in a Hugh Paddick hole which she'd just dug. The sergeant looked at his two companions – second lieutenant Bill Pertwee, he of the apple cheeks and pear-shaped body, and boyish, wistful Kenneth Williams, bent as always under the weight of the Vickers machine gun he'd borrowed from the vicar. ['Would relief never come,' thought Paddick.] Suddenly Williams leapt to his feet and, unbuckling the Sam Browne belt that held up Sam Browne's trousers and brandishing them above his head, he cried, 'I'm going over the top'. The censor got him before he'd gone two yards. The two survivors crouched there – then suddenly, when all seemed lost, they heard the cry that told them that the long-awaited succour was on its way –

KENNETH: Good evening. This is the long-awaited sucker – Kenneth Horne.

*Orchestra: Music (Applause over)*

That was Douglas Smith, England's only nudist kosher butcher and man about town. The town of course being West Hartlepool. Well now, as this is the first of a brand new series, here are the answers to last week's questions. The answer to question one – complete the first lines of the following songs – 'If I were a blackbird I'd——' The answer is 'I'd whistle and sing', and I positively will not accept any other suggestions.

The second song was 'There's a rainbow round my——' Now we got an amazing number of replies to this. We haven't had so many since we asked you to complete 'Over my shoulder goes——' Really, it makes it very difficult for us to keep up the high reputation for sophisticated comedy that we've never had.

And now back again hot foot from his thick army socks comes that debonair yobbo, Douglas Smith.

DOUGLAS: Hello again, fans. And now the further adventures of *Kenneth Horne – Master Spy.* [And here he is, the biggest bind of them all – Old Thunderball himself – Kenneth Horne.]

*Orchestra: Music*

KENNETH: I sat at the gaming table of my club [– The White Orang Utan in Jermyn Street.] I'd been losing heavily at chemmy – and not for the first time the thought crossed my mind – 'I wish I could chemmy like my sister Kate'. I was in trouble and I knew it – [if that was the best gag I could think of, I was in for a bad few minutes.] Opposite me sat my adversary – the head of STENCH, whose initials stood for Special Executive for Terrorism, Extortion, Nuclear Counter Espionage and Hand Laundry. So this was Kronkmeyer, the arch-criminal. He spoke –

KEN W: Come on, Mr. Horne, ducky, your deal –

KENNETH: I beg your pardon? Where does 'ducky' come in?

KEN W: I interpolated it. After all you said arch. If you wanted a butch criminal you only had to say so. I can be as butch as the next man, can't I?

HUGH: *(Fey)* 'Course you can.

KEN W: See? I'm not limited, am I? I've got range – I'm versatile.

HUGH: Bottomless, his versatility is. He can run the gamut. Run your gamut for him. Do your act. The one you do in the clubs up North.

KEN W: Alright. Ladies and gentlemen of Greaseborough – I went to a Hollywood party the other night with my roving microphone. Well, here I am at a Hollywood party and who's that over there? Why it's Tom Mix talking to lovely Theda Bara. *(American voice)* Hello, lovely Theda Bara. *(Deep gruff voice)* Hello, Tom Mix.

KENNETH: Did Theda Bara really sound like that?

KEN W: Yes. That's what ruined her when talkies came in. [Don't interrupt. Pushing my way through the throngs of celebrities – excuse me, Fatty Arbuckle, pardon me, D.W. Griffiths – why, who is that I see now deep in conversation in the corner – why, it's the late great George Arliss talking to the late great Al Jolson. *(Arliss)* Hello, late great Al Jolson. Why don't you sing us a song in your inimitable way? *(Jolson)* Alright late, great George Arliss. *(Sings)* Mammy, Mammy, I'd walk a million miles if I had your –

KENNETH: Excuse me.] I don't want to appear stuffy but we're in the middle of a James Bond parody. [I don't quite see a place for the late great Al Jolson – unless we play the sketch as a seance.] I mean, you've only got one line – no need to make a meal of it.

BILL: I'll do it, Mr. Horne. I'm very humble. I'm grateful for anything – please, Mr. Horne, please – however menial it is, I'll do it – I'm humble you see, humble –

HUGH: Oh here we go – the welcome return of Uriah Pertwee.

BILL: Did you hear that, Mr. Horne – the way they sneer at me 'cos I'm a provincial. [That Hugh Paddick with his glib London wave – and that Mr. Williams. He's a Piccadilly Johnny he is.] They look down on me – they laugh at my rude moleskin trousers and my clumsy manners. They mock me 'cos I'm not one of the fancy, but who would fancy anyone in rude moleskin trousers –

KEN W: A rude mole.

BILL: *(Dropping into affected rural accent)* Yes – you hates me Master Kenneth, you always did. ['Cos Miss Sibling up the hall preferred me to you. Ay, she spurned thee for oi –] Ar – Aha – ar – ahar. *(Suddenly switching to breezy compere voice)* And now ladies and gentlemen – *The Hunchback of Notre Dame* – *(Guttural voice)* Why am I so ugly, why am I so ugly?

BETTY: Answers please on a postcard to *Round the Horne* – care of the BBC.

KENNETH: Please, Betty – don't you start. I thought I could rely on you.

BETTY: Yes, you thought you'd bought my loyalty – among other things – with a plate of oysters and a bottle of milk stout. *(Start to shout)* I was a good girl till I met him. Selling flowers in Covent Garden I was. Then 'e come along. 'E 'ad a wager with his fine genl'man friend, Colonel Edwin Braden –

KEN W: Great hairy fool!

BETTY: He said [I'd never be a lydy while I kept dropping me aspirates – he said] he'd pass me off as a duchess.

HUGH: He promised me the same thing –

KEN W: Any luck?

HUGH: Well – so-so, but between ourselves I think the Duke's beginning to suspect something.

*Orchestra: Cymbal crash – into*

*variety type pay-off music in fast two*

BETTY: Mike and Bernie Winters are now appearing in *Bareskins and Frolics* at the Opera House, Glyndebourne.

DOUGLAS: Meanwhile, back at the plot –

KENNETH: Kronkmeyer and I stared across the gaming table at each other. His eyes smouldered fiercely. I stubbed them out in an ashtray. [My losses were heavy – I pulled out my bankbook – my adversary smiled –

KEN W: You are acquainted with the game of chess I believe, Mr. Horne –

KENNETH: Yes.

KEN W: Then of course you understand the term 'checkmate'.

KENNETH: Then you mean? . . .

KEN W: Yes. You know what you can do with your cheque, mate.

KENNETH:] Kronkmeyer's hand snaked under his jacket and re-emerged holding something small, black and shiny that I recognised with a tremor of fear.

KEN W: You know what this is, Mr. Horne?

KENNETH: Yes. A pickled walnut.

KEN W: Precisely. And I'm not afraid to use it.

KENNETH: There was only one thing could save me now. I had to go for my gun. Excuse me, Kronkmeyer – I have to go for my gun.

KEN W: Well, hurry back. I can't hang about here all night clutching a soggy pickled walnut.

KENNETH: I slipped out into the bar.

[It had been a close call. I knew that the next time we met, Kronkmeyer and I would have to have a reckoning. I propped my long, lean form against the bar, and sat on a stool next to it – the swarthy barman smiled and showed me his gold teeth –

HUGH: *(Gummy)* Here you are – have a look at my gold teeth.

KENNETH: Very nice. Now just slip them back and get me a drink – I'll have my usual – a small glass of Parrish's chemical food – stirred but not shaken – I drank it in one gulp – I was shaken but not stirred.] At that moment a waiter sidled over, sneezed discreetly in my drink and whispered up my nose – it was the message I had been expecting. 'M' wanted to see me – at once. I hailed a passing announcer and told him to step on it. Smith?

DOUGLAS: Yes, sir?

KENNETH: Step on it, will you?

DOUGLAS: Very good, sir.

*F/X: Something nasty being crunched underfoot*

DOUGLAS: There – I've stepped on it – it's quite dead now.

KENNETH: Good – then announce me to the headquarters of MI5.

DOUGLAS: Certainly, sir. Five minutes later – outside a small back room in the top security wing of Whitehall.

*F/X: Knock on door*

BETTY: *(Russian voice. Off mic)* Come in, Comrade.

*F/X: Door opens*

KENNETH: 'M's' new secretary sat behind the desk. [I surveyed her briefly and recommended immediate possession –] she had everything a tough virile man could want – big biceps, a huge black beard – not formally good-looking but interesting to a certain kind of man – Bertram Mills, Billy Smart, Barnum and Bailey. She spoke again –

BETTY: If you wish to see the decadent imperialist capitalist hyena, I'll tell him you're here.

KENNETH: She waved me in the direction of the office with her Communist Party membership card – there was something wrong – what was she doing here? I would have to ask 'M'. I strode into his office – he was bent over his work, but off duty, straight as a die.

HUGH: Ah Horne – glad you've come. [I've just had these plates sent over from the lab. What do you make of them?

KENNETH: Mmm. Baked beans I'd say.

HUGH: Just as I thought. The food in the canteen gets worse and worse every day.]

KENNETH: That girl outside – your new secretary –

HUGH: You mean Gladys?

KENNETH: Yes. Has she defected recently?

HUGH: Well, none of us is perfect. [No, she's a double agent for SMERSH and WHOOSH.

KENNETH: Whoosh?

HUGH: A new detergent.] But we've got something more important to worry about. Here – take these binoculars – look out of this window at the Houses of Parliament – what do you see?

KENNETH: I see the Earl of Arran's at it again –

HUGH: No. Look at Big Ben.

KENNETH: That's not Big Ben. What is it?

HUGH: It's just coming up to twelve o'clock – listen.

*F/X: Loud whirring of clock machinery – including very loud ticking & then – huge deep 'cuckoo – cuckoo'*

KENNETH: Good heavens – a fifty foot high cuckoo.

HUGH: Yes. Someone's stolen Big Ben and substituted a mechanical cuckoo – [at least we hope it's mechanical – nobody's dared to go near enough to find out. You realize what this means to the Empire – no Big Ben!

KENNETH: Yes. The end of the Big Ben Banjo Band as we know it.

HUGH: Precisely.] So far we've managed to cover it up. The BBC have been very co-operative. Before the ten o'clock news, Sir Hugh Greene himself comes into the studio and shouts 'Bong Bong' but if the poor chap gets laryngitis, it'll be civil war.

KENNETH: Who would have taken Big Ben? I mean it'd be very difficult to get it out of the country.

HUGH: Yes – we've alerted the police and customs officials to be on the look out for a very tall man with an enormous bulge in his waistcoat pocket – we have one slight clue to the identity of the thief – a visiting card left at the scene of the crime. Here –

KENNETH: *(Reading)* Doctor Chou En Ginsberg, International Clock Thief – 14 Station Parade, Switzerland. Hmm – not much to go on. But why Switzerland?

HUGH: I think the scriptwriters are planning some dreadful joke about 'What's the matter, Horne?' Be on your guard against it. Now you'll need some special equipment – Colonel Haverstrap of stores will be glad to fill you in – he's never liked you.

KENNETH: [The interview was over. 'M' smiled at me wryly – I smiled at his O'Hara – then together the two Irishmen, Riley and O'Hara, swaggered off arm in arm in the direction of Kilburn.] I hurried to the bottom of the page where Colonel Haverstrap was waiting for me, disguised as a greasy thumbprint.

BILL: *(Gruff army type)* Alright, Horne – here's your equipment. These are your small arms, these are your puny hairy legs and this is your [tiny bald head – you know how to use them I take it. Here's a] plastic Japanese junior spy kit, comprising a small plastic dagger, the egg-in-bag trick, a revolving bow tie, nail-through-finger trick, an exploding banjo – and this . . .

KENNETH: Good heavens – what is it?

BILL: [Ah well, the trade name is – Naughty Doggie – Fido Gets The Blame. Only use it if you're in a tight corner.

KENNETH: How does it help me escape?

BILL: While they're beating the daylights out of the dog, you can slip out unnoticed. But] if there's no other way out – use this card – but remember – you can only use it once.

KENNETH: *(Reads)* Get out of jail free.

BILL: [That's all then, Horne, except for these – a gun that looks like a transistor radio – a transistor radio that looks like a gun – and . . .

*Orchestra: Link*

. . . this umbrella.

KENNETH: Mmm. A cunning device. What's it for?

BILL: To keep the rain off, you bald-headed fool!] Right. Good luck, Horne. There's a plane leaving London Airport for Switzerland in eight bars time – be on it –

*Orchestra: Fast music link*

KENNETH: I relaxed in the luxury first-class compartment of the Super Constellation Pan World Airways swept-wing Sopwith Camel that was to take me to my rendezvous with fate. The hostess bent over me –

BETTY: We're about to take off, sir. Would you like a boiled sweet or cotton wool?

KENNETH: I won't have the boiled sweets. They just fall out of my ears. I'll just have some cotton wool.

BETTY: Here you are, sir.

KENNETH: Thank you. *(Sound of munching)* Delicious. Then suddenly I realised, too late, the cotton wool had been impregnated with a sleep-inducing drug manufactured from a blend of poppy seed, liquorice and senna pods. Well to be honest, it didn't induce sleep, but it seemed the safest thing to do. My head spun and then blackness engulfed me.

*Grams: Short dramatic sweep of strings*

KENNETH: When I came to, I found myself in a bare room strapped to an operating table. A face swam into focus – an evil yellow face [that I knew to be that of my adversary] – the inscrutable Doctor Chou En Ginsberg.

KENNETH: Ah, Mr. Horne – so we

meet again – [etcetera blah blah blah –

KENNETH: Why do you say that, Ginsberg?

KEN W: While you were unconscious we had to cut twelve pages for time. You are being kept plisoner in unglound seclet labolatoly. Yes, Mr. Horne – I lead the question in your eyes –

KENNETH: Thank heavens, I thought, he hasn't spotted the one up my nose.

KEN W: Yes, Mr. Horne –] I stole Blig Blen.

KENNETH: But why? Why?

KEN W: *(Screams)* Because I wanted to undermine foundations of Blitish Empire – because I wanted to show I am most powerful man in whole universe! *(Snide)* Besides my Mickey Mouse wristwatch has broken. *(Chou En Ginsberg)* But you will never live to tell, Horne – you are going to die – but before you die you will be tortured. Aha – aha – oho – aha – *(Snide)* There's about another half-dozen of those but I think we can take it as read. *(Chou En Ginsberg)* Alright, Mr. Horne – I clap hands *(Claps hands)* and here comes Charlie.

HUGH: Yers, guv?

KENNETH: Good heavens – Isn't that your concubine Lotus Blossom?

KEN W: Yes. But changed name by deed poll. Neighbours starting to talk. Now known as Charlie Girl, from hit musical of same name . . . 'I laughted till my sides ache' Halold Hobson – *Sunday Times*. Now my little bamboo shoot – my little Tsar double Tchin.

HUGH: Yers, oh mighty mandarin – what is your bidding – I await your behest.

KEN W: I'm never at my behest at this time of morning. Go my little nightingale and prepare the torture.

HUGH: Yes, oh warlord – I run like a fleet gazelle.

*F/X: Heavy clumping of boots running into distance.*

KEN W: If you can imagine a fleet gazelle with hobnailed boots on. Now, Mr. Horne – I shall leave you to await my little friend on whom no man has looked and lived. Goodbye, Mr. Horne – we'll meet again, don't know where, don't know when *(Sings in nasal Vera Lynn tones)* – but I know we'll meet again some sunny day –

*F/X: Door closes*

KENNETH: I was alone. I thought 'Horne – this is it –' I started to saw through my bonds – somewhere in Pinewood, Bond started to saw through his Hornes. When you're in show business you help each other. Then the door creaked open – a strange wild-haired creature with insane staring eyes and great fangs stood there. It opened its huge ravenous maw and from its throat issued a spine-chilling sound which made my blood turn cold . . .

BILL: *(As Ken Dodd sings)* Tears have been my only consolation . . .

*Orchestra: Music up to climax . . .*

[*(Applause over music)*

*Segue*

*Orchestra: 'Kenneth Horne Master Spy' theme – under following announcement . . .*

DOUGLAS: *(Over music)* That was Episode One of *Kenneth Horne – Master Spy* – will his reason snap under the strain of Ken Dodd's singing

– or will he escape and continue his pursuit of Big Ben? Will Chou En Ginsberg triumph over justice? Will Arkle win the Cheltenham Gold Cup? Will ye no come back again? And will the owner of car number 4233 BH please move it at once as it's blocking traffic in the announcers' washroom at Broadcasting House – tune in next week when we bring you Episode Two of *Kenneth Horne – Master Spy*.]

*Orchestra: Music up and out*

KENNETH: And here to pile their peculiar brand of pelion on this load of old ossa – it's alright, it's not dirty – I looked it up – are the Fraser Hayes Four – to sing you a track from their new LP – *Let's have a party* with the Lord's Day Observance Society Saxophone Octet. Ladies and gentlemen – the Fraser Hayes Four.

*(Applause)*

*Fraser Hayes Four & Orchestra: 'Plastic'*

*(Applause)*

KENNETH: Thank you the Fraser Hayes Four. [Well I must say that really took me back. I beg your pardon, I'll read that again. Took me <u>aback</u>. Smith –

DOUGLAS: Sir?

*F/X: Desk bell*

KENNETH: Shop!]

DOUGLAS: And now the part of the show that keeps you up to date with what today's people are doing – Trends!

*Orchestra: Trends Music*

KENNETH: First – the world of Art.

BETTY: Pop's out –

KENNETH: Well pop it back in again and let's get on with the show. Next, fashion.

BETTY: Balenciaga's dropped his skirts again.

KENNETH: Bad luck Balenciaga! And what are the trendy people doing?

HUGH: Jean Shrimpton still has that indescribable Stamp about her.[1]

BETTY: Actress Samantha Eggar is rumoured to be starting a company to promote her career – It is to be called the Eggar Marketing Board.

HUGH: So why not go to work on an Eggar?

KENNETH: Still leading the pop music trend is that doyen of folk singers, Rambling Syd Rumpo – we asked him to come along and sing some of his songs tonight but, unfortunately, he could – and here he is – Rambling Syd Rumpo.

KEN W: Well now my deario sing willow tit-willow for I've crumpled my doodle-oh.

KENNETH: Oh really, how painful for you. I'll give you the address of my garage.

[KEN W: I was just being picturesque, as is my wont. For I wander along life's highways a'culling of the simple folk melodies of our island heritage and a'cleaning 'em up for Saturday Club 'oh – a'posset me bodkin till I rumble me groats and the old grey goose is gone – oh, although to be frank I was glad to see the back of her.

KENNETH:] And what are you going to sing us this week?

KEN W: 'Tis a hoary old folk song

that I picked up from a home for hoary old folks. 'Tis a courting song or air which tells of the coming of spring to Clapham Junction, and 'tis about this young swain of they parts – who [every spring feels the sap rising and gets a kind of March Madness which is common to the young men of they parts and is known as swain-fever. He wanders among the bosky haunts and verdant pasturelands of Clapham High Street – and as he hears the little hedge-sparrows coughing and sees the young lambs hanging up in the butcher's shop, he feels a primaeval urge. And he] goes forth to seek his true love.

Suddenly he spies this winsome creature sitting in a window, with flaxen tresses flowing in the breeze. And he stands under the window in the moonlight, plighting his troth – and he sings – 'If you will marry me my love, I will give you a ruby ring, a single rose, a peacock in a cage, the moon to wear for a garland in your hair and three books of green stamps'.

And then the object of his desires looks all haughty at him, and tossing back the flaxen ringlets, sings this plaintive lament:

*Guitar accompaniment only: (While Ken W sings)*

Tho' you give me a single rose
And a ruby ring to wear – oh
A peacock in a cage of gold
And moonbeams for my hair-oh
I cannot marry thee sir
I cannot marry thee sir,
For I am promised to someone else –
Besides I am a geezer.
Geezer
Geezer

---

1. Model Jean Shrimpton and actor Terence Stamp were a well-known couple at the time.

Because I am a geee-eee-zer –
oooooOOOh! I think I've ricked
meself.

*(Applause)*

KENNETH: Thank you, Rambling Syd –
and they say romance is dead. Now
for trendy people, the final accolade is
to appear on one of the late night
television shows where exciting, fun,
with-it, super-type people get together
and make boring, flat conversation for
an hour. I tuned in last Sunday night,
just in time to hear . . .

*Orchestra: Colourable imitation of
Eamonn Andrews sig. tune . . .*

DOUGLAS: And now – embalmed from
London – *The Seamus Android
Show* –

[*Grams: Applause*

*Orchestra: Fade sig. tune*

HUGH: And tonight Seamus's guests
are Anatole De Gruntfuttock, the
celebrated dog forger, Puberty
Griswold 'the Boxing Rabbi', a pop-
singer Ruff Trayde and the Cruisers,
and philosopher and racing tipster
Captain Spock of the Nudist Racing
Pink –] and here is your host – Seamus
Android –

*Grams: Applause*

BILL: *(Irish)* Well now, we've got a
really dull show for you tonight, and
you'll be meeting some extremely
lifeless personalities with some off-the-
cuff Sunday night rubbish that I'm
sure will bore the pants off ya. [But
before I introduce the first nonentity, I
was going to tell you one of my long
boring pointless anecdotes, but luckily
for you I've forgotten the ending, so

I'll just get on with introducing.] My
first guest is one of the original Gaiety
Girls and now starring in a new West
End musical at the age of ninety-eight
– Gladys Runt!

*Orchestra: Music*

BILL: Well Gladys, you're ninety-eight
– how does it feel . . .

BETTY: *(Old crone)* I can't remember –

BILL: . . . to be back in the West End?
You must have some wonderful
memories.

BETTY: Yes, I have. I have some very
wonderful memories. Some very, very
wonderful memories.

BILL: Really? Is that so. Well, would
you like to tell us some of your
wonderful memories?

BETTY: I'd like to. I'd like to very
much. But I can't remember them.

BILL: But surely there is an anecdote
told about you and Bernard Shaw –

BETTY: Oh yes – that one – well, I was
playing in *Captain Brassbound's
Conversion* – and one night Mr. Shaw
himself watched the performance from
the wings – when I came off we stood
together for a few moments and then
he leant very close to me and
whispered in my ear – in that gracious
way of his – he said 'Get off my foot
you silly old tart.'

BILL: How wise! How true those
words are even today. And <u>talking</u> of
hamster-breeding in West Sussex
brings me to our next guest – the well-
known stuttering Irish raconteur –
Paddy Handbell.[2]

*Orchestra: Music*

---

2. Patrick Campbell, aka the Third Baron Glenavy, was a popular broadcaster, despite (or perhaps because of) his stammer.

BILL: Now Paddy – how about telling us one of those wonderful and interminable anecdotes of yours?

HUGH: Well, I was in the Isle of W-W-W–

[BILL: Wight?]

HUGH: Dogs the other W-W-W-W–

BILL: Week?

HUGH: Day. When this w-w-w–

BILL: Man?

HUGH: Woman, said to me – I'm a great f-f-f-f-fan of y-y-yours . . .

BILL: Yes, go on –

HUGH: That's all there is.

BILL: What a wonderful example of that quick-fire wit we've all learned to live with. Tell me Paddy, does being a TV celebrity affect your life at all –

HUGH: *(Ad lib stutters)* Yes. I'm often invited to parties to show off my s-s-s-spon . . .

BILL: Yes, your spon. And very handsome it looks.

HUGH: I haven't finished yet. My s-s-s-spon – t-taneous wit.

BILL: I noticed before the show, when we were knocking back the – er – having a preliminary discussion – you didn't stutter at all.

HUGH: No, that's quite t-t-true, but when I'm on TV I always make a p-p-point of it.

BILL: May I ask why?

HUGH: C-c-c-certainly. I get paid by the minute.]

BILL: Thank you, Paddy. Well, that's all we've got time for this week. But tune in again next week when you'll be meeting some more Sunday night people who make you long for Monday morning.

*Orchestra: Eamonn Andrews-type play-off*

*(Applause)*

KENNETH: There's nothing like good conversation and I think you'll agree that the *Seamus Android Show* is just that. Nothing like good conversation. The trouble with trends is that they change so often. And so last week I thought it was time to pay another visit to Carnaby Street to equip myself with a new wardrobe – so, taking my Courrège in both hands I went along to a men's boutique that calls itself 'Bona Drag'.

*F/X: Shop bell*

KENNETH: Hello – anybody there?

HUGH: Hello – I'm Julian and this is my friend Sandy.

KEN W: Oh it's Mr. Horne – [how fabe – I thought you'd retired.

KENNETH: Retired? Didn't you see me on television last week?

KEN W: Yes, that's what made me think.] Well, how bona to vada your eek again. Of course, we're only filling in here between acting jobs. But it's been a bit slack lately.

HUGH: Sand had a tickle from the tenants last week.

KENNETH: What – H.M. Tennant the impressario?

HUGH: No, the tenants upstairs. The ones on his half-landing. They're in advertising. They got us a commercial on telly – you may have seen it – we just do the voices –

KEN W: Jule says, in this great gruff voice, it doesn't come natural to him, does it Jule?

HUGH: No, I'm more your light baritone –

KEN W: He says 'What you doing?' And then I say 'I'm the pea that can't get into the packet'.

HUGH: Into the packet. Took his part lovely. He makes a very convincing pea. Anyway, Mr. Horne, what can we do for you?

KENNETH: Well, with all these new clothes coming out, I thought it was about time I got up to scratch.

HUGH: Don't let us stop you. Yes, well I think Sand and I can show you something fairly kinky if you hang on for a second –

KENNETH: Thank you. And I'd like to see some clothes as well.

KEN W: Oh bold! Now let's see – [to start with – what would be really unusual in a gents' suit?

KENNETH: Danny La Rue?

KEN W: I think we'll treat that crude pleasantry with the contempt it deserves, don't you Jule?] How about a nice [casual jacket?

HUGH: Yes, D.B. knitted, reefer or lumber?

KEN W: Oh lumber. He's definitely a lumber type. A right lumber. Here's a nice] Paisley army-style battledress jacket.

KENNETH: Army style?

HUGH: Yes. We call it Aldershot Camp. [Would you like to try it on?

KENNETH: Right – there – what do you think?

KEN W: Well, I don't know – it's quite cheeky isn't it?

HUGH: Cheeky yes – quite cheeky – it cocks a snook at convention round the collar and cuffs.

KEN W: Collar and cuffs, yes. And it provides him with that modern anti-heroical peacock look with its hunky arrogance –

HUGH: Hunky arrogance – yes. It proclaims his empathy with the nouvelle-vague.

KEN W: Nouvelle-vague, yes.

KENNETH: Yes, I must admit that it's sybaritically autocratic but it tends to bind me under the armpits.] Haven't you got anything more conservative?

KEN W: Only in bespoke. Go on Jule, show him your swatch.

HUGH: Well, [there's your denim – comes nice in your burnt marmalade.

KEN W: All the browns are very fetching. Comes beautiful in your donkey. And then there's your silks; you have the shot silk, the wild silk – well fairly wild – and then there's the raw. How do you think he'd look in the raw, Jule?

HUGH: I'm not besotted by the idea.] The fawn tweed's nice. Why not fawn?

KEN W: On him? I wouldn't cheapen meself. I've got it – show him your Op.

KENNETH: No, thank you, I've just had breakfast.

HUGH: Op-Art he means. Here we are – PVC with bulls-eyes all over it. Very trendy and inner than in, isn't it Sand?

KEN W: Fantabulosa! We can do that for you ready-made – here – try this on – it's a PVC raincoat.

HUGH: And you'll want these PVC thigh-length boots –

KEN W: Oh and here – a PVC cap to complete your toute plastic ensemble. There – look at yourself in the mirror. What do you think?

KENNETH: I look like an eccentric fireman, but I suppose if it's the thing to wear, I'd better have it – one problem though, how do I get it dry-cleaned?

KEN W: You don't. But don't worry – we have an arrangement with the garage next door. As soon as it gets grubby, you just nip into the five-minute car wash and half a dozen Pakistanis'll hose you down.

*Orchestra: Punctuating Chord*

*(Applause)*

KENNETH: [So that's what I did. I popped into the car wash – and while I was at it I had some anti-freeze put in.] Well that's the end of this week's show, except for a police message. If any passer-by in Lisle Street last Saturday night witnessed a middle-aged man stagger out of the Peeperama strip club and get knocked down by a passing cyclist, would you please keep quiet about it as my wife thinks I was in Folkestone. Goodbye. See you next week.

*Orchestra: Sig. tune*

DOUGLAS: That was *Round the Horne*, starring Kenneth Horne, with Kenneth Williams, Hugh Paddick, Betty Marsden and Bill Pertwee. On the musical side you heard the Fraser Hayes Four and Edwin Braden and the Hornblowers. The script was written by Barry Took and Marty Feldman and produced by John Simmonds.

*Orchestra: Sig. tune up and out*

*(Applause)*

# SERIES 2
# PROGRAMME 4

*FIRST BROADCAST* – Sunday 3 April 1966

## INTRODUCTION

*Round the Horne* drew many complaints from a small minority of listeners for its supposedly filthy gags – and, indeed, for its quite plainly filthy gags. Unrepentant, and perhaps even aggrieved at what they thought was unfair criticism, the writers delighted in scripting digs at the would-be censors and self-appointed moral guardians of the day, as we see in the pre-announcement sequence of this episode: 'Muck, that is. Muck.'

When we also consider Took and Feldman's general lack of reverence for the institution of the BBC itself, it's easy to imagine that producer John Simmonds' job was not the easiest in light entertainment. He must have possessed considerable diplomatic skills to keep the show on air and relatively unbowdlerized; though certainly the liberalizing mood of the times made this an easier task than it would have been ten years earlier – or, come to that, thirty years later.

This episode brings the first mention of that miracle product, Dobbiroids, the Magic Horse Rejuvenator, as announcer Douglas Smith tries to earn a few bob on the side, making commercial announcements. Smith really was a BBC announcer, but in *RTH* he was called upon to do far more than simply read the credits. His scripted asides and interactions with the cast are an essential part of the comedy. His assumed pomposity (he was anything but pompous according to those who knew him) contrasts to great effect with his frequent lapses from propriety. It's as if he is gradually getting sucked into the general madness of *RTH*, and can't quite decide whether or not to surrender to the inevitable.

That Douglas Smith could do all this while always remaining thoroughly credible as an announcer is evidence of considerable talent, and of a highly intelligent sense of humour.

HUGH: *(Cockney)* I see *Round the Horne*'s on in a minute, Dad.

KEN W: *(Very, very old)* Muck that is. Muck. [I wouldn't pollute me ears with it.

HUGH: I think it's quite clever, the way they do them voices – that Kenneth Williams –

KEN W: Muck he is. Downright muck.] They're all muck, every one of them.

HUGH: That Kenneth Horne isn't. He's educated.

KEN W: Well, he ought to know better, consorting with that other muck. It's all double entenders, incinuendoes and catchpenny horseplay.

HUGH: So you're not going to have it on?

KEN W: No. I shall just sit here and polish me boots with the cat.

HUGH: All right Dad, but I think you should listen to it –

KEN W: Why? Give me one good reason?

HUGH: Well, you are the Head of Broadcasting.

[KEN W: All right – switch it on – but it's a load of muck.]

*Orchestra: Sig.*

BILL: Ladies and gentlemen – it's the show that thumbs its nose at convention and cocks a snook at credibility – *Round the Horne.*

*Orchestra: Sig. tune*

*(Applause)*

DOUGLAS: The story so far. Beefy cowpoke Betty Marsden, Marshal of Dodge City, rode into town on her pinto Solly the Wonder Horse, played by Hugh 'The Wonder Horse'

Paddick, in an ill-fitting skin – his own. The marshal strode into the Last Chance Saloon and Heel Bar and was confronted by a masked stranger. Was it Wild Bill Pertwee, feared from Kansas City to the Rio Grande, and not too welcome at the All-Night Turkish Baths, Paddington? Or was the stranger Kenneth 'Gabby' Williams – after all, who could be stranger than Kenneth Williams? Then, after a pause, [for drinks and light refreshments,] the masked stranger spoke – in a voice that suggested the wide, open spaces – between his ears. He said –

KENNETH: My name is Kenneth Horne.

*Orchestra: Music link (Applause)*

KENNETH: That was Douglas Smith, or as he is better known, the Father of the Modern Bread Pudding, although he pleads the headaches.

Now for the answers to last week's questions – complete the following song titles. First, ['When I Leave The——' Well of course the answer was 'The World Behind' and not 'The bathroom as I would wish to find it' as one of you suggested. Question Two.] 'The Girl That I Marry Will Have To——'. Well, most of you thought that line was complete. [All except one plaintive cry from the heart from a man signing himself 'Disgruntled of Cheltenham', who says that he's told the lady in question what she will have to but she refused point-blank.]

Question Two. 'He's Got A Fine Brown——' The answer to that is 'Frame' and I will not enter into any correspondence about that with anybody. [If there's any lingering doubt in your mind, I refer you to the question of two weeks ago referring to 'The Sailor With The Navy Blue——']

Right, Smith – make the announcement.

DOUGLAS: Yes, sir. In a moment – *Kenneth Horne – Master Spy*. But first, the makers of Dobbins Medical Cummerbunds for horses present a new, exciting addition to their range – Dobbiroids Magic Rejuvenators. Is your horse listless?

[KENNETH: Smith!

DOUGLAS: Does he come from the office tired and run-down, or does he –]

KENNETH: Smith! Have you taken leave of your senses?

DOUGLAS: Don't forget that Dobbiroids will make your horse bounce with health –

KENNETH: Smith!

DOUGLAS: *(Sings)* So feed your horse on Dobbiroids, Dobbiroids, Dobbiroids –

KENNETH: *(Shouts)* Smith!

DOUGLAS: I'm sorry, sir. I had to do that. They offered me money. I can't live on what you pay me. *(Breaking down)* I'm sorry, I was driven – I had a wife and family once – now my friends shun me. My wife has left me. I have no job. *(Suddenly back to normal)* Read my story in the *Sunday Blag*. *(Brightly)* And now *Kenneth Horne – Master Spy*!

*Orchestra: Master Spy sig. tune*

HUGH: On the nineteenth of March, 1966, the World Cup was stolen[1] from the Central Hall, Westminster. It was subsequently recovered but what nobody knows is that it was stolen again yesterday. This was a job for MI5 –

KENNETH: I was summoned to an office in Whitehall where Colonel Haverstrap was waiting, a bulging dossier open on the desk in front of him.

BILL: All right, Horne, shall I run over it once more?

KENNETH: If you wouldn't mind, sir.

*F/X: Heavy running footsteps going off into the distance and then coming back*

BILL: *(Panting)* There. That's better. Nothing like a bit of exercise. Now Horne, [you'll want some information. Here are a few facts: soap is formed by the union of fatty acids with sodium or potassium; the bogwort sometimes reaches a length of nearly four inches; a stuffed porcupine tied to a stick makes the ideal thing for scouring out cold porridge from saucepans; those are all the facts I have.

KENNETH: Not much help in this case, sir.

BILL: No, but they'll be very helpful if you ever get on *Round Britain Quiz*. Now] the World Cup – it's been stolen and you know what that means?

KENNETH: Yes, sir – we'll have to drink out of the World Saucer. I had to move fast. I called Sir Andrew Sweet, head of the FA, at his headquarters –

*F/X: Phone rings: Phone up*

KEN W: *(On distort)* Hello – sweet – FA here. [Who's that?

KENNETH: Horne, FO.

---

1. The Jules Rimet trophy was stolen in March, and found a week later by a dog named Pickles.

KEN W: I'm afraid I can't answer that.]

F/X: *Phone down*

KENNETH: He was being evasive. I felt that he knew something. I had to get into FA headquarters somehow. But how? I needed to conceal my identity – I hurried to the disguise department of the MI5 Boutique. Their experts would take care of me.

F/X: *Shop door*

KENNETH: Hello? Anybody there?

HUGH: Oh hello, I'm Julian and this is my friend Sandy.

KEN W: How nice to vada your eek again. Absolutely bona, ennit Jule?

KENNETH: What are you doing in a top-security job with MI5?

KEN W: They sent us down here from the Labour. [It was either this or waiters up the Bun-In-The-Oven in Chelsea. So we're filling in here.]

KENNETH: I would have thought you might have been considered a slight security risk.

HUGH: Oh no, we've been screened. They went into our backgrounds and found that our fides were absolutely bona. We are your actual experts on disguise. We've had all the spies in here – when we've finished with 'em you wouldn't know them. That Siobhan Connery – we've done her –

KENNETH: I thought it was Sean Connery.

HUGH: That only goes to show how good our disguises are.

KEN W: And Modesty Blaise – that's David Niven in drag. Now first, you'll want your basic spy equipment – bulletproof waistcoat in your actual

Tattersall check, then you'll want your shoulder holster. Got a lovely range of shoulder holsters – show him your Spring Collection, Jule. Don't be modest, show him.

HUGH: Well, you have your mock-croc, encrusted with semi-precious stones.

KEN W: Comes nice in the mock-croc.

HUGH: You have your doe-skin, with your initials done in diamante.

KEN W: Comes beautiful in the doe-skin.

HUGH: And here's a nice off-the-shoulder for evening wear – black satin with an embossed rose done in bullion.

KEN W: Oh, it's a rave!

HUGH: Very gear!

KEN W: Fantabulosa, ducky!

KENNETH: I'll have that then. But will it support the weight of my gun?

KEN W: You don't want to go stuffing your Biretta in there, ducky.

HUGH: No, it makes such an unsightly bulge.

KEN W: And spoils the line of your jacket.

KENNETH: But surely, as a spy going on a dangerous mission, I'll need something to protect myself.

HUGH: Then you'll need this – it's small – fits into your pocket. If you're in trouble – press this little lever here.

KENNETH: What happens?

KEN W: You spray yourself all over. It gives you morn till night personal freshness. And it's nice to know you're nice to know.

KENNETH: Thank you. Now what about my disguise? Make-up – you know –

HUGH: [Well, let's have you in the chair. There. What do you think, Sand?] He needs a facial, don't he?

KEN W: Yes. Well, we won't have any trouble with superfluous hair. [We'll have to do something about them bags under his eyes –

HUGH: Yes. I think baggy eyes are so unbecoming in a spy. Smoothe 'em away with wrinkle-cream I think, don't you?

KEN W: Yes. About four hundredweight of it.

KENNETH: If it's all the same to you, I'll just have an ordinary disguise. I want to track down an arch-fiend, not win the Miss Universe competition.

HUGH: Oh! Bold!] Now, what do you want this disguise for?

KENNETH: I want to get into the Football Association headquarters. I'll need to look like a sporting personality.

KEN W: How about Tamara Press?

HUGH: Don't be facetious, Sand. Wait a minute, let me think, aaah – got it! Do you think he'd lend hisself to Kenneth Wolstenholme?

KEN W: Not if he's got any sense he wouldn't. Don't worry, Mr. Horne – we'll think of something.

*Orchestra: Short music link*

KENNETH: Two hours later, I emerged looking exactly like Billy Wright. The resemblance was fantastic. For a while, Joy Beverley and I were deliriously happy, but I knew it couldn't last. And besides, I couldn't stand her sisters coming round sitting in the living room singing about hand-cream all night. I hurried to the FA headquarters in Lancaster Gate on the trail of the World Cup. Once inside the building, I headed for the office of the England Team Manager – Alf Ramsay.

*F/X: Knock on door*

BETTY: *(Husky/sexy)* Come in, darling.

*F/X: Door opens*

KENNETH: Alf Ramsay?

BETTY: Yes, darling.

KENNETH: Mmm – that explains the way England are playing this year. [Then Alf Ramsay rose from behind the desk – wearing an off-the-shoulder gown, a collar of diamonds at her throat and a rattle in her hand emblazoned with World Cup Willie. But that didn't fool me for a minute.] Some sixth sense told me that this wasn't the real Alf Ramsay.

BETTY: So, you've rumbled?

KENNETH: Yes, I know, but it's a long time since I had breakfast. She came towards me; the air was heavy with the scent of musk; I took her in my brutal sinewy arms and pulled her roughly to me. Her sinuous body melted in my arms –

BETTY: Darling – I can live this lie no longer. I'm not Alf Ramsay.

KENNETH: And I'm not Billy Wright.

BETTY: Good. It's better this way. Otherwise it'd do absolutely nothing for the prestige of British football.

KENNETH: We kissed passionately like two Italian footballers after the winning goal. Who are you then, I murmured –

BETTY: I'm Grotty Thunderghast. [I'm from British Intelligence] – Demon Girl Spy. The real Alf Ramsay has disappeared – we think he took the World Cup. It's the only way he could get his hands on it.

KENNETH: It can't be true.

BETTY: It isn't. I slipped it in for a cheap laugh and a round of applause. I also do impressions. And now, Cicely Courtneidge as Jack Hulbert in *Dick Whittington. (Principal Boy)* Come along, puss – only six more miles to London.

KEN W: Bring back the cat!

[BETTY: *(Sings as Cicely Courtneidge)* Cheer up, puss – Faint hearts ne'er won fair lady – you scamper off and find some mice – ha ha – oh ha ha – And now at last I'm on my own, I think I'll play my xylophone –

*Orchestra: Standard intro 'On the Track' – then solo xylophone with orch . . .*

BETTY: *(Shouts over music)* All together now, and if you don't know the words, just whistle – *(Whistles with music)*

KEN W: *(Interrupting)* All right, all right, that's enough, dear –

*Music stops*

BETTY: But Mr. Beaumont, you haven't seen my aero.

KEN W: Don't bother dear. We'll let you know.

BETTY: All right. You've got my number, haven't you?

KEN W: Don't worry, ducky, we've all got your number. Alright boys and girls, you've had a breather, back to the show – top of page nine.]

KENNETH: If what Grotty Thunderghast had told me was true, this was serious. With Alf Ramsay and the World Cup both gone, this would undermine Britain's prestige as a footballing nation. There was only one man who could conceive such a fiendish scheme – Doctor Chou En Ginsberg.

*F/X: Gong*

KEN W: Aha, Mr. Horne – so you have tracked me to my secret lair on the North face of the Jungfrau –

BETTY: [*(German)* How are you? My name is Hilda.

KENNETH: Ah you must be the Jungfrau.

BETTY: Jawohl. Be careful where you put those alpenstocks. *(Yodels)*

KEN W: Lives in a world of her own, she does.

KENNETH: You know, I've been thinking. Doing this show's like spending half an hour in a spin dryer.

KEN W: Yes –] in answer to your unspoken question – I have Alf Ramsay as my plisoner – also have World Clup.

KENNETH: Clup?

KEN W: Yes. Clup. The sort you cleep in the clupboard.

KENNETH: Don't you think you're overcharacterising a bit?

KEN W: *(Own voice)* Look ducky, I don't tell you how to play your part. [I don't just rush at it, you know. I'm trained. I've been to the method school. Before I came here I went to the Stanislavsky.] If I say I've stolen the clup, the clup it is!

KENNETH: I didn't mean to offend you.

KEN W: Alright. *(Chou)* Now you have discovered my secret, you must die – but before you die – a little entertainment. I will summon most exquisite geisha – Lotus Blossom.

*F/X: Gong*

HUGH: Yers, cock. I stand before you in the first blush of my maidenly humility, mate. Do you wish for love songs to issue forth from my rose petal lips – or would you like me to shake it abaht a bit?

KEN W: Gives you the creeps, doesn't she? You should see her first thing in the morning. Ah, my little flower, my lychee nut, my Peking Duck. *(Own voice)* – More like a Bombay Duck, still you have to use your imagination on radio. *(Chou)* Come Lotus Blossom, before Mr. Horne dies, do your exotic and tantalizing version of the Dance of the Seven Veils. After two – a-one, a-two . . .

*Orchestra: 'A Pretty Girl is Like a Melody' (with oriental overtones)*

*F/X: Two distinct clumps as boots are dropped on floor*

*Music stops*

HUGH: Phew, that's better. Got me boots off. Now me feet can breathe.

KEN W: Takes all the titillation out of it, doesn't she – ah so – back to the plot. Now you die!

KENNETH: He leapt at me with a fierce cry.

KEN W: Aha!

KENNETH: We struggled –

KEN W: Aha! Oho!

KENNETH: I gave him a rabbit punch. He drank it thirstily and then, [staggering back, he threw his hands into the air, caught them deftly and balanced them on the end of his nose.] While my attention was thus distracted, he leapt on to a passing glacier and shot off down the valley at the rate of two miles a century.

The World Cup has so far not been recovered and so, the winning country at Wembley this year will be presented with a plastic Yogi Bear toothmug, in which to keep their Yogi Bear teeth.

*Orchestra: Play-off*

*(Applause)*

KENNETH: And now here are the Fraser Hayes Four to sing a track from their new LP – *Doing the Frug with Mrs. Bandaranaike*[2] – The Fraser Hayes Four.

*(Applause)*

*Fraser Hayes & Orchestra: 'Hear that Band'*

*(Applause)*

DOUGLAS: And now the part of the show that keeps you up-to-date with what today's people are doing. But first, a message from our sponsor – Does your horse suffer from dandruff? Or ill-fitting dentures? Give him Dobbiroids for that look-alive –

KENNETH: Smith!

DOUGLAS: *(Resigned)* Oh alright. There's no room for the little man in this show – *(Bored)* and now ladies and gentlemen – Trends –

*Orchestra: 'Trends' music link*

---

2. Sri Lankan politician Sirimavo Bandaranaike became the world's first female prime minister in 1960.

KENNETH: First – the teenage scene. Doctors are worried that many teenagers have been chewing Morning Glory seeds for kicks. We asked gardening expert Percy Thrower if, in fact, these seeds contained stimulant properties. His answer was simple and to the point –

*Orchestra: Solo walking bass behind next speech*

HUGH: *(Hipster)* Like, don't bug me, man. *(Sings)* Come fly with me, come fly, come fly away – ool ya boo da dooh.

KENNETH: Gardening Club this week comes to you from the Whisky A' Blue Jeans Discotheque – Soho. Meanwhile letters are still pouring in from people who want information about trendy things and people. The first query reads:

KEN W: My name is Gruntfuttock – J. Peasmold Gruntfuttock.

KENNETH: I'm afraid I can't answer that question; moving rapidly on – our second letter comes from a Mr. –

KEN W: Gruntfuttock. Anticipating that you would not answer my first missive, I have written another, to whit and viz, this greasy bit of paper you are now holding. My question is this. Can you let me have the private telephone number of Judith Chalmers, whom I would like to get my hands on and . . .

KENNETH: At this point, the writing becomes indistinct, [but I can make out odd isolated words like – broom cupboard – loofah – and something about the advantages of herbal tobacco.] But it's signed –

KEN W: Yours as ever – J. Peasmold Gruntfuttock, [Prince Consort.

KENNETH: Hmm, I can't see why any prince would consort with Gruntfuttock. Oh wait a moment – there's a P.S.

KEN W: P.S. I am not actually <u>the</u> Prince Consort, I am not even <u>a</u> Prince Consort. It is merely a pose.] P.S. And how long shall the men of money rule us? Nay, rise up and throw off your chains and drive the usurers forth with whips and scorpions – and if you have no scorpions, a plate of shrimps'll do as well. P.P.S. Must close now as have set the bed on fire and the flames are licking around my hot water bottle.

KENNETH: And there the pathetic message ends. [What became of the intrepid Gruntfuttock? Will the icy wastes ever give up their secret. We can only hope not.] The next letter I opened came from 'Worried ex-Gaiety Girl' and reads as follows:

BETTY: *(Gladys Lunt voice)* I am ninety-three and my husband is ninety-four and just lately we haven't . . .

KENNETH: And that's all there is –

BETTY: No. There's more on the other side of the page.

KENNETH: Oh yes.

BETTY: . . . been hitting it off too well. We disagree about our youngest boy. He's turned seventy-two – [but every week he squanders his pension on wild-living – staying up drinking cocoa with his friends 'til sometimes seven at night.] His one ambition in life is to do the ton up the M1 in his bathchair, an attempt doomed to failure as over six miles an hour the rims of the wheels get too hot to handle. What shall we do about him?

KENNETH: Well, he's only seventy-two – it's just a phase he's going through. [You'll find that when he's in his eighties, he'll settle down. I understand your problem, we had the same problem with Edwin Braden.

KEN W: Him? Great hairy catchphrase!]

KENNETH: Finally we had a rather sad letter signed 'Awkward of Tufnell Park' which reads –

HUGH: I feel terribly awkward in company. I can never think of anything to say. I'm gauche, shy and rather clumsy and I think people are avoiding me –

KENNETH: Well, 'Awkward of Tufnell Park' – you're not alone in the world – there are others who have the same trouble. If you don't believe me, you should watch *The Seamus Android Show* –

*Orchestra: Eamonn Andrews theme*

DOUGLAS: And now, the makers of Dobbiroids present – tonight from London, the *Marie Celeste* of Showbusiness – *The Seamus Android Show*.

*Orchestra: Music up*

HUGH: And tonight, Seamus's guests are – Rameses Gumbril, the whistling vicar of All Souls, Ludmilla Dogtrouser, the celebrated ballerina and copper's nark, [Miriam Van Creep – the Nose-drop heiress,] and Abdul Von Goldberg the well-known puzzle. And here's your host – Seamus Android.

*(Applause)*

BILL: Well hello there – and excuse me a moment while I answer this unexpected phone call, which none of us expected. *(Pause)* Well now, this phone call comes as much of a surprise to me as it does to you. *(Pause)* I wonder who it can be?

*(Pause) (Hisses)* The phone call!

*F/X: Phone rings*

BILL: Oh, bother! There goes the phone, I wonder who that can be?

*F/X: Phone up*

BILL: *(Into phone)* Hello. Why, it's Frank Sinatra phoning unexpectedly in person personally all the way from Hollywood himself. Hello Frank? Well that's incredible news. Good gracious, that's fascinating. They did? You have? You will? Well, that really is exciting news. Goodbye to yez.

*F/X: Phone down*

BILL: That was Frank Sinatra from Hollywood. Alright. [Now my next guest is somebody who I'm sure you all, er – I know I have – and so – er – without further – what more can I, er – than – er – and so here he is – the author of many sophisticated plays and so many unforgettable songs like – er – er – and others, equally well known – Noel Tramwicket.

*Orchestra: Music link (Applause)*

HUGH: *(Noel Coward)* How terribly, terribly, heart-warmingly nice of you to invite me here, dear, dear boy – whatever your name is.

BILL: Now, you're famous for your songs and plays about England and the English. Now, tell me, what is it that makes you keep writing about the same subject?

HUGH: Well, you may think me a sentimental old fool, but in fact, I am. And there's something in London that inspires me – makes me frightfully gay. The pitter-pattering of soot on the pavements, the pitter-pattering of tiny little cockney sparrows on the passers-by, the happy cries of costermongers as they're run in by the police, the old street cries like 'Who'll buy my sweet lavender', and 'Hello cheeky face, coming up for a drink'. I weave all this into a magic tapestry of sound. And these songs about dear old London that I write, make me enough money to get out of this dreadful place and live in Switzerland.

**BILL:** Thank you Noel. Alright. Now,] while we're on the subject of the Israeli lemon harvest – I'd like you to meet my next guest – actress eighty-four times married, Miss Zsa Zsa Poltergeist –

*Orchestra: Music (Applause)*

**BETTY:** Hello lovely, lovely English people. How are you all darleenks? Am I not delightful?

**BILL:** All right. Now, Zsa Zsa, I see you were quoted in the week as saying that you and millionaire Piggy Dipthong the Third were just good friends – is there any truth in that?

**BETTY:** No. Is a misquote. We're married. That is, we <u>were</u> married on Tuesday, but on Wednesday I discovered he hadn't got any money, so I divorced him.

**BILL:** I thought he was a millionaire?

**BETTY:** He was on Tuesday. But people have been so kind – since the news accidentally leaked out through the Zsa Zsa Poltergeist World Press Service. I have had seventy five proposals – some even of marriage. But to all of you who have written in, I'd just like to say – Don't worry darleenks, I'll get around to you all in time.

**BILL:** And how true those words are even today. Alright. And now, moving

lugubriously on to yet another aspect of string-vest poaching, brings us to our next guest – Hollywood fillem producer – Darryl F. Claphanger.

*Orchestra: Music link*

**KEN W:** *(Hal Roach[3])* Hi everybody. Grand to be back on this show. Just being here makes me feel kinda humble – yessir – humble – H-U-double-M-B-U-L – Humble.

**BILL:** Welcome back, Mr. Claphanger.

**KEN W:** Who are you, buster? Sachay your fat can out of here and let a man do the talking. Now what is it you want to know?

**BILL:** Well you've been making pictures for forty years now – but you've never had an actual box-office success.

**KEN W:** I been unlucky. But I've been pretty near – back in the '30s, I made that great musical – *43rd Street.*

**BILL:** I thought it was called *42nd Street?*

**KEN W:** Mine was called *43rd Street.* How d'ya like that – one lousy street out. Then I made that Western with Gary Cooper called *Eleven A.M.* – a floperoo – I was before my time. I been dogged by misfortune my boy, look at my record. I made *Lawrence of Israel, Nanook of the South, The Spy that Went Out in the Cold.* Each time my sense of direction let me down.

**BILL:** But you haven't given up, Darryl?

**KENNETH:** No my boy – I'm still in there pitching – ya got to have tenacity – T-E-N-N-A-S-Y. Boy, am I stupid! No, I'm coming back with a

---

3. The writers based Claphanger on Kenneth Williams' account of his meeting with silent film producer Hal Roach.

real biggie B.O.-wise. It's got everything – religion, music and horror – and I'm getting Debbie Reynolds to play the title role.

BILL: And what's that?

KENNETH: *Rasputin, the Mad Singing Monk.* But the hell with culture – everybody back to my place – big party after the show.

*(Applause)*

BILL: Alright. And now, talking of grouse-battering in Shropshire, my next guest is lovely sepia songstress, dusky nightingale, all the way from America – Miss Lena Horne!

*Orchestra: Music link (Applause)*

BILL: Well now, Lena –

KENNETH: I think there's been some mistake. Actually, it's Kenneth Horne. I was a bit worried when I got the invitation but I thought –

BILL: Well Lena – ya haven't changed a bit. Joost as loovely as ever.

KENNETH: Very good of you, but the name is Kenneth Horne.

BILL: Well, Lena, seeing yez in the flesh for the first time, I find it difficult to believe that you are the mother of a girl in her twenties.

KENNETH: You find it difficult to believe – how do you think I feel? Look – the name is Kenneth Horne –

BILL: Alright. But it seems incredible Lena, looking at yez – that ya still have the figure of a young girl.

KENNETH: Well, I keep myself up. But I am Kenneth Horne.

BILL: And good luck with it. I hope it has a long run. Alright. Now people wouldn't forgive me if I didn't ask ya to sing Lena –

KENNETH: Kenneth.

BILL: So what's it going to be Lena?

KENNETH: Look for the last time I – oh well! . . .

KENNETH *& piano: (Sings)* Do I love you, oh my, do I? Honey – 'deed I do.

*Orchestra: Play-off*

*(Applause)*

KENNETH: Apparently, I was so convincing as Lena Horne that I was offered the lead in a revival of *Green Pastures*, playing opposite Louis Armstrong – but I turned it down – I didn't feel I could combine a singing career with that of wife and mother. Well, that brings us to the end of the show, except for a message to all shipping in the region of Wolverhampton – what on earth are you doing there? Cheerio, see you next week.

*Orchestra: Sig. tune*

DOUGLAS: That was *Round the Horne* presented by the makers of Dobbiroids –

KENNETH: Shut up, Smith!

DOUGLAS: The show starred Kenneth Horne, with Kenneth Williams, Hugh Paddick, Betty Marsden and Bill Pertwee. On the musical side you heard the Fraser Hayes Four and Edwin Braden and the Hornblowers. The script was written by Barry Took and Marty Feldman and the show was produced by John Simmonds.

*Orchestra: Sig. tune up and out*

*(Applause)*

*Orchestra: Play out 'Round the Horne'*

*(Applause)*

# SERIES 2
# PROGRAMME 5

*FIRST BROADCAST* – Sunday 10 April 1966

## INTRODUCTION

The answer to last week's 'odd man out' question, according to this script, is 'Robin Day – all the others swell up in water'. It's just possible I suppose that there exists somewhere on this planet someone who would not dissolve into laughter at reading that line – though it is hard to picture such a person.

They tend to be overlooked in favour of the showier set pieces, but the various bits of non-narrative nonsense at the start and end of each episode do contain some of *RTH*'s funniest jokes, and certainly some of the most typically Tookian and Feldmanish. Even if you don't know who Robin Day was (a rather self-important current affairs interviewer), the above gag is likely to produce an involuntary explosion of laughter, as the image it conjures, or rather *half*-conjures, is so liberatingly insane.

At first glance, many of the jokes in *RTH* seem to depend on references to people or events now largely forgotten. I could quite legitimately put an explanatory footnote on just about every page of every script. I've restricted my annotative urges because I feel that only rarely is the topical reference itself central to the humour. Often, I suspect, the exact choice of politician or film star for inclusion in a punch line or throwaway gag was more or less irrelevant, even at the time of writing. The sound of the name, its place in the rhythm of a sentence, is more important than the exploits of the person it belongs to.

On the page perhaps even more than on the air, it is obvious that *Round the Horne* was a highly intelligent, language-based comedy, which invited listeners almost to provide their own jokes, using the scripts as launching pads for their imaginations.

HUGH: And now ladies and gentlemen – the show that makes your budgies bounce with health, but does nothing for human beings – *Round the Horne*.

*Orchestra: Sig. tune*

[DOUGLAS: *(Very fast)* The story so far: Gregory wants to marry Sally but Sally, still afraid of the mysterious Jeremy McHorseprivet, tells him that Nosmo Gonzalez, posing as a mechanical bread-pudding salesman, has kidnapped winsome fun-loving Rabbi O'Houlihan, and that Esmond Spong and Myfanwy Toulouse-Lippincott are not his father. Will Gregory get his true love in the end? What is McHorseprivet's grisly secret?

BILL: *(Dramatically)* Who is Sylvia? What is she?

BETTY: *(Dramatically)* Whatever became of Baby Jane?

HUGH: *(Dramatically)* How much is that doggie in the window? The one with the waggly tail?

KEN W: What is it that's got four wheels and flies all round?

DOUGLAS: These are only a few of the things you won't find out in the next half-hour as we take you *Round the Horne* –

*Orchestra: Music*]

KENNETH: Hello again – and here are the answers to last week's questions.

First, the odd man out. That was, of course, Robin Day – all the others swell up in water. Question two – the 'Where do you stick it' question. Well, the answer of course was in the family album – although I would have accepted 'on the wall' but not 'up the spout' because it gets covered in fluff.

Question three came in five parts, the answers were – over the waves, under the bed, between two slices of toast, across the Alamo and up the Edgware Road as far as the Trappist menswear boutique, and then ask again.

Finally, the 'Complete the following quotations' question. Well, the quotation was – 'Hark Hark the dogs do——'. Well, 'Pedestrian' of Chatham – I realise that the dogs do – you can't stop them – it's in their nature. [Personally, I'd recommend earplugs, and if that doesn't work, try throwing a boot at them.] Nevertheless, the answer is 'bark'. [That's what the dogs do – at least in this quotation.] Anything else that dogs do is a matter for the Borough Council. Ask them to hark. And anyway, it doesn't rhyme. Smith – would you announce the next section of this grim farrago?

DOUGLAS: Certainly, sir. Housewives – is your horse red and unsightly? Has he the fetlocks you love to touch? No? Then give him Dobbiroids, the magic horse rejuvenator – with the soft chewy centre – *(Sings)* Feed your horse on Dobbiroids, Dobbiroids, Dobbiroids –

KENNETH: Smith. I've warned you about introducing commercials into the show.

DOUGLAS: I need the money, sir. [I have to. *(Shouts)* Look out – the White Dobbiroid Man is coming your way – If you can produce a horse and answer one simple question, you will receive –

KENNETH: Stop it, Smith. What's wrong with you?

DOUGLAS:] I'm sorry, sir, I can't help it. I want things – I need things – things that other announcers have got. Look at Alvar Liddell – he's got a pair of underpants with the names of drinks on them. I want a pair like that. Is that just vanity and pomp, sir?

KENNETH: 'Course not, Smith – I understand.

DOUGLAS: *(Breaking down)* No, you don't. Nobody understands. Look at McDonald Hobley – we went to announcers' school together and look at the way he's got on. You see him on television turning up his nose at people who use –

*F/X: Cuckoo*

DOUGLAS: – It's all very well for him – I can't even afford – *(F/X: Cuckoo)* – I have to shave with – *(F/X: Duck noise)*

KENNETH: What on earth's a –

*F/X: Duck noise*

DOUGLAS: It's a – *(F/X: Cuckoo)* – that's gone rusty. Oh, it's too much, I can't go on.

KENNETH: Well, somebody's got to do the announcement – Ken? Be a good chap?

KEN W: Be a good chap? I should cocoa, ducky – I'm not a common announcer. I'm a trained thespian. You wouldn't ask Dame Edith to do an announcement. *(Dame Edith)* Here are the football results – League Division One – Arsenal 3 – West Bromwich Albion 4. *(Own voice)* You wouldn't go up to her and ask her to be a good chap. No, ducky, it's just not on. You see, I'm not functional – I'm decorative – ask Pertwee, he's not particular what he does –

KENNETH: Bill? You'll help out won't you.

BILL: *(Unctuous)* Oh yes, Mr. Horne sir, I'm not too proud. I'd do it for you, sir. *(Rustic)* The likes of me is beholden to the likes of you. You're a genl'man, sir, good luck, sir, bless you, sir, [I know you'll see me alright –

KENNETH: Here Pertwee, my man – here's a halfpenny wrapped in silver paper to look like a shilling.

BILL: Thank ee, sir – thank ee. Oi be easily taken in. This'll come in roight handy, sir – ar-ahar –] 'tis bin a bad year at Bleak Acre Farm. The sheep's gone dry and the cow won't lay. [There be a blight on the land – a blight I tell ee. And who will tend Old Jem's hollyhocks when oi be gone?] Ar – oh – ar – ar – ar – *(Briskly)* And now – Hutch. *(Sings)* They asked me how I knew, my new love was –

KENNETH: Pertwee!

BILL: Oh alright. And now *Kenneth Horne – Master Spy*!

*Orchestra: Music – 'Master Spy'*

KENNETH: My lean brown body[1] scythed into the limpid blue water. I turned over on my back and floated lazily and then, adjusting my snorkel, I plunged below the surface. Suddenly I saw it coming towards me – a killer shark. I slipped off the safety catch of my harpoon and pulled the trigger. The deadly trident cleaved through the water and buried its fangs in the hide of the monster. I was safe – I could breathe easily again. I surfaced – pulled out the plug and got out of the bath. As the water gurgled down the plughole, it left a ring. I answered it immediately. Hello – this is your friendly neighbourhood spy here.

---

1. Interestingly, this is a parody of the Bond books, rather than of the films.

BETTY: *(On slight distort)* Oh, Mr. Horne. Thank heavens you're there – sob–sob–gasp–gasp – I'm in terrible trouble – gulp – gulp – sob – gasp. I'm in the apartment opposite.

KENNETH: Would you come across?

BETTY: At the drop of a hat. But right now, I'm desperate. I came home five minutes ago to find my father, the well-known atomic scientist, missing – the butler and maid dead, and the chauffeur has disappeared.

KENNETH: Why are you phoning me?

BETTY: Well, you know how bored you can get on your own. I thought a bit of company would be nice.

KENNETH: I'll be over immediately. [I started to dress, selecting my favourite tweed suit – and then I slipped on my Harris and, picking myself up, I hurriedly threw a few things into a bag – some orange peel, peanut shells, a few toffee papers and some tealeaves. Then I headed for the Miss X's apartment.]

*F/X: Knock on door: Door opens*

BETTY: I thought you'd never get here. I'm Doctor Sigmund Ayer's daughter – Freda – free to my friends.

KENNETH: Oh I see – Free Ayer –

BETTY: Yes, but you have to buy four gallons.

*Orchestra: Drum roll and cymbal crash*

HUGH: The authors wish to thank the publishers of the *Occult Gazette and Amateur Fishmonger* – in which this joke first appeared in 1911. But back to the – if you'll excuse the expression – plot.

BETTY: I think my father has been kidnapped by a certain un-named foreign power which we cannot name, called Russia. They're after his nuclear-powered-remote-control-guided banana. They must not get it. Only you can stop them.

KENNETH: She raised a tear-stained face to me – on the end of a pole. She was lovely but wanton, but I knew that if I had my way, she wouldn't be wanton long. She kissed me and fanned my ardour – I returned the kiss, fanning <u>her</u> ardour. Then she spoke – her voice a husky whimper of entreaty –

BETTY: Would you mind fanning me a bit ardour? It's 'ot.

KENNETH: I caressed that swanlike neck, I stroked that cute tip-tilted little nose, I ran my fingers through that luxuriant silky hair. She spoke again –

BETTY: Stop fiddling with yourself and pay some attention to me.

KENNETH: I pulled her roughly towards me in my bronzed sinewy arms and pressed my cruel lips against her – er – Smith.

DOUGLAS: Yes, sir.

KENNETH: Draw a veil over what transpires next will you?

DOUGLAS: Certainly, sir. The makers of Dobbiroids proudly but humbly draw a veil over what transpires next. That evening found Master Spy Horne at MI5 headquarters being briefed –

BILL: There you are Horne – you are now briefed. And very nice they look on you too. Now, you need to be vested, socked and booted, a fate you richly deserve after that joke about fanning her ardour.

KENNETH: [I'm sorry, sir.] Now about the missing physicist. I have reason to believe he's being kept prisoner by STENCH in East Berlin. It's going to be a tough assignment –

[BILL: Yes. You'll need to brush up your karate. How long since you've had any Randore?

KENNETH: Not since last pay day, sir.

BILL: I'm talking about unarmed combat.

KENNETH: So am I. You don't know the wife like I do.

BILL: Well, get down to the special training gymnasium. There's a couple of instructors there that'll look after you.

KENNETH: You mean –

BILL: Yes.

*Orchestra: Very short link*

*F/X: Door opens*

HUGH: Hello, I'm Julian and this is my friend Sandy.

KEN W: Oh, it's Mr. Horne – what brings you trolling in here?

KENNETH: They sent me to be toughened up – but I think I must have come to the wrong place.

HUGH: Oh no, we're your actual experts in unarmed combat. What do you think we're wearing these judo outfits for?

KENNETH: But shouldn't they be made of white canvas?

KEN W: Oh, couldn't be doing with all that naph drag, ducky. Besides, shocking pink goes much better with the black belt.

HUGH: Alright, Mr. Horne – let's see what you know. We'd better have you on the mat. Run through your holds with Sand. Just think of him as a great hairy member of OGPU.

KEN W: Right. Now before the bout what do we do?

KEN W & HUGH: We make an obeisance.

KENNETH: Like this?

HUGH: No – you bow – not curtsey.

KEN W: I'm a great hairy member of OGPU remember? You're about to engage in mortal combat. You're not some grotty deb being presented at Court. Right – now come at me – *(Sounds of combat)*

HUGH: That's it, Mr. Horne – go for him. Go on, gel – hit him with your handbag.

KENNETH: I beg your pardon?

HUGH: I'm sorry – I forgot myself. The last one we taught was Honor Blackman. Now grapple with him, Mr. Horne. That's it – that's bona – don't give him no quarter – grab him by the wrist.

KEN W: Ooh – ahh – stop it – you've broken it –

KENNETH: Your wrist?

KEN W: No, me fingernail.

*Orchestra: Short link*]

DOUGLAS: Two days later, Master Spy Horne made contact with his opposite number at Checkpoint Charlie –

KENNETH: *(Urgently)* Horne MI5.

HUGH: *(German/American)* Fritz Wolfgang Von Schlattzenhoffer im Grunwald und Halberstadt – American CIA.

KENNETH: I shall want some help over the wall into East Berlin.

HUGH: That's what I'm here for. OK synchronise your watch mit mine – twenty-three hundred hours.

KENNETH: Right.

HUGH: Siegfried and out.

KENNETH: Shouldn't that be Roger?

HUGH: No, Roger is drunk – you can rely on Siegfried. Right – are you ready to go over the wall? Gut. Climb on my shoulders.

KENNETH: *(Sounds of effort)* There. I still can't reach.

HUGH: Alright. Stay where you are. I'll climb on your shoulders. *(Sounds of effort)* There. [Still not quite high enough. Now you climb up again on my shoulders –

KENNETH: *(Sounds of effort)* Yes – I – think – if I – stretch – I – just – might] – *(Pause)* hang on a minute – what are we both standing on?

*F/X: Swanee whistle and thud of falling bodies*

HUGH: You picked a fine time to bring that up.

KENNETH: Well, how do I get into East Berlin now?

HUGH: There are several ways – you can tunnel your way under the wall – you can sneak through disguised as an old apple woman – it's an old trick but it might just not work. You can dynamite your way in – you can bulldoze your way through in a tank, or you can go on the tram like everybody else does. There's an all-day spying excursion leaving tomorrow morning. Go on that, but be back before midnight or else –

*Orchestra: Dramatic chord*

HUGH: – you have to pay six pfennigs extra.

*Orchestra: Short music link*

KENNETH: Once in East Berlin, I headed for a bar called the Pig, Dog and Whistle, where I knew I could pick up some information. The barmaid, a buxom Rhinemaiden, brought me a beer stein and plonked it down on the beer-steined table cloth –

BETTY: *(German)* You are a stranger here?

[KENNETH: How did you know?

BETTY: That Union Jack you are waving] – what do you want, mein herr?

KENNETH: Your hair – anybody's hair –

BETTY: You want to buy American cigarettes? You are looking perhaps for a little female company?

KENNETH: Actually I'm looking for a nuclear physicist –

BETTY: Will be difficult, but I fix. Come – follow me.

KENNETH: She led me down some steps and through a door into what looked like a garage. Suddenly I realised – too late – it was a trap! Before me stood my adversary – the head of STENCH – Doctor Chou En Ginsberg.

KEN W: Ah, Horne!

KENNETH: Ah, Chou!

KEN W: Bless you. Aha – welcome return of old joke.

KENNETH: I thought we'd heard the last of that one.

KEN W: Not knowing our writers. Look at my script – Aha – Oho – goes on for pages. Rubbish, it's utter rubbish. They won't service me. I've asked 'em – pleaded with them. It's your fault – you let them get away with any old tripe. They've never had it so good. Before they came on this show, they'd never had it at all. [I give 'em all my cast off clothes and the scraps from my frozen telly dinners and this is how they repay me.

HUGH: Don't get yourself worked up, Ken. It brings you out in angry blotches.

KEN W: Well honestly, Hugh] – look what they've written. Just maudlin sentimental twaddle. Listen to this. Marty and me are starving in a cellar in Westbourne Grove. These good people in the audience don't want to hear that. They want to be taken out of themselves. There's enough misery in the world without Took and Feldman adding to it. I think I'll make the rest up as I go along. Instant Kenneth Williams – just add an egg – Right – eyes down for a flash finish –

KENNETH: Alright Chou En Ginsberg – what have you done with the nuclear physicist and the atomic banana?

KEN W: *(Chou)* Ah yes, the at . . . *(Own voice)* The what?

KENNETH: The atomic banana. Pay attention Williams, it was on page fifteen.

KEN W: I don't remember it. Oh no, that must have been while I was out the back having my sandwiches. Atomic banana is it? Oh, they've hit a new low this week. *(Chou)* Yes, Mr. Horne – I have the nuclear physicist here. I have blainwashed him. And now I am going to blainwash you.

KENNETH: Blain?

KEN W: Blain. As in Chil. You see this machine over here. Giant new automatic five-minute blainwash – only twelve and six.

KENNETH: I'm sorry – I haven't got any change.

KEN W: Foiled! Blast!

KENNETH: I see. As in brast-furnace.

KEN W: Plecisely. But have still one tlick up my sleeve. Will summon loveliest of my concubines – Lotus Blossom –

*F/X: Gong*

HUGH: Yers, oh mighty droopydrawers –

KEN W: Got no lespect. Modern girls all the same. Alright, darling – Mr. Horne must not be allowed to escape – you know what to do? Give him old one two –

HUGH: Right. One – two – Keep your sunny side up, up – hide the side that gets blue –

*Orchestra: Picks up tune – hold under announcement . . .*

KEN W: *(Felix Aylmer)* In *Fun at Clacton*, you heard Dame Sybil Thorndike and the Yardbirds – Tito 'Silly Thing' Gobbi – Alf and Lyn Lunt, accordionistically yours – and Bobby Bo-jangles Helpman's Taps in Tempo. Hitting the high notes were Otto Klemperer and the Tiger-ragamuffins. Striking a blue note was yours truly Felix 'Daft as a brush' Aylmer, who joins the boys and girls in saying –

*Cast & Orch:*

Stand upon your legs
Be like two fried eggs,
Keep your sunny side up.

*(Applause)*

KENNETH: And now it's goodbye Clacton – hello Fraser Hayes Four, who are going to sing a track from their new LP – *Pinky and Perky, Live at Smithfield*! The Fraser Hayes Four.

*(Applause)*

*Fraser Hayes & Orchestra: 'The Mood I'm In'*

*(Applause)*

**DOUGLAS:** And now the part of the show that keeps you up to date with what today's people are doing – Trends!

*Orchestra: Music – 'Trends'*

**KENNETH:** First – trendy people. In the studio with us today we have celebrated society and show business astrologer – Morris Woodrot –

**HUGH:** *(Dentures)* Greetings. Particularly to those born under the sign of Scorpio, Sagittarius and Pisces.

**KENNETH:** Now, you've made some absolutely amazing predictions in the past, Mr. Woodrot –

**HUGH:** Yes. That is quite true. Last year I prophesied the actual date on which Christmas would fall – eight months before the actual event. And do you know – I was only one day out.

**KENNETH:** Absolutely amazing.

**HUGH:** Not really. I'm gifted with second sight. For instance, it was me who forecast that Colin Jordan[2] would <u>not</u> be the next Chief Rabbi. I also stated quite definitely that George Brown would not be England's first woman Prime Minister. [I correctly forecast that the Duke of Edinburgh himself would not fall into a vat of calves' foot jelly at three o'clock on the afternoon of April the third – and at exactly three o'clock on that day, he didn't.

**KENNETH:** Couldn't that have been a coincidence?

**HUGH:** Oh no. The stars are never wrong. The answers to all our problems are up there in the heavens.

**KENNETH:** Well, could you give us some of your predictions for the coming twelve months?

**HUGH:** Yes, certainly. In the coming year, Jimmy Tarbuck at the London Palladium will get a joke the right way round – Wilkie Bard[3] will not be asked to appear at the Royal Command Performance – the Derby will be won by a horse with <u>exactly</u> four legs –

**KENNETH:** Well, that really narrows the field, doesn't it?] But would you care to stick your neck out and make a personal prediction – about me for instance –

**HUGH:** Let's see, you're Virgo, aren't you? [That's bad luck, I'm afraid. Uranus comes into contact with Venus and Ursa Minor is in the ascendant –

**KENNETH:** What does that mean?

**HUGH:** It means that] a sudden surprise is in store for you as a result of which you will have to take immediate and dramatic action. All this will take place about ten seconds from now –

**KENNETH:** How can you be sure?

**HUGH:** I've just slipped a ferret down your trousers –

**KENNETH:** [Well, thank you *(Screams)* Morris Woodrot.] Now, trends in music. Today we are delighted – perhaps delighted is an understatement – horrified to welcome back that doyen of folk singers – Rambling Syd Rumpo.

---

2. A leading figure on the extreme Right fringe of British politics.
3. A music hall comedian who died in 1944.

KEN W: Well, hello me deario, for I'll whirdle me scroop till the grusset-man comes.

KENNETH: You do that. [And when he comes, ask him to leave me one – and a carton of yoghurt. And] where have you been rambling lately?

KEN W: Well, after I got my last golden disc-oh, I felt I had to throw off the trammels of urban civilisation and get back to the essential rudiments, the simple necessities –

KENNETH: Like what?

KEN W: This bird I got in St. Tropez. But I have been rummagin' in my ganderbag for a ditty with which to gladden your ears. I'm going to sing a very picturesque and amusing old country song. It tells the story of an orang-utan who would a-wooing go. And so off he goes in his best top hat, singing 'Dingle me dando, follow me leader, rumpelstiltskin, heigho – gammon and spinach.'

KENNETH: That doesn't make sense.

KEN W: No, but you must admit it's not bad for an orang-utan. Then he comes to Old Mrs. Owl's door, and he says to her – 'Oh Mrs. Owl – I would fain take you for my wife'. Only Mrs. Owl don't want him – not surprising really – I mean an orang-utan in a top hat's not much of a bargain.

[KENNETH: Quite – and there's the matter of the offspring.

KEN W: Precisely. I mean, what would be the outcome of such a match? A great feathered orang-utan with huge staring eyes flapping about among the trees at night.] So anyway, off he goes again – hippity hoppity gammon and spinach – and he proposes to Old Mrs. Pussy Cat.

KENNETH: Please don't go on – the thought of what the children would look like –

KEN W: They might look a trifle bizarre but they wouldn't half keep the mice down. Anyway me deario, he tries 'em all – [Mrs. Camel, Old Widow Yak, Mrs. Hedgehog – when you're an orang-utan you can't be all that particular –] but they all say to him nay. So he runs away to sea in a sieve. And of course he drowns. But as he goes down for the third time, he sings –

*Ken W & guitar: (sadly & in a minor key)*

Now all you gay bachelors listen to
  me –
Dingle, dangle, gammon and
  spinach –
Never get wed if you want to stay
  free –
With a dingle dangle, riddle me posset
I'll wallow my gammon and rattle my
  splee –
Splee-Oooooooh.

*(Speaks)* I think I've rattled it.

KENNETH: You should oil it. Thank you, Rambling Syd. And we all look forward to what we hope will be your next record – *The Rambling Syd Rumpo Memorial Album*. And now – live from London – if you call that living – *The Seamus Android Show* –

*Orchestra: Eamonn Andrews sig. music*

HUGH: And tonight – Seamus's guests are – Lord Genghis Wilkinson, the well-known dancing cloakroom attendant, [Spatula Whitethigh, celebrated smoked-salmon impersonator,] Dorita y Alf, with Clarissa the performing senna pod, and Sid Jubb, the Bishop of Tel Aviv.

But now, here's your host – Seamus Android.

*Orchestra: Music*

*(Applause)*

BILL: *(Eamonn)* Well now, hello and welcome. [After last week's show we were absolutely inundated with a flood of letters and I'd like to read it now. It's a very amusing letter – and it goes – Dear Eamonn – er *(Chuckles)* – signed Constant Viewer – Chatham. Well, keep those letters pouring in. We certainly enjoy them on the show and it helps to pad out the time. Now we did have one phone call after last week's show – a viewer who asked, 'What was he up to during the show when the camera wasn't on him'. Well, none of us are quite sure what he was doing and, when we asked him afterwards, he – er – pleaded the headaches.]

Now our first guest who has come here personally to be here, himself, now, in person, all the way from the pub next door – shy, bespectacled, ex-Smithfield porter, now star of fillems like *The Ipswich File* – Michael Bane.

*Orchestra: Music*

*(Applause)*

BILL: Hello and welcome to the show, shy, bespectacled ex-Smithfield porter – [now the type of part you're known for playing is what is known as an anti-hero. What exactly does that mean?

HUGH: *(Quiet cockney)* Well, it means that I appear in anti-dramas giving my usual anti-performance, for which I've raised my ante to abaht hundred thousand a time.]

BILL: Well, you've come a long way

from your beginnings in the East End, Michael. Has it changed you at all?

HUGH: Nah. See, I mean we're all living under the shadah of the bomb ennit? I mean, it's futile struggling – it won't get you anywhere – at least that's what I tell all the birds I lumber back to my flat.

BILL: And you have quite a reputation with women, haven't you? You're constantly being seen in smart night-spots with models and fillem stars and the like?

HUGH: Yers. Well, it takes yer mind off living under the shadah of the bomb.

BILL: Well today, you, yourself, are a big star personally. Do you find it any easier?

HUGH: Yers. Now I just have to snap me fingers and they come running.

[BILL: I mean in your career –

HUGH: Well, it's like this. When I was a Smiff Field porter, I used to spend all day humping great carcasses abaht. Nah I'm a star, I don't find it no different.

BILL: How's that?

HUGH: I'm making a picture with Kim Novak and Sophia Loren.

BILL: Alright. And <u>talking</u> of chub fuddling in Bognor,] my next guest is lovely ageing fillem star – Miss Zsa Zsa Poltergeist.

*Orchestra: Music*

*(Applause)*

BILL: Welcome back on the show Zsa Zsa –

BETTY: Hello sweetheart, it is my pleasure –

HUGH: That's what I've heard, darling.

BILL: *(Nervous laugh)* Er – ha ha – yes, <u>alright</u>. Now – er – Michael and I have just been discussing marriage.

HUGH: No we wasn't – we was talking about birds.

BILL: . . . and Zsa Zsa, we'd like to know what you think are the qualities of the perfect wife – *(Small pause)* no, don't show us – just tell us.

BETTY: Well, first of all, I theenk she should be a woman.

BILL: How true those words are even today –

BETTY: And she should take an interest in her husband's business. I do. About seventy-five per cent generally.

BILL: Now this is something you should know about because I believe you've been married several times. How many exactly?

BETTY: After the last recount it came out at eighty-four. But there was no Liberal standing. I divorced my last husband yesterday.

BILL: And now you're free?

BETTY: Reasonable. [I believe in every marriage there should be give and take. I've practised this principle throughout eighty-four perfect marriages. When my husband's given me all he's got, I take him to the divorce court.]

BILL: Well, thank you Zsa Zsa and good luck with it. Now have we got a surprise for you – because sitting up there we've got some of your ex-husbands.

BETTY: What? In the audience?

BILL: They <u>are</u> the audience. Alright.

Now our last guest tonight is a Hollywood fillem director. [If I was to say that he'd directed *Ben Hur*, *What's New Pussycat*, *Tom Jones* and many other hits – it can only mean one thing – I'm a liar. As he is, in fact,] Darryl F. Claphanger.

*Orchestra: Music (Applause)*

BILL: Well, hello Darryl –

KEN W: Hello yourself, buster! Sachay your fat can outa here and let a man hog the camera.

BILL: Now you were quoted as saying recently that you were going to make specialized films for the overseas market. Would you like to elucidate?

KEN W: Don't give me them ten-dollar words, mac! You're just as ignorant as I am. I-double-G-N-U-R-R-E-N-T. Ignorant. Yup. And proud of it. I'm a simple homespun small-town boy who's made good. I'm part of the American dream – the part you have just before you wake up screaming. Is that funny or is that funny? Boy, I'm a riot! R-Y-E-T riot.

BILL: Alright. What sort of pictures are these that you're making?

KEN W: Well, m'boy – there's a whole new market in the Middle East. I'm re-making big pictures specially for showing in Israel. [Of course they've got to be kind of slanted – they don't want Westerns, they want Easterns.]

BILL: How do you mean exactly?

KEN W: Well, for instance – we're re-making the *Yellow Rose of Texas*. We're gonna call it *Yellow Mose of Texas*. And then we're re-doing some of the other classics – *Morry Poppins*, *How Golders Green Was My Valley*, *Never on Saturday*, [*Sol Flanders*, and then we're doing that epic saga of the sea – *Moby Ben Dick, the Great Pink Smoked Salmon.*] But my biggest is going to be adaptation of Ian Fleming's *Thunderball* – we're calling it *Matzo Ball* – with David Kossoff playing Oy Oy Seven.

BILL: Well, I'm sure we could go on talking all night if only we could think of something to say. But before I sign off, I have a postcard here from a viewer who makes a very interesting suggestion. But in spite of that, I'll be back next week [when my guests will be – as boring as usual. Goodnight.]

*Orchestra: Link*

*(Applause)*

KENNETH: And who says television is killing conversation? That sort of conversation is killing television. Well, that brings us to the end of our show except for the hangover question – which is 'Whatever was I doing dancing naked in the fountain in Trafalgar Square last night?' Answers, please, to my solicitors, Grossharbour, Grossharbour, Landlust and Gladys, Cell Block 3, Dartmoor. Cheerio. See you next week.

*Orchestra: Sig. tune*

DOUGLAS: This show came to you by the courtesy of Dobbiroids Magic Horse Rejuvenators –

BETTY: I like a horse who likes me enough to give me a Dobbiroid.

KEN W: *(Sings)* Buy one for Arkle!

DOUGLAS: Appearing in it were Kenneth Horne, with Kenneth Williams, Hugh Paddick, Betty Marsden and Bill Pertwee. On the musical side you heard the Fraser Hayes Four and Edwin Braden and the Hornblowers. The script was written by Barry Took and Marty

Feldman and the show was produced by John Simmonds.

*Orchestra: Sig. tune up and out*

*(Applause)*

*Orchestra: Play out 'Round the Horne'*

*(Applause)*

# SERIES 2
# PROGRAMME 6

*FIRST BROADCAST* – Sunday 17 April 1966

## INTRODUCTION

Early on in this episode Horne suddenly starts spouting Australian clichés, explaining that he does so 'in the hope that we get an Australian repeat.' He needn't have worried – to this day, *RTH* continues to play on radio stations all over the English-speaking world. It even has a loyal knot of fans in the USA, where much of the programme is surely incomprehensible, except to the most dedicated Anglophile.

Clearly, for all its topical and cultural references, there must be something universal about *Round the Horne*'s comedy, something that transcends the restraints of time and space, provoking laughter from people who know little or nothing of the characters and concerns of 1960s London. The only 'something' that seems to fit this bill is *daftness*. No matter where you live, the puncturing of self-importance, the exposure of human absurdity, and out-and-out silliness always give pleasure. Of course, gags about certain parts of the body seem to travel pretty well, too.

Jimmy Tarbuck and Ken Dodd are lampooned in this instalment of 'Kenneth Horne – Master Spy'. Predictably, neither are treated with excessive reverence by Took and Feldman, though that doesn't seem to have done much harm to the careers of these two 'much-loved and popular funsters'. At the time of writing, Mr. Tarbuck still appears on our television screens occasionally. He has slightly less hair than he used to have, but roughly the same number of jokes. Mr. Dodd, meanwhile, continues to attract full houses all over the country to his one-man shows, which frequently overrun by several hours.

Famously, Dodd is a keen student of the history and psychology of comedy – hence the set-up here in which his gag books are stolen. In fact, some years later, a famous comedian did have his joke books stolen – but the victim was Bob Monkhouse, not Ken Dodd.

*Orchestra: Cymbal crash*

DOUGLAS: Good news for all horses – Dobbiroids magic horse rejuvenators are down threepence this week –

*Orchestra: Cymbal crash*

HUGH: Remember, Dobbiroids melt in your mouth[1] – not in your hoof.

*Orchestra: Cymbal crash*

BILL: What are you feeding your horse – chocolates?

BETTY: No. Dobbiroids. The magic horse rejuvenator with the less fattening centre.

*Orchestra: Cymbal crash*

KEN W: *(Whispers)* Hot – Dobbiroids – Hot – Dobbiroids – Hot – Dobbiroids –

HUGH: *(Bernard Miles)* Good drop of horse rejuvenator this. Looks good – *(smacks lips)* tastes good *(smacks lips)* And by golly it – *(whinnies)*

*F/X: Horse's hooves galloping off into distance –*

HUGH: *(Going off mic)* . . . Does you gooooooooood!

BILL: Yes, the makers of Dobbins Medical Cummerbunds announce a new exciting addition to their range – it's *Round the Horne.*

*Orchestra: Sig. tune*

DOUGLAS: The story so far: Wizened, stooped old crone, Mad Meg, played by Kenneth Williams without artificial aids, stumbled through the dense, gloomy forest, played by dense, gloomy Bill Pertwee, with ivy up his trunk. Pausing to collect a bundle of

faggots, played by the Fraser Hayes Four and Betty Marsden, she suddenly spied a tiny frog, played by tiny but perfect Hugh Paddick. ['Help, Help,' quoth the frog – 'I've got my flipper caught in a bramble.' The old lady was amazed to hear the frog speak thus. Quickly she freed it and the frog was overjoyed.] 'Take me back to your cottage,' he said – 'Let me sleep at the foot of your bed, and when you wake up in the morning you'll have such a surprise.' And sure enough, when Mad Meg awoke next morning, the frog had turned into a handsome prince. 'Why,' she exclaimed, 'you're not a frog at all.' To which the prince replied –

KENNETH: I was wondering when you'd tumble. My name is Kenneth Horne.

*Orchestra: Sig. chords*

KENNETH: That was, of course, Douglas Smith – one of the Brothers Grimm. They don't come any more grim than Douglas Smith.

And now for the answers to last week's questions. First – the 'What sound was it' question. Well, the sounds were – the mating call of a female bread pudding, a trouser manufacturer flying south for the winter and, of course, Peregrine Worsthorne taking his socks off. The only one of you who got that was a Mr. Peregrine Worsthorne.

Secondly, we had the 'Where do you find it' question. The answer came in six parts, as follows: under the bonnet of your car, in an individual fruit pie, under the double eagle, up the junction, hanging in the wardrobe and

---

1. All sorts of contemporary TV ads are being plundered here, including several commercials for chocolate, and a particular favourite of Took and Feldman's – Bernard Miles' 'By golly, it does you good' adverts for Guinness.

behind a bush on Wimbledon Common. At least I found one there and if it's not claimed in three days, I shall present it to the nation.

Alright, Smith – on with the motley.

DOUGLAS: Hello again, fans. This is Douglas 'Smoochy' Smith, the announcer whose skin you love to touch, whose warm cultured voice sends little frissons down your spines, whose eyes are like great limpid pools of –

KENNETH: Smith. I can't bear you in these narcissistic moods.

DOUGLAS: I'm sorry, sir, but if you can't say something nice about someone –

KENNETH: Smith! The announcement.

DOUGLAS: And now, *Kenneth Horne – Master Spy.*

*Orchestra: Music – 'Master Spy' sig.*

KENNETH: I was in the bathroom of my luxury penthouse suite overlooking Park Lane when the phone rang. I stepped out of the sink and answered it.

*F/X: Phone up*

KENNETH: Hello cobber, this is Digger Horne. It's fair dinkum to hear your old billabong again. Come in Flying Doctor, Chips Rafferty[2] with everything and out –

HUGH: *(On distort)* Why do you say that Horne?

KENNETH: In the hope that we get an Australian repeat.

HUGH: Something rather disturbing has just landed on my in-tray. Get over here immediately.

KENNETH: Right away, sir.

*F/X: Phone down*

KENNETH: Well, here I am. It's marvellous what you can do on radio. It certainly licks the television.

HUGH: What does?

KENNETH: My cat. I think it's something they put in the polish. But what did you want to see me about?

HUGH: Well, that thing I was afraid of has come up again rather suddenly. What do you think I ought to do?

KENNETH: Put a bread poultice on it and if that doesn't work, try egg and chips.

HUGH: Righto, Horne, thanks for the advice. There is one other thing –

KENNETH: Yes, sir?

HUGH: Well, I've been given something rather awkward to handle. I don't like this but I'm going to have to drop it right in your lap.

KENNETH: Go ahead, sir.

*F/X: Short swanee whistle & splosh of blancmange hitting Horne*

HUGH: It's alright. It doesn't stain.

KENNETH: *(Sounds of tasting)* Ah, raspberry blancmange, isn't it?

HUGH: No. It's a custard pie. Of the sort normally thrown at comedians.

KENNETH: I don't understand, sir.

HUGH: Well, a pie of this exact description was used this morning in a vicious and unprovoked attack upon that much-loved popular funster – Ken Dodd. While he was wiping the custard off his face, the assailant loaded his gag files on to six

---

2. A ubiquitous Australian actor.

pantechnicons and made good his escape.

[KENNETH: Have you sent the fragments of pie over to the lab for tests?

HUGH: Yes. Ballistics say that they're from a 3.7 ex-army custard pie.]

KENNETH: Any fingerprints?

HUGH: Yes. We've arrested the owner of the fingerprints – Milo Nostradamus, an Armenian pastry cook of no fixed abode. He admitted under pressure that he had, in fact, manufactured this pie for a foreign agent.

KENNETH: Lew Grade?

HUGH: We don't know. That's for you to find out. All we know is that much-loved and popular funster Ken Dodd's gags are highly dangerous. [If these jokes get into the wrong hands, they can cause untold suffering.]

KENNETH: But who, in his right mind, would want much-loved and popular funster Ken Dodd's jokes?

HUGH: A comedian perhaps. Although it's unlikely, it's our only lead.

KENNETH: And with that the interview was over. [He leaned back, spread his hands on the blotter and ate it with every evidence of enjoyment.] I hurried to a theatrical club I knew, the Chuzzlewit in Great Newport Street. The bar was packed with celebrities. At one table sat Bernard Braden chatting satirically as he drank soup out of a tin. Close by was Alan Freeman busily washing David Jacobs' shirt in a fingerbowl. On the crowded dance floor, I spied Richard and Liz dancing cheek to cheek, while nearby Dudley Moore and Ursula Andress danced cheek to knee. I elbowed my

way to the bar. The barmaid came over.

*F/X: Crowded bar*

*Orchestra: Tinkling piano*

BETTY: *(Husky)* Yes, sir? Can I get you anything?

KENNETH: I took her in my arms and kissed her passionately.

BETTY: *(Husky)* And to follow?

KENNETH: I'll have my usual – a glass of Parrish's chemical food. Stirred but not shaken.

BETTY: *(Husky)* Coming up, sir.

KENNETH: I drank it in one gulp. I was shaken but not stirred. Then I beckoned her to follow me into the back room.

*F/X: Door opens – closes. Music stops*

BETTY: What do you want?

KENNETH: Some information about Ken Dodd.

BETTY: I've never heard of him.

KENNETH: Perhaps this will jog your memory. From my wallet I produced a handful of the green stuff and offered it to her.

BETTY: Oooh, a bit of lettuce. That's nice. Got a tomato to go with it?

KENNETH: If you tell me what I want to know. Can you tell me something about Ken Dodd's movements?

BETTY: Yes. He sort of prances about waving his arms and then he fluffs his hair up and twists it into a topknot.

KENNETH: She was holding something back. I pressed a slice of cucumber into her hand and she started to talk – and talk fast.

BETTY: *(Fast incoherent gabble like speeded-up record – and then suddenly switching to normal tempo)* and that's all I know.

KENNETH: That's all I needed to know. I grabbed her roughly, ran my tapering fingers through her long, tawny hair and then took her gently in my bronzed, sinewy, three-litre Bentley down to Brighton for the weekend. We booked into the hotel and registered. Smith.

DOUGLAS: Yes, sir?

KENNETH: No, not you. That was the name we registered under. Oh, but while you're here, draw a veil over the next two days would you?

DOUGLAS: Certainly, sir. Excitingly fragrant Douglas Smith, he of the schoolgirl complexion, all over – draws a veil over those two fateful days.

KENNETH: I had no sooner reached home and unpacked when the phone rang again.

*F/X: Phone ring and phone up*

KENNETH: Hello, Horne here. [Happy birthday, Grannie Bandersnatch. May every little wish come true – good luck, good health from me to you. All the best from Master Kenneth and three kisses.

HUGH: *(On distort)* I beg your pardon?

KENNETH: Sorry, Hugh. It's my old nanny. I forgot to send her a birthday card.

HUGH: Alright,] Horne – I think we've got a clue. One of Ken Dodd's jokes was done by the compere of the *New Sunday Night at the Pandemonium Show*.

KENNETH: Jimmy Armfluff?

HUGH: He! It's up to you to find out where he got that purloined joke from.

KENNETH: How?

HUGH: You'll have to infiltrate into the show. You could pass yourself off as one of the dancers –

KENNETH: But I'm awkward, clumsy. I can't dance a step.

HUGH: Then the resemblance is complete. But just to be on the safe side, you'd better take a couple of lessons. Get down to the Aida Poston Academy of the Dance – MI5 Branch.

KENNETH: Where actually is it?

HUGH: Go to the end of the following musical passage and turn right.

*Orchestra: Short link*

*F/X: Door opens*

KENNETH: Hello? Anybody there?

HUGH: Oh hello, I'm Julian and this is my friend Sandy.

KEN W: Why, it's Mr. Horne. How bona to vada your eek again. What brings you strolling into this shrine of Terpsichore?

KENNETH: Headquarters say I've got to dance.

KEN W: Well, you carry on ducky, we'll just sit here and watch.

KENNETH: No – I want a rush course in modern dancing.

HUGH: Well, we just can't go rushing at it like a mad thing. It takes years of hard work and dedication. I mean, look at Sand – he was a Beams Babe till he was thirty, wasn't you Sand?

KEN W: I've given my life to the

dance, I have. It's an art form. It's one of the highest cultural manifestations of man. You can't manifest yourself in five minutes. It's not just a matter of step-ball-change, dainty wrists, bat your eyelids and hope for the best. Take your actual greats – Dame Margot – Rudolph Nureyev. Old Marg and Rud didn't just do it over-night.

HUGH: Take Lionel Blair. It isn't easy to be like Lionel Blair. But if you're set on it, we'll start you off.

KEN W: We'll give you your rudiments and after that, it's up to you. Right. Roll up your trouser leg.

KENNETH: I don't want to become a Mason.

KEN W: No, ducky – we want to have a vada at your calves. Oooooh, he's got dancer's calves, I'll say that for him.

[HUGH: Bit gnarled for your Covent Garden, but they'll do for your common or garden wallop.

KEN W: He's well turned out, you have to admit that, Jule.

HUGH: Oh yes,] his scotches may be a bit naph but his plates are bona.

KEN W: Well, Mr. Horne, let's start off with a simple time step. Like this –

*Drums: Tap-dancing*

KEN W: Do you think you can manage that?

KENNETH: Yes. I think so.

KEN W: Right Jule – get on the piano. With a one and a two and away we go –

*Piano: 'Avalon' (stop chorus)*

*Drums: Tap-dancing effect*

KEN W: *(Over music)* Dainty wrists now – come on – keep your head up – smile – that's it – buck and wing – now trenches – watch your trenches. Now your splits – splits I said – well do as much as you can –

*Music and taps stop*

KEN W: Fantabulosa, ducky. What do you think, Jule?

HUGH: I think he's got it. By George, he's got it.

KEN W: Yes. P'raps doing the splits was a bad idea. Still, it's only the seams gone. Come on – we'll try again.

*Orchestra: Music link*

KENNETH: The next day I auditioned at the Pandemonium Theatre as a boy dancer.

KEN W: Oh bold! A boy dancer – did you hear that *(Peals of laughter)*.

KENNETH: Alright, Williams, your sketch is over.

KEN W: I'm sorry I spoke.

KENNETH: I was hired immediately and the following Sunday Night I made my debut in the show. After the opening routine, in which I figured as an Easter Bunny, I stood in the wings and watched the compere – Jimmy Armfluff – as he went through his routine to howls of hysterical apathy from the audience.

BILL: *(Jimmy Tarbuck)* . . . he said, Missus, if I walked that way, I wouldn't need talcum powder. But seriously, it's celebrity time and we've got some really smashing celebrities out there in the audience. [Down there is the entire British Women's Over-Forties Leapfrog Team. Give 'em a big hand – good luck next week in the boat race. What? Oh, have I? I mean, good luck in the International Free Style Leapfrog Championships in Ramsgate. Now who else have we got?] Why, isn't that Frankie Vaughan sitting down there? Let's have a look. Well, we <u>are</u> in luck tonight. It isn't. That means you won't have to hear us singing 'Side by Side' yet again. Smashing. [And, by Jove, isn't that Sabrina up in the circle? – No – I'm wrong – it's two bald-headed men sitting together.]

KENNETH: I recognised that joke immediately. [It had been broken down and put into a new setting, but] fundamentally it was the same as that stolen from Ken Dodd – er – that much-loved etc., etc., etc. I would have to take this up with Armfluff. After the show, I went straight to his dressing room and knocked on the door.

*F/X: Knock on door*

BILL: *(Tarbuck)* Come in, wack. Pull up a chip butty and sit down.

KENNETH: I'll come straight to the point, Mr. Armfluff – that joke you did – that was stolen from Ken Dodd.

BILL: I didn't steal it. I bought it in good faith from my scriptwriters Galton and Simpson.

KENNETH: Not Ray Galton and Alan Simpson, those two whimsical and much loved laughsmiths of *Steptoe* fame, whose merry quips have echoed round the nation?

BILL: Why do you say that?

KENNETH: I'm anxious to avoid a libel action.

BILL: You can talk to them if you like – they're through there in the office.

*F/X: Door opens*

KENNETH: I went into the next room. Two figures sat crouched over a typewriter. As I entered, they turned –

KEN W: *(Chou)* Aha, Mr. Horne, we meet again.

KENNETH: You – Ray Galton?

KEN W: Ah no. Chou En Ginsberg – and this –

*F/X: Gong*

HUGH: Lotus Blossom Simpson.

KEN W: You see – not leally liters – merely flakes and implostors. Have disposed of leal Galton and Simpson by simple device of persuading them to lite TV series on BBC2. Nobody will ever hear of them again – aha, ahaah! Ahaah!

KENNETH: Then it was you who stole Ken Dodd's gagfiles?

KEN W: Yes. I admit it. Am going to become most famous scliptliter in world.

KENNETH: You'll never get away with it. Somebody's bound to find out sooner or later.

KEN W: Who's going to tell them?

KENNETH: I am.

KEN W: No, Mr. Horne. Now you are here, I will never let you go.

KENNETH: Why?

KEN W: *(Sings)* Because I love you –

KENNETH: *(Harmonising on last note)* Doo-wah, doo-wah.

KEN W: Thank you.

KENNETH: A pleasure. Whilst his attention was distracted, my hand slid down my trouser leg and groped for something concealed in my sock – it was my foot.

KEN W: Why are you taking your socks off?

KENNETH: One false move and I shall wiggle my toes at you – and you know how you hate that.

KEN W: Alright, Mr. Horne, you've won, for the moment. But you haven't heard the last of Doctor Chou En Ginsberg, M.A. Failed. Come, Lotus Blossom.

KENNETH: Gathering the lovely creature into his arms and with a last despairing cry of –

KEN W: (Screams) Aaaaaaaah!

KENNETH: He leapt into the filing cabinet, filed himself under 'M' for 'Missing' and was never seen again. [Ken Dodd's jokes were returned to him, older but wiser. The real Galton and Simpson have not, so far, turned up, judging from the BBC handout.] We, in MI5 believe that Chou En Ginsberg and Lotus Blossom are, at this moment, preparing a new series for Harry Corbett and Wilfred Brambell. It's going to be called *Steptoe and Number One Son.* [They're still junk men – but this time the junk will be moored in Hong Kong harbour.]

*Orchestra: Play-off*

*(Applause)*

KENNETH: And now here are the Fraser Hayes Four to sing a track from their new LP – *Twist and Shout with Ian Macleod.* The Fraser Hayes Four.

*Fraser Hayes & Orchestra: 'Pass Me By'*

*(Applause)*

DOUGLAS: And now the moment you've all been waiting for – Douglas

Smith sings *(Sings)* If I ruled the world, every day would be like –

KENNETH: Smith!

DOUGLAS: *(Angry)* Oh alright! And now, Trends!

*Orchestra: 'Trends' music*

KENNETH: First – show business. One of the trendiest people in London's West End is club-owner and female impersonator Manny La Scroop. Well Manny, it really is quite extra-ordinary the way you manage to look like a woman, sound like a woman and even act like a woman. What is your secret?

BETTY: Well you see, I am a woman.

KENNETH: Thank you. And now we're fortunate to have another trendy person with us tonight. Well-known show business astrologer – a man whose predictions have astounded everybody – Morris Woodrot.

HUGH: Greetings. Sorry I'm late but something unexpected happened.

KENNETH: Now in the past you've made some absolutely amazing predictions.

HUGH: Yes that is so. Hardly an event of world importance occurs without my having predicted it, sometimes as long as six months afterwards. For instance, I stated categorically last year that 1966 would be an uneventful year for Benjamin Disraeli. And so far nothing much has happened to him.

KENNETH: Ah, but the year's not over yet.

HUGH: No. But I'm sticking my neck out when I say that – I have to otherwise I'd soak my shirt front.

KENNETH: Well, would you like to make some more predictions for the coming year?

HUGH: Certainly. I predict that in the next few months, man will find intelligent life on Juke Box Jury. I also forecast that Kenneth Wolstenholme will not win the Miss World Competition for the fourteenth year running, and furthermore I prophesy that Cassius Clay will not become Governor of South Carolina or – and here I'm sticking my neck out again – Mississippi.

KENNETH: I don't want to dampen your ardour –

HUGH: That's alright, it'll soon dry out.

KENNETH: – you have been wrong in the past – noticeably before the General Election when you said the Tories would get in.

HUGH: Yes. Actually I did prophesy a landslide.

KENNETH: When you say it, it's more like a tidal wave. How do you explain this startlingly wrong prediction?

HUGH: Ah, but I wasn't wrong. I said the Tories would get in – but I didn't say in what.

KENNETH: Thank you, Morris Woodrot.

HUGH: Please. Don't thank me. It's all in the stars.

KENNETH: We move on now to trends in music. It's time again to meet folk-singer Rambling Syd Rumpo, one of the all-time grates – and I think you'll agree nobody grates like Rambling Syd.

KEN W: Hello me deario, chirrup chirrup for the fox be away with a goose and the fly be on the termutt.

KENNETH: Well, what can you expect if you leave it out all night? Now what are you going to sing for us today?

KEN W: Well, I was a-rummaging in my ganderbag for a gladsome ditty to bend your ear-oh with. It's a song of the Royal Scottish Pretender –

KENNETH: Bonnie Prince Charlie?

KEN W: No, this were an old Scotch tramp called McWhirter. He pretended to be Queen Frederika in order to get free orange juice. You can't drink metal polish straight, you know.

KENNETH: It does tend to dull the palate.

KEN W: Anyway, we fell to chatting by the wayside and over a rude meal of hedgehog paté, [washed down with a simple, unpretentious bottle of paraffin rosé,] he sung me it. It tells the story of a simple Highland lass, who one day espies a man in a kilt sitting up an oak tree. 'Hello,' quoth she to herself, 'it's Bonnie Prince Charlie' – well she could tell it wasn't Mary Queen of Scots.

KENNETH: Of course. A different tartan.

KEN W: Yes. So anyway, she takes him in and hides him, and gives him sustenance for three months. But lackaday, there's a sorry end to this tale that will wring your withers.

KENNETH: Good. They haven't been wrung for years.

KEN W: It turns out that he isn't Bonnie Prince Charlie after all but a cabinet maker from Huddersfield called Alf Posselswaite.

KENNETH: How tragic.

*Guitar: Vamp*

KEN W: And to this very day, almost six months later, the Highlanders still sing the Posselswaite Lament, which goes after this fashion:

*(Sings in minor key – slowly & sadly)*

Ye mucky doon a braw me lummock
A scorpit beastie through the rye
For there's a tatty bogel in me
    trussoch
Over the sea to Skye –
Pull away
Pull away me sporran
Till the seas run dry –
oooooooooooooooooooh!

*(Applause)*

KENNETH: It makes you catch your breath, doesn't it? And now once again, as our gorge rises slowly in the East, we present *The Seamus Android Show* or, as it's known in millions of homes – Never on Sunday.

*Orchestra: Music*

HUGH: And tonight, Seamus's guests are – Rancid Counterstroke, the celebrated navvy and lay brain surgeon; Battling Syd Mousetrousers, the frozen faggot millionaire; pop singer, Whimpering Lord Grope and the Underthings; and Her Royal Highness, Lil Mossop, belly dancer and Maharanee of Muswell Hill. And here is your host – Seamus Android.

*Orchestra: Music (Applause)*

BILL: Well, hello. Now before we start, I heard an amusing little story that I thought might amuse you and I'd like to tell it to you tonight. I'd like to – but I've forgotten it. Well, now, we've had our bit of fun and now – on with the rest of the show. My first guest is romantic lady novelist, health food expert and lecturer, the lovely and overdressed Barbara Cartload.

*Orchestra: Music*

BILL: Well, Barbara, it's nice to have you here, personally, in person, yourself personally.

BETTY: *(Barbara Cartland)* Thank you, Seamus. And as my family are watching, I'd just like to say 'Hello mummy – hello Boojie, hello Poppet *(Shouts)* Hello granny!' *(Quietly)* She's upstairs having her bath, you know.

BILL: Alright. Now Miss Cartload, I believe that you're England's greatest lady novelist.

BETTY: Yes. I believe that too.

BILL: And I understand that you've actually written, yourself, in person, personally – two hundred books.

BETTY: Well, actually darling, I've written one book two hundred times. And they all have the one theme – romantic love – no sex – I don't believe in it. There's too much of it going on nowadays. In my books the hero gets the heroine on the last page, but all he does is kiss her hand. After the book's finished what they do is their own affair.

[BILL: You've been quoted as saying that there's too much emphasis on sex in modern novels.

BETTY: Yes, there is. Much too much. If people stopped reading this trash and followed my principles, this country would be a much healthier and better place – and what's more you'd be able to get into an hotel in Brighton when you wanted to.]

BILL: Well, talking of Weston-super-Mare leads me to our next guest, [who by coincidence is actually about to make a film in Dar-es-Salaam.] It's shy, bespectacled ex-Smithfield porter, now fillem star – Michael Bane.

*Orchestra: Music (Applause)*

BILL: Hello again, shy, bespectacled ex-Smithfield porter and welcome to the show. Now you and Miss Cartload, I believe, have a lot in common. She's a novelist and I believe you once read a book.

HUGH: Yers, but I haven't got much time for reading. I mean we're all living under the shadah of the bomb; what chance have you got? You may as well give up – that's what I tell all the birds I lumber back to my flat. For instance, last night I picked up this bird, then I . . .

BILL: *(Hurriedly)* Er – ha-ha – I believe Barbara wanted to make a point, didn't you Barbara?

BETTY: No, I was just trying to hog the camera.

BILL: Now Michael, this fillem you've come to plug – I believe that you're getting a record fee for it?

HUGH: Who cares abaht money? Money don't mean nothing to me. They offered me forty thousand pahnd – I said 'What good is money when you're living under the shadah of the bomb?' I said, 'Keep your forty thousand pounds – I want sixty thahsand, [five percent of the gross and first crack at the leading lady.']

BETTY: What are you going to do with all that lovely money when you've got it?

HUGH: Well, darling, I'm going to fulfil a lifetime ambition. See I come from a working-class backgrahnd. I was born in Keir Hardie street in Stepney. Well, I've never forgotten the people who live in that street. And particularly the old lady what brought me up and made me what I am today. I'm going to go down there – I'm

going to buy up the lease of her house – and then I'm going to evict the old slagheap.

BETTY: I think that's an absolutely lovely thought.

[HUGH: Who's asking you, granny?

BILL: Well, I can see you two are getting on like a house on fire, so I'll leave youse two having a chat while I introduce our last guest – Hollywood impressario and producer – Darryl F. Claphanger the Fourth.

*Orchestra: Music (Applause)*

BILL: Hello and –

KEN W: Can it, fatso. Hey, where can a fella get a drink around here? Who's that snazzy broad sitting over there – Hi baby – sachay your can over here and sit on Daddy's knee.

BETTY: Really, Mr. Claphanger – a girl wants to be wooed.

KEN W: Wooed-schmooed, who's got time at our age? I like you kid, you got class. K-L-A-H-S-E – class.

BILL: Er – Mr. Claphanger – I believe you're over here, yourself, personally, to make a new fillem.

KEN W: Yup. Gonna make a whole string of low-budget pictures. *Two Coins in the Fountain* – and to show you how low the budget is, I had to borrow those. And after that I'm gonna make *The Moon and Threepence*, *Snow White and the Dwarf*, and *The Three and a Half Commandments*. But first, I'm gonna make a war picture – *The Shortest Day* – the whole picture will be shot in a pawnbroker's in the Balls Pond Road. Boy am I an iconoclast – I-K-K-O – Let's face it, I got no chance with that one.

BILL: Now, why are you making this film in a pawnbroker's shop?

KEN W: Got to m'boy – I can't afford to redeem my camera. Boy, am I illiterate –

BILL: And how true those words are even today. And while we're on the subject of tripe-skeining, you're all pretty successful at what you do – to what do you attribute your success? Michael?

HUGH: Well, being one of the best actors in the world and one of the richest, and being good-looking like I am, and gifted and charming and intelligent, I put it down to my natural humility.

BILL: Yes. Yes. Yes, yes. Yes. Mmm. Yes. Uhuh. Yes. Alright – Barbara?

BETTY: I attribute it all to health foods and a wholesome mind. In short, romance and honey. You see, I get everything I need from honey; honey keeps me fit and young and content.

BILL: Really?

BETTY: Yes. Every morning, I say to my husband 'Honey . . .'

BILL: Yes, well. Finally – Darryl?

KEN W: Well m'boy, ya got to be able to think on your feet. I remember once when I was making a picture called *Seven Brides for Seven Brothers*, and we ran out of money – six of the actors walked out on me. But I pressed on and I finished it. I called it *Seven Brides for One Brother*. It was a flopperoo B.O.-wise, but on the set – oh brother! I remember once that great producer and gentleman Cecil B. De Finkelbaum said to me, 'Darryl, it's a short life, we only pass this way once, so while we're here, what say we pick up a couple of broads and go back to my place. Big party after the show.'

BILL: I think there's a lesson for us all there.] And on that note, I'm afraid I must close because all good things come to an end, but so does this show. Goodnight to yez. See yez next week.

*Orchestra: Music*

KENNETH: Well there we are. That was *The Seamus Android Show* – would anyone who witnessed the accident . . . [and that's the end of our show too, except for this week's teaser – Miss Ecstasy Le Moko.] Oh yes, there was another thing – a few weeks ago I left you with a 'What is it' question – the what is it being a creature with an orange body, eight tentacles and hairy legs that made a noise resembling *(Does noise)*. I did mention that the reason I wanted to know was that it had just crawled up my trouser leg – at which you dutifully laughed. Well, so far I've heard nothing from any of you. For heaven's sake hurry up because it's crawled up as far as my – aaaaaaaaaaagh!

*Orchestra: Sig. tune*

DOUGLAS: And there the pathetic message ends – as does [this pathetic show which passes itself off under the title of] *Round the Horne*. Appearing in it were Kenneth Horne, with Kenneth Williams, Hugh Paddick, Betty Marsden and Bill Pertwee. On the musical side you heard the Fraser Hayes Four and Edwin Braden and the Hornblowers. The script was written by Barry Took and Marty Feldman and the show was produced by John Simmonds.

*Orchestra: Sig. tune up and out*

*(Applause)*

*Orchestra: Play out 'Round the Horne'*

*(Applause)*

# SERIES 2
# PROGRAMME 13

*FIRST BROADCAST* – Sunday 5 June 1966

## INTRODUCTION

'It's not every day you see a giant duck with a wooden leg.' Yes, for the last programme of the second series, we have one of Took and Feldman's best-remembered literary pastiches, loosely but affectionately based on *Moby Dick* by Herman Melville.

It's narrated by Ebenezer Kukpowder: 'I come of a West Country seafaring family, but I can't do the accent.' Compare that to the tape, and you'll be able to spot a Kenneth Horne ad lib that actually made it on to the air. (But only if you've nothing better to do this afternoon, obviously.) Of course, if Kenneth *did* do the accent, the comic effect would be lessened; the fact that he always uses the same rich, amused, modulated voice, no matter the age, occupation, race or even sex of the character he's playing, is one of the most charming ingredients of *Round the Horne*'s magic.

The *Moby Dick* skit contains some superbly surreal and imaginative jokes, and some highly quotable lines: 'I was fancy free – that is, if it was free, I fancied it.' There are also some truly ancient puns and groaningly predictable tags, which are rendered fresh and funny by being filtered through the personas of the cast that we have come to know so well – which is only a long-winded way of saying, 'It's the way they tell 'em.'

As you read the script, by the way, be sure not to skip the instructions relating to sound effects and non-verbal noises, as they are frequently amusing in their own right. I'm sure Williams and Paddick must have relished the challenge of acting out 'Ad lib sounds of man & duck in a fight to the death.'

HUGH: *(Dentures)* My lords, ladies and gentlemen – your highnesses, your graces, Father Thames, Mother Macree, Sister George, the President of the Balls Pond Road Temperance Society would like to take Irish whisky with his honoured guests – but he daren't. So please be upstanding and charge your glasses with Dr. Cattermole's Vitaminized Tonic Wine – the kiddies love it – ladies and gentlemen, the toast is – *Round the Horne.*

*Orchestra: Sig. tune (Applause)*

DOUGLAS: And in this edition, you'll be able to meet Dermot Stavacre and Renee – thrills and spills on the Mighty Bacon Slicer – [Banderanaika Lippincott, his ferret and his gluepot, in a mystifying melange of melody. There'll be – tumbling from Ali Ben Globule and the Whirling Postules] and music will be provided by Captain Peregrine Simcox and the massed pipes of the 14th Mounted Sanitary Inspectors. But here now is your own, your very own, Kenneth 'the tiddley-winkey girl' Horne.

*Orchestra: Music*

*(Applause)*

KENNETH: That was Douglas Smith, who has often been – but unfortunately always comes back. Now here are the answers to last week's questions. First, complete the following film title – *Whistle Down The——.* Well, of course, it was wind and most of you had it. Bad luck. Needless to say I had a letter from Mr. Gruntfuttock. What he whistles down is of no possible interest to anyone except Bertram Mills and perhaps the Director of Public Prosecutions.

The well-known phrase or saying was – 'People in Glass houses shouldn't——' – and of course that is

complete as it stands.

All right, Smith – make the announcement.

DOUGLAS: Certainly. And now, since this is the final programme of the series, this is positively your last chance to throw yourselves at the feet of D. Smith, demon boy announcer, and demonstrate the esteem in which you hold me. What – no one? Oh well – *The Kenneth Horne Theatre of Suspense.*

*Grams: Electronic Music*

HUGH: Terror is a strange emotion. It is different things to different people. It can be a creaking on the stairs, it can be something rustling in the attic – but for most people it is *(Ghastly chuckle)* Mrs. Thursday. Come with me now through the creaking door of the unconscious, where lurks the ghastly naked spectre of insanity –

BILL: *(Gruff cockney)* Good evening, sir. I am the insanity spectre. I've come to unblock your libido.

HUGH: Through here, spectre – you'll find it in the Twilight Sanctum-um-um-um.

*Grams: Electronic music*

KENNETH: My name is Ebenezer Kukpowder, but we won't go into that now. I come of a West Country seafaring family, but I can't do the accent. The story I am about to relate took place when I was but a slip of a lad, the lad in question being my father, and the slip being me. The year was 1863 and I had arrived in Portsmouth. I was footloose – in fact my kneecaps were only held on with sticky tape – and fancy free – that is, if it was free, I fancied it. Ready for adventure, I made my way to a low tavern on the quayside frequented by rough swarthy seafaring men.

*F/X: Low tavern noises*

**BILL:** *(Dame voice)* Pink gin, dearie.

**BETTY:** *(Barmaid)* Coming up, Black Jem. How about you, Tobago Jack?

**HUGH:** *(Shy)* I'll have the same as him . . . and a packet of crisps. Don't forget the salt.

*F/X: Door opens: Howling Gale: Door closes*

[*Clumping of hobnailed boots approaching*]

**KEN W:** *(Robert Newton)* Shiver me timbers! Avast, me maties! Clear a path for Scarface Rufus, me boyos – avast, I say – I'll put me hook through any man jack who dares to stand in me way. Ahah – ahah – ar – a pint of grog, me beauty. Ah, come here me dear, give us a kiss, ar – ar –

**HUGH:** *(Shy)* Evening, Vicar.

**BILL:** *(Gruff voice)* What brings you in here, Scarface?

**KEN W:** I be looking for a crew to sail with Captain Ahab – he be shipping out tonight. Which of ye stout-hearted lads'll sign on? Shanghai Charlie? Frisco Sam? Yokohama Mike? Weston-super-Mare Alf[1]? What? Be ye all afeared? Curse your black hearts for a pack of lily-livered jackals. Who will take ship with Captain Ahab?

*F/X: Door opens*

**KENNETH:** Good evening. Ebeneezer Kukpowder at your service.

**KEN W:** No thanks, I never use it. [But I'll have the green stamps.]

**KENNETH:** I eyed him curiously. Aye Aye, Scarface.

**KEN W:** Aye Aye, Kukpowder.

[**KENNETH:** He was a small, wizened creature with dangling greasy ear locks. I wondered why he wore them. As if in answer to my unspoken question, he said –

**KEN W:** To lock up my dangling greasy ears. They'll nick anything in this pub.] Well, [Kukpowder,] what brings you here?

**KENNETH:** I'm looking for a ship.

**KEN W:** Ar – then come in, me hearty. Ah, and who be this young Kukpowder, who puts ye all to shame – this fine stripling with his apple cheeks and his long blonde hair and his – *(Own voice)* – Gaw! You don't half have to use your imagination with this script. *(Back in character)* You'm be a likely lad to sail aboard the Golden Help Glub Glub.

**KENNETH:** A curious name for a sailing boat –

**KEN W:** Aye – the woman who was launching it fell off the rostrum and drowned.

**HUGH:** *(Seafaring type)* Aye – and ever since the ship be accursed. Nobody who sails on her ever be seen again. 'Tis like a floating Eamonn Andrews show.

**KEN W:** Take no heed, young Kukpowder. *(Own voice)* Oh, it's ludicrous. *(Back into character)* Have a drugged drink matey – what'll it be?

**KENNETH:** I'll just have a grog and bitter lemon.

**KEN W:** Here, lad –

1. The Somerset seaside resort is not only a universally acknowledged 'funny-name town', it was also where Barry and Marty's long friendship first blossomed, when they were both young music-hall comics.

KENNETH: I quaffed the foaming tankard eagerly, and then suddenly, everything blurred and the figure of Scarface started to dance in front of my eyes.

*Grams: Highland Reel*

KEN W: *(Highland dance-type shouts)*

KENNETH: When I came to, it was to find myself lying on a bunk surrounded by the faces of as ruffianly a band of desperadoes as one could wish to meet – outside of Eddie Braden and the Hornblowers. One of the scoundrels leant over me –

HUGH: *(Ancient toothless and evil)* Hello matey, be ye feeling better?

KENNETH: Where am I?

HUGH: You're in the evil-smelling fo'csle of Captain Ahab's ship and these are some of the evil-smelling fo'csle be your shipmates – this be One-Eye Culpepper.

BILL: *(Irish)* Hello, matey.

HUGH: This be Blackhearted Obadiah Loombogel –

DOUGLAS: Hello, matey.

HUGH: And this be the first mate – Ironteeth Rumspigot.

BETTY: *(Sexy)* Hello, darling.

HUGH: You've been shanghaied, young Kukpowder. We be four weeks out of Portsmouth bound for the China Seas – we be going after Moby Duck.

KENNETH: Shouldn't that be Dick?

HUGH: No. This be the Great White Peking Duck that haunts them waters. Eighty foot long it be, with a two-hundred foot wingspan, and they do say as how when it lays an egg in the China Seas, there be tidal waves at

Scarborough. Cap'n Ahab be sworn to slay the creature. You see, they had a tussle once before and he now wears a wooden leg. Oh, it be a fearsome creature.

KENNETH: I can imagine. It's not every day you see a giant duck with a wooden leg.

BETTY: It's not the duck, it's Captain Ahab.

BILL: Here he comes now.

*F/X: Man with wooden leg approaching mic*

*Door opening*

KEN W: Morning, scum.

ALL: Morning, Cap'n.

KEN W: Curse all they black hearts ye bunch of snivelling toadies.

ALL: Thank you, Cap'n.

KEN W: Any complaints?

BILL: The food, Cap'n Ahab – it be awful. [The biscuits got the weevil in 'em, the salt beef be blighted and the crepe suzette be burnt to a frizzle.

HUGH: There be no hot chocolate sauce for the ice cream and the champagne be non-vintage. It's more than human flesh and blood can stand.]

BILL: For the last four weeks, we've had nothing but baked beans. There's rumblings in the foc'sle every night.

KEN W: Silence, One-Eye. How would thee like a taste of the cat?

BILL: Thank you Cap'n – it'll make a change from all them baked beans.

BETTY: We can't go on like this.

OMNES: *(Rumble with mutiny)*

KEN W: Back, you mutinous dogs – where's Mr. Christian – Mr. Christian –

HUGH: *(Jewish)* So do me a favour, what do you want?

[KENNETH: He was a small dark man with a parrot on his shoulder. It regarded the company with a beady eye and spoke –

BETTY: *(Parrot)* Solly wants a cracker, Solly wants a cracker. Solly wants a cracker. Pretty Solly, Pretty Solly, Solly wants a cracker.

HUGH: *(Jewish)* Solly'll get a bunch of fives up the beak if she doesn't shut up.]

KEN W: Mr. Christian, take One-Eye Culpepper below and give him a few lashes, some mascara, and a tin of wrinkle cream. He looks awful.

BILL: No – no – no – please – not that – no –

KEN W: Take him away, Mr. Christian, [and when he's had his punishment, clap him in irons, applaud him in manacles] and put him to picking oakum.

*(Bill is dragged off protesting)*

*Orchestra: Short link – sea music*

KENNETH: For the next two weeks the poor wretch lay below picking away at his oakum. An unpleasant habit, but it passes the time at sea. The next morning I was awakened at a quarter to six bells by Captain Ahab shouting from the crow's nest.

KEN W: *(Shouts)* Avast! Avast!

KENNETH: *(Shouts)* Avast what?

KEN W: I dunno. But it's pretty big. Wait a minute, it be Moby Duck. Thar she blows –

KENNETH: What do you mean, there she blows? Ducks don't blow.

KEN W: Well, whatever it is they do – she's doing it. Look – duck-ho on the port bow. She's taking off – she's going to lay an egg.

HUGH: *(Quacking of giant duck)*

*F/X: Duck laying huge egg, ending in gigantic splash*

KEN W: *(In character)* Man the harpoon gun – we're going after her. She's getting away. More steam – more steam –

BETTY: This is a sailing boat.

KEN W: Oh – more wind! More wind! We're gaining on her – she'll not get away this time. Forty years I've awaited this moment – *(Insane laugh)* yes, I know what you've said about me – I know what's been whispered on this ship. You all think I'm a raving madam.

BETTY: It's a misprint, Ken – it should be raving *mad* man.

KEN W: *(Own voice)* Oh, I thought it was a bit bold. *(Character)* I may be mad but that duck be the cause of my madness. I will have vengeance. There she be alongside now –

HUGH: *(Giant duck quacks)*

KEN W: Stuff me in the harpoon gun, Kukpowder – I'm going after her myself.

KENNETH: Aye aye, sir. Ready, aim – fire –

*F/X: Harpoon gun going off:*

*Whoosh of body through air*

HUGH: *(Painful quack)*

BETTY: Congratulations – a direct hit.

KENNETH: Where?

BETTY: Well, I can't actually say – but if Captain Ahab was an orange . . .

BILL: See them grappling – Cap'n Ahab and his leviathan duck, locked in mortal combat.

KEN W & HUGH: *(Ad lib sounds of man & duck in a fight to the death)*

KENNETH: For hours it seemed the duel continued, no quarter being given or asked, but at last, with a final flurry of its huge webbed feet, Moby Duck succumbed –

HUGH: *(Duck succumbing)*

KENNETH: And vanished beneath the waves, carrying Captain Ahab with it –

KEN W: *(Screams ending in 'glug glug' sounds)*

KENNETH: There endeth my chronicle. And even today, eighty years later, though I am old, bent and sore – I beg your pardon – another misprint, that should be sere – [and although I've lost a little hair since then – the one growing out of my ear – no great loss and anyway it was insured –] the memory of that giant duck stays with me. And whenever I eat duck à l'orange at the Ritz, I think to myself, with a quiet smile . . . 'It's amazing what you can get away with in *Round the Horne.*'

*Orchestra: Play-off*

KENNETH: By the way, the part of the duck was played by the accomplished Mr. Hugh Paddick – it was the part that most people throw away.

And now, here are the Fraser Hayes Four, who've spent all the morning polishing their scales, and cleaning

their little webbed feet, so as to be nice and smart as they sing . . .

HUGH: *(Dentures)* 'Super-cali-fragilistic-expiali-docious'

KENNETH: . . . Ladies and gentlemen – the Fraser Hayes Four.

*(Applause)*

*Fraser Hayes Four & Orchestra: 'Supercalifragilisticexpialidocious'*

*(Applause)*

DOUGLAS: And now – Trends.

*Orchestra: 'Trends' music*

KENNETH: First – [theatre –

BETTY: Noel Coward's new play *Song at Twilight* has taken London by storm. And while some critics say that it's controversial, others maintain that he has avoided the real issues –

KEN W: *(Noel Coward)* It's the Coward's way out.

KENNETH: In the cinema there's still a lot of trouble over certain love scenes –

BETTY: *(Common)* You do that again and I'll call the manager.

BILL: *(Old)* I'm sorry, madam – I was looking for my umbrella.

BETTY: Well, you won't find it there.

KENNETH: However,] the trend in films is still back to the Forties – the era when Fanny was By Gaslight and not Hill, and Hill was Doctor Charles[2] and not Fanny. The days when Jimmy Tarbuck was Ted Ray, and so was Charlie Chester. When [we all sat behind blackout curtains in three inches of bath water, doing nothing with this page until told what

2. Dr Hill was 'the radio doctor'; *Fanny Hill* is English literature's most famous pornographic novel. Published in 1748–9, its publishers were prosecuted for obscenity as late as 1963.

to do with it. When Cooper was Gladys and not Henry, when Clay was Keyes and not Muhammad Ali, when] everybody was our gallant ally except for people who are now our friends. Ah well – plus ça change – that's your actual French. Here now is an excerpt from one of the great films of that period, starring Dame Celia Molestrangler and ageing juvenile Binkie Huckaback.

*Tape: 'White Cliffs of Dover'*

BETTY: Oh, Charles – I thought you'd never get here.

HUGH: It wasn't easy, but I pulled it off. [I managed to swing a forty-eight.]

BETTY: How strong you are.

HUGH: Oh, Fiona, how I love you in these gay, madcap, antic, hoydenish, exuberant moods of yours. You just twinkle.

BETTY: Only for you, Charles. Only for you. Come – sit here by me – tell me, Charles, is it bad?

HUGH: At the Front?

BETTY: At the Front.

HUGH: Pretty bad. At the front. Not too good at the back. But the sides he's done it beautifully.

[BETTY: You're pulling my leg, Charles.

HUGH: I'm sorry, darling, I thought it was mine. *(Hollow laugh)*

BETTY: Is it – hell – the trenches?

HUGH: Yes. The trenches are hell. The buck and wing's not too good either, but fortunately they're not too particular in ENSA.]

BETTY: *(Tinkling laugh)*

HUGH: Oh, it tickles you does it?

Perhaps I should have shaved it off. How I love to hear you laugh, Fiona – [it's everything most wonderful – it's a rainbow after rain, the first cuckoo of spring, a field of corn in the sunlight, the dappled dancing of moonbeams on a mountain lake – it's jam and crumpets in front of the fire – it's Christmas Day – it's like a fairy tinkling in an enchanted glade – a sunset over the Cairngorms, – the Taj Mahal by moonlight, it's – it's – I don't have the words for it.]

BETTY: I know.

HUGH: I know you know.

BETTY: I know you know I know.

HUGH: Yes, I know.

BETTY: Oh, Charles – I want to make you happy for these few brief, fleeting moments that we're together. How can I make you happy?

HUGH: You know, Fiona.

BETTY: Yes – I know I know. Kiss me, Charles – kiss me –

HUGH: Oh, Fiona – if only this could go on forever. Tell me, Fiona – have you ever loved like this before?

BETTY: Not like this. Not quite like this. Not on the top of a 73 bus.

*Orchestra: Link*

*(Applause)*

KENNETH: Yes. It beggars description, doesn't it? And now we move on to the world of folk music – summer is icumen in – loud sing Rambling Syd Rumpo.

KEN W: Well, hello me deario – for I'll fusset me trusset and whirdle me groats, and if that don't work, I'll poke it down with a stick.

KENNETH: I wouldn't. It might turn

nasty if it's disturbed. And what ineffable ullage have you got for us this week?

KEN W: 'Tis a Runcorn splod cobbler's song. Sung by the splod cobblers of Runcorn as they pump their cordwangle bellow afore cobbling their splods. It's best to do it in that order – see, the splod has to be white hot, otherwise it gets the bogel in it and you can't do nothing with a bogelled splod.

KENNETH: No. I believe that even the dustman won't take it away. What exactly is a splod?

KEN W: [Now that's an interesting question and I only wish I had an interesting answer to give you. However,] a splod is a kind of spottle guard or shreeve hoof worn by a Lummockshire Nobtiddler or work goat as it prefers to be known. Understandable really – you'd feel embarrassed too, if you was called a Lummockshire Nobtiddler.

KENNETH: Yes. You would be wide open to all sorts of curious nicknames.

KEN W: Precisely. *(Own voice – to audience)* Sometimes I swear he understands every word I say – *(Back into character)* Now me deario – [I have dipped into my ganderbag on many happy occasions, but none more so than tonight, when I have come up with what is undoubtedly the most uninteresting song in my whole niggardly repertoire.] *(Guitar vamp)* As the splod cobbler works his trumice, he sings this lugubrious ditty –

KEN W & GUITAR: *(Sings)*

I sing as I cobble and hammer my
    splod
Tho' my trumice glows hot and my
    trade be odd

I sit as I gorble and pillock my splee
For a cobbler's life is the life for
    me-ee –
Sing lickety-lickety-splod me boys
Sing wackety-wackety – *(Cry of
    anguish)*

KENNETH: Why the *(Cry of anguish)*

KEN W: Well, that's the sad part of the narrative. Alas, he misses his splod and impales hisself on his own cordwangle.

KENNETH: I imagine that could be very painful.

KEN W: Fatal most often as not. As a result of which he dies – lackaday – and they do say as how his ghost walks abroad in a minor key, as follows:

KEN W & GUITAR: *(Sings mournfully in a minor key)*

Now his ghost still sits and cobbles his
    splod
Tho' his trumice grows *(Quavering)*
    cold, and he's on his tod.
He sings as he gorbles his ghostly
    splee
'Oh a cobbler's life was the death of
    me –'
*(Quavering)* Sing lickety-lickety splod
    me boys
Sing wackety-wackety – *(Moans)*
    Splod!

*(Applause)*

KENNETH: I think there's an awful warning for us all there. Moving on now [from the ineffable Rambling Syd to something far more effable] – recently I was asked to organize a cabaret for the Director General of the BBC. They said they wanted something different, so I popped down to a little agency in the Charing Cross Road that I'd heard of. It was called – Bona Performers.

*F/X: Door opens*

KENNETH: Hello, anybody there?

HUGH: Hello, I'm Julian and this is my friend Sandy. We're Bona Performers.

KEN W: Oh, it's Mr. Horne. How nice to vada your dolly old eek again. What brings you trolling in here?

KENNETH: Well, I've been asked to organise a cabaret for the BBC on the fifteenth. I was wondering if you could fix me up.

KEN W: Oh yes, ducky. We'd be glad to fix you up anytime. BBC is it? Oh you'll want something a bit risqué for that mob. How about Queenie? I think she's at liberty.

KENNETH: What does Queenie do?

HUGH: Striptease with a difference. See, normally she's the bearded lady at Blackpool; long beard she's got, right down to her ankles.

KEN W: And instead of stripping, she just comes on and shaves. She can't do it often. It takes her two years to grow the beard again, poor love.

KENNETH: It's not exactly what I had in mind. A little less exotic, I think.

[HUGH: Well, would you like to have a leaf through me files? See if there's anyone you fancy?

KEN W: Yes Jule – get out your immediate vacancies and let the gentleman have a vada.

HUGH: How about him? Nemesis Groatblast – England's Premier Yodelling Archbishop – he's V.A.F. you know.

KENNETH: Variety Artistes Federation?

KEN W: Oh, is that what it means – we thought it meant 'Vada! Absolutely Fantabulosa'.

KENNETH: And what does he do?

HUGH: Well, it's difficult to describe, but it involves feats of incredible agility and dexterity with a fire extinguisher, a frankfurter sausage and a goat.

KEN W: Yes. Unfortunately though, the goat's got a prior engagement on the fifteenth.] But we can get you the Great Omipaloni – he's one of ours, isn't he, Jule?

HUGH: Oh yes. He's your actual strong man. Beggars description, he does.

KENNETH: Could you give me some idea of his act?

KEN W: Well, he comes on wearing this leopard skin, see – he's a great huge butch ome, with thews like an oak and bulging lallies –

HUGH: Then he bends an iron bar – tears two telephone directories in half, drives a nail through a plank with his bare fist, and then, as a finale – for his *pièce de résistance* –

KEN W: There's your actual French –

HUGH: He's harnessed between two teams of wild horses – pulling in opposite directions. But does he budge? Budge he does not. We bill him as the strongest man on earth –

KENNETH: I'll take him then.

KEN W: But you can't have him on the fifteenth. That's his night for washing his hair.

KENNETH: Well, who else have you got that's available?

HUGH: Well, we're available, aren't we Jule?

KEN W: Extremely. We'll be happy to oblige on the fifteenth. We are your great all-round entertainers – Sand and Jule – a show in theirselves – the brightest stars in the show business firmament. We can be seen nightly at the Marine Commando Club in Paddington, can't we Jule?

HUGH: Yes. Come and see us. Drag yourself up there one night. We have to be seen to be believed.

KENNETH: And what, I shudder to ask, do you do?

KEN W: Oh bold! He goes too far, doesn't he? Well, we are versatile, Mr. Horne. You name it – we do it.

KENNETH: Sing?

HUGH: Not your actual singing. No.

KENNETH: Dance?

KEN W: No. [The muse of Terpsichore has not actually lighted on our shoulders. That is to say, we don't do your actual wallop.]

KENNETH: Juggle?

HUGH: No.

KENNETH: Conjure?

KEN W: No.

KENNETH: I thought you said if I named it you could do it?

KEN W: Ah yes, ducky, but you haven't named it yet.

*Orchestra: Play-off*

*(Applause)*

KENNETH: Well, eventually I named and they did it. But happily the plaster should be off in a couple of weeks. [Anyway the BBC cabaret problem was solved. The Director General decided that the most suitable thing was to have an actress coming out of the cake. Unfortunately, I made a mistake in booking and so, at the appropriate moment, out leapt an actress – *(Pause)* – only it turned out to be Dame Edith Evans covered in marzipan. Which wasn't what they had in mind at all. Most of the programme committee can't bear marzipan. Which is one of the reasons that this is the last of the series.

Before we go, in answer to certain suggestions that this show, from time to time, is not as pristine as driven snow – all I'd like to say is – remember 'Evil is in the eye of the beholder'. *(Small pause)* Thank goodness.] Finally the 'What is it' question, in which I asked you 'What is it that has a great hairy body, two huge staring eyes, sixteen legs and an eight-foot wingspan'. Well, I only got one answer to this which came from a Major E.R. Larkshaunch of North Borneo. He said 'the creature you describe is common in these parts and is known as the giant man-eating – aaaaaaaaaaaagh!' I assume he was right as the letter was sent by his next of kin. Cheerio. With any luck, see you next year.

*Orchestra: Closing sig.*

DOUGLAS: That was *Round the Horne* starring Kenneth Horne, with Kenneth Williams, Hugh Paddick, Betty Marsden and Bill Pertwee. On the musical side you heard the Fraser Hayes Four and Edwin Braden and the Hornblowers. The script was written by Barry Took and Marty Feldman and the show was produced by John Simmonds.

*Orchestra: Sig. tune up and out*

*(Applause)*

*Orchestra: Play out 'Round the Horne'*

*(Applause)*

# CHRISTMAS 1966

*FIRST BROADCAST* – Sunday 25 December 1966

## INTRODUCTION

Kenneth Horne suffered sporadic ill health through the last decade of his life, but this is the only episode in which he did not take part. Rather than bring on a sub (as was sometimes done in other comedy shows; for instance Harry Secombe occasionally stood in for an indisposed Tony Hancock), the writers re-jigged the script, sharing out the great man's burden amongst the rest of the cast. The result is . . . well, the result, in fact, is a classic episode.

Took has said in the past that, once he and Feldman had hit their stride, *RTH* 'almost wrote itself', and while it's interesting to go through this script trying to figure out which lines should have been Horne's ('I am a marquis – which means I can be hired for parties and functions'), it's more interesting to wonder at the sheer mechanical efficiency of a machine that can continue functioning faultlessly even when its head has been chopped off.

Not that this script is robotic at all, either in sound or in print; on the contrary, it's full of life. Any *RTH* fan would agree that Kenneth Horne was central to the success of the show, and yet his absence from this edition really doesn't seem to matter. This can only be because the structure of the series is so firmly established, and its diverse components are so perfectly fitted together, that even a crisis like the loss of its lead player can, on a temporary basis, be dealt with without difficulty. Indeed, despite his physical absence, Horne's character seems to be present throughout the script in spirit. Of course, it does help if you have available the services of the best writers, producer and performers in the business. And let's not forget announcer Douglas Smith, who in this episode plays an absolute blinder!

# The Trailer

**DOUGLAS:** 'Twas Christmas at the BBC – and in the *Round the Horne* studio, presents were being exchanged –

**HUGH:** *(Charles)* This is for you, Fiona. I hope you like it.

**BETTY:** *(Fiona)* Oh, Charles – what is it? It's such an unusual shape – but what a pretty ribbon.

**HUGH:** I had them put it on in the shop. Do you want it now, or will you wait till after the Queen's speech?

**BETTY:** Now, Charles, now. Quick, pass me the scissors.

*F/X: Rustle of paper*

**BETTY:** Oh, how lovely. You shouldn't have.

**HUGH:** I wanted you to have it, Fiona. It belonged to my grandmother.

**BETTY:** Thank you, Charles. But what is it?

**HUGH:** It's – my grandfather.

*Grams: Sounds crazy*

**BILL:** Meanwhile – in another part of the trailer, other gifts are changing hands –

**KEN W:** Merry Christmas, Jule.

**HUGH:** Merry Christmas, Sandy – here, this is for you –

**KEN W:** Oh, Jule – how thoughtful – it's absolutely bona.

**HUGH:** I made it especially –

**KEN W:** What with your own hands? Oh you're so good with your hands. I envy people who can do things with their hands. Now what shall I wear it with?

**HUGH:** Well I don't know . . .

**KEN W:** How would it go with me velour trouser suit, or me crushed strawberry PVC ensemble with the bell bottoms. What shall I wear it with?

**HUGH:** Please yourself. It's a Christmas pudding.

*Grams: Sounds crazy*

**BILL:** *(Breezy Radio Caroline-type compere)* If you want another earful of this zesty fun-packed, rib-tickling Yuletide family filth, tune in tonight at six o'clock – to Radio BBC, Light Programme, your station of the stars – when you'll be able to hear a special edition of *Round the Horne* – until then – *Bon Noel*!

**KEN W:** That's your actual Christmas French.

# The Show

**HUGH:** *(Dentures)* My lords, ladies and gentlemen, Field Marshal Loompoper, General Klaus Von Runstedt und Halberspiegel of the Royal Welsh Fusiliers, Colonel McGanderpoke, not forgetting his good laddie wife – er I beg your pardon – good lady wife – Brigadiers, Brigadarlings, officers, non-commissioned officers, men, non-commissioned men, other ranks, Comrades of the Khyder – the toast on this festive occasion is Enid, the regimental goat, with whom I should like to couple General de Gaulle – not to mention – *Round the Horne*.

*Orchestra: Opening sig.*

**BETTY:** *(Christmas message voice)* As this is a special show specially mounted for this very special occasion, we're going to mark this very special day by doing the same old rubbish we do the rest of the year – First . . .

DOUGLAS: Around Town – a quick round up of what's been happening in Swinging London, as opposed to Dangling Bootle. Here with the inside info is trendy show biz columnist Peter Nodule – come in Peter Nodule.

KEN W: And shut the door after you. There's a draught.

BILL: *(Peter Noble)* Well, it's all happening this week.

KEN W: Not here it isn't.

BILL: Yes, it's really popping all over town –

HUGH: *(Mutters)* Plead the headaches.

BILL: Hot news! Trendy trumpeter Herb Alpert is in town staying at the Balls Pond Road Hilton with the Tijuana Brass. His only comment – 'We're just good friends.'

DOUGLAS: And on the sporting scene – Daphne Whitethigh reports –

BETTY: *(Horsey voice)* At Wembley yesterday, the Dobbiroids-sponsored Horse of the Year Show was won by Pamela Ormsby-Foot. Her horse came second.

DOUGLAS: Finally – man-on-the-spot Brad Smallpiece with news of current events.

HUGH: *(Lotus Blossom voice)* There have been no h'events this week concerning currants, with the possible exception of an incident concerning a Christmas pudding and a workhouse master, but there is 'owever many exciting 'appenings to titillate the visitor – porridge tasting in the crypt of St. Paul's, a traffic wardens' wine and cheese party at the Wigmore Hall, a torchlit display of ferret sexing at the White City, and Otto Klemperer at the Albert Hall, playing selections

from the 'Well-Tempered Liver Sausage'. But I myself would plump for the Aldershot Tattoo, which can be seen nightly on the arm of Lance Corporal Brutt at the Jolly Embalmer, High Street, Aldershot, and depicts two heraldic camels entwined and the motto 'Up the Liberals'.

KEN W: Well worth a visit, but here now to announce our next item is our own trendy announcer – Douglas Shh you know who.

DOUGLAS: Thank you. That was, of course, Kenneth Shh you know what.

KEN W: He's no right to say that. He's only an announcer.

BETTY: Take no notice, Doug. Don't let him throw you.

BILL: No. You get on with it, Doug. Come on – gird up your loins.

DOUGLAS: Well they're not actually mine. I'm breaking them in for Kenneth Williams.

KEN W: I'll thank you not to bandy my loins about. I won't have me loins made a laughing stock. I'm not having me loins pilloried to make a Roman holiday. It's cheap and uncalled for. Especially when you consider my stature – am I not part of Britain's Great Heritage? I should be above ridicule – I am a sacred cow. I am a myth in my own time.

BETTY: What you do in your own time is your own affair, Ken. Doug, make the announcement.

*Orchestra: Timp roll*

DOUGLAS: Ladies and gentlemen – it's . . .

*Orchestra: Very grandiose theme. Four bars*

DOUGLAS: . . . *Armpit Theatre*[1] . . .

BILL: *(Dramatic/American)* The BBC – the studios which gave you epics like *Les Miserables, Crime and Punishment*, and *Does the Team Think*, would now like them back in exchange for their pathetic production of –

*Orchestra: Music up to climax*

BILL: *The Hunchback of Notre Dame.*

*Music out*

HUGH: My name is Henri de l'Abbatoir. I am a marquis – which means I can be hired for parties and functions. I'm known all over Europe as a rich powerful lecher.

BETTY: Yes, darling, but what part are you playing in this piece?

HUGH: In medieval Paris, I am called a despot – but I don't make a habit of it. I have a small, unpretentious four-thousand roomed château in the Place Notre Dame – it's convenient for the cathedral. One day I was in my chambers, which is something like being in your cups, only larger, and I was poring over an old, finely chased, bow-fronted peasant girl when there came a knock on my door.

*F/X: Knock*

HUGH: Entrez.

*F/X: Door opens*

BILL: Milord, the Bishop of Paris wants to see you. He is without.

HUGH: Well, I'm afraid that's his problem. I've got barely enough for myself. What does he want?

BILL: He desires an audience.

HUGH: Well, tell him he can have the one on *Take Your Pick*. I'd be glad to see the back of them. You'd better show His Most Reverend and Noble Grace in.

BILL: *(Shouts)* Oi! Gracie – you're on!

KEN W: *(Felix Aylmer[2])* Ah, good my liege, allow me to greet you in the traditional manner –

*F/X: Kiss*

HUGH: On the hand, Ken. You're supposed to kiss me on the hand.

KEN W: *(Own voice)* I'm only doing what it says in the script, ducky. I assure you there's no pleasure in it for me. It's the writers' faults – if they can't be bothered to do a bit of historical research I can't be held responsible. *(Back into character)* Ah, good my liege, I have grave tidings.

HUGH: What is it, good Bishop?

KEN W: *(Aylmer)* Quasimodo.

HUGH: The poor ugly hunchbacked bell-ringer at whom the townspeople scoff?

KEN W: The same.

HUGH: Well, that's established who he is. Now, what's he done?

KEN W: He's been insolent and rude. Yesterday at evensong, I was leading the choir through the nave, swinging my censer, and do you know what the impudent wretch shouted? 'Go it gel – your handbag's on fire.'

HUGH: What did you do?

---

1. *Armchair Theatre* was a hugely influential series of one-off TV dramas, celebrated (and ridiculed) for its gritty realism.
2. A distinguished, elderly actor with perfect diction.

KEN W: *(Aylmer)* What could I do, my liege? I give him a mouthful of knuckles. *(Own voice)* That's fine period dialogue that is. Mouthful of knuckles – that's nice palare for a medieval bishop. See, these writers have got no sense of period – anything outside of a four-ale bar is shrouded in mystery to them. You want Christopher Fry for a job like this – you know, him who wrote *The Palone's Not For Burning*. He'd understand me, old Chris would. He could service me. I need servicing. How can I take a bishop without the proper servicing? Mouthful of knuckles – you wouldn't get a bishop saying that. It's ludicrous. He'd be unfrocked. He would. Unfrocked. They'd have his frock off him in no time.

HUGH: All right, take out mouthful of knuckles. What would you say in its place?

KEN W: *(Aylmer)* I belted him one with my episcopal crook.

HUGH: Yes. That's much better. Has the right ecclesiastical nuance about it.

KEN W: *(Aylmer)* Quasimodo must go. He's ugly, he smells, he's dirty, he has the evil eye.

HUGH: The rest of him doesn't sound much to shout about either.

KEN W: He's the devil's familiar. *(Own voice)* And you know how I hate people being familiar. *(Into character)* He's a witch. He ought to be burned.

HUGH: This is a matter for the church. You, good bishop, must try Quasimodo.

KEN W: *(Own voice)* Try him? I wouldn't even try him on approval. You must be joking, ducky.

HUGH: Look, Ken, you're supposed to be playing my aide-de-camp. Could I have a little more aid and a little less camp?

KEN W: I'm sorry I spoke. *(Character)* I bid you good day, my liege.

HUGH: And turning haughtily on his heel, he gathered up his mini-cassock and swept out of the room. I forgot about Quasimodo in the next few days. I had other matters on my mind – a troupe of Spanish gipsies had come to town – their caravans made a gay splash of colour in the square below my window, and at night all the townspeople would gather to hear their wild gipsy music and see their exotic gipsy dancing –

*Flamenco guitar. Hand clapping. Shouts of 'Olé', etc. Segue into orchestra playing* Come Dancing *sig. tune*

BETTY: *(Judith Chalmers-type voice)* And representing South East Europe is Sonny Zahl and Edna Lippincott who dances under the name of Esmeralda. She is wearing a dress that she made herself out of a hundred and forty yards of sequined horse blanket, her balaclava helmet is encrusted with gilded senna pods which she tells me she sewed on herself. She and Sonny run a cat's meat boutique and formation horse knackers school in Palmers Green. They were last year's runners up. Well done Sonny and Esmeralda. Keep taking the tablets.

HUGH: Watching from my window I was entranced by the fiery Esmeralda. She was beautiful, untamed. Her lips were a sensual scarlet wound set in a perfect oval face – her eyes held a smouldering invitation to forbidden delights.

KEN W: I should have played that

part. It describes me perfectly.

HUGH: Well, why didn't you get it?

KEN W: I failed the medical.

*Orchestra: Corny chord*

BILL: *(Bill Gates[3] voice)* Elsie and Doris Waters are now appearing in *The Naked World of Harrison Marks*[4] at the Hollywood Bowl, Great Yarmouth.

HUGH: Meanwhile, back at the plot – one sight of Esmeralda set my pulses racing, my blood pounding and my corn throbbing. I determined that she should be mine and mine alone – I think it's best when there's just the two of you . . . I sent my servant to bring her to me.

*F/X: Knock on door. Door opens*

BILL: *(Gruff cockney)* Good my liege, I have obeyed your command – I got the gippo bodger outside.

HUGH: Show her this way.

BILL: I think she already knows that way. In here missus – woman.

HUGH: Ah, so you are the lovely Esmeralda whom all men desire?

BETTY: *(Old crone)* That's right, dearie. Wanna buy some clothes pegs?

HUGH: Perhaps we should have given the part to Kenneth Williams.

BETTY: Cross me palm with silver and beware the gipsies' curse.

HUGH: That's not the kind of gipsy we had in mind, Betty. Start again from your entrance. Ah – Esmeralda.

BETTY: *(Sexy Spanish)* Si señor – you

wish to see me?

HUGH: Among other things, yes. I'm getting on in years, I admit I'm not handsome but I can give you things, things you've never had – like a good bath. Come to my arms my proud beauty.

BETTY: No – I am promised to another – I am betrothed to Sonny Zahl[5], King of the Gipsies.

HUGH: A fig for Sonny Zahl.

BETTY: Oh ta. I'll give it to him when I see him.

HUGH: Come here, wench.

BETTY: Don't touch me, señor – I warn you – if you lay one finger on me I shall kill you. I have a stiletto concealed in my – blast! I forgot to put them on this morning.

HUGH: Oh Esmeralda, let me smother you with kisses – there – there – there –

BETTY: Ooops!

HUGH: I beg your pardon. Not there. Just a trick of the light. Let me hold you like this – close to me. How do you feel now?

BETTY: *(Own voice)* I wish they <u>had</u> given the part to Kenneth Williams.

KEN W: It's a disgrace!

HUGH: Well Esmeralda, you have but one choice – take me as your lover or I shall see that you're burned at the stake as a witch.

BETTY: I shall never submit to you – burn me if you will – better dead than bed.

---

3. A radio announcer.

4. A producer of films which starred people who'd forgotten to get dressed. A sort of prehistoric version of Channel 5, only with better picture quality.

5. A theatrical agent; he represented Feldman at one time.

HUGH: Very well. *(Calls)* Executioner!

BILL: Yes, master. What is your bidding?

HUGH: This wanton wretch is to be burnt in the market place – or if wet, in the scouts' hut.

BILL: How do you want her done, master – medium or rare?

HUGH: I leave it to you. You know how to go about it. Surround her with faggots.

BILL: Well, everybody to their own taste – what time's fry-up?

HUGH: At noon today. Right, take her away, executioner. Do what you have to.

BETTY: You may do your worst with me, executioner.

BILL: Yes, I may very well. Come on, darling.

*Orchestra: Music sting*

DOUGLAS: Meanwhile in yet another part of the plot, other eyes were watching, or should I say other eye – it was Quasimodo, enter Kenneth Williams with cushion stuffed up his jacket –

*F/X: Ringing of church bells, up and then fade for dialogue*

KEN W: Ah! Ahaah! The bells! I must ring the bells – that's all I do from morn to night – ring the bells. That's how my life is spent – but I love the sound of the bells – yes I do like a good ding dong. Oh woe is me! This burden I carry has been the cause of the trouble I'm in –

BETTY: Psst – Ken – you should have the cushion stuffed up the back of your jacket, not the front. You're giving people the wrong idea of the sort of trouble you're in.

KEN W: Oh yes. I thought it was a bit odd. Yes, now where was I? Ahah, ohoh, pity poor Quasimodo! Why am I so ugly? Why do people run away from me? Is it just because I'm bent? I may be bent but I have a heart. Ahah – aagh – who would have my lot? What a lot I got. Oh! Ah! *(Aside)* It's a tour de your actual force this is. Must be worth a knighthood at least. *(Back into character)* Ah – ooh – ooh ah – but am I not human? Have I not parts and passions . . . *(Own voice)* well don't take a vote on it . . . *(Character)* I love Esmeralda, I know I'm not much to look at, nothing to see *(Sings)* But I'm funny that way – well, I'm glad I got that out of me system – you can get on with the story now.

DOUGLAS: The scene changes to the square in front of the cathedral. Esmeralda is about to be tied to the stake, the executioner prepares to ignite the faggots, when suddenly a hunched figure bursts through the crowd, seizes the object of his desires and rushes up into the belfry of Notre Dame.

*F/X: Footsteps running upstairs*

KEN W: *(Quasimodo)* You'll be safe with me, my little beauty.

BILL: *(Executioner)* Here, what's your game, mate? Put me down.

KEN W: Blast! Wrong one.

*F/X: Footsteps running off – pause.*

*Footsteps running back*

KEN W: *(Panting)* Darling!

HUGH: Wrong again.

KEN W: Beg pardon.

*F/X: Footsteps running downstairs.*

*Small pause*

*Footsteps running back*

KEN W: *(Panting)* There, Esmeralda. You'll be safe with me.

BETTY: *(Startled)* Who are you? Why have you saved my life?

KEN W: Because – because –

*Grams: Romantic strings behind following dialogue*

KEN W: I love you Esmeralda. I want you. I need you. Stay here with me. Oh I know I can't give you what other men can give you – fine clothes, jewels, gold, *(Music stops abruptly)* but I can ring the bell. What do you say?

BETTY: *(Artificial laugh)*

KEN W: *(Own voice)* All right, don't overdo it, girl. Give her a line, she makes a career of it. It's the producer's fault. She wouldn't carry on like this if she was under Tyrone Guthrie[6]. May we continue with the performance –

BETTY: *(Character)* Me? Stay here with you, no it could never be . . . I have already plighted my troth –

BILL: *(Radio doctor)* Then bathe it three times a day in hot water.

BETTY: I am betrothed to the King of the Gipsies.

KEN W: Sonny Zahl?

BETTY: The same! But soft – here he comes even now –

*F/X: Galloping hooves approaching*

*F/X: Door opens*

HUGH: *(Jewish)* Esmeralda – I've found you at last. Quick we must fly from the mob. I have saddled these two thoroughbred Arabian hedgehogs who will carry us to safety and heartsease at the end of the rainbow. Come my beloved. To far Tuscany – hard by leafy Whitechapel.

KEN W: Go with him, my child.

*F/X: Galloping hooves off*

KEN W: *(In character)* Alone – poor Quasimodo's left alone. Up in the belfry – all I've got is me bells. Is that how I'm destined to end my life – just an old lonely campanologist?

*F/X: Distant babble of mob*

KEN W: What's that? The mob. They're down there in the square. They're coming for me.

BETTY: *(American) (On loud hailer effect)* All right, Quasimodo. We know you're up there. Are you coming down or do we have to come up and get you?

KEN W: Come and get me, copper. I've got a loaded gun here and I'm not afraid to use it.

HUGH: You can't have a gun. It's an anachronism.

KEN W: All right, I've got a loaded anachronism here.

DOUGLAS: *(On loud hailer)* Come down Quasimodo, son – This is your mother talking.

KEN W: Mother?

DOUGLAS: Yes – it was the only part left. Come down, son.

KEN W: Too late. I'm going to jump.

CAST AND ORCHESTRA: *(Ad lib)* Don't jump! Don't jump!

---

6. British theatre director, noted for his experimental approach.

KEN W: Oh, all right. If you insist. Instead *(Dropping into concert party tenor voice)* I shall waft you round the world on a magic carpet of melody – *(Sings in strangled voice with sobs)* My song, goes round the world . . .

CAST & ORCHESTRA: Jump! Jump!

KEN W: In that case I shall leap on to the bells and have A Resounding Tinkle from the play of the same name by N.F. Simpson, amateur rights available.

*F/X: Bell chime*

KEN W: *(Scream)*

*F/X: Bell chime*

KEN W: *(Scream)*

*F/X: Bell chime*

KEN W: *(Final death agony)*

HUGH: *(Sonny Zahl – King of the Gipsies)* Don't look, Esmeralda – it's not a pretty sight. Don't look. Wail! He's been crushed by the giant clappers.

[BETTY: What a terrible, terrible end.

HUGH: Yes it is. But we couldn't think of anything better. Besides it's only *Round the Horne* – they'll applaud anything.]

*Orchestra: Pay-off chord*

*(Applause)*

DOUGLAS: And now it's time for the Fraser Hayes Four – a sort of Gin-Trapp Family Singers with their own contribution to Christmas. Here to sing 'It Happened in Sun Valley' – the Fraser Hayes Four.

*Fraser Hayes Four and orchestra*

*(Applause)*

DOUGLAS: And now the *Round the*

*Horne* Christmas Colour Supplement.

*Orchestra: Short link*

DOUGLAS: This part of the show can only be heard in colour, and like the newspaper supplements, is slipped in entirely free . . . So if you don't like it, remember it's costing you nothing, and don't come whining to us. First – the lively Arts. Here in the studio tonight is that doyen of folk singers – a man who is no stranger – than he ever was – here he is . . . Rambling Syd Rumpo.

KEN W: Well hello me deario. Sing rue-me-down and spong-atwitty-oh, for green grows the moss on my true love's corbangle.

HUGH: Have you tried scouring it with steel wool?

KEN W: I did but it took the varnish off. Well, since I been here last, I been a'wandering over hill and dale, through bush through briar, where the spotted curd wings low over the bosky fields of groat and turve to where the high spume blows and the curlews grunge.

BILL: Grunge?

KEN W: Yes, – grunge.

BETTY: I didn't know curlews grunged.

KEN W: Oh they do. You can't stop 'em. It's their diet. You'd grunge an' all if you lived on a diet of seaweed and worms. Anyway 'twas there, close by fabled Clacton, that I picked up this ditty. It is the 'Clacton Bogel Picker's Lament' sung by the itinerant lummock mongers of they parts, who hang about the foreshore scroping their lummocks and monging them at the passers-by. Which is one of the reasons why more people are going abroad than ever before. This lament is sung by an old lummock scroper and goes as follows . . .

*(Sings to a small guitar)*

When I was one and twenty boys
My bogle did I plight
And many's the lummock I did scrope
Beneath the pale moonlight.
Sing haul away me posset Meg
There's limpets on me dando.

*(Next verse to be sung sadly and in a minor key)*

Now I am old and sere me boys
My bogle's silvered o'er.
I cannot scrope me lummocks
And me heart it is full sore.
Sing pull away me posset Meg
There's barnacles on me dando.

*(Brightly)*

Now all you jolly sailormen
Who listen to my song,
Come plight your bogles while ye may
They don't stay fresh for long.
Sing hurry up with that posset Meg
There's an octopus up me dando –
    oooooooooh!

*(Applause)*

**DOUGLAS:** Thank you, Rambling Syd Rumpo. You are part of England's living folklore.

**HUGH:** If you ask me it's a lore that should be repealed.

**BILL:** Well, Christmas is a time of nostalgia, when the memory of those wartime Christmases comes flooding back. How well one remembers those dark days of the '40s when Edward G. Robinson was Little Caesar and Harold Wilson wasn't – when Powell was Sandy and not Enoch and when Franco was accompanied by Monte Crick at the piano – when Day was Dennis and not Doris –

**KEN W:** Talk about the longest day.

**HUGH:** Those halcyon days when Noel was Gay, Roy was Rich and Thora was seen but not Hird. One can't help but look back a little nostalgically.

**KEN W:** No, I can't, for it seems like only yesterday we were going to the cinema to see those 'There's a U-boat on the port bow number one, I've been seven nights without sleep, the convoy must get through, don't worry about Felicia sir, I'll look after her, God what a mess, what a ghastly mess'-type of film.

*Grams: 'I'm Dreaming of a White Christmas' (cracked record)*

*Orchestra: Short link*

**BILL:** It gets you where you live, doesn't it?

**BETTY:** Well, it's your own fault for living there.

**DOUGLAS:** Finally, *Round the Horne* Christmas Colour Supplement takes a look at the occult. Here tonight are two celebrated clairvoyants and seers who are going to talk about their work –

**HUGH:** Good evening. I'm Julian and this is my friend Sandy.

*(Applause)*

**KEN W:** Or, to give us our professional names – I am Madame Bona and Jule here is the Great Omipaloni – natural sensitive.

**DOUGLAS:** I believe you can see into the future.

**HUGH:** Oh yes. I'm a seer. I am occupied by your actual mystic forces.

**KEN W:** He is. Occupied. Frequently. Cross his palm with silver and he will reveal all, won't you Jule?

HUGH: Gladly.

KEN W: You see, it's a gift with him. Some have got it, some haven't. He's got it – by George he's got it.

DOUGLAS: Well, I'm afraid I haven't got any silver on me –

HUGH: Oh, don't worry. You can cross me hand with a Diners Club Card. They trust you up there. Now, how would you like me to prognosticate? Through the tea leaves, a spot of palmistry or would you like Sand here to have a vada in his crystal?

KEN W: I'll have a vada in me crystal. Right. Whip it out of its chamois, Jule. There. There's your actual crystal ball. Now let's see what it foretells – It's cloudy – 'Scuse me, I'll just hurr on it *(Heavy breath)* There, it's clearing – I see a man – it's you – you're in a room – a dark room – but you're not alone – there's two strange weird creatures – one of them is peering into a crystal . . . Oh sorry, it's a reflection. How mortifying.

HUGH: Don't castigate yourself, Sand. Nante's coming through. Shall we try the Ouija?

KEN W: Yes. Get out your Ouija, Jule. Let's have a palare with the spirits. Come on, all sit round and hold hands – you sit next to me, Mr. Smith. Jule will be going off.

HUGH: Yes I do, you know. I go right off. Right up the astral plane.

KEN W: He does. Right up there. He's limp for days afterwards. It takes it right out of him. Right, nisht the chat now, he's going into his trance.

HUGH: *(Groan)*

KEN W: He's going. He's going. It's coming over him in waves. *(More groans)* Look at him. He's in touch with what we do not know. He's gone beyond. He's being possessed now by his spirit guide. He's a great butch Red Indian you know – look – look – Geronimo's occupying him now. It's very uncomfortable to be occupied by a Red Indian. And it lowers the value of the property. *(More groans)* Hello – Geronimo – it's Sand here – have you a message for any of us? Speak, Geronimo.

HUGH: *(Haltingly)* Mr. Geronimo is out[7]. Leave your name and number. He will call you when he comes in. This is a recorded message.

*Orchestra: Link*

KEN W: *(Pickles)* Well, lads and lasses that brings us to the end of the show, and on behalf of the company I'd just like to say that if you've enjoyed listening to the show as much as we have performing it for you – then we've all had a pretty boring half-hour. Goodnight, Macclesfield.

OMNES: Goodnight, Wilfrid.

*Orchestra: Play out*

*Down for announcement*

[HUGH: *(Cheery compere voice)* You have just been listening to the *Franz Kafka Bandshow* – among those appearing were Bishop Podghast with Solly the Educated Ferret, King Freddie of Buganda and the Dreamers, Jaroslav Brovnik – the Dog-Toothed Ozech, and Miss Ecstasy La Bootstrap in the forbidden dance of the Giant Flue Brush – once seen never forgotten. Hitting the high notes were

---

7. Is this the first gag about an answering machine to appear in a British comedy show?

Werner von Braun[8] and his Band of Renown, and your compere was that zesty, curvaceous little armful, Lord Artemus Posture – 'She knows you know'.]

*Orchestra: Signature tune*

DOUGLAS: That was *Round the Horne*, starring Kenneth Williams, Hugh Paddick, Betty Marsden and Bill Pertwee. On the musical side you heard the Fraser Hayes Four and Edwin Braden and the Hornblowers. The script was written by Barry Took and Marty Feldman, the show was produced by John Simmonds and your announcer was me – lovely Douglas Smith – younger than springtime am I – gayer than laughter am I –

KEN W: Yes ducky, we've all got your number.

HUGH: Kenneth Williams is now appearing in the Fairy Grotto at Belfridges.

*Orchestra: Sig. tune up and out*

*(Applause)*

*Orchestra: Play out*

*(Applause)*

---

8. Nazi rocket engineer who, at the end of World War II, instead of being prosecuted as a war criminal, was employed by the US government. Subject of a famous satirical song by Tom Lehrer.

# SERIES 3
# PROGRAMME 4

*FIRST BROADCAST* – Sunday 5 March 1967

## INTRODUCTION

Some of *Round the Horne*'s film spoofs were of recent releases, but in this episode we are firmly in the 1930s, when Alexander Korda made *Sanders of the River*, which starred Leslie Banks and Paul Robeson, and Merian C. Cooper filmed *She*, which didn't.

I suspect Took and Feldman were more comfortable with the classics because, although both of them were still young men, many of their joint obsessions and fascinations were not exactly bang up-to-date, including as they did the music halls and the nineteenth-century novel.

At this stage in their careers, Barry and Marty are writing so well it almost hurts, with lines like 'My name is Dr. Gandermole Lipharvest the Third. The other two died of embarrassment.' The script reads as it was apparently written – quickly, fluently, with a joyful ease of invention.

Hugh Paddick gets his fair share of the best lines, though he was also able – as the writers well knew – to make a 'best line' out of almost anything. His contribution to *RTH* is to some extent overlooked; never mind 'we're all living under the shadah of the bomb', Paddick's reputation has to cope with the shadow of Kenneth Williams. Of course, Williams was the loudest, liveliest, most compelling element of *RTH* – but when you read these scripts, and listen to the shows again, I think you'll agree that without Paddick *Round the Horne* couldn't have happened.

Many of his contemporaries are even more celebrated today than they were at the height of their careers. I can think of no comic performer of that generation more deserving of 'rediscovery' than Hugh Paddick.

DOUGLAS: Here's a warning to all shipping. 'It's *Round the Horne.*'

*Orchestra: Sig. tune*

HUGH: And tonight, Kenneth's guests are – [Monsignor Monty Greenspan, the nude cyclist of Polperro – Major General Vidal Nightsock at the electronic corset of St. Paul's –] the Reverend Unseemly Dogposture, conducting the Massed Pumas of the Women's Institute, Edgbaston – and Dame Sweeny Eggblast, the Clacton dripping heiress.

DOUGLAS: And here's your host – Cardiff's dusky queen of song – Kenneth Horne.

*Orchestra: Signature tune*

KENNETH: Thank you. That was, of course, Douglas Smith, who would like to get it straight – but unfortunately it has to stay in plaster for another two weeks. Here now are the answers to last week's questions. First, the 'Where do you find it in Scotland' question. The answers were:- [in Loch Ness, North of Kenneth McKellar, flung over a highlander's shoulder, and held in the right hand. Andy Stewart has a long, gnarled curly one which he uses when impersonating the late Harry Lauder[1], but this is only for comic effect. The other answers were] – hanging down in front of the kilt, tucked under the arm and blown, stuffed down the sock – except on Burns night when it's used to cut the haggis. Finally, the 'Where would you find it written' question – and the answers were: on the base of the great pyramid – halfway along the great wall of China, in whitewash – and in a tobacconist's window in the Edgware Road. At least that's where I

read it, and if you're listening Miss Lolita, I rang and rang but there was no answer, so I've joined the Photographic Society of Chalk Farm Polytechnic instead.

*Orchestra: Armpit Theatre theme*

DOUGLAS: At this point, we were going to do *The Three Musketeers*, Episode Three, but we got fed up with it[2], so here instead is a thrilling story of Africa. We proudly present Kenneth Horne as *Lipharvest of the River.*

KENNETH: My name is Dr. Gandermole Lipharvest the Third. The other two died of embarrassment. I was christened James Obadiah St. John Abraham Spike Loomis Cyril Angus Ali Ben Moses Rastus Paddy Heinrich Giovanni Fun Man Noger – after my father. My mother wasn't too sure – apparently he kept his hat on throughout the brief acquaintance. However, dear reader, I digress. I am a [fellow of All Souls – if I have deciphered this manuscript correctly – and am a] keen botanist . . .

KEN W: We've all got your number, ducky.

KENNETH: . . . and zoologist. In the spring of 1883, I was in the Umpopo country looking for the great White Rhino which I'd sent up the road for the newspaper and which had never come back. One evening I was in the bar of Dutch Pete's Waterfront Dive having a sundowner, when a strange figure lurched in. [His ragged Eton tie and moth-eaten trousers showed at once that he was a gentleman. Curious to see such a man in such a place –] I crossed to him and smiling politely asked him if he fancied a jigger.

---

1. Two well-known Scots entertainers of the time.
2. This, apparently, is the unvarnished truth!

KEN W: No thanks I never dance with strange men. But I'll have a drink. I need one. My name is Gaylord Ffitch. What I have done no white man has done and lived. I've been up the Umpopo with Yellow Yack.

KENNETH: How is he?

KEN W: *(Own voice)* Not bad, considering. He sends you his regards. *(Character)* I have seen things up there that would make you blanche. [See this shrunken head?

KENNETH: Yes and your wizened body and puny hairy legs. What a pathetic sight.]

KEN W: I have seen the lost city of Watalumbas, the fabled lost jungle city ruled over by a white woman – known by the superstitious natives as She.

KENNETH: Who's She?

KEN W: The cat's mother. They say she's over three hundred years old but as beautiful as she was when she was two hundred and fifty.

KENNETH: I must meet her –

KEN W: Why?

KENNETH: I'm attracted to older women. Will you lead me to her?

KEN W: It's a dangerous journey – through fever-ridden swamp – through trackless jungle – over mountains, across deserts, through crocodile-infested rivers.

KENNETH: Is there no other way?

KEN W: Well, a 73 bus passes the door.

KENNETH: I haven't any small change, and you know those conductors – they'll never take a note.

KEN W: Then we must go by river.

We'll sail at dawn tomorrow.

KENNETH: The next morning we set off in the African Queen played by Douglas Smith with cocoa on his face. He nosed his way lazily upstream – Ffitch and I relaxed in the s-s-stern.

DOUGLAS: Chug – chug – chug – phut – phut – phut –

KENNETH: Phut phut, Smith?

DOUGLAS: Yes sir, it's the engine –

KENNETH: Well, give the old boiler a kick.

DOUGLAS: Yes, sir.

*F/X: Boot hitting old boiler*

BETTY: Aah! Thank you, sir. When you're an old boiler you don't get many kicks.

KENNETH: Isn't that the one who played Grannie in *The Three Musketeers*?

KEN W: Yes – she gets about a bit for an old un.

DOUGLAS: Meanwhile, halfway up the Umpopo – phut phut chug chug – ker fong!

KENNETH: All right, Smith. What was that supposed to be?

DOUGLAS: I think a crocodile has fouled the propeller. What shall I do?

KENNETH: Hit it on the nose with a rolled-up newspaper.

KEN W: From here on we'll have to go by foot. Follow me.

*F/X: Splash*

KENNETH: I think we should have moored the boat first.

KEN W: Help! I can't swim.

KENNETH: Well, tread water.

KEN W: I can't. A crocodile's gnawing me leg.

KENNETH: Well, hop water.

F/X: *Water splashing*

KEN W: *(Shouts for help)*

Orchestra: *Music link*

KENNETH: We scrambled ashore more dead than alive – and set off on foot through the tangled undergrowth of the Umpopo country. Ffitch and I made slow progress.

KEN W: Well, it's not easy to walk when you've got a crocodile hanging on to your leg. Ooh – aah – I can't go on. I'm done for.

KENNETH: Come on, Ffitch.

KEN W: No – I'm f-finished.

KENNETH: He was bent double with agony. Suddenly there was a ssst and a pft. For a moment I thought he'd expired but fortunately he was only transfixed by a poison dart.

KEN W: *(Howls in agony)*

KENNETH: Where did the dart hit you, Ffitch?

KEN W: *(Own voice)* Well – if I was a dartboard it'd be – treble 19.

KENNETH: Then suddenly from out of the bush, or rather, from under the bush, came the tiny naked figure of a man riding a hedgehog. He was 30 inches high and he brandished a small but deadly blowpipe. He galloped across the clearing, reined his hedgehog to a halt and dismounted – with a sigh of relief.

HUGH: Cor – I have a warning for you, white man.

KENNETH: What is it?

HUGH: Never ride a hedgehog with no clothes on.

KENNETH: Who are you?

HUGH: I am Sonny Zahl, King of the Umpopo pygmies. Observe – tiny but perfect in every detail. What brings you here?

KEN W: We're looking for the lost city of the Watalumba – and the white goddess – She.

HUGH: Oh, her. But you are injured, you need a doctor. I'll summon my tribe. *(Calls)* George, Arthur, Sidney, Solly.

F/X: *Tiny running feet*

*Babble of tiny voices (like chipmunks)*

KENNETH: Hundreds of tiny figures swarmed out of the undergrowth, and in a trice we were up to our knees in Umpopo.

HUGH: Take these white men to our village.

KENNETH: But this man is injured. He can't walk.

HUGH: Don't worry – I'll give him a pygmy back.

Orchestra: *Jungle drums*

KENNETH: That night found us ensconced in a rude hut. Ffitch was raving.

KEN W: I've got f-fever.

[*Grams: Peggy Lee 'Fever' (one bar)*]

HUGH: Your friend delirious but witch doctor will soon cure him.

KENNETH: Where is he?

HUGH: At witch surgery. Is coping with epidemic among pygmy tribe. German measle.

KENNETH: Measle? You mean measles.

HUGH: No, pygmy so small only room for one.

KEN W: Water – water.

KENNETH: Here, old chap.

KEN W: It's not for me it's for the crocodile. Aah – ooh (etc.). Mother!

KENNETH: Thank heavens he recognizes me.

KEN W: I can't feel my legs – help me.

KENNETH: Help him to feel his legs, will you?

KEN W: I'm going – I'm going – it's slipping away. It's coming back. It's going again –

KENNETH: I wish it'd make its mind up.

[KEN W: Lipharvest, dear old friend, I'm going away on a long journey – hold my hand and we're halfway there – *(Sings)* There's a place for us –

KENNETH & HUGH: *(Hum)* Zoom!

KEN W: *(Sings)* Somewhere – somewhere – etc. Lipharvest, you'll find something in my trouser pocket – it's a tablet, give it to me.

KENNETH: No Ffitch. Not that.

KEN W: Don't argue, do as I tell you. It's better this way. There. *(Smacks lips)*

KENNETH: What is it?

KEN W: *(Own voice)* A curiously strong peppermint. I want to be at me best when the doctor comes.]

KENNETH: At that moment the witch doctor arrived – he stood framed in the doorway towering over three foot tall – a giant of a man – for a pygmy. His ears were pierced with elephant tusks. He wore a headdress of fine ostrich plumes – and he carried a

matching handbag. From his waist dangled his curious medicaments. He spoke –

BILL: *(Frenzied African gibberish)*

KENNETH: What was that?

BILL: I said – and how's the patient today?

KENNETH: Will you examine him?

BILL: Certainly. Now does it hurt when I do this?

*F/X: Loud thud*

KEN W: *(Yells in agony)*

BILL: Well, his reflexes are all right. Ah ha – um – hum.

KENNETH: What do you diagnose?

BILL: Not well at all. Patient has a bad case of galloping.

KENNETH: Galloping what?

BILL: Don't know. It goes too fast. I suspect beri-beri.

KENNETH: Beri-beri. Is it bad?

BILL: Not beri-beri bad – not beri-beri good. So-so.

KENNETH: How are you going to treat it?

BILL: As follows – first I smear myself in sacred chicken fat – then I make cabbalistic sign –

KENNETH: There's nothing cabbalistic about that sign.

BILL: Then I summon devil drummer. *(Calls)* Devil drummer!

HUGH: Yes, baby.

BILL: Give me a steady four – and easy on the hi-hat. A one – a two – a one two three four –

*Orchestra: African drums*

BILL: *(Ad lib African chants)* One more time – *(More chants)*

KENNETH: And he leapt about the room brandishing a chicken above his head. Ffitch stirred – his eyes opened, he slowly sat up and then, as if possessed by evil spirits, he screamed.

KEN W: Shut up! Have a bit of consideration. I'm not well.

*Orchestra: Music link*

KENNETH: The next morning we set off again in search of the lost city – and She.

*F/X: Jungle noises*

KENNETH: For days we hacked our way through the undergrowth until finally there in a valley below us lay the fabled city of Watalumba, its marble domes and gabled minarets glinting in the sunlight. I heard a movement behind us and turned to see four grinning dark faces. The leader spoke –

BILL: Ah, white men, we were expecting you. Would you accompany us?

KENNETH: Delighted.

*Orchestra: Piano arpeggio*

BILL & FRASER HAYES BOYS: *(Sing in manner of minstrel troupe – opening bars of 'Camptown Races')*

KENNETH: And then mercifully came oblivion. When we came to, Ffitch and I found ourselves lying on the marble floor of an enormous chamber. At the far end of the room was an ornate throne on which sat the three-hundred-year-old white goddess – played by Betty Marsden, without any artificial aids. On either side of her stood a huge nubian. As if answering my thoughts, Ffitch spoke.

KEN W: Cor – what an enormous pair of nubians!

BETTY: That which I am is – that which is not shall be – for I am that which has always been and what I have done I have done – many, many times. I am She, but you can call me Lil. See, I am old – three hundred years have I lived – but with age there are compensations – I can get in up the pictures free on a Thursday. I am old, I am wrinkled, I am hideous, but . . .

KENNETH: But what?

BETTY: Don't rush me, I'm thinking. There must be something. [Ah yes, I am powerful. My whim is law – and my desire is that one of you shall be my consort. Even now the nuptial bed is being prepared. Which is it to be?] One of you shall be my lover, the other shall be thrown to the sacred shark. Which is it to be? Me or the man-eating shark?

KENNETH: Don't rush me. I'm thinking.

BETTY: See this pool beneath the throne – there waits the sacred shark played by Douglas Smith, with teeth cut out of orange peel. My little pet is hungry.

DOUGLAS: Snap-snap.

KENNETH: Well done, Smith.

DOUGLAS: Thank you, sir. I also do sheep.

KENNETH: Thank you, Smith.

BETTY: Well gentlemen, have you decided?

KENNETH: Well, Ffitch?

KEN W: Well, Lipharvest?

KENNETH: It seems there's no choice. Last one in's a cissy.

*F/X: Two splashes*

KENNETH/KEN W: *(Screams)*

BETTY: Funny – they all do that.

*Orchestra: Pay-off music*

*(Applause)*

KENNETH: What a way to go. To perish in the awful gaping jaws of the sacred Douglas Smith . . . and talking of awful gaping jaws, here are the sacred Fraser Hayes Four to sing –

BILL: *(African gibberish)*

KENNETH: Which freely translated means 'Serenata'. The Fraser Hayes Four.

*(Applause)*

*Fraser Hayes Four and Orchestra: 'Serenata'*

*(Applause)*

DOUGLAS: And now the *Round the Horne* Colour Supplement.

KENNETH: This is the section of the show which you can pull out – and if you don't like it – throw away. First, show business. [Here, hot from the studio floor is Daphne Whitethigh.

BETTY: Despite misgivings by the distributors, film critics all agree that it was an inspired idea to put Hayley Mills in *The Family Way*. Asked how she came to play the part, Hayley's father, plucky John Mills said –

BILL: After her first screen kiss in *The Moonspinners* one thing led to another.

KENNETH: Thank you, Mr. Mills, and tell Mrs. Mills I've always admired the way she plays 'Knees Up Mother Brown'. Who's where?] Here now interviewing a well-known personality at London Airport is that Sunday

Night person – Seamus Android, whose very name is a synonym for –

HUGH: *(As in advert)* Deep Sleep.

KENNETH: Come in, Seamus Android.

BILL: All right. Now I am here at London Airport personally, myself in person to meet someone who I know you will as I have, so without further ado, here is a world-famous personality who I am dying to meet as much as you are – and who is dying to meet you as much as you are and indeed I am. *(Chuckles)* All right. So here without further ado – is the one and only – oh he's gone. And with that I return you to the studio.

KENNETH: Thank you, Seamus. I won't miss your TV show this week. What you don't see you don't miss. Now this week, the Colour Supplement's special feature is devoted to: 'The Englishman and Art'. Throughout history the English have been connoisseurs of the arts.

KEN W: *(Very old)* Come in, Gregory – there's something I've just acquired – and I'd like your opinion on it. In here. Look, next to the Degas.

HUGH: *(Very old)* Good heavens, a Constable.

KEN W: Genuine do you think?

HUGH: Let me see – hmm – ah lovely, lovely. No doubt about it. It's a genuine Constable. Absolutely beautiful.

BILL: Thank you, sir – I try to keep meself nice.

*Orchestra: Brief link*

KENNETH: Love of arts is deeply embedded in the Englishman's soul – and many films have been made depicting the inner struggles and romantic agony of the painter. Here now is an excerpt from that great film of the Forties, *The Moon and Sixpence Reduced to Fourpence This Week Only*, starring Dame Celia Molestrangler and ageing juvenile, Binkie Huckaback.

*Tape: 'Pagan Love Song'*

BETTY: Can I come in, Charles?

HUGH: Yes, Fiona. I'm glad you came – it's finished. I think I've pulled it off.

[BETTY: Oh good, Charles. You've been at it so long.

HUGH: Yes. I think I've done something quite magnificent, and now it's ready for you to see – I want you to be the first, Fiona.

BETTY: Do you, Charles?

HUGH: Yes. I think you'll appreciate it. But be careful. It's only just been varnished.

BETTY: Where is it, Charles?

HUGH: Here –

*Grams: Dramatic strings*]

BETTY: Oh Charles, I think you've captured it. It's a small masterpiece.

HUGH: Thank you, Fiona.

BETTY: I mean, you wouldn't see anything like this hanging in the Royal Academy.

HUGH: I don't <u>want</u> it hanging there.

[BETTY: It may be ugly but it's got colour – warmth – life. How did you get that impasto mottled effect?

HUGH: I used a palette knife. Nobody knows the agony of the artist, Fiona.]

BETTY: But Charles, I'm not quite sure that I understand what you're doing.

HUGH: Ha! Surely it's simple enough.

BETTY: For you, Charles. You're an artist – you painted it. I'm only a woman. What does it mean?

HUGH: What it says – 'Gents Wash and Brush-Up 6d'.

*Orchestra: Brief link*

KENNETH: Ah, the agony of the artist, and here is an artist who's been responsible for more agony than almost anybody alive – Rambling Syd Rumpo.

KEN W: Hello, me deario. Sing Bogle tit willow and lackaday for the fly be on the turmutt.

[KENNETH: Have you tried whacking it with a broom handle?

KEN W: I did – but it raised a nasty bruise.]

KENNETH: Now, you're a great exponent of the art of folk singing. What are you going to give us this week?

KEN W: 'Tis a taddle gropers' dance, sung by the villagers of Musgrove Parva and it heralds the coming of the oak apple fairy or sanitary inspector, as he is known. The taddle gropers grope round [taddling each other] while the turve maiden merrily whirdles her splod. They dance to a roundelay that goes after this fashion:

*(Sings to an approximation of 'Here We Go Round The Mulberry Bush')*

There's cordwangles in my possett
   bag,
What shall I do my Mary O –
And I can't woggle my artifacts
What shall I do my darling.

*(Spoken)* So the turve maiden sings back:

*(Sings)*

Stove it with a gander hook
That's what to do my Billy O –
Then you can woggle your artifacts
As good as new my darling.

*(Spoken)* So he stoves it with a gander
hook but it don't do no good as a
[stoat's nibbled the end off and] he's
forgot to put anti-freeze in so
plaintively he sings to her:

*(Sings)*

I stoved it in with a gander hook
That's what I've done me Mary O –
But now I've nadgered my artifacts
What shall I do my darling?

*(Spoken)* So she tells him what to do
with his artifacts and he does it – and
they dance off woggling and groping
their taddles to the following refrain:

*(Sings)*

Billy cock Billy cock
Nadger me danda
Boggle me loomer me jolly boys
And possett me splee – in the
       morning.

*(Applause)*

KENNETH: Thank you, Rambling Syd.
I can find the words to express my
feelings – they're in the script of *Till
Death Us Do Part*[3]. Well now, art is
subject to changes of fashion [and
things that were thrown out by my
grandmother – my grandfather for
instance – but that's another story –
are considered beautiful today] – and
hence the current vogue is for
Victoriana, old uniforms and so on.
Last week I paid a visit to a shop near
the Portobello Road. The sign over the
door read Bona Antiques. I entered
gingerly. Hello. Anybody there?

HUGH: Hello, I'm Julian and this is my
friend Sandy.

KEN W: Hello, Mr. Horne. Come to
have a browse through our bric-a-
brac?

HUGH: You want it, we've got it – if
you don't see it just ask for it.

KEN W: Did you have anything in
mind? Hm – I see you're eyeing that
piece in the corner. It's beautiful, ennit
Jule?

HUGH: Beautiful it is – a thing of
beauty that is. It's a wangee rocker.

KENNETH: I don't rock my own
wangees – I have a little woman round
the corner who does it for me.

KEN W: Oh bold.

HUGH: The older they get the cheekier
they are. Well have a vada at our nick-
nacks – no obligation.

[KEN W: Hello – Jule – see I told you –
he's having a vada at your whatnot.
They all do. They're all taken by it.

HUGH: Everybody's taken by my
whatnot. But I'm not keen to part
with it. I want it to go to a good 'ome.

KEN W: He's a good ome, Jule. One of
the best. Give him a price.

HUGH: It's very difficult to put a price
on it. I don't know.

KEN W: But you've got the pair, Jule.
You could let one go.

HUGH: All right – you can have it, Mr.
Horne. There – a fiver. I can't say
fairer than that.

KEN W: He can't – not fairer than
that.

---

3. The new BBC sitcom was proving very controversial, not only for its outspoken political comment
but also for its use of 'strong language' not previously heard on television.

KENNETH: Thank you but it wouldn't fit in – I mean I wouldn't know where to put it.]

KEN W: Jule – change the subject. Here, I got it. Uniforms.

HUGH: Oh yes – very In – very chich.

KEN W: The chichest. Fantabulosa. Uniforms are the utmost.

KENNETH: Yes, I've heard that wearing old uniforms is the latest craze.

HUGH: And we've got the craziest.

KENNETH: Good heavens – soldiers' uniforms – sailors' uniforms. [How do you get them all?

KEN W: Through the trade.]

HUGH: How do you fancy yourself as a Gay Hussar?

KEN W: Oh he'd take a lovely Hussar with great bullion epaulettes and frogging down his lallies.

HUGH: Or there's this – a fireman's uniform – very butch. Comes complete with fourteen yards of hosepipe and a dinky little chopper.

KENNETH: I can't see myself wearing that to the Junior Carlton Club – unless of course it was on fire.

KEN W: Then how about this naval uniform?

KENNETH: Do you think it's me?

KEN W: Do you think it's him, Jule?

HUGH: It is him. A naval uniform just does something for you.

KEN W: Here just slip it on – ah! Fantabulosa!

KENNETH: I'll take it – in fact I'll wear it now.

KEN W: Ta ta, then. We'll send our account.

F/X: *Shop door open and shut*

KEN W: There he goes – doesn't he look an absolutely perfect example of a . . . what's the phrase, Jule?

HUGH: – great steaming nit.

KEN W: That's it exactly.

*Orchestra: Pay-off music*

KENNETH: In my second-hand naval uniform I got many admiring glances, several compliments and arrested for impersonating a Wren officer. Well, how was I to know? I was in the RAF. Cheerio. See you next week.

*Orchestra: Signature tune*

DOUGLAS: That was *Round the Horne* starring Kenneth Horne, with Kenneth Williams, Hugh Paddick, Betty Marsden and Bill Pertwee. On the musical side you heard the Fraser Hayes Four and Edwin Braden and the Hornblowers. The script was written by Barry Took and Marty Feldman and the show was produced by John Simmonds.

*Orchestra: Signature tune up and out*

*(Applause)*

*Orchestra: 'Round the Horne' playout*

*(Applause)*

# SERIES 3
# PROGRAMME 10

*FIRST BROADCAST* – Sunday 16 April 1967

## INTRODUCTION

Took and Feldman were mystified, in the early days of the show, to receive a bizarre complaint from anti-obscenity campaigners that members of the *RTH* cast were guilty of 'putting emphasis on certain words'. The opening sketch in this episode is a perfect answer to such nonsense, as Kenneth Horne is called to account for using such blatantly smutty words as 'Hello' – and we all know what that means, don't we?

Over the years, *Round the Horne* presented parodies of many great works of literature and drama, but here they are having fun with that epitome of melodrama, *Gaslight*. It's a good choice, perfectly fitted to the *RTH* style, with its absurdly sinister characters and plenty of openings for silly names and double meanings.

The first ever colour supplement magazine had recently been launched by a London newspaper – obviously, an idea absolutely made for radio (at least Barry and Marty thought so). *Round the Horne*'s colour supplement contains much the same sort of stuff as can be found, even today, in any Sunday newspaper: outlandish recipes, celebrity gossip, publicity stills from unwatchable films, and other assorted rubbish.

Students of Palare, the dialect of Jules and Sand – and not forgetting their friend Gordon – should pay particular attention to this episode. Anyone tuning in halfway through would probably have thought they were listening to a foreign language station, when faced with lines like, 'Then they drag him up the King's lattie, and chain his lallies to a pillar.' But don't worry, it must be clean: it's a Bible story.

*F/X: Knock on door*

HUGH: Come in.

*F/X: Door opens*

HUGH: Aah, Horne.

KENNETH: You sent for me?

HUGH: Yes. As Controller of Thought, Word and Deed at the BBC I'm afraid I have to reprimand you over the use of certain words and phrases [used in your show, which are capable of misinterpretation.

KENNETH: I'm surprised to hear that, sir. Was it something the Fraser Hayes Four sang, sir?

HUGH: No, I'm referring to double entendres] contained in last week's show.

KENNETH: What specific phrases did you have in mind?

HUGH: Well, last week in your show, you distinctly said 'Hello'.

KENNETH: Well, what's wrong with that?

HUGH: Come off it, Horne. We all know what 'Hello' means. We all know what it suggests. It suggests 'Hello, what's this I see through the keyhole – it's a scantily clad female doing an exotic dance with a ball of wool.'

KENNETH: Good heavens, is that what it suggests?

HUGH: That's what it suggested to me. Immediately. And later in the programme, you said you were going to introduce someone without further ado – which suggests immediately that there had been some ado going on previously – [and what sort of ado might I ask? I know what sort of ado I had in mind.] Which brings me to

your name –

KENNETH: My name? What's wrong with Kenneth Horne?

HUGH: Yes. Everybody knows that ground-up moose's horn is an aphrodisiac – the very title of your show is an incitement to loose living and carrying on – I've found. You'll have to change your name.

*Orchestra: Signature tune*

DOUGLAS: Ladies and gentlemen – for the next thirty minutes it's *Round the Larksleigh-Fortinbrass* . . .

KENNETH: I can't wait until the Controller gets round to *Housewives' Choice*. Well, today as everybody knows is the start of Coat-A-Sheep-In-Raspberry-Jam week, and to celebrate the occasion the City of London has gone gay and organised a really exciting festival. There'll be [Loophole Nobbling under Floodlights at the Kensington Round Pond – an Exhibition of Rare Miniature Kneecaps at the Victoria and Albert Turkish Baths – weather permitting –] Swan Upping at Downham – Swan Downing at Upham. Streptococcus racing at the BMA Recreation Grounds, Walthamstow – and an auction of Rembrandt's dentures at Sotheby's Horsemeat Boutique, Hungerford Arches and for racing fans the week's events will be crowned by the Nudist Annual Point-to-point at Kempton Park. I can't wait to see them jogging round the course. Right – Smith – make the announcement.

DOUGLAS: And now Armpit Theatre presents a story of horror and lurking fear – more spine-chilling than the *Eurovision Song Contest*, more macabre than *The Late Show*, more grisly than *Call My Bluff* – we give you – *Gaslight – Son of Flicker*.

*Orchestra: Music link*

BILL: The year is 1890. The place – Victorian London – which as anyone who's ever been to the cinema knows, means gas lamps, frock coats, barrel organs, Basil Rathbone trotting through the fog in a hansom cab driven by Alfie Bass, [and Vincent Price shuffling up alleys murdering an assortment of Rank starlets.] In his office at Scotland Yard, Inspector de la Rose of the CID was going through his file of unsolved crimes with his dour cockney assistant, Sergeant Molecule.

KENNETH: Well Sergeant, [any fresh clues in the strange affair of the 'Brides in the Pudding' case?

HUGH: No, sir – I've tested the goat for fingerprints.

KENNETH: Find any?

HUGH: Yes, sir – mine.

KENNETH: Have you 'put a tail' on yourself?

HUGH: Yes, sir – there it is sir, tucked into me boots.

KENNETH: And very nice it looks too. Well done, Sergeant.

HUGH: Thank you, Inspector.]

KENNETH: What about the Chalk Farm case? Have you dragged the hip bath?

HUGH: Yes, sir. We've sent frogmen down but all they've come up with is a sliver of carbolic, a pair of flippers, a bar of chocolate, one roller skate, a waterlogged copy of *Memoirs of a Harem Girl* and a false beard, but there's no sign of the Bishop himself.

KENNETH: Have you tracked down the hooded finger bogler of Brixton yet?

HUGH: We traced the footprints in the semolina to the boudoir of Lady Crabthrobber – and in the wardrobe we found <u>this</u>.

KENNETH: Oh, that's where I left it. Once I get the tea leaves out it'll be as good as new. That only leaves the strange business at Fourteen Ganderbody Square still unsolved.

HUGH: What do we have on that case, sir?

KENNETH: Precious little. The Countess of Ponders End was foully done to death with a blunt instrument . . . namely a blunt instrument. The house was ransacked but we never found the assailant. [I believe he didn't find what he was looking for and will return to the scene of the crime.

HUGH: And what if he doesn't?

KENNETH: The Fraser Hayes Four will have to sing three encores to pad out the time.

HUGH: Then let's hope you're right, sir – for all our sakes. By the way, sir –] did you know that a couple have moved in to the house?

KENNETH: Yes. The Grunter-Pulpits – just married. She seems a sweet little thing – but Polyp Grunter-Pulpit, her husband, he's odd. Very odd indeed. Cue orchestra.

*Orchestra: Music link*

*F/X: Smashing china*

*Splintering wood*

KEN W: *(Laughs insanely)*

BETTY: Good morning, Polyp.

KEN W: Good morning my dear – *(Laughs insanely)*

*F/X: Smashing china, etc.*

BETTY: I'm glad you're in such a good mood this morning. Aren't you coming down to breakfast, dear?

KEN W: No. I'll have it up here, where I am – on the chandelier. Did you sleep well last night?

BETTY: Not really, Polyp – I was frightened.

KEN W: Frightened? What was there to be frightened of? I was out.

BETTY: I heard noises – and the gas light went very low.

KEN W: Nonsense – you imagine things, my dear.

BETTY: I didn't imagine it. I heard footsteps coming from the attic –

KEN W: Mice.

BETTY: – and foul oaths and cursing.

KEN W: Ill-bred mice. I'm worried about you, my dear. You're not well. Here, lay down on this bacon slicer – let me get you something.

BETTY: What?

KEN W: Sliced.

BETTY: Polyp – we've been married for six weeks now but every night you go out – not returning until the dawn. Where do you go?

KEN W: To work.

BETTY: But you're an upholsterer.

KEN W: I'm an all-night upholsterer. You worry too much, my dear. [Come, sit beside me.] Let me comb your hair with this axe.

BETTY: Why are you looking at me so strangely, Polyp?

KEN W: [You're not wearing it.

BETTY: What, Polyp – what?

KEN W: The snake shaped like a bracelet I gave you.

BETTY: You didn't give me anything.

KEN W: You're forgetting things again.] You forgot to give old Spot his weekly bath yesterday.

BETTY: But why should I have to bathe him – he's your father.

KEN W: When I come home at night all I hear are excuses, evasions and boring, senseless, rambling and hysterical ranting.

BETTY: Well if you will watch *Panorama*, what do you expect? I know what you're up to, Polyp. You're trying to drive me mad. But yesterday when you were out I tried the attic door. It was locked, Polyp. Why was it locked?

KEN W: Because I say so. You must never go in there.

BETTY: But the room next door is locked too.

KEN W: You must never go in there either. No never – never ever – not ever – on any account, do you hear? You must never go in that room. *(Pause) (Snide)* Well, not till the plumber's been. [*(Character)* Besides, if you go in there you'll see something you won't like – no you won't like what you see at all. It's not a pretty sight. *(Laughs)* Not a pretty sight at all. Ah ha ha ha *(Own voice)* there's seven or eight more ha has here – but I won't bother with them. Cor, playing a loony doesn't half take it out of you – you need a good pair of lungs for it. *(Character)* No, my dear, there's something in that room too awful for human eyes to see.

BETTY: What, Polyp – for pity's sake – tell me what it is.

KEN W: It's Dad – washing his feet. But let us think of pleasanter things, my dear – see, look what Polyp's got for you.

BETTY: *(Gasp of delight)* Oh, Polyp.

KEN W: Let me put them round your neck.

BETTY: What are they?

KEN W: My hands. Don't worry, it will look like an accident.]

BETTY: Polyp, you're mad.

KEN W: Did you say mad? Is that what you said – mad? Did you call me mad?

BETTY: Yes.

KEN W: I thought so. Only you'll have to speak up. I'm not wearing the appliance. But it's not me who's mad my dear, it is you.

BETTY: Me?

KEN W: Yes. You keep losing things.

BETTY: What have I lost?

KENNETH: Answers please on a postcard to the Lost Property Office, Baker Street . . . New Guinea.

KEN W: I'm going to have you put away. Dr. Otterbland will do the necessary. Come in, Dr. Otterbland.

KENNETH: *(Narrating)* A secret door in the whatnot opened and into the room stepped the kindly old family physician, Dr. Otterbland. An imposing man with beetling brows that met in the middle – of his back. [His ruddy cheeks were adorned with mutton chops and a leg of lamb stuck out of his ear. He lit a crêpe suzette and puffed on it reflectively.]

BILL: *(Peter Lorre)* Ah my dear, your husband has told me all about you.

[KEN W: Yes doctor, her mind's wandering.

BILL: And you want a certificate, eh?

KEN W: In her case I think a certificate X . . .]

BILL: Come with me, my dear.

BETTY: Where are you taking me?

BILL: To Somerset and Dr. Croakraven's Private Residential Hotel, for loony gentlefolk. Don't worry my dear, it's a trust house – all our residents are trussed.

KEN W: Go with him, my dear – the doctor will never be far away. He has a private practice in Bath.

BILL: Every morning . . . the acoustics are better in there.

BETTY: I won't go. You can't make me.

KEN W: Oh can't I? Grab her otterbland . . . I mean grab her, Otterbland . . . and give her an injection.

[KENNETH: *(Narration)* The doctor opened his Gladstone bag and produced a gleaming frankfurter sausage. Filling it with a colourless liquid, he plunged it between two slices of bread and munched it greedily.

BILL: Right, now the hypodermic.]

BETTY: No, no.

BILL: Don't shrink away, my dear – it's only an eight-inch hypodermic needle. It won't hurt a bit. There.

BETTY: *(Screams)*

BILL: It only goes to show how wrong you can be.

KEN W: Ah, she's gone limp – help me carry her out – there's a horse-drawn minicab waiting.

KENNETH: [At this point we were going to do the joke about there's a horse outside with a hansom behind – but we've already done it twice this series and people are beginning to tumble us. 'But what were the police doing all this time?' you are asking. Well, Hugh made a phone call and I popped up the road for a newspaper] but meanwhile a watch was being kept on the house by Edwin Braden disguised as Epping Forest – without any artificial aids to speak of. Seeing the unfortunate Mrs. Grunter-Pulpit being bundled into a hansom cab, he paused, only to knock back 18 pints at the Captain's Cabin[1] before making his way speedily to the Yard.

EDWIN: Excuse me, sir.

KENNETH: He speaks! Ladies and gentlemen, you're in the presence of history. It's as if Zeus had descended from Mount Olympus disguised as a water buffalo. Speak on, O Braden.

EDWIN: They've done a moonlight flit.

KENNETH: I beg your pardon?

EDWIN: That's what it says here.

KENNETH: Is that all?

EDWIN: Yes.

KENNETH: Hardly worth getting off your podium for. Right Sergeant Molecule, we haven't a moment to lose!

F/X: *Two whooshes*

KENNETH: Not so fast, Grunter-Pulpit, we're on to your little game.

[HUGH: We know what you've been up to in the attic. We've grilled the butler and fricasseed the chamber maid.

KENNETH: We know you foully slew the former owner of the house, as established on page four. We know you tried to unhinge your wife's reason – pages eighteen to twenty-three.]

KEN W: Yes, but what you don't know is what I did on page thirty-five.

HUGH: Look out, he's got a bottle of liquid paraffin.

KEN W: And it's loaded. One false move and we all go together.

BETTY: Drop that liquid paraffin. I've got a Biretta here – and I'm not afraid to wear it.

BILL: Drop that Biretta – I've got a Tommy gun –

KENNETH: Drop that Tommy gun I've got a 12-bore Douglas Smith here – and it's cocked.

HUGH: But it's only a sawn-off Douglas Smith, sir.

KENNETH: Then it's half cocked – but this is no time to haggle.

KEN W: Drop that sawn-off, half-cocked Douglas Smith – I've got a stick of dynamite here –

KENNETH: Drop that stick –

BETTY: No!

F/X: *Huge explosion*

Orchestra: *Play-off music*

KENNETH: That was the end of the affair. The others were never seen again. But blasts play funny tricks. My trousers were blown off and the blast threw me several hundred feet in the

---

1. A pub not far from the Paris Studio, where the *RTH* gang would slake their thirsts after recordings.

air. I came to rest in the drawing room of a Mrs. Evadne Spigott of 'Mon Repos', Sidcup. At least that's what I told Mr. Spigott when he came home unexpectedly from work. But enough of my problems – you've got your own – because here are the Fraser Hayes Four – Dozy, Beaky, Mick and Tich[2] – judging by their appearance, that is. So here to sing 'Goodbye Charlie' are the Fraser Hayes Four.

*(Applause)*

*Fraser Hayes Four with Orchestra: 'Goodbye Charlie'*

*(Applause)*

**DOUGLAS:** And now the *Round the Horne* Colour Supplement.

**KENNETH:** First, with a few new wrinkles on cookery, and a great many old wrinkles elsewhere – here is Daphne Whitethigh.

**BETTY:** Good news for all housewives – rhino is down in the shops this week and you can give hubby his favourite cut – my suggestion best end of rhino. The difficulty is, of course, to know which is the best end. Rhinos know, but their cause is not ours.

Other good buys are escalope of vole, water buffalo chestnuts, and hippo in its shell.

For those of you who fancy something a little more exotic in the way of poultry, why not try duck-billed platypus – flambé?

**KENNETH:** I've tried it but they keep blowing the match out. If you want details of the recipes mentioned, write, not to me but to Daphne Whitethigh c/o The Hospital for Gastric Disorders, Addis Ababa. Now once

again, it's over to Sunday Night TV personality Seamus Android who is waiting at London Airport to interview yet another celebrity – come in Seamus Android.

**BILL:** Hello – all right – ha ha. Well, yet again it's welcome back for the first time to someone who's so well known that even I've heard of her – so [here without much ado – right now, here, at this moment, as it's happening,] I'd like to . . . now . . . so if someone would hold the microphone I will – if it takes me all day.

**KENNETH:** Thank you, Seamus Android – the man with a fluent tongue – trouble is, the cat's got it.

**KEN W:** Yes. Pity they don't put the cat on on Sunday nights.

**KENNETH:** This week the *Round the Larksleigh-Fortinbrass* Colour Supplement turns its attention to the cinema – [how well I remember those days long ago, when a bunch of us would save up our money and sit in a stuffy little hall, and watch those flickering silent images on the screen – chuckling at their merry antics and whimsical pranks – until somebody tipped off the police and they raided the place.] Now, when I was young our values were clear cut – we always knew who to hiss, the goodies wore white and the baddies wore black – it's a bit confusing nowadays – recently I spent the first twenty minutes of *The Singing Nun* booing Debbie Reynolds – I don't think the time was entirely wasted. Legal note – common abuse is not libel. [These days, with the competition from television, the cinema-goer is becoming far more choosy about what he goes to see.

---

2. Dave Dee, Dozy, Beaky, Mick & Tich had a number of chart hits in the mid-Sixties.

HUGH: Seats in all parts! Seats in all parts! This way, sir –

KEN W: *(Old)* Excuse me. Is this film suitable for the whole family?

HUGH: Yes, sir. Good wholesome clean family entertainment.

KEN W: Blast! Isn't there a single provocative scene with flimsily attired loose women prancing about in a house of shame?

HUGH: No.

KEN W: What are the usherettes like?

HUGH: Married.

KEN W: What's the flavour of the month?

HUGH: Curried mongoose.

KEN W: On a stick?

HUGH: Yes.

KEN W: Who's in the film?

HUGH: Julie Christie.

KEN W: Yes, I don't mind her. Who else?

HUGH: Omar Sharif.

KEN W: Oh no. I'm not having him.

HUGH: Well, I'm afraid there's nothing we can do about it.

KEN W: Never mind. While he's on I can amuse meself having a poke about the ashtrays – and have a crawl under the seats – see what I can find – and if I get tired of that, I can sit next to courting couples in the back and light matches. Don't worry about me – I'll find something to keep my mind occupied. Oh by the way, what's the film called?

HUGH: *Doctor Zhivago.*

KEN W: Is he good? I mean – is he a specialist? I mean I don't want to waste my time watching a GP.

HUGH: *Doctor Zhivago* is very good, sir.

KEN W: Well, I'll give it a try.

HUGH: Hey – come back here, sir – you haven't paid!

KEN W: I'm not paying to see *Doctor Zhivago.* I'll see it on the National Health.

*Orchestra: Punctuated chord*]

KENNETH: We in England have a great tradition in film making. Particularly during the war when we made those never-to-be-forgotten epics of the 'Keep it up, stick it out, take it on the chin, I knew you'd all volunteer, [but sir my granny was on that tanker, there's something I've got to tell you Reggie, action stations,] good heavens an orange, Jack darling what's happening to us' school of film. Here is an except from one such naval drama, starring Dame Celia Molestrangler and ageing juvenile Binkie Huckaback.

*Tape: 'White Cliffs of Dover'*

*F/X: Door opens*

BETTY: Oh, Charles.

HUGH: Oh, Fiona!

BETTY: Oh Charles, Charles – you're back!

HUGH: Yes, would you mind scratching it?

BETTY: There, darling. Better?

HUGH: Yes, darling. Oh, how I've missed that. It seems years since I was home on leave last –

BETTY: [What was it like out there?

HUGH: Pretty damn grim out there. What was it like back here?

BETTY: Empty, Charles. Pretty damn empty back here.] Did you think of me out there?

HUGH: Yes. Constantly, incessantly, never-endingly I thought of you back here. And did you think of me out there back here?

BETTY: Yes. All I could think of back here was you out there thinking of me back here thinking of you out there – back here. Needing you, wanting you, wanting to need you, needing to want you.

HUGH: I want to feel you need me. I want to feel that you're there behind me, leading the way. And how are the children? All I know of them is what you've written to me – Emily – how's she? And Peter, Roger, Sidney, Jonquil, Rupert, Abdulla and . . . you know, I've wondered a lot about young Abdulla while I've been away – and Buster. How's young Buster? Is he in long trousers yet? Is he going out with girls? Does he look like me?

BETTY: Buster's the dog, darling.

HUGH: Forgive me, Fiona – I'm not – I can't . . .

BETTY: Charles! You're limping!

HUGH: Yes. I didn't want you to find out this way. But you'd have to know sooner or later. I've got *(Stifles a sob)* an ingrowing toenail. The MO says I'll never be a normal man again.

BETTY: Oh, Charles! Hold me!

HUGH: I can't, Fiona. Curse this gammy toe! I must go now.

[BETTY: Must you, Charles?

HUGH: Yes. I must. Kiss the children for me, Fiona.]

BETTY: When will you be back?

HUGH: I don't know. I have a funny sort of premonition I won't be coming back –

BETTY: You mean?

HUGH: Yes. But if I don't get back – don't grieve – just think 'At last he's found a little rest – a little peace'.

BETTY: A little peace, Charles?

HUGH: Yes. She's a barmaid at Chatham.

*Orchestra: Chord*

KENNETH: These days making films is no longer the prerogative of the large Hollywood companies. Today many of the best films are made by the small independent film units. Recently I visited the office of one such company – the sign on the door said 'Bona Prods.' . . . So I prodded and entered. Hello – anybody there?

*F/X: Door*

HUGH: Oh hello, I'm Julian and this is my friend Sandy.

KEN W: We are in the forefront of your nouvelle vague. That's your actual French.

HUGH: It means we are of the new wave.

KENNETH: And very nice it looks on you too.

HUGH: Yes. Vidal always looks after me.

KEN W: You see, we've got a small independent unit.

HUGH: We are the Cecil Bs of the sixteen de mille. Small-budget pictures mainly.

KENNETH: Would I have vada'd any of them, do you think?

KEN W: Oh, he's got all the palare, hasn't he?

HUGH: I wonder where he picks it up.

KEN W: You may have vada'd one of our tiny bijou masterpiecettes, heartface – we made *Funny Eek, My Fair Palone*. And then we done one on Chopin and his love for George Sanders –

KENNETH: Shouldn't that be George Sand?

KEN W: He's right, you know. He's not wrong – he's right. I told Jule that, but he wouldn't listen –

HUGH: No wonder Rock Hudson turned the part down.

[KEN W: It also explains the cuts the censor made in the script. We had the same trouble when we made *Useless*, Mr. Horne.

KENNETH: *Useless*?

KEN W: Yes – James Joyce's *Useless*. Could not get Sean Connery to play the part of Molly Bloom.

HUGH: She just wasn't interested.

KENNETH: She? Surely you mean Siobhan MacKenna?

KEN W: You're right, Mr. Horne. We'll have to get photos next time.]

KENNETH: I take it you're engaged in something pretty exciting at the moment.

HUGH: No, not really, we're just standing here with our hands on our hips, talking to you . . .

KENNETH: Oh bold! Very bold.

KEN W: I wonder where he spends his evenings? Oh, you mean subjects – well frankly Mr. Horne, at the moment we are dickering, aren't we Jule?

HUGH: Yes. We're dickering. We've got one or two germs and we're dickering with them. We was thinking of a biblical subject – in fact I was up all last night working on me outline.

KEN W: Show it to Mr. Horne – show him your outline.

HUGH: Well, how I see it is this . . .

KEN W: This is how he sees it, Mr. Horne – you are present at a moment of cinema history. He is about to create – look, his features are getting all tortured – he's getting all worked up – the muse is fluttering about him – looking for a place to perch – there she is – go it gel – there she's lighted on his shoulder –

HUGH: I've got it!

KEN W: He's got it, Mr. Horne. It's coming over him in waves.

HUGH: We're going to do Samson and Delilah.

KEN W: Did you see how he came out with that, Mr. Horne? The way he does it is frightening. Samson and Delilah. Go on Jule, how do you see it?

HUGH: Well, I see Samson as huge and all butch, with great bulging thews and whopping great lallies, with long blonde riah hanging right down his Jim and Jack –

KEN W: That's rhyming slang for 'back'. Or for France – down his Jules and Jim, but I won't go into that. Yes – so what happens?

HUGH: I'll tell you what happens – the film opens with him lying there spark out in his palliasse – suddenly there's a movement behind the arras, and who comes trolling in but this palone Delilah – she vadas his sleeping eek, and she pulls out this pair of scissors and lops off his riah.

KEN W: Yes. I can see that. Great close up of his head – nante riah. That's your cinema verité.

HUGH: Suddenly he comes round – 'Who's had me riah off?' he squeals – 'It's all ebbing away.' And then the Philistines come and mock him, Mr. Horne.

KEN W: What a figure of tragedy he presents –

HUGH: Then they drag him up the King's lattie, and chain his lallies to a pillar. Then he gets his wild up, and with one mighty heave *(Grunts)* he brings the whole lattie tumbling about their heads. End of film.

KEN W: *(Applauding)* Bravo Jule, bravo! It's an Oscar winner. I shall go and go again. How about you, Mr. Horne?

KENNETH: Yes. It makes me want to go. And who do you see playing the role of Samson –

KEN W: Well let's see – the description says – big, butch, muscular and blond. There's only one person it can be.

KENNETH: Who's that?

KEN W: It's you, Jule – it's you.

HUGH: It's a pity. I saw myself as Delilah.

*Orchestra: Brief link*

KENNETH: They've promised me a couple of tickets for the sneak pre-vada [– and naturally I shall go, providing I can find another sneak to accompany me.] Well that brings us almost to the end of the show but for this week's musical adventure up the highways and byways of folk music – and stopping off in a layby what else would we find but Rambling Syd Rumpo.

KEN W: Well hello me deario – and I expect you're dying to know what I've pulled out of my ganderbag this week . . .

KENNETH: We're all agog – well, half agog anyway.

KEN W: Well, the air with which I am about to burst forth is traditional in Lincolnshire. 'Tis the song of the bogle clencher – and goes after this fashion . . .

KEN W AND GUITAR: *(Tune of 'Lincolnshire Poacher')*

When I was a clenchers' bogle man
In famous Lincoln Town,
I often clenched my bogling fork
For less than half a crown.
And I would woggle and nurk my
    boys
As I shall quickly tell,
Oh 'tis my delight on a shining night
And a foggy night as well.

Oh once I took my moulies
And I set them in a snare.
'Twas then I spied a scroper's man
A' whirdling a hare.
But I was not afeared my boys
Of that there is no doubt.
Oh 'tis my delight on a shining night
When the coppers aren't about.

Although I'm over eighty now
My bogles still I clench.
And I will flutter my artifacts
At any passing wench.
I've tickled many a screebling nut
As on my way I go.
Oh 'tis my delight on a shining night
At one and nine a throw – oooooooh!

*(Applause)*

KENNETH: I'm afraid I don't have one and nine on me, do you take credit cards? Well, that brings us to the end of the show for this week except for a police message. Police are still looking

for the Nude Cyclist of Polperro –
they wish to interview a tall
distinguished, middle-aged radio
comedian with a bald head and a deep
fruity voice – oh! *(Falsetto)* So until
next week then – cheerio.

*Orchestra:* Round the Horne *signature
tune*

DOUGLAS: That was *Round the Horne*
starring Kenneth Horne, with Kenneth
Williams, Hugh Paddick, Betty
Marsden and Bill Pertwee. On the
musical side you heard the Fraser
Hayes Four and Edwin Braden and
the Hornblowers. The script was
written by Barry Took and Marty
Feldman. The programme was
produced by John Simmonds.

*Orchestra: Sig. tune up and out*

*(Applause)*

*Orchestra: 'Round the Horne' playout*

*(Applause)*

# SERIES 3
# PROGRAMME 13

*FIRST BROADCAST* – Sunday 7 May 1967

## INTRODUCTION

If you have sides, prepare to split them now. Barry Took has stated elsewhere his opinion that series 3 was some of the finest work he and Marty ever did, and many *RTH* connoisseurs would argue that this very episode represents the best of the best.

First, though, by way of a word of warning, a statement of the obvious: this script was written by two white, middle-class Londoners in 1967. Comedy was, in many ways, a more robust beast in the 1960s than it has become since, and it's quite possible that the main sketch in this script would cause nervousness amongst broadcasting executives if it were presented to them today. The idea of Kenneth Horne playing 'an old Negro trumpeter', while Betty Marsden takes the role of a 'fat coloured nanny', might well raise eyebrows, if not hackles.

Well, language changes as society changes, and terms considered polite in one decade are often taboo to later generations. The crucial point, however, is that Took and Feldman have written here a *film spoof*. They'd grown up watching Hollywood pictures that routinely represented black Americans, especially rural Southerners, as grinning idiots, or naughty children. It is that cinematic genre, and the (already dated) attitudes behind it, which these two well-informed, left-of-centre writers are mocking here.

As for any 'Georgia crackers' or 'po' white trash' who might read this – well, yes, sorry, in your case the insulting stereotypes should indeed be taken at face value.

Incidentally, this episode contains not only three or four of the finest jokes in the whole *RTH* canon, but also some of the most staggeringly bold innuendoes ever heard on the wireless. If you understand all of them, you must be deeply depraved – but probably quite cheerful with it.

DOUGLAS: My name is Douglas Smith – I come among you earthlings in peace –

KEN W: It's all right, we've all got your number, ducky. Oh, she goes too far, that one. Get on with it.

DOUGLAS: The BBC presents – more in sorrow than in anger – *Round the Horne*.

*Orchestra: Signature tune*

KENNETH: That was Douglas Smith – known to the girls of the BBC Typing Pool as 'Old Tail End Charlie', for reasons we won't go into. [I think it must refer to his RAF career.] Well, today as everybody knows is the beginning of Unzip a Hyena for Peace Week – [and to celebrate it, London is in festive mood. On Tuesday there'll be a display of Old Tyme Frog-Bottling in-the-round, at the Downing Street Slipper Baths; on Wednesday there's the International Freestyle Gnome-Curling competition at the five-minute hippo wash in Brompton Oratory.] At the Wigmore Hall, Mrs. Ganderlip Whaletrouser will be talking about the mating habits of the savage man-eating pygmies of Upper Norwood. This will be followed by a talk, given by the savage man-eating pygmies of Upper Norwood on the mating habits of Mrs. Ganderlip Whaletrouser. At the Albert Hall there'll be the Gynaecologist Annual Concours d'Elegance. [There'll be Chip Fumbling in the great Vat of St. Paul's and,] at the Do-it-yourself Smoked Salmon Boutique, Edgware, Over-Eighties Nudist Leapfrog teams will be taking on all-comers – er within reason – right – [sufficient unto the day are the evils thereof –] Smith –

make the announcement . . .

DOUGLAS: And now Armpit Theatre presents . . .

*Orchestra: Trumpet solo. Blues. Badly played*

DOUGLAS: A story of jazz and the men who made it. A story of how jazz came up the river from New Orleans to Teddington, via Stoke Poges. Based loosely on *Young Man with a Horn*[1], we present *Young Horne with a Man*.

*Orchestra: 'South Rampart St. Parade'*

KENNETH: New Orleans 1919. The New Orleans of Storeyville – and Basin Street. Where all the dark and light folk meet. [New Orleans – land of those dreamy queens – so the song tells us – and who are we to argue?

KEN W: Who's arguing?]

KENNETH: I am an old negro trumpeter –

KEN W: You could have fooled me.

KENNETH: – which will come as a surprise to my wife if she's listening – my name is Jelly Roll Pank Stukely, pronounced Chumley – but not very often. [I would have preferred a nickname like Snake Lips or Snake Eyes, but unfortunately the part of the snake I most resemble – a snake doesn't have. Just as well really, it'd make nonsense of Darwin.] However, they call me 'jelly roll' for reasons I won't bore you with – and I lead a small combo in downtown New Orleans. My story is of Bix Spiderthrust – a young white kid who learned to play my people's music. De blues as it's sometimes called. It all began when young Bix and his nanny were watching a New Orleans street parade.

---

1. A 1950 film about the life of Bix Beiderbecke. In the UK, it was re-named *Young Man of Music*, presumably on the grounds that British people have filthier minds than Americans.

*Orchestra: New Orleans street parade-type music (approaching)*

KEN W: *(Southern child)* Look, Nanny. Look, Nanny [Goatsbreath] – a street parade.

BETTY: *(Fat coloured nanny)* Why lan' sakes Massa Bix, sho' is. Sho' enough. Yich, yich, yich – dog my cats, dang my possum.

KEN W: Dang your own possum, Nanny – hold me up so I can see.

*Orchestra: Parade music to climax and fade into distance*

KEN W: I never heard that kind of music before. What's it called?

BETTY: Jazz, Massa Bix. It's my people's music.

KEN W: I want to play music like that, Nanny [Goatsbreath].

BETTY: You, young massa – yich, yich, yich – well hush my mouth.

KEN W: *(Own voice)* I wish you would.

BETTY: But you're a white boy. You can't play like that.

KEN W: But I wanna, Nanny. I wanna play the blues on one of those big shiny things that man's got.

BETTY: You ain't never gonna play the blues on one of them.

KEN W: Why not?

BETTY: Dat's a horse.

*Orchestra: Short New Orleans-type link*

KEN W: You wanted to see me, Pappy?

HUGH: Yes, son – pull up a burning cross and sit down. What's this I hear about you wanting to play this new-fangled jazz music?

KEN W: I got to, Pappy. [When I hear it I get a feeling inside me I can't describe. It's like . . .

*Grams: Strings romantically in background*

KEN W: . . . Gee I don't know – it's a roller-coaster ride – it's a double-whipped chocolate malted – it's turkey and cranberry sauce on Thanksgiving Day. It's the Fourth of July and Christmas and toasted marshmallows all in one – it's . . .

*Grams: Music ends*

HUGH: Well, if you won't talk about it, I can't make you.] You see son, this here jazz music, it ain't respectable – we Spiderthrusts are leading citizens, we're Georgia Spiderthrusts – your grandpappy was a Georgia Cracker – I'm a Georgia Cracker, you're a Georgia Cracker. In our family we're all Crackers. We don't go messing round with what don't concern us.

KEN W: What about Beulah the maid? Is she a Cracker?

HUGH: She sho' is son, but of a different kind. Now don't let me catch you messing round with those no-good jazz musicians, or I'll whop your hide.

KEN W: I'm too big.

HUGH: Well, in that case I'll hide your whop. [I'm a-going now, son – if you want me I'll be down on the levee.

KEN W: *(Own voice)* Well, don't be all night.]

KENNETH: [So much for our grasp of the nuances of Southern dialect.] Later that night, young Bix sneaked out of the house and made his way to Storeyville, and Mahogany Hall where a few of us cats were having a jam session. All right – one, two, a one two three.

*Orchestra: 'In the Shadows'*

KENNETH: *(Over)* Play that thing. Yeah, yeah. *(Music ends)* All right cats, take five.

KEN W: Excuse me, Mr. Jelly Roll.

KENNETH: I put down my liquorice stick and my bag of sherbert and stared at the pale young kid who stood before me. He looked like po' white trash – Poe as in Edgar Allen – I ran my ebony fingers through my frizzy hair –

KEN W: The mind boggles.

KENNETH: I looked into his eyes. A look of query came into his. What do you want, young massa?

KEN W: I want to sit in with you. I want to play this thing I've got tucked under my arm.

KENNETH: You can't. Not with us.

KEN W: Why not?

KENNETH: It's a horse.

KEN W: No – I mean this.

KENNETH: He produced a battered trumpet from a green baize bag – and put it to his green baize lips.

*Orchestra: Trumpet cadenza à la L. Armstrong – only badly*

[KEN W: Well?

KENNETH: Now try blowing it.

KEN W: *(Snide)* Oh – is that how you do it?]

KENNETH: I knew that this boy had something – I decided to give him a chance and introduced him to the rest of the band – Bix I want you to meet the boys. This is Mead Lux Panderbody.

BILL: *(Gruff negro)* Hi there, man.

KENNETH: This is Fats Hominy Grits.

HUGH: There you go, man –

KENNETH: This is Howling Charlie Swampfever.

BETTY: *(Debby)* Hello, darling.

KENNETH: This is W.C. Handy, or as the producer insists we call him, Bathroom Convenient. Over there is our bass player, Bayou Jack.

KEN W: How's Bayou Jack?

HUGH: *(Jewish)* Can't complain. How's by you?

[KENNETH: Over there tickling his ivories is old Massa Hotchkiss. Here, tightening his snares, Fats McWhirter – or as we call him, Massa Flesh. This one here is Douglas 'Stuff' Smith. That's not a stage direction, it's a nickname.]

KEN W: I want to join your band, Mr. Jelly Roll. I have a dream.

KENNETH: Would you like to tell me about your dream? Cue strings.

*Grams: Rhapsodic strings – behind speech*

KEN W: I see Carnegie Hall – everybody who is anybody is there. The cream of New York's High Society. They're all wearing diamonds and mink – even the women. On stage a big band, strings, woodwind, percussion, brass – and there in front leading them – you, Jelly Roll, in a mink bikini –

KENNETH: A mink bikini?

KEN W: Well, I told you it was a dream. Then on to the stage walks a solitary figure in a spangled leotard – his long blond hair framing his perfect oval face – it's me.

KENNETH: You?

KEN W: It's my dream. I don't interfere with your dreams, do I? Yes, it's me. They've all come to hear me perform on my golden trumpet. I whip it out – my fingers flash over my plungers – the audience goes wild. I purse my lips and they hear a sound that they've never heard before in Carnegie Hall.

KENNETH: And then do you play the trumpet?

KEN W: I'm playing it. A new sound. There's a note I'm after – it's up there somewhere – if only I can reach it. I can't reach it now, but I'll reach it one day. Mr. Jelly Roll will you make my dream come true?

KENNETH: I'll do what I can but I can't promise the mink bikini – not after the last time. Still, you can join the band. We're heading up river for . . .

*Orchestra: 'Chicago'*

KEN W: You mean?

KENNETH: Yes. Greasborough. And if we don't have any luck there we can try Chicago.

HUGH: Ah – Chicago in the Roaring Twenties. It was my town, I tell you – my name was legendary, Diamond Jim Legendary. Known to the customers in my speakeasy as Alice. It was very dark in that speakeasy. The year was 1926 – the Jazz Age – Al Jolson was thrilling the world with his impersonations of Dai Francis[2]. The crowd flocked to my club every night [to drink bath tub gin – from a bath tub and] to stamp their feet to the hot rhythm of Jelly Roll Pank Stukeley and the Original New Orleans Knee Tremblers. Everybody was doing a dance called the colour fundament.

KENNETH: The producer won't allow us to say Black Bottom!

[*Grams: Faint background music and chatter*

BILL: Shake that thing. Oh, shake that thing – come on and shake that thing.

DOUGLAS: I'm doing the best I can but I can't get the lumps out.

BILL: Never mind. I'll drink it as it is. Black Bottoms up. *(Drinks and screams)* What is this stuff?

DOUGLAS: Bath tub gin.

BILL: Well I think I've swallowed the loofah. It tastes terrible.

DOUGLAS: It was all right when I bathed the dog in it. Cheers!]

KENNETH: Suddenly the crowd was hushed as into the spotlight stepped the dusky Queen of the Blues, Lobelin 'Lead Belly' Mutterbucket, played by Betty 'Lead Belly' Marsden in rather a lot of burnt cork. She sang huskily, her voice choked with emotion, the music of her people that had come from Africa to the cotton fields of the Deep South.

BETTY: *(Sings)* My Yiddisher Momma –

KENNETH: Er – via Golders Green. As she sang, young Bix played behind her supplementing catch phrase with his tender obligatos.

BETTY: *(Sings)* I miss her more than ever *(Squeals)* You do that again mate, and I'll really make your obligatos tremble.

KEN W: I was looking for that note that I've been searching for.

BETTY: Well, you won't find it there.

---

2. One of the main stars of *The Black and White Minstrels*.

KEN W: But I love you. You're my kind of woman – in fact we could be taken for sisters. Could you learn to love me?

BETTY: Yes. But not up here on the bandstand.

KEN W: I know what you're going to say – you're going to throw those ugly words at me like 'race', 'bar'.

BETTY: Yes, I am. I'll race you to the bar. Last one there buys the drinks.

HUGH: Hi there, Bix.

KEN W: Evening, Mr. Legendary.

HUGH: You see that man over there?

KEN W: Yes. Who is he?

HUGH: Norbert Potwalloper –

KEN W: The King of Jazz?

HUGH: He. He wants you to join his band. This is the big time, Bix.

KEN W: You're asking me to leave Jelly Roll? The man [who taught me everything I know – well at least the things I can talk about here. The man who's been like a father to me,] who's had faith in me – who's shared his last crust of bread with me. You want me to walk out on him just like that?

HUGH: Not like that, you'll get arrested. Put some trousers on first.

KEN W: I can't do it.

[HUGH: You can't leave Jelly Roll?

KEN W: No, I can't put my trousers on – they're at the cleaner's.]

BETTY: You don't understand. There are things a man can't do – and there are things a man must do – there are things that a man don't like to do but he's got to do and things that he won't do that he must, and he's got to do what he's got to do.

HUGH: Is that true, Bix?

KEN W: Yeah – but I'll be finished in five minutes. Tell Mr. Potwalloper I'll see him outside.

*Orchestra: Brief link*

KENNETH: And so Bix Spiderthrust left the Knee Tremblers and joined Norbert Potwalloper and his Collegiates. They toured all over America.

*Orchestra: Train effect*

BILL: Denver.

HUGH: Palm Springs.

KENNETH: Kumquat Junction.

BILL: Medicine Bend.

HUGH: Allberkewker – er – Alkewkerberk – Alber – Alker – oh the hell with it – Boston.

BILL: Washington.

KENNETH: Kansas.

HUGH: St. Louis.

*F/X: Hugh splash*

*KENNETH:* Niagara Falls. If only that train had stopped – he'd have become a star. But forced to play the commercial music that he despised – Bix took refuge in the bottle.

*F/X: Knock on bottle*

BILL: Come out of that bottle. I can see you hiding behind that twig.

KEN W: Leave me alone. I can't go on, Mr. Potwalloper.

BILL: But this is Carnegie Hall. Remember your dream – you can't let those kids down.

KEN W: I can't play, I tell you – I've lost my lip.

[BILL: Don't worry, my boy – I've got another one here – go out there and play.]

KEN W: I can't, I can't. I had it once but it's gone. I lost it in Chicago.

BETTY: *(Off mic sings)* My Yiddisher Momma . . .

KEN W: It's – it's Lead Belly.

BETTY: *(Coming on mic)* Yes, it's me. I've come back to you, Bix. And I'll never leave you again. You can do it, Bix –

KEN W: I can't.

BETTY: Do it for me – pick up that trumpet and do it the way you used to.

KEN W: But will I ever get that note?

BETTY: Of course you will with me behind you. Play, Bix – play.

*Orchestra: Trumpet cadenza – notes getting higher*

KEN W: *(High-pitched squeal)*

*Orchestra: Trumpet top note*

BETTY: I told you you'd get it with me behind you.

KEN W: Yes, but I wish you'd cut your fingernails.

*Orchestra: Play-off. Trumpet dominant*

KENNETH: Gets you right here, doesn't it – [well perhaps a bit higher up but then Kenneth Williams is smaller than I am.] But here now with a familiar strain – you can hear it when they go for their top notes – are the messed voices of the Fraser Hayes Four. Ladies and gentlemen – the Fraser Hayes Four.

*(Applause)*

*The Fraser Hayes Four with Orchestra: 'The Brotherhood of Man'*

*(Applause)*

DOUGLAS: And now the *Round the Horne* Colour Supplement.

KENNETH: First, Daphne Whitethigh with hints for party givers.

BETTY: If you're having a few friends over for the evening, why not do what the Duchess of Stainesforth does – but pull the curtains first. The Duchess specialises in unusual party games – Pin the Tail on the Orang-utan – [Deaf Man's Buff – which is like Blind Man's Buff only quieter, and then there's] Postman's Knock played with a real postman. It's not as much fun but it saves giving him a Christmas box. But if you want your party to go with a swing, here are some dos and don'ts – Do do do – don't don't don't.

KENNETH: Thank you, Daphne Whitethigh. I'll try not to not to not to. But here now an on-the-spot report from Sunday Night television personality Seamus Android.

BILL: Hello. All right. Ha ha. Well now, all right. Well, I could go on like this all night, so I probably will. But now while I'm waiting for my first guest to sober up I'd like to read you a lot of letters from viewers who watch me on TV and say how much they'd like to – but unfortunately they can't so I'd like to be the first but as you can see time has run out as have the studio audience and with that – goodnight.

KENNETH: Thank you, Seamus Android, the sage of television and we all know where the sage goes – with the onions. And now the *Round the Horne* Colour Supplement turns its attention to the occult, and to start the crystal ball rolling, here with me once again is the Colour Supplement's resident astrologer, Madame Osiris Gnomeclencher.

HUGH: Osiris brings you lots of luck and many roses. Well, what of the zodiac? Neptune's in Scorpio with Venus.

KENNETH: Is he.

HUGH: Yes. Sent me a postcard. Says the weather's lovely.

KENNETH: Well, it is at this time of the year.

HUGH: If you're a Sagittarian, look out – your node's rising. Be on your guard against sitting on rusty razor blades, bathing in vats of boiling syrup of figs and men who try and set fire to your trousers.

KENNETH: Thanks for the warning – I shall put the vicar off tonight.

HUGH: Well advised.

KENNETH: Have you any personal predictions for me?

HUGH: Well, you're a Virgo in conjunction with your Aries, aren't you? So – Capricorn rules your head, Pisces rules your heart – Libra rules your kidneys and Britannia rules the waves.

[KENNETH: Which part of me do the Heavenly Twins look after?

HUGH: I can only divulge that in a plain envelope, but suffice it to say it's not a sought-after job. That's why there's two of them – it's company. Scorpio had the job but he's been redeployed to an area of you where there's more going on – anyway your lucky number is – 01-229-1922 – and ask for Colette – your lucky flower is cauli – as is your lucky dog.]

KENNETH: Thank you, Madame Osiris.

[HUGH: Don't thank me – it's all in your hand.

KENNETH: So it is . . . and they're supposed to melt in your mouth.]

There are many stories of the occult in fiction – Who does not know Poe's 'Raven' . . .

KEN W: I never listen to gossip, ducky.

KENNETH: The cinema has long specialised in stories of the supernatural. Especially in the '40s. [How well we remember those 'Why have you brought me to this house – I just saw a face at the window Sir James – there's something in my drink – the spirits are quiet tonight – why do you keep the east wing locked – let me take you for a walk along the clifftop in your bathchair Cynthia'-type of film?] Here is an excerpt from one such film starring Dame Celia Molestrangler and ageing juvenile Binkie Huckaback –

*Grams: Suitable dramatic music of period*

BETTY: I'm afraid, Charles – terribly afraid.

HUGH: Afraid, Fiona? Don't you like living here?

BETTY: No, Charles. I feel something odd – here – something very odd indeed. Something I can't put a name to. Do you feel it here?

HUGH: Here?

BETTY: Not there, Charles – here. Oh, Charles – [I don't like it – it's suddenly gone cold.

HUGH: Don't worry – I'll make you another cup.]

BETTY: Don't leave me, Charles I – *(Screams)* [I just felt something touch my foot – something cold.] Look, Charles – the door's opening – the light's gone on – there's someone there – every night the door opens, the light goes on and he's standing there. What does he want? For pity's sake, Charles, ask him.

HUGH: What are you doing there?

BILL: I might ask you that. After all, you're in <u>my</u> fridge.

*Orchestra: Very short link*

KENNETH: Turning now to songs of the supernatural, here is Rambling Syd Rumpo, a man who is neither super, nor particularly natural – good evening Rambling Syd –

KEN W: Hello me deario, for my heart is heavy and my cordbangle is full sore –

KENNETH: [An application of Doctor Loomore Blend Cordbangle Alcohol Rub should do the trick.] Now what are you going to sing for us this week?

KEN W: 'Tis an eerie song, so spine-chilling that it'll make the bogles on your posset stand on end. It's the story of a bold highwayman called the Black Grunger of Hounslow, tells of his exploits –

*Orchestra: Guitar vamp*

KEN W: – and it goes after this fashion . . .

*(Sings to tune of 'Too-ra-lae-aye')*

Oh list while I sing of a highwayman bold
His feats were remarkable, so we are told.
He'd whirdle the ladies and scrope all

the men
Then he'd straddle his nadger and ride off again.
Too-ra-lae, too-ra-lae
Singing fiddle me grummits
And scrumple me floot.

They caught him and hung him from Old Tyburn Tree
But e'er the noad screevelled his moulie, quoth he:-
'If I had my time to live over again
I'd scrope all the ladies and whirdle the men'
Too-ra-lae, too-ra-lae
Singing fiddle me grummits
And scrumple me [(*Squawks*).

KENNETH: Scrumple your *(Squawk)*?

KEN W: You'd squawk an' all if your moulie'd been screevelled with a length of hemp. However – they strung him and his horse up – and they do say as how his ghost rides abroad even to this day haunting the place where he once straddled his nadger so gaily. Only unfortunately they've built a supermarket on the site, and on early closing day his wraith can be seen a'galloping along the bacon counter and manifesting itself behind the crystallized fruits. And as he gallops he sings:-

*(Slowly)* My tale it is ended, my song it is sung,
As me and my horse we have both been well hung
And as I'm a phantom my only recourse
Is to scrope by myself and to whirdle my horse.
Singing fiddle me grummits
And scrumple me[3]] – *(Sepulchral tones)* – Flooot!

*(Applause)*

---

3. This speech was used in a later programme.

KENNETH: [Well, I don't know about you, but the bogles on my posset not only stood on end but I got goosepimples on my cordwrangle. Now,] any survey of the occult would not be complete without a look at the medium – and that's why when I saw an advert in my copy of *Physique Pictorial* – I buy it for the gardening section – it was an advert actually for Bona Seances – I rushed out of my lattie and trolled down there.

*F/X: Knock on door. Door opens*

KENNETH: Hello – anybody there.

HUGH: Oh hello. I'm Julian and this is my friend Sandy.

KEN W: Or to give us our professional names – I am Madam Bona – and Jule here is the Great Omipaloni – natural sensitive.

KENNETH: I believe you can see into the future.

HUGH: Oh yes. I'm gifted with second vada. I am occupied by your actual mystic forces.

KEN W: He is. Occupied. Frequently. He's got the waves, he's got telepathy. You see, it's a gift with him. Some have got it, some haven't. He's got it – by George he's got it. [Go on heartface – cross his palm with silver.

KENNETH: Well, I'm afraid I haven't got any silver on me –

HUGH: Oh, don't worry. You can cross me hand with a Diners Club Card. They trust you up there. Now, how would you like me to prognosticate? Through the tea leaves, a spot of palmistry or would you like Sand here to have a vada in his crystals?

KEN W: I'll have a vada in me crystal. Right. Whip it out of its chamois, Jule.

There. There's your actual crystal ball. Now let's see what it foretells – it's cloudy – 'Scuse me I'll just hurr on it *(Heavy breath)* There, it's clearing – I see a man – it's you – you're in a room – a dark room – but you're not alone – there's two strange weird creatures – one of them is peering into a crystal . . . Oh sorry it's a reflection, it's us. How mortifying.

HUGH: Don't castigate yourself, Sand. Nantes coming through.] Shall we try the Ouija?

KEN W: Yes. Get out your Ouija, Jule. Let's have a palare with the spirits. Come on all sit round and hold hands – you sit next to me, Mr. Horne. Jule will be going off.

HUGH: Yes I do, you know. I go right off. [Right up the astral plane.]

KEN W: [He does. Right up there. He's limp for days afterwards. It takes it right out of him.] Right, nisht the chat now, he's going into his trance. Are your vibrations quite favourable? Oh bona.

HUGH: *(Groan)* Yes I'm going off. I'm going one step beyond.

KEN W: You go, Jule. Don't worry about us. We'll be all right on our own. He's going, he's going . . . he's coming back.

HUGH: *(Groans)*

KEN W: What do you want, Jule?

HUGH: I forgot to leave a note for the milkman.

KEN W: He's going again. He's going. It's coming over him in waves . . .

HUGH: *(More groans)*

KEN W: . . . Look at him. He's levitating. He's in touch with what we do not know.

KENNETH: Neither do we particularly want to.

KEN W: He's gone beyond. He's being possessed now by his spirit guide. He's a great butch Red Indian you know – look – look – Geronimo's occupying him now. It's very uncomfortable to be occupied by a Red Indian. And it lowers the value of the property.

HUGH: *(More groans)*

KEN W: Hello – Geronimo – it's Sand here – have you a message for any of us? Speak, Geronimo.

HUGH: *(Haltingly)* Mr. Geronimo is out. Leave your name and number. He will call you when he comes in. This is a recorded message.[7]

*Orchestra: Play-off*

KENNETH: The flesh was willing but the spirits were a bit weak. But I wonder if it is possible that there is a limbo where strange wraith-like creatures flit about in a twilight world of their own.

KEN W: Mind your own business. We don't ask you how you spend your evenings.

*Orchestra: Round the Horne signature tune*

DOUGLAS: That was *Round the Horne* starring Kenneth Horne, with Kenneth Williams, Hugh Paddick, Betty Marsden and Bill Pertwee. On the musical side you heard the Fraser Hayes Four and Edwin Braden and the Hornblowers. The script was written by Barry Took and Marty Feldman. The programme was produced by John Simmonds.

*Orchestra: Sig. tune up and out*

*(Applause)*

*Orchestra: 'Round the Horne' playout*

*(Applause)*

---

7. If the previous section looks familiar, it is because it also appeared in the Series 2 Christmas programme.

# SERIES 3 PROGRAMME 16

*FIRST BROADCAST* – Sunday 28 May 1967

## INTRODUCTION

*The Muffplaster Saga* echoes *The Clissold Saga* of the show's earliest days, in using an elderly loony's unreliable memoirs as a framing device for all manner of sketches, long and short. In this episode, we discover that the dreaded Spanish Inquisition employed methods strikingly similar to those of quiz-master Michael Miles on the TV game show *Take Your Pick*. There's a rare treat for Douglas Smith, as he gets to play an animate object for once – a seal.

You'd have to feel sorry for anyone attempting to learn English from studying this script. Not only is there the usual gibberish from Rambling Syd Rumpo ('In Hackney Wick there lives a lass, Whose grummitts would I woggle'), but there's also a page of frankly unlikely sailors' argot: 'Staunch fast the mizzen whelping grumions'.

Kenneth Williams is full of complaints – 'It's him that cheapens the show. It's so denigrating for an artiste of my stature' – and some of the writers' favourite running jokes prove they've still got legs ('Take that! And that!').

Horne introduces the half-time song in usual barbed fashion: 'And now the moment we've all been waiting for, but first the Fraser Hayes Four.' The idea of a sketch show having a straight musical interlude seems odd today, but in the 1960s it was still usual – and remember, even the rule-breaking *Goon Show* used to take a break from its madness to listen to Max Geldray's harmonica. It was a chance for the audience, even more than the cast, to catch their breath, so as to ensure that laughter-fatigue did not inhibit their 'performance' in the second part of the show. Resident bands are now out of fashion in radio comedy – but perhaps more significantly, they are beyond the reach of most producers' budgets.

DOUGLAS: Here is a trailer for a forthcoming BBC adventure series.

*Grams:* Big Country-*type music (estab. then under)*

BILL: The fastest man in Wyoming – what he had seen no man had seen before – what he had done no man had done before and lived. A face at the window, a scream, running footsteps in the night, are an invitation to adventure with –

HUGH: Hawkeye – Last of the Peeping Toms.

DOUGLAS: But here now is the show that came second in the Tristan da Cunha Festival of Light Entertainment – the first prize went to Finland for a report on Guttapercha farming in medieval Latin – ladies and gentlemen – *Round the Horne.*

*Orchestra: Signature tune*

KENNETH: Hello and welcome to the show. That was, of course, Douglas Smith the Bane of Britain. Well now, today is the British Legion Barbecue a Bishop for Lent day, and all over England there'll be events to commemorate it. There'll be Toad Grappling at Sadlers Wells – Subterranean Beaver wiping in the steam room at Girton – Dowager cuffing at the Rotherhithe Slipper Baths, and a demonstration of Knothole Freezing given by the Mountford Holmes Formation Liver Sausage Chorale at the Hatfield College of Applied Technology and Curate Bleaching. [The event that I'm looking forward to is the Over-Eighties Nudist Leapfrog Team's Annual Old Tyme Dance. I can't wait to see them 'bobbing up and down like this'.] And now –

HUGH: By permission of the trustees

of the Tomtiddler estate and in association with Brian Epstein Miracle Plays Limited, Hampstead Garden Suburb – we present –

DOUGLAS: *The Muffplaster Sage.*

*Orchestra: Stately music*

KENNETH: Here with us in the studio is the last surviving member of the Muffplaster family – Sir Aardvark Muffplaster. Talking to him is Nemone Mousehabit.

BETTY: Now, Sir Aardvark –

KEN W: Now, Miss Mousehabit? All right, if you say so –

BETTY: *(Squeals)*

KEN W: Sorry my dear, it was just an old man's whim – you were saying?

BETTY: Now, I wonder if you would . . .

KEN W: Certainly, me dear –

BETTY: *(Squeals. Indignantly)* I suppose that's another old man's whim?

KEN W: No – same old man – same old whim.

BETTY: Your family have always been prominent in English history.

KEN W: Oh yes – [my grandfather was in the van at Waterloo. They caught him trying to steal a mailbag. But wherever history has been made, there you will find a Muffplaster. The Great Fire of London – that was started by a Muffplaster. The Great Plague – he was a Muffplaster too, and of course] as everyone knows it was a Muffplaster who discovered America.

BETTY: But surely that was Columbus?

KEN W: That's what the history books say, but in fact it was Sir Triffid Muffplaster – the year was 1491 – the place, the Court of King Alphonso the Incontinent, and his queen Isabella. It was the time of the dreaded Inquisition.

*Orchestra: Fifteenth-century link*

KENNETH: Good evening and welcome to the Spanish Inquisition. First, the Yes/No Interlude – will you bring on the first contestant.

BILL: And the first contestant is an old age pensioner and heretic from Seville – Father Lacrymoso Throbwalloper.

*F/X: Clanking chains and moaning as first contestant is dragged on*

HUGH: *(Groans)* Evening, Michael.

KENNETH: Now, you did say you were a heretic didn't you?

HUGH: I did.

KENNETH: And you come from Seville?

HUGH: That is correct.

KENNETH: You didn't say yes?

HUGH: I did not.

KENNETH: Are you going to recant?

HUGH: I am not.

KENNETH: Then you won't object to a little torture.

HUGH: I will not.

KENNETH: *(Cheerfully)* Does it hurt when I stick this lighted match up your cassock?

HUGH: Ooh! . . . Aaah! . . . Urgh! . . . eeaah!

KENNETH: Did you say yes?

HUGH: *(In extreme agony)* I did not.

*F/X: Gong*

KENNETH: Well done, Father Throbwalloper. Now for four pieces

of eight or two pieces of four or one piece of two – just answer this question. Brothers and sisters have I none, but this man's father is my father's son – who am I?

HUGH: Mrs. Boggis the char?

KENNETH: No – shall we give him another try, Cabal?

ALL CAST: Yes, Michael.

KENNETH: Come on then. Who am I?

HUGH: Torquemada?

KENNETH: Correct.

*All cast and orchestra (cheer)*

KENNETH: Now, let's open the box and see what you've won. Well, you haven't won the star chamber prize – being burnt at the stake.

CAST: Aah.

KENNETH: And you haven't won the do-it-yourself torture kit consisting of thumbscrews, boiling oil and a complete set of Lady Dartmouth[1] speeches.

CAST: Aah.

KENNETH: But never mind because you have won four days – four whole days for two – on my own private rack.

ALL CAST: Oooh!

HUGH: Just what I wanted – you've made a young masochist very happy. Bless you, Michael.

KENNETH: Drag him out and drag in the next contestant.

*F/X: Chains rattling as next contestant is dragged in*

KENNETH: And what's your name?

KEN W: Triffid Muffplaster.

---

1. Barbara Cartland's daughter.

KENNETH: Why are you here?

KEN W: Because I said the world was round. I can prove it. I have been studying Mercator's projection.

KENNETH: Yes, he told me. And you should be careful what you do with your dividers.

KEN W: *(Self)* It's disgraceful the way he twists my words – and I get the blame. I shudder to think what he'll make of the <u>next</u> line. *(Character)* Look, it's round.

KENNETH: Anything I say here is bound to be misconstrued. Take him to the Queen.

*Orchestra: Trumpet fanfare*

BILL: Your Majesty, I have a Muffplaster outside.

BETTY: How painful for you.

BILL: It's a sailor. [He says he's found a new way . . .

BETTY: Show him in –

BILL: . . . to the Indies.

BETTY: Well, show him in anyway.]

*F/X: Feet on marble floor*

KEN W: Allow me to genuflect before Your Majesty – you can do it too as soon as I've finished.

BETTY: Brave Muffplaster. You may kiss my seal.

KEN W: I don't like to. He looks all damp, and phaw . . . he's been eating herrings.

DOUGLAS: *(Oinks as seal)*

BETTY: Down seal – bad seal. Now, what did you want to see me about?

KEN W: I know that Your Majesty is interested in trade. Look at this map. I've found a new route to the Indies – it avoids the Exeter by-pass. Give me two dozen stout seafaring men or four dozen thin ones or three dozen mixed . . . I don't mind, but [let me get together a bunch of rough sailors and I'll –

BETTY: You'll what?

KEN W: You could er – we could er – never mind, we're bound to find a use for them and meanwhile] they could man a ship and I can cross the Atlantic. I might discover a new world.

BETTY: A new world?

*Grams: 'Star-Spangled Banner' (estab., then under for speech)*

KEN W: Yes, it's a hope, a dream – a new world where all men can be equal and free – free to eat jumbo nutburgers and whippsy malties twenty-four hours a day – I see as if in a vision George Murphy tap-dancing his way up the steps of the White House while Barry Goldwater waves his old glory on the roof. I see Lincoln at Gettysburg, George Peppard at Tobruk – I see all men marching together down the freedom road, Martin Luther King arm in arm with Governor Wallace[2], Sammy Davis arm in knee with John Wayne, James Baldwin and Lincoln Rockwell holding hands, Batman and Robin . . . stop it, Batman . . . A land where men are free to . . . stop it, Batman . . . free to live in peace and harmony the American way, under American rule – the American way of life.

---

2. Various prominent Americans of the day, chosen for their incompatibility; for instance, Baldwin was a black writer and civil rights activist, while Rockwell was a leader of the American Nazi Party.

**BETTY:** And what are you going to call this land?

**KEN W:** England. [*(American accent)* Gee Whillikins Queenie baby, can I go huh? Can I go? Huh?

**BETTY:** Yes.

**KEN W:** Gee, thanks. Huh!]

*Orchestra: Sea music*

**KENNETH:** And so young Triffid Muffplaster set sail in command of a small fleet – the *Nina*, the *Harold Pinter* and the *Santa Saucy Mrs. Trusspott*. I was his aide de camp. The men under my command were a rough and ready lot.

**BILL:** I'm rough.

**BETTY:** And I'm ready.

**KENNETH:** She was known as Midshipman Easy for reasons I won't go into. But the biggest scoundrel aboard was the bosun – Iron Liver McVitie – day after day he drove the crew relentlessly.

*F/X: Ship at sea*

**HUGH:** Staunch fast the mizzen whelping grumions.

**BILL:** Mizzen whelping grumions staunched fast.

**HUGH:** Loop your nooky pinnions.

**BILL:** Nooky pinnions looped.

**HUGH:** Double cleat your main top'sle halliards and jumble home your stench knots.

**BILL:** Do what?

**HUGH:** Tie a bit of string round that nail.

**BILL:** Oh.

**HUGH:** Right, now haul fast the mizzen sheet.

**BILL:** Aye aye, sir.

**HUGH:** Tack down the main sheet –

**BILL:** Aye aye, sir.

**HUGH:** Haul down all – now plump up the pillow – right – night night all.

**BILL:** Night night, bosun.

**KENNETH:** Meanwhile, Muffplaster stood on the poop, brooding – you look downcast, Captain.

**KEN W:** Who's there?

**KENNETH:** I'm your aide de camp. You seem unhappy, sir. You've been here alone all through the dog watch.

**KEN W:** Yes. Eight hours and I haven't seen one dog. What do you want, Number One?

**KENNETH:** Turn back – please turn back.

**KEN W:** Why?

**KENNETH:** We missed the chance of a cheap laugh on the last page – when I came on and said, 'I'm your aide de camp', you could have said, 'I don't need any aid I can manage by myself.' *(Chuckles)* Get it?

**KEN W:** Did you hear that? Oh it's a burden having him on a voyage. It's him that cheapens the show. It's so denigrating for an artiste of my stature – I was Playmate of the Month in *Horse and Hound*.

[**BILL:** Sail ho!

**KEN W:** Where?

**KENNETH:** There look on the port bow. *(Calls)* Who are you?

**HUGH:** Vasco da Gama. Out of Lisbon with a cargo of fresh spinach.

**KEN W:** What did he say?

KENNETH: Hey ho – it's Vasco da Gama and spinach.

KEN W: He'll be pleased with himself now he's thought of that one. Oh, it makes you sick.]

HUGH: Excuse me, Cap'n.

KEN W: What is it, bosun?

HUGH: The men want to turn back. They want to go home.

KEN W: But why?

HUGH: They think they've left the bath water running.

KEN W: You're lying. That's merely an ingenious excuse to hide your real reason. You're afraid.

HUGH: Afraid? Nobody calls Iron Liver McVitie a coward and lives. How would the feel of cold steel . . .

KEN W: You wouldn't.

HUGH: Oh, wouldn't I? There.

KEN W: Aaah!

KENNETH: Has he? Has he?

KEN W: Yes, he's put a cold key down my back. All right Iron Liver, you've asked for it.

[KENNETH: You're not going to fight him are you?

KEN W: Why not?

KENNETH: He's got a hook for each hand – two peg legs each with a spiked tip –

KEN W: Well, if he leaves them off, I'll fight the rest of him. There,] take that and that.

HUGH: And you take that.

KEN W: And you take that – and that.

HUGH: Oh, don't you want them?

KEN W: No I've got a drawer full. Besides you've got the height to carry them.

HUGH: You don't think they're a bit tight round the hips, do you – I don't want to look cheap.

KEN W: No. It's you.

HUGH: Well, all right then, but I must give you something in return.

KEN W: Oh, what is it?

HUGH: A quick thrust with me cutlass.

KEN W: Aaaah!

BILL: Land ho!

F/X: *Crunch of boat hitting beach*

KENNETH: You've done it, Muffplaster. Against all the odds you've discovered the New World. Quick, on to the beach and claim the land for Queen Isabella.

HUGH: There – I've got the flagpole.

KEN W: I name this land America.

KENNETH: And just think Muffplaster, one day a proud city will stand on this spot – here the statue of Liberty, there the Empire State Building. What are you going to call it, Muffplaster?

KEN W: I don't know – what about New Grimsby?

KENNETH: No –

KEN W: What about New Ashby de la Zouche – New Leighton Buzzard? New careful with that flagpole – er – New Manchester?

HUGH: I don't like it.

KEN W: I've got it. Watch what you're doing with that flagpole. Now – careful – New – watch it – New Yawk!!

*Orchestra: Play-off*

KENNETH: And so it was that for a long time the Goodwin Sands were known as the United States of America – but that's another story and probably funnier. And now the moment we've all been waiting for, but first the Fraser Hayes Four – ladies and gentlemen, to sing 'Gotta Travel On' – the Fraser Hayes Four.

*(Applause)*

*The Fraser Hayes Four with Orchestra: 'Gotta Travel On'*

*(Applause)*

DOUGLAS: And now the *Round the Horne* Colour Supplement.

KENNETH: First, Daphne Whitethigh.

BETTY: Hello – there's been a lot of controversy aroused by the film version of *Ulysses*. People say this sort of thing shouldn't be allowed. I quite agree – it should be done in whispers.

KENNETH: Thank you, Daphne Whitethigh, and come in Sunday Night TV personality Seamus Android.

BILL: Hello – all right – hello. I'm here on the set of, and here beside me is the star of the fillem, a beautiful young lady who I know you're dying to as I am, and this seems like the perfect opportunity to – so without further ado, this is Seamus Android returning you to the studio.

KENNETH: Thank you, Seamus Android, a man who has few peers except at his prompt card every ten seconds. This week the Colour Supplement takes a look at London. Here are some interesting facts about our capital.

KEN W: Did you know that if you stand in Piccadilly Circus long enough it's said that you'll be arrested for loitering?

HUGH: Did you know that London boasts the largest home for distressed gentlefolk in Britain – where people of breeding, too old for useful employment, can spend their declining years pottering harmlessly about collecting OBEs? It's called Broadcasting House.

BILL: Did you know that if Nelson's Column was laid on its end in Whitehall, the tip of Nelson's hat would block the entrance to the gents washroom at Scotland Yard?

BETTY: Did you know that Archer Street was once the haunt of Archers, that Brewer Street was the centre of the Brewing trade, and that Mincing Lane has an interesting history too?

KENNETH: So has Queensway I believe – however – there's lots in London to interest the visitor – the waxworks, where lifelike effigies of former politicians can be seen – it's called the House of Lords. Next door is the Chamber of Horrors – or House of Commons. A great tourist attraction, of course, is the London Zoo – where although in captivity, the animals receive the finest care.

BILL: And how are the patients today, Dr. Pewterblast?

KEN W: *(Snide)* Well, I'm a bit worried about that horse in the east enclosure. He's got a nasty swelling on his back. I tried to lance it but he didn't take kindly to that – so I put a bread poultice on it but it hasn't gone down.

BILL: I'm not surprised. That horse in the east enclosure is a camel.

KEN W: How mortifying –

BILL: Yes, isn't it. How's the giraffe?

KEN W: Oh, I diagnosed that all right. He's got a sore throat. I shall paint it with iodine – just as soon as the scaffoldin's up. But I'm worried about that dog.

BILL: The dog?

KEN W: Yes, the one by the lion house. He's hysterical.

BILL: That's the laughing hyena.

KEN W: Oh –

BILL: Has Keeper Jenkins told you about the boa constrictor – apparently he's been off his food.

KEN W: Yes, Keeper Jenkins told me. I've had a look at him – he's all right now except for a nasty protuberance in his stomach –

BILL: What do you think it is?

KEN W: [Well, from the shape of it I think it's] Keeper Jenkins. I'm more worried about Cornpasture, the elephant. He's lost his memory – thinks he's a baby kangaroo. Keeps hopping about on his hind legs punching people.

BILL: Good heavens.

KEN W: It's the other kangaroo that frightens me. Cornpasture keeps trying to get into her pouch. But I've got worries of my own.

BILL: What's the matter?

KEN W: I've got to resign.

BILL: Why?

KEN W: Well, yesterday I thought that Lulu, the giant orang-utan, was expiring so I leapt into the cage and gave her the kiss of life. It turned out she was only asleep – when she woke up she misunderstood the situation entirely – and now she's suing me for breach of promise.

*Orchestra: Brief link*

KENNETH: I think there's a lesson for us all there. Of course, for many people, London spells romance.

*Grams: 'London Pride'*

HUGH: Come here, Fiona – Look down there – it's like a necklet of diamonds on a velvet cushion – stretching away as far as the eye can see.

BETTY: Oh, Charles – it's lovely at night – London.

HUGH: I love it at any time – London. In the fog, in the rain – I even love it in the winter when Jack Frost touches it all with his icy finger.

BETTY: I love it too, Charles – It's <u>our</u> London.

HUGH: All those plucky cockneys – costermongers, ironmongers, fishmongers – they're all monging something. And how did Noel Coward put it – ah yes – I remember – cheerful little Cockney Sparrows. Look at those two – aah – oh. No wonder they're so cheerful.

BETTY: Oh, Charles I want to remember this moment – and keep it always, to pluck it out of time and lock it away in my heart for ever.

HUGH: For ever?

BETTY: Yes, Charles. For ever and ever and ever.

HUGH: Never let me go.

BETTY: No, Charles never – never ever – never never, never ever –

HUGH: Ah, London what strange magic you weave – Fiona, have you ever loved like this before?

BETTY: Not like this – not quite like this – not on top of Big Ben.

*F/X: Big Ben*

HUGH: Don't worry – it's only the half.

*Orchestra: Brief link*

KENNETH: There are many songs, airs and doggerel about old London – and here with the air of the doggerel is Rambling Syd Rumpo. Well me dearie, and how is your cordwangle this week.

KEN W: Nadgered.

KENNETH: Oh dear – then you won't be able to scrope your woggling iron for us.

KEN W: Oh, there's no problem. I've grunged it at the all-night bogle wash in Paddington.

KENNETH: And listeners, if you think that's a lot of rubbish, remember you get the sort of show you deserve. Now what are you going to sing for us this week?

KEN W: 'Tis a Master Fumbler's traddling air – and tells of a fair young maid from Hackney Wick for whom he'd gladly whirdle his stunging troon and it goes after this fashion –

*Ken W & Guitar: (To tune of 'Lass of Richmond Hill')*

In Hackney Wick there lives a lass
Whose grummitts would I woggle
Her ganderparts none can surpass,
(and) her possett makes me boggle.
Her moulies fine,
Her grunge divine,
The way her loomers tick,
I'd give up work
For one quick nurk –

*(Spoken)* I won't go into a long explanation of the precise meaning of the word nurk as it would weary you

*– (Sings)*

Sweet Lass of Hackney Wick.
I'd give a groat
for one quick scroat
with the Sweet Lass of Hackney Wick.

*(Applause)*

KENNETH: Thank you, Rambling Syd – now, the best way to see London is to go on a guided tour. Last week I was leafing through my copy of *Forbidden Flesh Monthly* – it's a vegetarian magazine. The latest edition has a rather daring front cover – an unretouched photograph of a Scotch egg in the nude. Anyway, I saw this advertisement which read . . . 'Guided Tripettes – Troll round London with Us', so I hurried to their address in Chelsea.

*F/X: Door open*

KENNETH: Hello – anybody there?

BILL: *(Gruff)* Hello – what do you want?

KENNETH: Oh, I was expecting somebody else – this <u>is</u> Guided Tripettes?

BILL: Oh yes. You want Master Julian and Master Sandy – I'll call them. *(Calls)* Oi – one of your regulars down here.

*F/X: Feet coming downstairs*

HUGH: Oh, it's Mr. Horne.

KEN W: So it is – how nice to vada your dolly old eek again.

KENNETH: Er – who's your friend?

HUGH: That's Gordon.

KENNETH: The one that used to be the attendant in the slipper baths?

KEN W: Yes, that's him – he's working for us now.

KENNETH: A sort of gentleman's gentleman.

KEN W: You <u>could</u> say that – but he's more of an odd job ome. Here's a pound, Gordon – go and tinker with your motor bike.

BILL: Ta, Master Sandy –

*F/X: Footsteps clumping off*

HUGH: You'll have to talk to him about his clothes, Sand. What with them studs in his jeans and them studs in his jacket – he's got more rivets in him than the Q4.

KEN W: That's your actual fourth queen.

HUGH: They're scrapping the other two queens you know.

KEN W: Yes, I know. When I read the headline 'Queens to be scrapped' my stomach went over – [till I realized they was talking about ships.]

HUGH: He's a devoted royalist, Mr. Horne. Anyway, I take it you're interested in a guided tour of London.

KENNETH: Yes I am.

KEN W: Our motto – see London and die.

KENNETH: Surely that's Naples.

KEN W: No, London.

HUGH: You'll die when you see the places we take you.

KEN W: We start off with all the usual sights. The latties of Parliament, Buckingham lattie – the lot.

HUGH: Yes, we cruise round all the latties – having a quick vada – then down your Birdcage Walk and up your Mall (Pronounced Maul).

KEN W: That's your Paul Maul.

HUGH: Then a quick mangare up the top of the GPO Tower and back to the Palace to vada the Changing of the Guard.

KEN W: When he's changed – it's off to the City to see the Old Palone of Threadneedle Street.

KENNETH: The Bank of England?

KEN W: No, Mrs. Gnomesfriend – keeps a very understanding pub in the City. It's called 'The Gay Bargee'.

HUGH: It's always full of chums.

KEN W: They do a very good draught crème de menthe.

HUGH: Thus revived the weary traveller is whisked up the West End for the gay round of the nightspots.

KEN W: The Marine Commando in Paddington –

HUGH: The Pink Gin A-Gogo –

KEN W: Reynard la Spoon's club.

KENNETH: Reynard la Spoon[3]. Is that the famous female impersonator?

HUGH: That's right – with our tour you spend a whole evening at Rene la Spoon's.

KEN W: Yes, it's fantabulosa. What a spectacle – the lighting, the costumes, the make-up, the jewellery – the fabe hairdos.

KENNETH: It sounds remarkable.

KEN W: It is – particularly when you consider that that's only the waiters.

*Orchestra: Play-off*

---

3. Loosely based on female impersonator Danny La Rue.

KENNETH: Anyway, I went on the tour
– and I really got to see places that the
normal visitor to London would never
see [– sober – Bow Street Magistrates
Court, the Dock at Old Bailey –] from
the inside, and that's why next week
*Round the Horne* will be an outside
broadcast from Pentonville Prison –
cheerio. See you – Governor
permitting – next week.

*Orchestra: Signature tune*

DOUGLAS: That was *Round the Horne*
starring Kenneth Horne, with Kenneth
Williams, Hugh Paddick, Betty
Marsden and Bill Pertwee. On the
music side you heard the Fraser Hayes
Four and Edwin Braden and the
Hornblowers. The script was written
by Barry Took and Marty Feldman.
The show was produced by John
Simmonds.

*Orchestra: Sig. tune up and out*

*(Applause)*

*Orchestra: 'Round the Horne' playout*

*(Applause)*

# SERIES 3
# PROGRAMME 19

*FIRST BROADCAST* – Sunday 18 June 1967

## INTRODUCTION

In preparing these notes, I have mostly been working from typescripts. However, in some instances – including this penultimate episode of a very long series, which ran from February to June – I have been able to compare the typed version of the script to Barry Took's original, hand-written version. Naturally, such priceless artefacts are normally kept in the Ancient Scrolls room of the Department of Mundane and Tepid Buffoonery at the National Museum of Corn – but they were loaned to me, as a bona fide scholar, on condition that I agreed not to smear them with Marmite and set light to them.

Took and Feldman preferred handwriting to typing because (as Barry says in his foreword) it allowed them to 'write literally as fast as we thought'. Writing in blue ink on white foolscap, Barry produced a remarkably orderly script. There are crossings-out, scribbled corrections and the occasional full-scale obliteration – but the finished product, as reproduced here, differs very little from its pen-and-ink forebear.

The typescripts themselves were subject to further changes during rehearsal. Cuts were often made at this stage, sometimes to increase the funniness or reduce the lewdness of the show; more often simply because the programme was overrunning. In a few places, the typescripts include the direction 'To be explained', meaning that a particular 'bit of business' would be easier to demonstrate than to put in writing. Every now and then, lines have been left entirely blank, and later filled in (presumably during rehearsal) in ink or pencil.

If the boys had known that what they were writing would still be being scrutinized decades later, would they have written with more care, I wonder – and if so, would their work have been better, because more polished, or worse, because more inhibited?

*F/X: Thunderstorm*

*F/X: Heavy door creaks open*

KEN W: Come into my laboratory, my dear.

BETTY: What is it, Baron Frankenstein?

KEN W: Look!

BETTY: Ugh – it's horrible. I don't want to see . . . 'it'.

KEN W: You must. People say I have a sick mind but I've done it. *(Mad laugh)* I took a few bits from here and a few bits from there – I stuck them together anyhow. It's crude but at last it's complete.

BETTY: It's monstrous. What are you going to call it?

KEN W: What else can I call it but – *Round the Horne.*

*Orchestra: Signature tune*

KENNETH: Hello and welcome to the show. Now, today as everybody knows is Commonwealth Sennapod Day – and all over London the bunting is up. To celebrate the centenary of the noble sennapod they are holding a goose fair in the grounds of Lambeth Palace. Among the many attractions will be Five-a-side Mitre Fingering – Knock a Sexton Out of Bed – Guess the Weight of a Bishop – Rabbi Shaving in the Round – [Cloister Traddling in the Great Marquee at threepence a go] and in the evening under floodlights, our old friends the Over-Eighties Nudist Leapfrog Team are giving a display of ballroom dancing – their programme includes the Dashing White Sergeant, the Blue Danube Waltz and the Red-Hot Polka. I myself am looking

forward to the finale where they all join hands in the grand chain. Right, Smith, make the announcement.

DOUGLAS: And now a story of the fastest gun in the West and how justice was brought to the wild frontier by the man they called the Palone Ranger.

*Orchestra: Western music*

KENNETH: My name is Wild Alf Pubes[1]. I'm an old panhandler –

KEN W: You don't have to tell us, ducky.

KENNETH: One day I was panhandling up the creek, crouched over my pan looking for gold.

KEN W: You won't find any there, ducky.

KENNETH: [Be quiet, Williams.] I had staked out a claim in the Black Hills of Dakota – [Dakota Station actually –] and my daughter and I were hoping to strike it rich . . .

BETTY: Gee Paw, shucks doggone my hide and cat on my hot tin roof.

KENNETH: What is it, Hoss?

BETTY: Do you think we'll ever find gold?

KENNETH: Of course we will.

BETTY: But Paw – we've been out here prospecting for months – [I'm so tired, and I get them headaches all the time. I've had 'em since I was scalped by that Apache –] I'm plumb tuckered out.

KENNETH: Well, plumb tuck it in and fix us some vittles.

BETTY: Look Paw – strangers on our land.

---

1. Quite a common surname. At least, it is in *RTH*.

*F/X: Horses approaching*

KENNETH: I looked up as a group of horsemen approached. The leader towered over five foot high – including the horse. I took in his sombrero'd head, his leather-jacketed body and his chapped legs. His high-heeled boots boasted ornate silver spurs. Who was this sinister stranger? He spoke.

HUGH: *(Dentures)* I am Buffalo Sidney Goosecreature, the celebrated desperado who's feared and hated from Kansas City to Sacramento – and none too popular in Finchley I might add.

KENNETH: What do you want of me?

HUGH: I want your land – the railroad is coming through – Soon the Black Hills will reverberate to the sound of the iron horse.

KENNETH: If your iron horse sets so much as an iron hoof on my land I'll plug you more times than the BBC plugged 'Puppet on a String'.

HUGH: Don't mess with me Pubes[2]. We're desperate men.

KENNETH: He gestured at his swarthy companions.

HUGH: This is Mexican Solly Mutterbucket – he was with Villa.

KENNETH: Pancho Villa?

HUGH: No – Aston Villa. He was transferred to me in the close season. And this is Two Gin Panderbody – he's a hired gun – he works for anyone, don't you Two Gin?

KENNETH: Two Gin – surely you mean Two Gun.

BILL: *(Dame)* No dearie, two gins and I'm anybody's.

KENNETH: She's a fine figure of a woman – and who are the others?

HUGH: These are my cow hands. These are my cow feet – and that's my cow heel. I'll give you twenty-four hours to get out of this territory.

KENNETH: Twenty-four hours?

HUGH: Well to you – twenty-three. Adios amigos. [Gee up Neddy.]

*F/X: Horses hooves thundering off into distance*

BETTY: Gee Paw, what are we gonna do?

KENNETH: There's only one thing we can do. Send for the Palone Ranger.

*F/X: Galloping hooves*

BILL: A streak of light – a flash of white and a cry of –

KEN W: *(Ginger Muffplaster voice)* Hi Ho Sylvia!

BILL: It's the Palone Ranger!

KEN W: Whoa, Sylvia. Allow me to introduce myself. I am the Palone Ranger and this is Sylvia the wonder horse – played by Douglas Smith in blinkers.

DOUGLAS: *(Whinnies)*

KEN W: Steady, girl. Look at her! Cats meat manqué.

KENNETH: She looks run down.

KEN W: Well, we've ridden five hundred miles to get here and she's due for a service. But we are at your command, me and my trusty paloyourno.

KENNETH: Palomino.

KEN W: Well, any paloyourno is a palomino.

---

2. Shouldn't there be a comma there somewhere?

KENNETH: You've ridden five hundred miles to say that? A fool's errand.

BETTY: Tell me Palone Ranger, why do you always wear a mask?

KEN W: Some say it's because I am a wanted criminal seeking to atone for my crimes, some say I wear it to prevent unsightly crow's feet but the real reason is that the elastic's caught round me ears and I can't get the damn thing off. I ride from place to place righting wrongs, protecting the strong, attacking the weak – taking from the poor and giving to the rich.

KENNETH: Shouldn't that be the other way round?

KEN W: I know which side my bread's buttered, ducky – What's your problem?

KENNETH: The wicked rancher, Buffalo Sidney Goosecreature is trying to drive us off our land. If you can help us I'll give you everything I have, land, gold, my daughter –

KEN W: You drive a hard bargain. But I'll do it. I'll summon my Indian friend, Squatting Duck. Oi, Ducky!

HUGH: *(Lotus Blossom)* Hello?

KEN W: You're wanted.

HUGH: I come in answer to your bidding oh white brother, cock. How do.

KEN W: He was educated abroad.

[HUGH: Do you wish to have pow wow with me?

KEN W: Business first – pleasure afterwards.

HUGH: Come let us suck boiled sweet of peace.

KENNETH: Shouldn't that be smoke a pipe?

HUGH: No. I give up smoking, O little white father from over the water near Hammersmith Reach.]

KENNETH: Can you find Buffalo Sid Goosecreature for us?

HUGH: I can, oh white brother. For have I not the nose of an eagle – the eye of a hawk, the feet of a gazelle, the ears of a puma, the chest of a buffalo – let's face it, I'm not much to look at but I can't half go. I can swim like the fish, climb like the mountain goat and run like the clappers.

KEN W: Yes – he sees like a lynx, hears like a roebuck and smells like a badger.

HUGH: Follow me.

KENNETH: All right – but at a distance. *(Narration)* The amazing Squatting Duck set off – and even though we were on horseback we found it hard to keep up with him – he was driving an E Type. [At the river he lost Goosecreature's spoor –

HUGH: That's done it. I've lost his spoor in the river.

KENNETH: That's all right. Fish it out with a stick.

KEN W: I have another tin here – look, instant horse's spoor. Just add an egg. I sprinkle it on the ground so, and quick after it – there it goes.

*Orchestra: Music link*]

KENNETH: We rode into the small town of Outlaws Creek.

KEN W: Eh?

KENNETH: Outlaws Creek.

KEN W: Only when they wear corsets.

KENNETH: And while we nipped in for a quick shave and hot towels the Palone Ranger swaggered into a bar called the Last Chance and Hartebeest in search of Goosecreature.

*Grams: Honky-tonk piano*

*F/X: Bar room sounds*

BILL: It's the Palone Ranger – what'll it be?

KEN W: Give me two fingers. Of rye you idiot – I want a drink not an opinion.

BETTY: Hello, pardner. What brings you down to these parts?

KEN W: I've got a lousy agent. I just thought I'd have a mosey around. I'm looking for Buffalo Sid. D'you know where he is?

BETTY: You know Indians Bend?

KEN W: I don't know – I've never bent one but I'll take your word for it.

BETTY: That's where you'll find Buffalo Sid. [He has a shack up there with his gang.

KEN W: Well chacun à son goût.]

BETTY: Don't fool with Buffalo Sid. He packs a 45 – he never wears it – he takes a 33 – he only packs it to impress the chambermaid.

KEN W: I'm not afraid. I've got a 45 too. Well, to be honest it's a double-barrelled twenty-two and a half. I'll five o'clock shadow him to his lair and beard him in his den.

[KENNETH: The Palone Ranger summoned a posse.

KEN W: Here posse posse posse.

BILL: All the boys are here. Where are we headed, Palone Ranger?

KEN W: The outlaws' camp in the hills. Now everybody on to their horses and ride for the hills.]

*F/X: Horse galloping into the distance*

DOUGLAS: The scene changes. Come

with us now dear listener through bosky woods, and fairy dell, over hills, over dales, to where the curlew cries its soft impeachment and –

KEN W: Oh, get on with it – stop hanging it out.

DOUGLAS: Ah, all right. Goosecreature's shack some hours later.

KEN W: *(Off mic)* All right Goosecreature, we've got the place surrounded. Are you coming out?

BETTY: *(Old crone)* Sidney's not coming out – not till he's eaten his rice pudding.

HUGH: *(Dentures)* Oh Mum –

BETTY: I'm not having you playing with that Palone Ranger – he's rough.

HUGH: Oh Mum – go on –

BETTY: All right – but put your wellingtons on.

HUGH: Thanks Mum. *(Calls)* All right Palone Ranger, I got me wellies on. I'm coming.

*Grams:* High Noon-*type music*

KENNETH: The two fastest men in the West faced each other, their hands hovering over their hips – not like that Williams – then slowly, inexorably they walked towards each other –

HUGH: All right Palone Ranger, you draw first.

KEN W: No.

HUGH: Draw, I say.

KEN W: Oh, all right – It's ticket number 304.

KENNETH: Well done. [You've won a bottle of invalid-type Yokohama sherry.

KEN W: Oh, just what I wanted.

HUGH: OK Palone Ranger, this is the end of the line – you're on a one-way ticket to Boot Hill – changing at Crewe.]

KENNETH: Goosecreature's hand snaked to his holster – and quicker than the eye could follow, he drew his ivory-handled 'Peacemaker' and fired.

*F/X: Gunshot*

KENNETH: But the Palone Ranger was even faster.

*F/X: Gunshots*

KEN W: Pow!

HUGH: Oof! Kersplat –

KEN W: Grunt.

HUGH: *(Yelps and dies)*

KENNETH: You got him, Palone Ranger.

BETTY: Oh, Palone Ranger – but you're hurt.

KEN W: It's nothing. He's just winged me in the heart. This is the end of the trail old buddy – old pal. But we'll meet again in that great corral in the sky – if not my place for drinkies at si . . . x.

KENNETH: And that was the end of the Palone Ranger – clutching the hole where he'd been plugged, he ran round in ever diminishing circles and with a final gurgle disappeared down his own plug hole.

*Orchestra: Play-off*

KENNETH: They took him to Boot Hill and on his tombstone they inscribed this awful warning – ladies and gentlemen, it's the Fraser Hayes Four.

*(Applause)*

*The Fraser Hayes Four with Orchestra: 'Italian Street Song'*

*(Applause)*

DOUGLAS: And now the *Round the Horne* Colour Supplement.

KENNETH: News from the fashion front. At a recent gala film opening, Twiggy wore a topless dress. Asked for her comments, she said –

BETTY: I was mortified. Nobody noticed.

KENNETH: At the same affair there was an unfortunate mishap.

BETTY: *(Daphne Whitethigh)* Dusty Springfield's eyelashes fell off and stabbed Sandie Shaw in the foot.

KENNETH: And now over to trendy Sunday night TV personality, Seamus Android.

BILL: Well now, all right – hello. Well, tonight I've got someone rather special who I know you'd like to – so without further ado, I'd like to give her a big warm – because I know she'd appreciate it and I'd like to add – but I can't – or subtract or divide, and I'm not very good at reading either – but I have a warm spot – and it gives me a great thrill – but that's none of your business, and with that, goodnight.

KENNETH: Every Sunday evening I think 'Seamus Android you should be living at this hour' or at least awake. This week the Colour Supplement turns its bleary eye on the subject of the BBC. What is the BBC? It is something you turn to when you're faced with the cold grey reality of David Frost on commercial, only to find that he's beaten you to it, and he's there on BBC as well. And then there's BBC Radio – the elephants' graveyard of entertainment. To be fair, the BBC are always searching for new talent – take the script department.

HUGH: So you're our new scriptwriter Mr. . . . er –

KEN W: Gruntfuttock. J. Peasmold Gruntfuttock.

HUGH: Well, well, well – er – welcome aboard – now I've been looking at some of the scripts you've sent in and, well, I know you're new at it but – er – there are limits. I mean look at the synopsis you sent in for The Dales. The incident you envisage in the bathroom between Mrs. Dale, Bomber Harris and Dr. Adam York concerning the loofah, the mirror on a stick and the inflatable rubber duck – whilst not without its dramatic highlights would – I should think – be extremely dangerous to all concerned.

KEN W: Not at all. I tried it out. The loofah snapped but the rubber duck came through it unscathed.

HUGH: What about this scene? You can't have Mrs. Dale and Mrs. Freeman crouched on a bomb site swigging meths.

KEN W: That's the trouble with you lot – you're stuffy and hidebound – you don't want the fresh clean wind of reality blowing up your corridors of power.

HUGH: But look at this dialogue –

KEN W: Let me read it to you. You'll get the full flavour of it then. 'Enter Mrs. Dale in her flimsy night attire, her bronzed young . . .'

HUGH: Yes, quite. We can skip the stage directions.

KEN W: Mrs. Dale speaks – 'Why hello Jim – cor stone me, what a booze up we had last night up the BMA. My mouth's like the bottom of a parrot's cage.' To which her better half replies – 'Shut up you silly old tart – or I'll give you a mouthful of knuckles.' There – what's wrong with that?

HUGH: It hasn't quite the nuance we expect. [And look what you've done to The Archers. You can't have Walter Gabriel discovered on the roof of the Tithe Hall without his trousers.

KEN W: What's wrong with it?]

HUGH: It just won't do, Mr. Gruntfuttock. Your work is obviously the product of a one-track degenerate childish mind.

KEN W: I suppose that means you're giving me the sack?

HUGH: Good heavens no – you're just the chap we need to write Round the Horne.

*Orchestra: Link*

KENNETH: A lot of people think of the BBC as a heartless institution staffed by automatons – and a lot of people are right – but love can still blossom even in such an unlikely place as the sound effects department.

[*Grams: 'Room With a View' (vocal version) punctuated with F/X. e.g. 'A room with a – F/X – and – F/X – with no one to – F/X' etc.*

HUGH: I'll just try a . . .

*F/X:*

HUGH: . . . and if that doesn't work I'll use a . . .]

*F/X: Door open*

*F/X: (Long) (Raspberry?)*

BETTY: Charles – am I disturbing you?

HUGH: No. I'm just trying out a few sound effects for Midweek Theatre.

BETTY: Don't let me interrupt but – Charles – I had to see you.

HUGH: Well, close the . . .

F/X: *Door close*

HUGH: . . . and . . .

F/X: *Clumping footsteps*

HUGH: . . . over here. Now, what's the matter, darling?

BETTY: Roger knows everything.

HUGH: Everything?

BETTY: About us.

[HUGH: Does he know that you and I have been . . .

F/X: *(Comedy kiss with squelchy pop at end)*

HUGH: . . . every Wednesday afternoon?

BETTY: Yes, I'm afraid he does.] He had us watched by a detective – he's signed an affidavit to the effect that he's seen us . . .

F/X: *As above*

BETTY: . . . on four separate occasions and . . .

F/X: *As above*

BETTY: . . . in the grill room of the Ritz.

HUGH: Come, my dear, don't . . .

F/X: *As above*

HUGH: . . . yourself. It'll ruin your make-up. Here, let me take you in my . . .

F/X: *As above*

HUGH: . . . and kiss you on the . . .

F/X: *As above*

HUGH: . . . and dry your . . .

F/X: *As above*

HUGH: . . . on my . . .

F/X: *As above*

BETTY: Am I being a foolish little . . .

F/X: *As above*

BETTY: . . . Charles. I just want to know that you still . . .

F/X: *As above*

BETTY: . . . me and that you'll always . . .

F/X: *As above*

BETTY: . . . me even when I'm old and . . .

F/X: *As above*

HUGH: Yes I'll always . . .

F/X: *As above*

HUGH: . . . you as long as there's a . . .

F/X: *As above*

HUGH: . . . in my body. Life will be one long . . .

F/X: *(Comedy kiss)*

HUGH: . . . and we'll find a little peace.

Orchestra: *Link*

KENNETH: Makes you feel absolutely . . .

F/X: *As above*

KENNETH: . . . Well, it does me – but then I'm a sentimental old . . .

F/X: *As above*

KENNETH: . . . and talking of . . .

F/X: *As above*

KENNETH: . . . here's Rambling Syd Rumpo. The folk singer who is no longer – and no shorter than he was last week. He's about the same length – in his stockinged moulies. Good evening, Rambling Syd.

KEN W: Hello me deario – for I'll whirdle tit willow and jump Jim Crow.

KENNETH: You do. They can always edit it out of the recording. Now, what are you going to sing us?

KEN W: 'Tis an air that I shall be doing on my new LP – but, of course, there I shall be accompanied by the Loomer-Fairfax Spondling Chorale – unfortunately they cannot be with me today [as they're taking part in a twenty-four hour spondle at Wembley Pool]. So if you and the boys and girls will join me – we shall all burst forth together – so grundle your parts and away we go . . .

KEN W WITH GUITAR: *(To tune of 'Green Grow the Rushes-O')*

KEN W: *(Sings)*

I'll sing you one-oh!
Green grows my bogling fork.

CAST: *(Sings)*

What is your one-oh?

KEN W:

One's the grunge upon my splod
Masking my cordwangle.
I'll sing you two-oh!
Green grows my bogling fork.

CAST:

What are your two-oh?

KEN W:

Two are my looming thrums
See how they gangle,
One's the grunge upon my splod
Masking my cordwangle.
I'll sing you three-oh!
Green grows my bogling fork.

CAST:

What are your three-oh?

KEN W:

Three are the times
I've lunged my groats,
Two are my looming thrums
See how they gangle,
One's the grunge upon my splod,
Masking my cordwangle.
I'll sing you four-oh!
Green grows my bogling fork.

CAST:

What are your four-oh?

KEN W:

Four for my whirdlers bent,
Three are the times
I've lunged my groats,
Two are my looming thrums,
See how they gangle,
One's the grunge upon my splod,
Masking my cordwangle.
I'll sing you five-oh!
Green grows my bogling fork.

CAST:

What are your five-oh?

KEN W:

Five are the wogglers
Up my spong,
Four for my whirdlers bent,
Three are the times
I've lunged my groats,
Two are my looming thrums,
See how they gangle,

CAST: *(Slowly)*

One is the grunge upon my splod –

KEN W: *(In tempo)*

It's ruined my cordwangle!

CAST: *(Quasi-religious)*

Wangle.

*(Applause)*

KENNETH: That's better out than in.

Now, we in the entertainment business have every cause to be grateful to the backroom boys of the BBC – especially those unsung heroes of the wardrobe and make-up department. Recently I was appearing on BBC television and before I went on I popped into the wardrobe department.

*F/X: Door open*

KENNETH: Hello, anybody there?

HUGH: Oh hello – I'm Julian and this is my friend Sandy.

KEN W: Look it's crocheted on our smocks. Are you one of the Daleks from *Doctor Who*? Oh no, it's Mr. Horne. Nice to vada your eek.

HUGH: Come for a fitting, have you?

KENNETH: Yes, I've been sent up by the producer.

KEN W: I'm not surprised, ducky.

HUGH: He's got an acid tongue that Ned. What show are you doing, Mr. Horne? You come for *Suivez la Piste*?

KENNETH: Not particularly but – if you've got the kettle on . . .

KEN W: Oh he's bold.

HUGH: And cheeky with it. What sort of programme are you doing?

KENNETH: It's an interview programme.

KEN W: You're not on *Omi Alive*?

HUGH: Course he isn't. He's much more your *Vada of the Week*, aren't you, Mr. Horne?

KENNETH: To be honest I'm not sure – they just said report to Studio Six.

KEN W: Let's see what's on the schedule – look up your call sheet,

Jule.

HUGH: Hmm, let's have a vada. Well, he's not a Black and White Minstrel.

KEN W: And he's not one of your Likely Lads – quite the reverse. Most unlikely.

HUGH: Most. Hmm. He wouldn't be on *Vada with Mother* –

KEN W: He's more your Vada with Granny.

HUGH: I wonder if he's on BBC2. [Do you think he's *Something Special*?

KEN W: Not really. *Points of Vada*?

HUGH: No.] What cossie did they say?

KENNETH: They said a dinner suit.

KEN W: Sorry ducky, that's out.

KENNETH: Out?

KEN W: Yes, the Director General's wearing it.

HUGH: And I hope he doesn't put his hand in the trouser pocket.

KENNETH: Why?

HUGH: Channing Pollock had it last.

KEN W: You know – that one that produces the doves from the most unlikely places.

KENNETH: Wait a minute – do you mean that the BBC only has one dinner jacket?

KEN W: Yes. It's part of the economy drive – they all wear it – Eric Robinson[3] – Ronnie Corbett –

HUGH: Not at the same time, of course.

KEN W: I don't know though – you can't tell, Ronnie could be in there somewhere.

---

3. A bandleader, frequently seen on TV.

HUGH: Anyway it's out. Most of our stuff's out. Let's look through the wardrobe and see if we can find you some bona drag.

KEN W: Here what about this – very chich.

HUGH: Only been worn once.

KEN W: By Kathy Kirby[4]. You've got much the same measurements.

HUGH: Distributed differently.

KENNETH: I think not.

KEN W: Well it's either that or this outfit – worn by Jimmy Saville.

KENNETH: Of the two I'd rather have Kathy Kirby's.

KEN W: Now you'll want your baubles to go with it.

HUGH: And this wig –

KEN W: Now a few dabs of make-up – there you look a picture.

KENNETH: Of the sort you buy in Tangier. Well it's too late to do anything about it.

HUGH: Off you go. Bona luck.

KEN W: Don't worry, you'll be fantabulosa!

*F/X: Door shut*

HUGH: Here, did he say Studio Six?

KEN W: Yes. Why?

HUGH: Well he'll certainly make an impression on the viewers.

KEN W: Why?

HUGH: He's reading the Epilogue.

*Orchestra: Play-off music*

KENNETH: I think I'm the only man who read the Epilogue in gold lamé

and a henna-rinsed wig – [it was all right though – I dropped my voice an octave, scowled at the camera and flexed my muscles, – and people thought I was Fanny Craddock.] Cheerio, see you – [Johnny permitting –] next week.

*Orchestra: Sig. tune*

DOUGLAS: That was *Round the Horne* starring Kenneth Horne, with Kenneth Williams, Hugh Paddick, Betty Marsden and Bill Pertwee. On the musical side you heard the Fraser Hayes Four and Edwin Braden and the Hornblowers. Special effects by Ken Gregory and Andy Cartledge. The script was written by Barry Took and Marty Feldman. The programme was produced by John Simmonds.

*Orchestra: Sig. tune up and out*

*(Applause)*

*Orchestra: 'Round the Horne' playout*

*(Applause)*

---

4. A singer.

# SERIES 4
# PROGRAMME 4

*FIRST BROADCAST* – Sunday 17 March 1968

## INTRODUCTION

The fourth (and as it turned out, last) series sounds a little different from its predecessors. One of the BBC's periodic cost-cutting crusades has left the show without the services of Bill Pertwee and the Fraser Hayes Four (while Edwin Braden and the Hornblowers have been replaced by the Max Harris Group) – and at the same time, Marty Feldman is no longer one of the writers.

The other side of Marty's career, that of performer, had taken off, and he was now much in demand for TV comedies – including in 1968 his own award-winning show *Marty*, written by Took and Feldman. He ended up in Hollywood, making films with Mel Brooks and Gene Wilder. Marty Feldman died in 1983. His short life had seen many professional triumphs, as well as a few disappointments, but with hindsight it's hard to avoid the conclusion that *Round the Horne* was his most accomplished and lasting achievement.

Barry stayed on as script editor, and writer of the Julian and Sandy and Rambling Syd sketches, while much of the rest of series four was written by Johnnie Mortimer and Brian Cooke, who were then part-time radio comedy scriptwriters as well as newspaper cartoonists, with additional material by freelance writer and former teacher, Donald Webster. After *RTH*, Mortimer and Cooke wrote some immensely popular TV sitcoms, including *Father Dear Father* and *Man about the House*.

Reading the scripts from this series, I don't think you'll be able to see the joins – Mortimer and Cooke slip into the *Horne* style with confident ease. Highlights of this episode include Douglas Smith's animal impressions, and a 'Movie-Go-Wrong' spoof of *Camelot*, in which Kenneth Williams plays Sir Mincealot.

HUGH: As we have a few moments in hand before the next programme, here is a warning to all shipping . . . *(Imitates foghorn)* <u>Vooooom!</u> <u>Vooooom!</u> Thank you. And for my next impression, a BBC announcer performing a rather distasteful duty . . .

DOUGLAS: Ladies and gentlemen . . . *Round the Horne*!

*Orchestra: Signature tune*

KENNETH: Hello and welcome to the show. First, a late sports result. Lions . . . three. Christians . . . nil. And now, an apology. In last week's programme we said that Sir Armitage Bulstrode likes to go and feel the pigeons in Trafalgar Square. This of course was a typographical error. It should have been 'feel the pigeons in <u>Soho</u> Square'. None of which brings us to the results of last week's 'Complete The Title' competition. The first title we asked you to complete was *The Girl With Green——*. Yes. The correct answer was 'Eyes'. Though I must congratulate the Very Reverend Ignatius Dangle for an inspired if highly improbable guess. [The second title was *Across the River and into the——*. As most of you correctly stated, the answer was 'Trees'. All other suggestions have been forwarded to the Director of Public Prosecutions.] The other title was *The Man with the Golden——* and this produced such a volume of mail that I haven't been able to sort through it. Particularly as my secretary is away suffering from shock. Smith! Announce the next item.

DOUGLAS: Shan't.

KENNETH: What?

DOUGLAS: Shan't. You promised I could do <u>my</u> bit first. You promised.

Granny is listening specially.

KENNETH: Oh, very well. Go on.

DOUGLAS: Thank you, sir. *(Clears throat)* As I walk down the country lane, I hear the birds twittering . . . *(Does bird imitation)* And look, here comes Rover the dog. Woof! Woof! Hello, Rover. And yonder I spy Brock the Badger. Oh, he's gone. Just as well, really, I can't do badgers, but see, here comes Nelly the Cow . . . Mooo, moo! . . .

KENNETH: And look, coming towards us, John the Producer, carrying your notice to quit.

DOUGLAS: Oh, yes. Well, I'd better announce the latest in our 'Movie-Go-Wrong' series. A film adaptation to stir the heart, quicken the pulse and agitate the peritoneum. Horneographic Productions, in association with British Mouse, proudly present . . .

*Orchestra: Brief fanfare*

DOUGLAS: *The Knights of Camelot*!

*Orchestra: Medieval intro music*

[KENNETH: I should point out that our version doesn't have any songs in it, so that in that respect it does differ from the original film . . . Oh, I don't know, though.]

DOUGLAS: This is the story of King Arthur, the man who told the sea to go back while he watched the spider burning the cakes.

KEN W: They don't exactly go in for historical accuracy, do they?

DOUGLAS: We open with a panoramic view of King Arthur's seat in glorious colour. Yes, Camelot. In the narrow streets, bold knights flaunt their escutcheons and serving maidens hang out their wimples to dry.

[KENNETH: Smith!

DOUGLAS: It's a hat, sir.

KENNETH: OK.] I'm playing Arthur. I spent a happy boyhood roaming about in oak forest and poppy wood . . . Iris would, too, sometimes, but mostly it was Poppy. It was on one of these childhood jaunts that I first discovered my mighty Excalibur.

DOUGLAS: I, Douglas Smith, play the part of Excalibur, the shining sword. I am buried up to my pommel in granite.

KENNETH: I was skipping down the woodland path with poppies in my hand, when suddenly . . .

KEN W: *(Merlin)* Stay, young master, stay!

KENNETH: You, Williams? I thought Hugh Paddick was playing Merlin.

KEN W: *(Self)* Well, he was, but I wouldn't have come in till page five. So we did a swop. I'm doing Merlin and I've told him he can play Gruntfuttock.

KENNETH: But we're not doing Gruntfuttock this week.

KEN W: Shh . . . <u>He</u> doesn't know that. He only reads his own lines. *(Merlin)* Stay, young master! See this Douglas Smith buried in the granite? Now's your chance. If you can pull it out, you shall be king!

KENNETH: I gripped the thing by its curiously carved hilt . . .

DOUGLAS: Do be careful, sir.

KENNETH: With one mighty heave, I dislocated my shoulder. But I had the sword. Excalibur was mine!

*Orchestra: Excitement link*

KENNETH: Of course, many years have

passed since then. Now I sit at the Round Table, my gallant knights around me. Sir Gawain, the gentle knight, Sir Insomnia, the sleepless knight . . .

HUGH: *(Sir Gawain)* My liege! By your leave, I crave a boon!

KENNETH: Certainly. There's a plate of them over there. Buttered boons . . . currant boons . . .

HUGH: No, sire. I seek an opportunity to show off my derring-do! I haven't derring-done for weeks.

KENNETH: Very well, I decree that a grand tourney be held. My knights shall go out into the field, wearing full armour and carrying heavy shields. You shall tilt, some of you may even fall over.

*F/X: Door opens*

KEN W: *(Sir Mincealot)* Hold! Hold! I demand that you hold!

KENNETH: I held. Who are you, intrepid knight with the pointed black face?

KEN W: I've got me helmet on, y'fool! I am Sir Mincealot, the pure knight.

KENNETH: Of course, I dubbed you myself . . . for the foreign language markets. What do you want, Mincealot?

KEN W: I have heard of the exciting deeds done by your bold company, and I wish to take up my position on the Round Table!

KENNETH: A deadly silence fell. Mainly because the producer had cut the next line. Later that day I hurried to see my court magician, Merlin.

HUGH: *(Merlin)* Eye of newt and toe of frog, wool of bat and tongue of dog . . . Greetings, sire. Care for a sandwich?

KENNETH: No, thank you, Merlin . . . Just a minute – Kenneth Williams was playing Merlin just now.

HUGH: *(Self)* Yes, but the less said about him and his little devices the better! Gruntfuttock!

KENNETH: Oh. Anyway, Merlin, I come to you because I need good counsel.

HUGH: I'll try and get you one. When does your case come up?

KENNETH: I need advice. This knight, Sir Mincealot, he fills me with foreboding. I don't know . . . there's something about the way he holds his lance that makes me uncomfortable. [And I refuse to elaborate on that statement.]

HUGH: Never fear, for nothing is hidden from Merlin. [I have here something which a man may look into and see all!

KENNETH: By Jove, yes. A peephole into the damsels' changing room. Merlin, I never thought you could stoop so low!

HUGH: Well, it does make my back ache a bit. But do not condemn me, sire. Was it not I who first led you to Excalibur, the sword which now hangs at your side?

DOUGLAS: Still played by myself, Douglas Smith. A little older, a little tarnished, perhaps, but my edge is still keen, and my point still sharp.

KENNETH: Thank you, Smith.

DOUGLAS: Swish, swish, snicker . . . See how the firelight plays on me as I dance in your hand . . .

KENNETH: Oh, shut up, Smith. Now, good Merlin, cast your runes and tell me.] What doth this knight Sir

Mincealot at my court?

HUGH: Even now he is with your wife, the Lady Guinevere, whom men call Guinevere the generous.

KENNETH: And I'd give a lot to know how that name got about.

*Orchestra: Brief link*

BETTY: Greetings, bald knight!

KEN W: *(Self)* Bold knight, do you mind? *(Sir Mincealot)* Greetings, Lady Guinevere. I am Sir Mincealot, the pure. See me in my shining armour . . . I am pure, pure. The pleasures of the flesh are not for me. I resist all temptation . . . I am pure! Mainly because I can't get out of this rotten armour.

BETTY: Oh, Sir Mincealot, I have heard of your intrepidity. Is it true what they say about your great feat . . . that you went out and rescued a dragon and slaughtered a fair maiden?

KEN W: Yes, well, you can't see what you're doing with these visors down.

BETTY: Come, stand by me . . . closer . . . closer. Look into my eyes. Do you not see beauty there?

KEN W: Oh, yes, yes. Such beauty! I could gaze upon it all day . . . two little reflections of me.

BETTY: *(Piqued)* Verily, thou art a right bighead. Come the day of the tourney, my champion will demand satisfaction from you.

KEN W: Oh, will he now.

*Orchestra: Link, leading into fanfare*

HUGH: *(Dentures)* Your majesties . . . my Lords, Knights of the Round Table, Damsels of the octagonal stool, Squires, Serfs, Archers, Dales, Franciscan Friars, Blackfriars,

Mansion House, Cannon Street and all stations to Upminster. Announcing the first joust. On my left, Sir Mincealot, seven stone three in dripping wet armour. And on my right, the Queen's Champion, Sir Cular!

*Grams: F/X: Cheers of crowd*

KENNETH: Guinevere and I watched from the Royal Box. To the South, Sir Mincealot rode. To the North, Sir Cular Road . . . North Circular Road . . . *(Amused)* . . . I missed that at rehearsals . . .

*F/X: Thunder of hooves gathering speed*

KENNETH: . . . It was an inspiring sight, the knights astride their gaily caparisoned coconut shells. We watched with bated breath . . . they gathered speed . . . lances held ready . . . faster and faster . . .

*F/X: Hoofs quickly going into distance*

BETTY: Shouldn't they have been galloping towards each other?

KENNETH: Yes, but don't worry, they're turning back. See, they're fighting.

*F/X: Clang of swords on armour: Continue under*

KEN W: *(Sir Mincealot) (Sounds of effort)* Ha! Thrust and parry . . . thrust and parry . . .

HUGH: *(Sir Cular) (Sounds of effort)* Why do you keep saying thrust and parry?

KEN W: They're my tailors. I thought you'd be interested. Ha! Take that!

*F/X: Particularly loud clang*

HUGH: Aaaah!

KEN W: I have cleaved your armour!

Your end is in sight.

HUGH: I yield, I yield!

*F/X: Grams: Crowd cheer*

BETTY: Sir Mincealot! He's won! He's won!

KENNETH: Who would have thought it. We should throw something in his honour. A rotten tomato, or better yet, a feast!

*Orchestra: Medieval party music*

KENNETH: *(Starting over music)* What a banquet it was! Oxen roasted whole, wine flowed like water. The board was groaning . . .

HUGH: *(Business man)* The shareholders won't like us spending all this money!

KENNETH: Nonsense. Give me wine, give me venison, give me sweetmeats, give me the moonlight, give me the girl and leave the rest to me. But stay, where is my Lady Guinevere?

HUGH: *(Merlin)* I did see a slim girlish figure flit away into the shadows, sire . . . and Lady Guinevere was with him!

*Orchestra: Very brief link (on party music)*

BETTY: They will never find us here, Mincealot. Another goblet of mead?

KEN W: Well, I don't know, Guinevere, we've already had seven goblets of mead.

BETTY: Oh, Mincealot, we can't go on meading like this! If Arthur suspects I am lacking in chastity he will belt me!

KEN W: Quite. Oh, Guinevere.

BETTY: Oh, Mincealot!

KEN W: Guinevere, Guinevere!

BETTY: Mincealot, Mincealot!

KEN W: Guinevere! Guinevere! Guinevere!

BETTY: Mincealot! Mincealot! Mincealot!

KEN W: Oh, Guinevere . . .

BETTY: Oh, Mincealot . . .

*F/X: Door opens*

KENNETH: Mincealot!

KEN W: Arthur!

KENNETH: Mincealot! Mincealot!

KEN W: Arthur! Arthur! Arthur!

KENNETH: Well, so much for the introductions. What are you both doing? And on the Round Table, too. You know how easily it marks.

KEN W: Fear not, my liege. It's this rotten armour – I can't get my visor up! Your wife has been chaste.

KENNETH: I know, I saw you chasing her. You leave me no alternative but to punish you both!

*Orchestra: Doom link*

*F/X: Grams: Muffled drum beats as of execution: Fade and hold under*

DOUGLAS: Picture the awful scene. The crowded public square in Camelot. Faggots are piled high around two solitary stakes in the centre of the square. The torch is applied . . . the wood blazes . . . smoke and flames hide the stakes from our view . . !

KENNETH: Yes, this is your punishment for Guinevere and Mincealot. We're having a barbecue and you haven't been invited!

BETTY & KEN W: *(Ad lib ending)*

'. . . find the way out of this armour.'

*Orchestra: Pay off*

KENNETH: *(Ad lib into)* 'I Remember it Well' *(Kenneth/Betty duet)*

DOUGLAS: Now for the go-ahead – don't look back it's right behind you – tingling scene of Radio Balls Pond Road!

*Orchestra: Jingle*

BETTY: And here is your number one DJ – that groovy, smoothie, swinging –

KEN W: Simon Dee –

HUGH: – Funct.

KEN W: Hello – Man: Waiter, there's a fly in my soup. Waiter: To get to the other side. That didn't go too well, eh, Terry? Still, must be good – can't be bad.

KENNETH: I beg your pardon?

KEN W: Well, it can't be any worse.

*Tape: 'Balls Pond Road is Wonderful'*

[BETTY: And now, the man who's always being rung – Jimmy Sponge.[1]

HUGH: Good morning, lovely housewives. Keep those requests coming even if I don't do what you suggest. And for those of you who tried last Tuesday's recipes – delicious, wasn't it? Sorry about that ptomaine poisoning but just lie back, try and forget the pain, and listen to Spig Jeans and The Stiffs 'At Twelve Twenty-Seven' . . .

CAST SINGS: 'Twelve Twenty-Seven'

KENNETH: That time was recorded. But now – *Nature Notes* with Daphne Whitethigh.

---

1. Based on the disc jockey, Jimmy Young.

BETTY: Hello. Well, spring is just around the corner and it's time for your early bloomers. If you have a stiff clay soil, top dress your mugwort and henbane, lop and poll your sequoias, and avoid moths and owls. If you're in a loamy or peaty area, block up disused mineshafts, sprinkle sparingly with a vitamin concentrate, and go to bed for twenty-four hours, stirring occasionally. Should the sun break through – spank him soundly and put him back in his cot. Speaking personally, my lawn's never been the same since I had my man sprinkle it with Instant Graunchex. But don't try it unless you <u>want</u> a patio ankle-deep in moribund worms. Next time I'll be telling you what to do with your old man's beard, and giving you the addresses of several good barbers.

KENNETH: Thank you, Daphne Whitethigh.]

This is the point in the show where we invite listeners to phone in with any queries or comments on topics of the moment. The Postmaster General has had a special hook-up, but what he does in his own time is his own affair. Ah, there's the phone now. *(Pause)* I said, there's the phone now. Well, it seems we're having a little technical difficulty . . .

*F/X: Phone rings – receiver up*

KENNETH: Hello –

KEN W: *(Slight distort)* I have a query regarding a member of your cast. Can Betty Marsden –

KENNETH: Yes – go on.

KEN W: That's all.

[KENNETH: If you send me a stamped addressed envelope, I'll send you a reply. If you send me a four and sixpenny postal order I'll send you Betty Marsden – you can find out for yourself.]

*F/X: Phone down*

*F/X: Phone rings – receiver up*

KENNETH: Hello –

HUGH: *(Slight distort) (Shy)* Me and my mates have been having an argument. Is C.P. Snow[2] the real mother of David Frost? I say yes, they say no.

KENNETH: It's not an easy question to answer, Mr. – er – what did you say your name was?

HUGH: Frost – David Frost.

*F/X: Phone rings*

KENNETH: That's my other phone –

*F/X: Receiver up*

KENNETH: Hello.

BETTY: *(Slight distort)* I'm answering your advertisement in *Posing Brief Quarterly*.

KENNETH: I think you've got the wrong number.

BETTY: *(Slight distort)* No. I've got the advertisement here. I'll read it. 'Mature sexy man about town wishes to meet petite young widow. Interested in photography, ballroom dancing and physical culture. Object . . .'

KENNETH: Well, I don't think we need to bore the listeners with all that.

BETTY: Well, I'm game.

---

2. British novelist and physicist who used the phrase 'the two cultures' to bemoan an absence of communication between artists and scientists.

[KENNETH: It's hard to tell on the phone whether you're the petite young widow or the mature man about town.

BETTY: I give this service to a number of gentlemen.]

KENNETH: Yes, I'm sure you are – but the – er – position's filled. Goodbye.

*F/X: Phone down*

KENNETH: [There's obviously been a mistake.] I wanted some keys cut. Funny – I wonder how she got my number?

KEN W: We've all got your number.

*F/X: Phone rings – receiver up*

KENNETH: Hello –

KEN W: *(Slight distort) (Heavy breathing)*

KENNETH: It's for you, Betty.

BETTY: *(Dramatically)* Is it a man?

KENNETH: Yes.

BETTY: Is he just breathing heavily over the phone?

KENNETH: Yes.

BETTY: Not saying anything? Just that infernal breathing?

KENNETH: Yes.

BETTY: *(Relieved)* Oh, that'll be the butcher. Tell him half a pound of stewing steak and some liver for the cat.

KENNETH: Did you get that?

KEN W: *(Breathes heavily)*

KENNETH: Yes, and the same to your good lady.

*F/X: Phone down*

KENNETH: Well, that's all the calls we've got time for this week, but if you've got anything you want to air – there's a cupboard on the landing. [And now I have beside me in the studio, Harvey Schmaltz, the theatrical agent who's had many a struggling young starlet through his hands.

HUGH: *(Harvey)* I've shown them the way, Kenny boy. But listen, listen, have I got hold of something!

KENNETH: Nothing of mine, as far as I can tell.

HUGH: No, no. I want you to hear about my latest discovery. A group, three boys an' a girl . . . or possibly three girls an' a boy, the way they look, who cares? Here's a photo of them. I tell you, they've got it!

KENNETH: It doesn't show.

HUGH: That <u>star</u> quality. You know me, I wouldn't give you a load of schlumpf!

KENNETH: That's true. You'd probably sell it to me.

HUGH: Believe you me, they're gonna start a rock revival.

KENNETH: You mean people will throw rocks at them?

HUGH: *(Unamused)* Oy, veh, you're a comical goyschmutter, Kenny boy. Look, can you use 'em on your programme next Saturday? It's important to me.

KENNETH: Why?

HUGH: That's the day they cut their first disc.

KENNETH: So?

HUGH: Well, I gotta keep 'em away from the recording studio somehow! They'll upset the session musicians

I've hired!]

*Orchestra: 'Balls Pond Road' link*

KENNETH: Here now is a man we'd all like to – he'd like to himself, but things being what they are, he's merely going to sing. Rambling Syd Rumpo, whom Dobbiroids preserve.

KEN W: Hello my dearios – here is a Sussex air about an old man who plays nick nacks in various places – and it goes after this fashion, brightly and with great nerve.

*Ken W sings with guitar accompaniment*

This old man, he plays one,
Plays nick nacks with a hot cross bun,
Nick nack ganderback
Give a dog a flute,
The old man whirdles like a newt.

*(Spoken)* They do, you know, when they get to a certain age, but what the eye don't see, the heart don't grieve over.

*(Sings)*

This old man, he plays two,
He plays nick nacks up the flue,
Nick nack ganderback
Give a dog a choc,
The old man nadgers round the clock.

*(Spoken)* Picturesque, isn't it?

*(Sings)*

This old man, he plays three,
He plays nick nacks for a fee.
Nick nack ganderback
Give a dog a punch,
The old man grunges after lunch.

*(Spoken)* You tend to after a heavy meal.

*(Sings)*

This old man, he plays four,

He plays nick nacks till he's sore.
Nick nack ganderback
Give a dog a kick –
The old man bogles with a pick.

*(Spoken)* I won't weary you with verses five, six, seven, eight or nine – sufficient to say that each verse gets more ethnic among other things, but eventually comes verse ten . . .

*(Sings)*

This old man, he plays ten,
See him trundling up Big Ben,
Nick Nack ganderback
Give a dog a bone,
If you want any more – you can woggle your own!

*(Applause)*

KENNETH: [Thanks for the offer, but I haven't woggled my own for years.] From time to time I clear those things out of my wardrobe that I don't really want. The milkman, several moths, a chap called Arbuthnot who appears to be a friend of my wife, and, of course, old clothes. Nobody will give you much for them, [particularly Arbuthnot, as he's been there since 1926 and now, I feel, is past his best.] So when a card was pushed through my door which read 'Bona Rags – we pay top prices for omes' left-offs', I called them up and the following morning they came round.

*F/X: Ring at doorbell*

KENNETH: The door's open – troll in.

HUGH: Oh, hello. I'm Julian and this is my friend, Sandy.

KEN W: Oh, hello, Mr. Horne, duck. We're gentlemen's misfits.

HUGH: He means we're interested in anything reasonable in gentlemen's clothing.

KEN W: We are the actual joint managing directors of Bona Used Clothing Limited. Branches in Queensway and Mincing Lane.

HUGH: Our motto – 'Before you throw it away, show it to us'.

KEN W: We may have an ome for it. For instance, that bundle of rags. It may seem a useless load of old tat, but we'll take it off you.

KENNETH: But it's the suit I'm wearing.

KEN W: Oh – if that's what he's hanging on to I'd dread to think of what he's throwing away.

HUGH: Let's have a vada at his zhush.

KENNETH: Clothing. Translator's note.

KEN W: Right – I'll just open the wardrobe. Here, look. *(Pause)*

KEN W AND HUGH: *(Laugh)*

HUGH: What a naff lot.

KEN W: Yes – it's a bit cod, isn't it.

HUGH: He never wears one of those!

KEN W: He does. You can tell by the bulge under his cardigan. Make a note, Jule. One gents' Edwardian foundation.

HUGH: Kinky.

KENNETH: If you want the correct name, it's a Bracerite Midriff Support.

HUGH: Is it? It's a bit Isherwood's Barlin if you ask me. Still, we'll give you half a crown.

KEN W: Yes – it's worth it for the scrap metal alone. Ooh – they're nice.

KENNETH: What?

KEN W: Those silver metallic high-heeled shoes. The ones with springs on them.

KENNETH: They're shoe trees.

KEN W: I thought they were a bit small in the ankle.

HUGH: Let's see what else there is. One gents' D.B. dinner jacket with contrasting skirt.

KENNETH: That's a kilt.

KEN W: Anything else, Jule?

HUGH: One moth-eaten Shetland tweed – and ooh, look, he's got a baggy old Harris.

KEN W: I'll say he has. Right, five bob the lot. Now, let's have a rummage through his drawers.

HUGH: Don't move.

KEN W: Why?

HUGH: There's something red and hairy lurking behind his socks.

KEN W: Oh, it's nasty! Hit it with the trouser press.

KENNETH: No, careful – that's – er – look, promise you won't tell anybody – that's my wig. I wear it for special occasions.

KEN W: Like Halloween? Put it down, Jule. One naff Irish.

HUGH: We don't want that, do we?

KEN W: Yes we do – it'll come in handy as a tea cosy. Or we can use it for wiping down the horse. And what are these?

KENNETH: My old rugby kit. I'll throw that in –

KEN W: Don't mention rugby to Jule. He's sworn never to touch a pair of rugby shorts again after what happened.

HUGH: You swore you'd never tell!

KEN W: Go on, tell him. Purge your soul.

HUGH: Well, when I was younger, I had a friend who was a Wasp.

KEN W: You mean Jock?

HUGH: Yes. He was a great butch ome with huge bulging lallies and an eek like a Greek god. We was in hairdressing school together. Any road, he used to play rugger on Saturdays and he asked me to make up the number one week. Everything went well till halfway through the match.

KENNETH: What happened?

HUGH: Well – I completely misunderstood the meaning of a forward pass.

KEN W: Don't worry, Jule. It's all eau under the pont now. That's your actual French. Now you feel better now you've told him, don't you, Jule?

HUGH: Yes, I feel I've purged myself. All right, we'll take the rugger kit and the suits.

KEN W: We'll take your entire wardrobe. Thirty shillings the lot.

KENNETH: Only thirty shillings?

KEN W: Tell you what – if you throw in that suit you're wearing we'll make it twenty-five bob.

KENNETH: Done. I know a bargain when I see one. And where will you dispose of the stuff? To distressed gentlefolk?

HUGH: No, there's no point in adding to their distress. We've got a different outlet, Mr. Horne.

KENNETH: Well, I'd like to know my cast-offs will go where they're appreciated.

KEN W: Oh, they will, Mr. Horne. You see, we've got a contract to supply the clowns at Bertram Mills Circus.

*Orchestra: Play-off*

KENNETH: I must say it makes me feel nostalgic every Christmas to see Bobo the clown slipping on a banana skin and falling on my Harris. Well, that's it, except for this week's motto, which is, 'Love is where you find it, if you know where to look.'

Cheerio. See you next week.

*Orchestra: Sig. tune – timp roll continues under*

DOUGLAS: That was *Round the Horne*, starring Kenneth Horne, with Kenneth Williams, Hugh Paddick and Betty Marsden. On the musical side you heard the Max Harris Group. The script was by Barry Took, Johnnie Mortimer and Brian Cooke, and Donald Webster, and the show was produced by John Simmonds.

*Orchestra: Sig. tune up and out*

*(Applause)*

*Orchestra: Play out*

*(Applause)*

# SERIES 4
# PROGRAMME 5

*FIRST BROADCAST* – Sunday 24 March 1968

## INTRODUCTION

Simon Dee (or Nicholas Henty-Dodd, as he was known to his parents) was, for a short time in the late Sixties, the most famous disc jockey and TV presenter in Britain. Ever since, he has been the most famous subject of 'Where are they now?' features in Britain. In this series, he has taken over from Eamonn Andrews as *Round the Horne*'s target-in-chief. It's not an entirely successful substitution; the character never really developed much beyond a single joke. Dee's main crimes, as far as the writers were concerned, seem to have been a big head, and a lack of comic timing so complete that it was almost impressive.

The film spoof is of the 1966 picture *Grand Prix*, which starred James Garner. This one, of course, stars Kenneth Horne, who denies that he is wearing a pink, shiny crash helmet. Jokes about Horne's supposed vanity (in real life, Barry Took remembers him as being reluctant to wear spectacles), and his undeniable baldness (which shows up surprisingly well on radio), provide plenty of opportunities for sharp exchanges throughout all four series – usually involving Kenneth Williams, either as himself or as various characters.

In the absence of the Fraser Hayes Four's soothing harmonies, in series 4 the cast fill in with renditions of sundry popular songs; suffice it to say that not even the most tone deaf listener would be likely to mistake the latter for the former. A good many of these ditties appear to have arisen in the greengrocery trade – cucumbers and marrows featuring prominently amongst their subject matter. Proof that in radio comedy, as in life, you gets what you pays for.

BETTY: Well, let's have the verdict. Have I got to have any out?

KEN W: *(Preoccupied dentist)* Hmmm? Yes, I think I'm going to have to extract that one. It's rotten.

BETTY: Oh, dear. That'll leave a gap.

KEN W: 'Fraid so. Can't be helped. If I leave it in, there may be trouble later. That one's going to have to come out too . . . and that one . . . and that one.

DOUGLAS: And now the producer has cut the lines he doesn't like, here is what's left of *Round the Horne*.

*Orchestra: Sig. tune*

KENNETH: Hello and welcome to the show. First, we're privileged to hear a short address from the Archbishop of Tring . . .

HUGH: *(Archbishop)* 105 Old Compton Street. Ring twice and ask for Colette.

KENNETH: Thank you, it's always useful to know where one can find a good chiropodist. [Now then, the results of last week's photo competition, in which we asked you to 'Guess Who They Belong To'. Well, as you might expect, the biggest one belonged to Sean Connery. The little tiny one belonged to Godfrey Winn[1] and I must confess the one in the middle was mine. It's a bit old now, but in its day it was the talk of the neighbourhood. Next week we'll ask you to guess the owners of three more motorcars. Forward, Smith.]

DOUGLAS: Sir. We continue with the latest in our 'Movie-Go-Wrong' series. This week a radio adaptation of a film that has recently been released, mainly

for lack of evidence. Horneographic Productions present a stirring story of racing cars and the daredevil men who drive them . . .

*Orchestra: Brief fanfare*

DOUGLAS: *Relatively Grand Prix!*

*Orchestra: Intro. music*

KENNETH: My name is Jones, and after some of the names I've been given in this series I can hardly believe my luck. My full name is . . . eh . . . Goosevestular Jones . . . oh, well. I build high-powered cars and race them. It's rather pointless, really, they always beat me.

*F/X: Grams: Motor racing in background: Keep under, then lose*

KENNETH: As our story opens, I'm standing in the pits at Silverstone. Beside me is the sleek, powerful brute with which my mechanic has been busy all night. My daughter, Wilhelmina.

BETTY: Oh, Daddy, we will win this race, if we just have faith! I know we will. Say you believe it too! Say we'll win! Say it!

KENNETH: I will if you like, but we haven't actually entered a car.

BETTY: Oh, Daddy, why not? Are you having trouble with blocked-up lubricating points again?

KENNETH: Not since I started taking the tablets, no. It's simply that the car isn't ready yet.

DOUGLAS: The scene shifts to 'Jones' Car Works'. Two mechanics work on a new racing car. One adjusts the gearbox, while the other is half-hidden under the long, green bonnet.

1. A camp columnist and pundit.

HUGH: *(Scots)* I wish ye wouldn'a wear that long, green bonnet. People are talkin' about ye.

KEN W: *(Young, keen)* Let them talk. One day I shall be a great racing driver! One day my name will be on everybody's lips!

HUGH: So ye say, young Filtertip. Now, get on with your work, or do I have to raise me sporran to ye again? Have ye tuned the engine?

KEN W: Of course. Listen . . .

*Orchestra: Musical notes rising in scale*

HUGH: D'ye call that tuning, ye young haggis? Your diminished B Natural is flat.

KEN W: It's the heat . . .

KENNETH: Ah, Jock, I've just returned from Silverstone. How are you getting on with my pride and joy?

HUGH: Well, yesterday I gave her a thorough going over . . . with an oily rag.

KEN W: He means the car, you fool, the car!

HUGH: Oh, that. Well, see for yourself.

DOUGLAS: I, Douglas Smith, am playing the car, hereafter known as the 'Douglas Smith Special'. I mention this for my many admirers, particularly, perhaps, Mrs. Jocasta Tweed of Peckham. Thank you for your charming letter and the Fair Isle sock. It was delicious.

KENNETH: Oh, get on with it, Smith.

DOUGLAS: Sir. I stand over the inspection pit, my well-waxed body gleaming. I have just been fully serviced by Mister Williams.

KENNETH: Good for you. All we need now is a driver for the big race at Marital, in the South of France. Everybody is interested in the *Prix Marital*.

DOUGLAS: That pun is the official entry for Britain in the Eurovision 'Most Contrived Joke Of The Year' contest.

KEN W: Oh, let me do it, sir! I can do it, honestly I can. I've often done it when nobody was looking . . . all round the garage and out into the street, sometimes.

KENNETH: You, young Jimmy? Drive at Marital? It's a tricky and skilful course.

KEN W: I'm tricky . . . and skilful . . . and coarse.

KENNETH: Very well. I'll give you a quick test on your knowledge of the car. What's the technical term for this?

KEN W: A wheel.

KENNETH: And this?

KEN W: A wheel.

KENNETH: And this?

KEN W: A wheel.

KENNETH: And this?

KEN W: A jam doughnut.

KENNETH: No, it's another wheel, actually. Still, three out of four isn't bad. You can drive in the *Prix Marital*!

*Orchestra: Link*

*F/X: Racing car engines revving up in background*

KENNETH: This is your big chance, Jimmy, but look out for Enrico Lasagne, the big Italian. He'll try to get on your tail.

KEN W: I'll watch it. I'll win this race, sir, not just for you, sir, but also for Miss Wilhelmina, your daughter, whom I have long worshipped from a distance . . . assisted by powerful binoculars.

KENNETH: I see. And how does <u>she</u> feel?

KEN W: I haven't had the chance to find out yet. If I win this race I shall go to her and press my suit.

KENNETH: I should press your suit <u>before</u> you go, if I were you. Incidentally, where is she?

HUGH: *(Scots mechanic)* Mr. Jones! The Italian driver is under the starter's flag, and Miss Wilhelmina is under there with him!

KEN W: *(Bitterly)* Oh, this is too much! For years I've watched her giving her favours to other men. And she doesn't even know I'm <u>there</u>! At least, I hope she doesn't.

HUGH: Never mind her, ye've a job to do. Get into the Douglas Smith Special and warm him up.

KEN W: You're right.

DOUGLAS: Vrooom, vrooom . . .

KEN W: I've got him going.

DOUGLAS: Vrooom, vrooom, vrooom . . .

KEN W: His bucket seat's comfy, I'll say that.

DOUGLAS: Vrooom, vrooom . . .

KENNETH: Young Filtertip selected his gear . . . a fetching duck-egg blue overall with lemon yellow driving gloves . . . and drove off to the starting line. My daughter approached.

BETTY: *(Coming on)* Oh, Daddy, surely <u>you're</u> not driving? Why are you wearing a shiny pink crash helmet?

KENNETH: I'm not.

BETTY: Oh, sorry.

HUGH: Yon young mechanic is driving. By heavens, he's got pluck. Ye've got to hand it to him.

BETTY: I haven't got to do anything of the sort.

F/X: *(Off) racing cars starting up*

KENNETH: *(Over above)* There goes the starter's flag! They're away!

F/X: *Very brief burst of racing cars*

KENNETH: And he's won!

BETTY: Eh?

KENNETH: It's a tricky course, but quite short. Ah, here he comes.

KEN W: I've done it! I've done it!

HUGH: Aye, ye've done it . . . in the seat of the Douglas Smith Special, too.

BETTY: Here, Jimmy, take the laurel wreath, the hardy wreath, and this large silver cup for your sideboard!

KEN W: Let us fill it with champagne!

KENNETH: Good idea. So we filled his sideboard with champagne and I toasted his victory from a brimming cutlery drawer. Here's to many more such races!

*Orchestra: Brief rising link*

DOUGLAS: Monaco!

F/X: *Roar of racing cars in background: Keep under*

BETTY: Oh, Jock, it's close, it's close, it's desperately close!

HUGH: I do beg your pardon, Miss.

BETTY: Jimmy's only half a lap ahead. He's . . . he's coming in for a pit stop!

*F/X: Racing car drawing up and stopping*

KEN W: Oil! Oil! I need more oil!

HUGH: Here y'are, Jimmy.

KEN W: Oh, that's better, my hair was blowing all over the place.

*Orchestra: Brief rising link*

DOUGLAS: Nurburgring!

*F/X: Roar of racing cars in background: Keep under*

BETTY: Oh, Daddy, look! Jimmy's got his nose in front!

KENNETH: Well, most of us <u>have</u>.

BETTY: I think he's going to pull it off! Wait! He's slewing all over the track!

KENNETH: Yes, that may well get him disqualified. No, no . . . he's heading for the finishing line.

BETTY: He's passed it! He's passed it!

HUGH: *(Self)* I've often thought that myself.

*Orchestra: Final brief rising link*

KENNETH: As success followed success, young Jimmy changed. There was something different about him. I couldn't put my finger on it . . . indeed, I didn't <u>want</u> to put my finger on it . . . but he wasn't the same shy lad.

KEN W: Call this a hotel? I put my boots out last night and they haven't been licked properly! And another thing, these autograph hunters . . . I'm sick and tired of having to run up and down the corridors. Put them in one place, where I can catch them easily.

BETTY: Oh, Jimmy, Jimmy, I think it's going to your head.

KEN W: What is?

BETTY: This vase, if you go on like that. What happened to that shy, freckle-faced, snub-nosed little fellow we all liked?

KEN W: He's in the wardrobe.

HUGH: Aye, I'm sortin' through some of his old socks. He wants 'em framed and presented to the nation. Och, ye've changed, Jimmy lad, ye've changed, but judgin' by these socks, not often enough.

[BETTY: Oh, come, come, Jock, he's not really conceited at heart, are you, Jimmy? Say you aren't. Let's kiss and make up.

KEN W: Oh, very well . . . Here.

BETTY: I'm not kissing your <u>foot</u>!

KEN W: Please yourself, your loss . . .]

*Orchestra: Link*

KENNETH: As a successful Grand Prix driver, young Jimmy was the toast of the continent. He was seen at the gayest parties. He began to give himself airs . . . he grew a moustache, for instance. *(Amused aside)* Give himself airs! He fell in with loose women . . .

*F/X: Loud splash*

KENNETH: The hectic pace began to affect his performance in the one thing he really cared about, and his driving suffered too. He lost race after race.

DOUGLAS: Speaking as the Douglas Smith Special, sir, I do resent his crude handling lately. [I'm as ready to give my all as the next racing car, but I must be coaxed, not bullied.]

KENNETH: Quite.

DOUGLAS: He doesn't give me a chance to warm up. He's got no consideration. And another thing, he takes so many chances. He never wears a crash helmet or anything.

KENNETH: I'll speak to him about it.

KEN W: Oh, what a fool I've been! Looking back, I see where I went wrong, I see it all!

KENNETH: Oh?

KEN W: *(Self)* Yes. I should have played that Douglas Smith's part. He got more laughs than I did.

KENNETH: Never mind that, if we don't win a big race soon, my company will go bankrupt. We'll have to change the name from 'Jones' Car Works' to Jones' Car Doesn't Work'.

KEN W: I'll do it, sir, I'll do it. Enter me for the big race next week!

*Orchestra: Quick link*

*F/X: Crowd hubbub and racing car zooming past: Keep under*

HUGH: He's doing it! By the great hairy legs of Flora MacDonald! He's up among the leaders!

BETTY: He's pulling away . . . into the straight . . . he's won!

*F/X: Crowd cheers: Racing car drawing up and stopping*

KEN W: I did it, Mr. Jones, sir. I won for you!

KENNETH: Well done, Filtertip. This will go down in racing history. The day the Douglas Smith Special, driven by you, beat every horse in the Derby!

*Orchestra: Sketch pay-off*

KENNETH: So much for this week's production. Next week, we'll be showing you something which deeply impressed our leading film critic and had him sitting on the edge of his seat. Yes, it's a broken spring.

And now let's roll back the carpet and see what that smell is under the floorboards. Why, it's a medley of old songs, rendered – in rather the same way as you render fat – by the *Round the Horne* Spondling Chorale.

ALL: *Song medley* 'A Nice Cup Of Tea'

HUGH:

I like a nice cup of tea in the morning,
For to start the day, you see,
And at half-past eleven,
Well, my idea of heaven
Is a nice cup of tea.
I like a nice cup of tea with my dinner,
And a nice cup of tea with my tea –
And when it's time for bed,
There's a lot to be said
For a nice cup of tea.

*(Applause)*

'A Little Bit Of Cucumber'

KENNETH:

I was weaned on cucumber, and on my wedding day,
Sitting down to supper when the guests had gone away,
My old darling said to me:

BETTY:

You must be hungry, Joe! What is it you fancy?

KENNETH:

I said, Fancy! Don't you know?
I like pickled onions, I like piccalilli,
Pickled cabbage is all right
With a bit of cold meat on Sunday night.
I can go termatoeses, but what I do prefer –
Is a little bit of cu-cum-cu-cum-cu-cum –

Little bit of cucumber.
Several years of married life have
  brought me lots of joys,
I don't know how many girls, I think
  it's fourteen boys.
When the last one came to town it
  nearly turned my head.
It was marked with a cucumber,
And the first words that it said . . .
  were . . .

BETTY:

I like pickled onions, I like piccalilli,
Pickled cabbage is all right
With a bit of cold meat on a Sunday
  night.
I can go termartoeses, but what I do
  prefer –
Is a little bit of cu-cum-cu-cum-cu-
  cum –
Little bit of cucumber.

*(Applause)*

'The Marrow Song'

KEN W:

(1) Down the road there lives a man
  I'd like you all to know,
He grew a great big marrow for the
  local Flower Show;
When the story got around they came
  from far and wide,
And when the people saw the marrow,
  everybody cried:

CHORUS:

Oh, what a beauty! I've never seen
  one as big as that before,
Oh, what a beauty! It must be two
  feet long or even more
It's such a lovely colour, and nice and
  round and fat,
I never thought a marrow could grow
  as big as that,
Oh, what a beauty! I've never seen
  one as big as that before.

(2) He was leaning on the garden gate

the other day
And beckon'd to a lady who lives just
  across the way.
Took her down the garden path and
  show'd it her with pride,
And when she saw the size of it, the
  little lady sighed –

*(Chorus as above)*

DOUGLAS: Now for twelve solid hours
of imitation commercial breaks –
fasten your seat belts and stuff in your
earplugs – it's Radio Balls Pond Road!

*Orchestra: Jingle*

BETTY: It's your number one DJ –
from a great height – swingy, ring-a-
ding-dingy –

KEN W: Simon Dee –

HUGH: – cayed.

KEN W: Hi there. A man came rushing
into a pub. Said to the landlord: 'Tell
me, are there any penguins round
here?' Landlord says: 'No, sir.' Man
says: 'Then I've just run over a
chocolate biscuit.' Er – is it my <u>timing</u>
that's wrong?

KENNETH: Yes – you shouldn't have
got up.

*Tape: 'Balls Pond Road Is Wonderful'*

[BETTY: And at the number two spot,
slaving over a hot turntable – Jimmy
Sponge!

HUGH: Good morning, swingers.
Sitting solidly at the bottom of the
charts this week it's Bread Pudding.
The Sponge-cake is rising fast, but the
Pink Icing is sure to top it. And here,
in person, is Mrs. Twinge of Wembley
with a dish for me. Why, it's custard
pie!

*F/X: Splosh*

HUGH: *(Sings thickly)* They try to tell

me I'm Jim Sponge.

*Tape: 'Jimmy Sponge Is Wonderful'*

KENNETH: And now, direct from Aucherlocherty, your friend and guide – Patience McGodfrey. Welcome, Miss McGodfrey.

BETTY: Thank you, thank you, Mr. Horne. Wat a lovely waird that is – 'welcome'. Aye . . .

''Twill bring a glow to ev'ry heart, If that's the way you make a start.'

KENNETH: Yes. And what rays of joy can you flash from your beacon this week?

BETTY: Och – <u>hope</u>! Hope for all those in need or trouble, especially this week for those wives whose husbands batter them about the head, in Dundee.

KENNETH: A touching reminder that the world is not all that it should be.

BETTY: Och, bless you – no!

'A humble home is all we ask, Where we can lend to every task A feeling of felicity, Mid scenes of domesticity.'

KENNETH: Very proper.

BETTY: And what a wonderful waird 'proper' is, to be sure!

'It makes my heart rejoice and burn To hear such a delightful term.'

I'll just clear my throat *(Rasp)*. It's the London air – so unlike the liquid of the glens.

'When all your life seems grey and love's asleep, When woes and troubles pile up heap on heap, When black depression wears a troubled brow, And all the universe seems empty now; When ogres grim and spectres vile attack, And foul lumbago grips your luckless back – When storm and clouds are all that you can see, Take Doctor Snoddie's Stimulex, BP.'

KENNETH: Thank you . . .

BETTY: . . .

'Available from Glasgow to Glenshiels – Three times a day with water, after meals.'

KENNETH: Thank you again, Miss McGodfrey. Next week she will be offering comfort to all those who have to watch Jean Morton and the Tree House family. And now an appeal. We should like you to collect and parcel up any of the following: old waistcoats, frayed fragments of hessian, lengths of old clothes line, dented plastic ducks, cleansed sardine tins, pieces of burnt or musty toast, holey vests, etc., and post them COD to Tony Blackburn, c/o BBC1.]

This is the point in our show where we invite listeners to phone in with any queries or comments on topics of the moment.

*F/X: Phone rings. Receiver up.*

KENNETH: Hello.

BETTY: *(Distort)* Hello. Would you be Jimmy Young?

KENNETH: No, would you?

BETTY: Not for a million pounds. You're Kenneth Horne, aren't you?

KENNETH: Yes.

BETTY: Can you answer a question about one of the cast of your show?

KENNETH: I'll try.

BETTY: Well, my question is this. Is Kenneth Williams the same person that I knew once in Houndsditch? He had long blond ringlets, little apple cheeks and wore the cutest little romper suit – and wouldn't be parted from his ragged old teddy bear that he always called Sebastian. He always used to sit on my knee and call me Nana.

KENNETH: How long ago was this, Nana?

BETTY: Last Tuesday.

F/X: *Phone down*

KEN W: It's a disgrace.

F/X: *Phone rings*

KENNETH: Ah, that's my other phone.

F/X: *Receiver up*

KENNETH: Hello –

HUGH: *(Distort)* I'm phoning to complain about the filth on radio and television – it seems that all you people think about up there is sex. It's all right for you theatricals but what about us decent ordinary people? We've had enough of sex and I'm not just speaking for myself but for my wife and forty-three children.

F/X: *Phone down*

KENNETH: That Basil Brush has a lot to answer for.

F/X: *Phone rings. Receiver up*

KENNETH: Hello – Horne here.

KEN W: *(Distort)* I know you but you don't know me.

KENNETH: That's an arrangement that suits me perfectly.

KEN W: I know where you were last Friday night. I have photographs of you with the feathers and an incriminating tape recording of you and the french loaf – and I know all about Purley and the dance on the mirrors. I even have a piece of salami as evidence. I know all about you and I shall tell what I know – I shall hound you remorselessly – unless we can come to some financial arrangement.

KENNETH: But this is blackmail.

KEN W: Call it what you like.

KENNETH: All right. This is Ipecacuanha[2], and Ipecacuanha is an ugly word.

KEN W: *(Own voice)* Well, how about Crêpe de Chine then, that's prettier.

KENNETH: All right, this is Crêpe de Chine, but you'll never get away with it. It clashes with your eyes.

KEN W: Oh, does it, Mr. Clever dick Horne? Unless the money is left in the usual place next Sunday morning, I shall nark to the rozzers.

KENNETH: Don't worry, there'll be an extra two shillings in the plate, and thank you for calling, Vicar.

[KEN W: *(Normal)* A pleasure! We're here to help.]

F/X: *Phone down*

KENNETH: Well, that's all the calls we have time for, but don't forget, if you have any queries – don't bother us – we've got enough of our own. But now a man whose work has been spread over many fields: it's double-yield Rambling Syd Rumpo.

---

2. *Cephaelis ipecacuanha* is a low-growing South American rubiaceous shrub, or a purgative and emetic made from the dried roots of same. Just thought you'd want to know.

KEN W: Hello my deario – since we last met I have been where few men have been and see what few men have seen – and got off with a five pounds fine. And my air this week tells something of my peregrinations. It goes jauntily but painfully.

*Ken W: Sings with guitar accompaniment to the tune of 'Strawberry Fair'*[3]

As I was going to Goosenadgers Fair,
Singing, singing, loomers on my
    possett, I met a maiden trundling a
    bear –
Fol de ree.
Her bogles were blue and they jangled
    about
Till the grunge on my cordwangle
    nearly fell out.
Singing, singing, nadger Julie Felix
Singing, singing, riddle Simon Dee.

Kind sir pray woggle my gimp if you
    can,
Singing, singing, loomers on my
    possett.
For you, I can see, are a free scroping
    man –
Fol de ree.
So I woggled her gimp till her welkin
    rang,
And as I woggled this tune I sang . . .

*(Spoken)* It's a good trick if you can do it.

*(Sung)*

Airy Fairy Peter Paul and Mary –
Airy Fairy whirdle Simon Dee.

KENNETH: And so say all of us. The other day I was leafing through my copy of the *Lady Wrestlers' Home Journal* – I buy it for the fat stock prices – and I noticed this advertisement which said – 'Bona

Male Model Agency. New eeks wanted.' I thought I'd give it a try – after all, my manhood is burgeoning and besides pin money is always handy. So I decided to pop down to their address in Chelsea. The sign on the door said 'Knock and troll gracefully in'. So I knocked and trolled.

*F/X: Knock and door open*

KENNETH: Hello – is there anybody there?

HUGH: Oh hello – I'm Julian and this is my friend Sandy.

KEN W: Oh hello. Why, it's Mr. Horne.

KENNETH: I'd like to register with you.

HUGH: Well, you won't looking like that.

KEN W: What's that you're wearing? A fun fur?

KENNETH: No, as a matter of fact it's an angora cardigan. It stretched in the wash.

KEN W: Well, you'll have to drag yourself up if you want to join our clientele. All our models are hand-picked.

HUGH: Through these portals have minced England's top male models. We trained Conrad Montfalcon.

KENNETH: I don't think I know the name.

HUGH: You must have seen him – does a lot of advertising work now – you seen that one where this great butch ome's on a building site and he's squatting there with his mates, rolling his own – well, that's Conrad.

---

3. Anthony Newley had been in the charts in 1960 with 'Strawberry Fair'. It was a different version, mind.

KEN W: Well, not all of him – it's his hands in the close-up. And it's his hands in that commercial – where they're pouring disinfectant down the sink – and it's his hands that stay as soft as your face. His hands have been everywhere.

HUGH: There's not an ome in the country who is not familiar with Conrad's hands.

KEN W: 'Course, he hasn't always been Conrad Montfalcon. We give him that name. When we first knew him he was just plain Wally.

HUGH: Wally McWhirter.

KEN W: It was very romantic how we first met him. Tell him about it, Jule.

HUGH: I don't like to – it's very hurtful looking back.

KEN W: Go on . . .

HUGH: Well, it is.

KEN W: Unburden yourself, Jule – bring it out in the open.

HUGH: It would never have happened if I'd had the change.

KENNETH: I'm afraid I don't quite follow.

HUGH: Change – for the milkman. That's what he was once, Conrad. I didn't have change for a pound – and he came round to my lattie for his Christmas box.

KEN W: So Jule invited him in while he raided his sixpenny bottle.

HUGH: Then I saw him – stood there on me half-landing – highlighted in the rays of the morning sun – and I could see his great possibilities.

KEN W: And of course the rest is history. We groomed him and trained him and now he's England's top male model.

HUGH: He's left us now –

KEN W: But what we did for him we can do for you.

KENNETH: But surely my possibilities are not as great as his?

KEN W: Don't run yourself down, heartface. Admittedly, you haven't got the fashionable flat-chested look.

HUGH: Nor the Pre-Raphaelite eek.

KEN W: You can say that again – he's more your Goya's *Horrors of War* – still, he's got something.

HUGH: He has. Something.

KEN W: Let's see you walk up and down.

KENNETH: Like this?

KEN W: No, no. Mince tall.

HUGH: And pull in your stomach – or whatever that bulge is.

KEN W: Let's see them hips go – ducky, you've got 'em, use 'em.

HUGH: Now, look haughty.

KEN W: Wet your lips . . .

HUGH: Smoulder . . .

KENNETH: Well, what do you think?

KEN W: Well, frankly, ducky – it's a bit Hildegarde Naph[4].

KENNETH: Aren't I any good for TV commercials?

KEN W: Hm. We might pass you off as the pea that can't get into the packet. Go on, Jule, you show him.

---

4. Hildegarde Neff was a film star.

Look at the way he trolls up and down. Vada that insolent eek – like a thoroughbred.

KENNETH: A thoroughbred what?

KEN W: Look, he's freaking out. Now he's freaking back in again – what a mover. He's a grand little mover, Mr. Horne. Faster, faster – now, do you think you could learn to do what he's doing?

KENNETH: What, split the seams of my trousers?

KEN W: Now turn, Jule. Watch him, Mr. Horne. He's on the turn. Beautiful. Fantabulosa!

HUGH: We'll have you walking like that in a few weeks, Mr. Horne.

KENNETH: Will you?

HUGH: Yes, well, you can hardly avoid it when you're wearing leather trousers.

KEN W: Now, do you want to sign on?

KENNETH: Hm. Well, do you think I should?

KEN W: Well, if you don't, we haven't got a tag for the sketch.

KENNETH: All right – I'll sign.

HUGH: Oh, no, don't sign 'Kenneth Horne'.

KENNETH: Why not?

HUGH: The name's not right. You'll want something more classy if you're going to be a male model.

KENNETH: What do you suggest?

KEN W: Something with a bit of glamour about it – like Garbo.

HUGH: Garbo Horne? No.

KEN W: Well, Jean Harlow, then.

HUGH: We can't call him Jean.

KEN W: No, Harlow –

HUGH: Harlow Horne – hm, it's got something. Horne's not right.

KEN W: What about thingy – that ome with Twiggy. What's his name? – Justin.

HUGH: Yes, him – Justin de Aston Villa.

KEN W: Aston Villa – Bossa nova – No, I'm wrong. Villeneuve.

KENNETH: It's a bit French for me – I'm backing Britain.

KEN W: Well, in that case our money's on Tristan da Cunha.

KENNETH: Well, couldn't you Anglicize it?

KEN W: Yes, all right. Let's see. Neuve is new.

HUGH: Ville is town.

KEN W: So there we are – that's your name now.

KENNETH: What is?

KEN W: Harlow New Town

*Orchestra: Play-off*

*(Applause)*

KENNETH: I didn't adopt it. I mean, if you're going to change your name to that of a place you might as well pick somewhere you feel at home. That's what I've done – so don't forget, tune in next week to the next episode of *Round the Leighton Buzzard*.

Cheerio – see you – rural district council permitting – next week.

*Orchestra: Sig. tune – timp roll continues under*

DOUGLAS: That was *Round the Horne*, starring Kenneth Horne, with Kenneth Williams, Hugh Paddick and Betty Marsden. The music was provided by the Max Harris Group, and the script was by Barry Took, Johnnie Mortimer and Brian Cooke, and Donald Webster. The show was produced by John Simmonds.

*Orchestra: Sig. tune up and out*

*(Applause)*

*Orchestra: Play out*

# SERIES 4
# PROGRAMME 8

*FIRST BROADCAST* – Sunday 14 April 1968

## INTRODUCTION

Inaudible in print is the ovation which by now always greets Rambling Syd Rumpo's entry – not to mention the waves of laughter which frequently force him to pause in his recitation, or else risk losing the next line under the cachinnations provoked by the previous one.

There's yet more painful singing in this week's Julian and Sandy sketch. If Rambling Syd caused the Paris Studio to echo with hilarity, that's nothing compared to what happens now. Almost every line is greeted with guffaws, as Williams and Paddick harvest the cumulative goodwill of three years' worth of perfect scripts and inspired performances. If ever fictional characters could be said to have taken on a life of their own, it's surely Jules and Sand.

Now, it's Horne who struggles just a little to ride the laughs, while an ad-libbing Williams ('Go on, come right out with it, love!') teases him with a straight face. Well, a straight face by Williams' standards anyway.

Sometimes the laughter of those audience members who are in the know – the 'Williams claque' which some listeners and BBC executives found so troubling – seems tinged with disbelief. Did they *really* just hear Sand describe Jules on national radio, on a Sunday lunchtime in 1968, as 'a miracle of dexterity at the cottage upright'?

Barry Took has said that the question he is most often asked about *Round the Horne* is 'How on earth did you get away with it?' In part at least, the answer must be that those who might have censored jokes about cottage uprights didn't do so simply because they didn't understand them. After all, in the previous decade the Goons had got away with introducing a character named Hugh Jampton, on the same basis of 'what they don't know can't hurt them'.

HUGH: *(American) (Off: As through megaphone)* Okay, Polowski! We know you're in there! Come on out!

KEN W: *(American: Calling)* You're gonna have to come in and get me! Keep away! Keep away! *(Near breaking point)* I never had a break, I tell ya! I was born on the wrong side of the tracks! We were so poor I had to wear my sister's cast-offs . . . I was dragged up in the slums! What've I ever got out of life? Reform school . . . prison . . . every man's hand turned against me! *(Sobs)*

HUGH: *(Still off)* This is your last chance, Polowski!

KEN W: *(A broken man)* Okay . . . Okay . . . I'm comin' out!

*F/X: Door opens*

KEN W: *(Normal)* I dunno why you can't wait your turn. I've only been in there ten minutes!

DOUGLAS: Ladies and gentlemen, [due to circumstances beyond our control,] it's *Round the Horne*!

*Orchestra: Sig. tune*

KENNETH: Hello and welcome to the show. First, a motoring flash. On the Great North Road a lorry loaded with strawberries has collided with a tanker full of cream. A police spokesman on the spot said 'Delicious'!

Now, your letters. A Mister or Miss P.J. Gripe of Wallasey writes in to say that he or she has a problem. And in all honesty I can't disagree.

A Mr. Groinwhippet of Leith sends a postcard telling me he's had a piece of bacon sticking out of his ear for several years and wants to know if it can be cured. I enjoyed that! *(Laugh)*

[Next, a charming letter simply signed

'A Well-Wisher', expressing the wish that I jump down a well, and finally a long and detailed letter from a Miss Bubbles La Rouge that really moved me. I changed my address the moment I got it.]

And now, spreading straight from the fridge but retaining ninety-nine per cent of household germs, it's Douglas Smith! Forward, Smith.

DOUGLAS: Sir. This week's film adaptation. Direct from a waste paper basket at the British Board of Film Censors, Horneographic Productions proudly, not to say impertinently, present . . .

*Orchestra: Fanfare*

DOUGLAS: *Around The World In Ten Minutes*!

KENNETH: Eh?

DOUGLAS: It's an edited version, sir.

*Orchestra: Around The World-type music*

KENNETH: The setting . . . London, under Victoria. A peaceful place, except when the trains run overhead. As our story opens, it's a bright sunny day. My name is Phineas Figg . . .

DOUGLAS: It was Fogg in the original version, sir.

KENNETH: Well, it's a bright sunny day in ours, Smith. I live alone, apart from my manservant, whose name is Passepartout . . .

KEN W: They call me that 'cos I spend a lot of me time round the pictures. I am a gentleman's gentleman. Will you be dinin' in tonight, Mr. Figg? Shall I lay on your dinner?

KENNETH: I'd rather you didn't. It does tend to bruise the Brussels sprouts. No, I'm off to the club for a game of cards, Passepartout.

KEN W: Right then, I'll call you a horse-drawn music link.

*Orchestra: Horse-drawn music link*

BETTY: Good afternoon, Mr. Figg. Let me take your hat, your cloak . . . *(With increasing intensity)* Your jacket . . . your waistcoat . . . your shirt . . . your trousers . . . your vest . . . your underpants . . . your flannelette kidney pad . . . your socks . . . your cornplaster . . . your spectacles . . .

KENNETH: Thank you, Albert.

BETTY: Perhaps you'd better have your spectacles back.

KENNETH: I went straight to the gaming room and purchased a hundred guineas' worth of chips. Well, I hadn't had much breakfast.

HUGH: Ah, Figg! There you are.

KENNETH: Ah, my old friend Alistair Chitwitherington-Ponsonby-Fitzpasture-Macmurdoch.

HUGH: Er, no, I'm Jones, actually. I say, Figg, I've just dropped a packet on the gaming table.

KENNETH: By Jove, how embarrassing for you.

HUGH: Quite. Are you coming into the card room? [I was thinking of having a rubber of brudge.

KENNETH: Brudge? No, no, it should be 'i', not 'u'.

HUGH: All right. You have a rubber of brudge and I'll watch.]

KENNETH: I don't think so, Jones. I'm bored with card games. No, what I want is something new to gamble on.

HUGH: New, eh? Tell you what, I'll bet you a shilling you can't run round this room in five seconds!

KENNETH: It wouldn't make much of a plot, would it?

HUGH: I see your point. Very well, then, a thousand guineas that you can't go round the world in eighty days!

KENNETH: Done! I hurried home to prepare for my historic journey. Passepartout! You and I are going to see distant places. We're going round the world!

KEN W: You mean, like Chichester?

KENNETH: Yes, and possibly even more exotic places than that!

KEN W: Cor! Round the world!

DOUGLAS: At this point, I, Douglas Smith, tackle my most testing role to date. I play the world. And I'll tell you this, it'll take Mr. Williams more than eighty days to get round me!

KEN W: Pig.

KENNETH: That'll do, Williams. You're sure you can manage this part, Smith? The world?

DOUGLAS: Oh, yes, sir, I've done it before. I played it in *The Day the Earth Caught Fire*. They force-fed me with curry powder for three weeks.

KENNETH: Splendid. Then let's go!

*Orchestra: Stirring link: Ending in balloon music*

KENNETH: A few days later found us drifting in a balloon high above the Alps. I knew it was the Alps because my manservant kept shouting . . .

KEN W: *(Off: Shouting)* Alp! Alp! Alp!

KENNETH: I'd flung him out of the basket in mistake for a sandbag.

KEN W: *(Coming on: Breathless)* Oh . . . oh . . . that was a bit of luck. I caught my plastic dickie in the wickerwork.

KENNETH: Good. Wait a moment, I think we're beginning to lose height! Yes . . . quick, Passepartout, put something over the side . . . not <u>that</u>, something a bit heavier!

KEN W: Too late! We're going to hit the ground!

*F/X: Heavy basket landing*

KENNETH: I managed to jump clear at the last moment, but unfortunately I broke a leg. It belonged to Passepartout, he was underneath me.

KEN W: Oh, my leg . . . my leg . . . it's broken! You'll have to put a cast on it.

KENNETH: A cast? Right . . . Smith, Paddick, Betty . . . get on his leg!

KEN W: *(Sourly)* Don't bother, I'll manage. I say, Mr. Figg, look, coming towards us, a Swiss milkmaid [carrying a yoke.

BETTY: *(Swedish – coming on quickly)* There was a yocular yewish yentleman whose car broke down near a farmhouse . . .

KENNETH: Don't tell me, I've heard it. Never with a Swedish accent in Switzerland, but I've heard it.] I say, miss, my servant and I are going round the world. What's the quickest way from here?

BETTY: Well, you veer right as far as Austria, left through Yugoslavia, take the first turning past Russia and then you'd better ask again.

KENNETH: Thank you. We left her and were fortunate enough to get a lift to Istanbul.

*F/X: Very brief hum of lift: clang of doors opening*

HUGH: *(Dentures)* Sixth floor. Ladies toiletries, electrical accessories, soft furnishings, reconditioned bicycles and Istanbul!

KENNETH: Thanks for the lift.

HUGH: It was a pleasure.

KENNETH: So this is Istanbul, city of glamour and mystery. Have you ever been here before, Passepartout?

KEN W: Only when I played the Ottoman Empire. But now we must obtain transport to continue our journey. Let's try in here, 'Sultan's Harem and Second-hand Car Hire, Ltd.'

*F/X: Door opened*

*Orchestra: Soft harem music: Carry under and lose*

BETTY: Hello, strangers, I am Fatima . . . I used to be Thinema, but they turned me into a bowling alley.

KENNETH: Quite.

BETTY: Here in this harem we have almost forgotten what a man looks like. Can either of you two girls remind us?

KEN W: Cheeky cat!

KENNETH: Actually, we're men.

BETTY: Then you must flee! We are guarded by a fearsome eunuch who misses nothing!

KEN W: Oh, he <u>must</u> do.

BETTY: Too late. Here he comes.

HUGH: *(Coming on: Self)* Mr. Horne, I positively refuse to play this part. After all, I have got my principles.

KENNETH: Yes, that does make it

difficult for you . . . But you'll do it, Hugh . . . I know you will. Because you're a trouper, because the show must go on, because I have photographs of you with the stick of celery and the bolsters . . .

HUGH: I'll do it . . . give me my cue line again.

BETTY: Here he comes!

HUGH: *(High-pitched)* Aha!

*F/X: Gunshot*

KENNETH: We shot him. It was the kindest thing to do.

HUGH: *(Going off: Piqued: Self)* It was hardly worth putting the baggy trousers on for!

BETTY: You must flee! Take this hubble-bubble car and continue your journey round the world.

*Orchestra: Brief rising link*

DOUGLAS: Across my trackless wastes they went. By car over parts of me that no man had ever seen before, by boat across the vast bosom of my oceans, by yak across my back, by punt across my front . . . but I care naught, I spin lazily on my axis at an angle of sixty-six degrees.

KEN W: *(Self)* Yes, we all know your inclination.

KENNETH: Where are we now, Smith?

DOUGLAS: You've just gone through my Khyber Pass travelling on a camel, sir.

KENNETH: Then we're in India.

HUGH: *(Pukka Sahib)* Hello. Colonel Haunchblast, Indian Army. [Care for a chota-peg?

KENNETH: Thank you. I hung my chota on it.]

HUGH: I'd like you to meet the Maharajah of Randibint.

KEN W: *(Indian Maharajah)* Greetings. I am the Maharajah. [I wear a ruby in my navel, an Ethel in my turban and a string of Gladyses round my neck.]

KENNETH: I'm Phineas Figg and this is my manservant, Passepartout.

KEN W: *(Passepartout)* We are travelling round the world, camping where we may . . . *(Self)* Quick change of voice to Maharajah. *(As Maharajah)* I will offer you transport to continue your journey. You may borrow my elephant, Fido. Here he comes now . . .

KENNETH: We leapt up and clung to the great flapping ears.

KEN W: *(Maharajah)* Let go my ears! He won't hurt you!

KENNETH: The incredible journey continued. [We got on well with the Burmese and the Malays, but there was an ugly incident with the Thais – we were thrown out of a restaurant for not wearing any. On we pressed.] Where would we arrive next?

*Grams: Snatch of 'Hawaiian Serenade'*

KENNETH: Ah yes, the Kalahari Desert.

KEN W: *(Calling hoarsely)* Water . . . water!

KENNETH: Across the Indian Ocean . . .

KEN W: Sponges . . . sponges!

KENNETH: Until, finally, England came into view. The familiar white cliff appeared . . .

*Grams: Snatch of Cliff Richard singing 'Congratulations'*

KENNETH: Thank you.

KEN W: Come on, Mr. Figg, we must get to London. It's only two hours before the eighty days are up. We can go on horseback. There's a couple of hacks over there.

KENNETH: No, leave them alone. They're the writers looking for a tag. We'll walk.

*Orchestra: Very short link – walking music*

HUGH: *(Jones)* Ah, there you are, Figg.

KENNETH: *(Breathless)* Yes, Jones, here I am. Remember our wager? A thousand guineas if I could go round the world in eighty days?

HUGH: Of course I remember. Off you go, then.

KEN W: We've <u>been</u>!

HUGH: Oh, well, tell you what, you're a sporting man, Figg. Double or Quits.

KENNETH: Done! Come on, Passepartout. This time we'll go the other way round. It's longer, but it's much prettier!

KEN W: Oh, no!

*Orchestra: Sketch pay-off*

*Lead into song*

KENNETH: *'Sing Us One Of The Old Songs'*

1. In a gilded hall of music sat a bright expectant crowd,
Waiting for the coming singer whom they hail'd with praises loud;
Years ago he'd been their idol – how his wit had made them roar!
Now this benefit performance kept him from the workhouse door.
What a storm of welcome greets him as he steps upon the stage –
But alas, how sadly altered what with

illness and with age,
'Cannot sing tonight,' he falters –
As he speaks he bows his head,
But his speech was interrupted –
Someone in the gallery said:

CHORUS:

'Sing us one of the old songs, George,
One of the songs we know –
Try, old man, do what you can,
And we'll let the chorus go.
We can't forget what you used to be
In the days when life was new . . .
Sing us a song, and if you go wrong,
We'll help to pull you through.'

2. At this show of recognition tears stole down the singer's cheek,
Twice he started, twice he faltered, neither could he sing nor speak.
[Maybe 'twas the glorious triumph that his memory still could trace,
Where he'd shone the best and brightest in the very self-same place.
Well he knew the doctor's warning – 'Singing would be fatal now,'
But the gratitude they'd shown him must be recognized somehow.
How could he essay to please them, All his wits were now appalled –
As he stood there hesitating Once again the gallery called:

*(Chorus)* 'Sing us one . . .']

3. Then, as tho' a ray of sunshine cast a halo round the place,
Stood a child before the footlights with a smiling angel face.
'Dad's been ill,' she murmured softly, 'And if me you will allow,
Just to let him rest this evening I will sing for Daddy now.'
Then a strain of sweetest music wafted o'er the spacious hall,
'Twas a child's pathetic story, but it reached the hearts of all.
As she bowed her thanks and left the stage, all eyes in haste were dried,

Those who heard her must have blest
    her on the night the gallery cried –

*(Chorus)* 'Sing us one . . .'

**KENNETH:** And now the *Round the Horne* Forum Of The Air where people from all walks of life phone up to discuss things that are troubling them.

*F/X: Phone rings*

**KENNETH:** Here's the first call.

*F/X: Phone up*

**KENNETH:** Hello –

**KEN W:** *(Heavy breathing)*

**KENNETH:** Hello, Mr. Gruntfuttock.

[**KEN W:** Hold on. I haven't finished yet. *(More heavy breathing)* There – I'm glad I've got that off my chest.]

**KENNETH:** What can I do for you?

**KEN W:** I'm getting out a circular.

**KENNETH:** A circular what?

**KEN W:** I don't know – it's too dark in here to tell. But when I do get it out I shall send it to you.

**KENNETH:** What am I supposed to do with it when I get it?

**KEN W:** Pass it on to two friends – they in turn pass it on to four friends and so on. If you keep it up for eight weeks you'll be surprised at the results.

**KENNETH:** In what way?

**KEN W:** At the end of that time you will receive three and sixpence in cash, an elk's tooth, three hundredweight of suet and nine thousand glossy art studies of General Bismarck doing the splits.

**KENNETH:** Could mortal man ask for more?

**KEN W:** But I must admonish you, Mr. Horne. Be warned. Do not break the chain – one man broke the chain – and had to use his braces.

**KENNETH:** Thank you, Mr. Gruntfuttock – one step beyond.

*F/X: Phone down*

*Phone rings*

*Phone up*

**KENNETH:** Hello –

**BETTY:** *(Refined)* Mr. Horne?

**KENNETH:** Yes.

**BETTY:** Is it just an old wives' tale that if you grind up elephants' hoofs and add the powder to bats' fluff gathered at midnight by a celibate fishmonger's assistant and mix it with essence of toad's bane it produces a deadly poison which, when added to a cup of tea, is completely undetectable?

**KENNETH:** Yes, it's true – such a mixture <u>is</u> deadly <u>and</u> undetectable.

**BETTY:** Thank you, Mr. Horne. *(Coaxingly)* Dad –

**KEN W:** *(Very old – off mic)* Yes.

**BETTY:** Here's your nice cup of tea . . .

**KEN W:** Aaah!! . . .

*F/X: Phone down*

**KENNETH:** It's nice to feel one is able to help. Finally we come [to our 'on-the-spot' report from Gerald Monkshabit in Zambali-land.

*F/X: Phone up*

**KENNETH:** Come in, Gerald Monkshabit – and wipe your feet.

**HUGH:** Hello – this is Gerald Monkshabit speaking to you from Central Zambali-land. The Zambali are a curious race with amazing –

*Vocal atmospherics*

. . . which no white man has ever seen. Although they are of small stature, they are immensely brave, especially when hunting and think nothing of –

*Atmospherics*

. . . under the hoofs of a charging rhino. But now, thanks to the efforts of U.N.O., each of the tribe will be able to grow his own –

*Atmospherics*

. . . in place of the pitiful –

*Atmospherics*

. . . he once had. This means that his –

*Atmospherics*

. . . will be relatively enormous. Their joy is tempered with a measure of –

*Atmospherics*

. . . as the village elders find it hard to grasp the –

*Atmospherics*

. . . in the face of the –

*Atmospherics*

. . . that is commonplace in Europe. The question facing them is, can they do it alone? Odd though it may seem, I have no –

*F/X: Beep beep of telephone*

HUGH: . . . So this is Gerald Monkshabit from Umpopo returning you to the studio.

*F/X: Phone down*

KENNETH: Thank you, Gerald Monskhabit. We'll be interested to hear more of your exotic doings next week. And talking of exotic doings leads us] inexorably to Rambling Syd Rumpo.

KEN W: Hello, my dearios.

KENNETH: What are you going to burst forth with this week?

KEN W: 'Tis a paean of praise to my grandfather's grunge. They don't make 'em like that any more. You can't get the drippets. But be that as it may, the song goes after this fashion, limply and cunningly . . .

*Ken W sings with guitar accompaniment* (to the tune of 'Grandfather's Clock')

My grandfather's grunge was too
  large for the house
So he left it outside by the door.
It was almost as big as the old fool
  himself,
And it weighed half a hundredweight
  more.
He would whirl it around with a
  mighty booming sound,
While my granny stood by in
  surprise –
But he lost – grip –
Dented the tip,
And it caused his untimely demise.

Now he's left it to me and it's plain
  for to see
I'm the pride and the joy of the
  Broads.
Every Michaelmas Day it is there on
  display,
It's already won several awards.
All the summer I munge, as I whirl
  that mighty grunge,
And my granny regards me with
  pride –
But I stop, short –
Never to grunge again,
When it's cold outside . . . oooh!

*(Applause)*

KENNETH: Thank you, Rambling Syd Rumpo. And more power to your whirdler. And now it's time to meet our young visitor from the Antipodes, Miss Judy Coolibah. How are you getting on? Found yourself a position yet?

BETTY: *(Coarse Australian)* What're you gettin' at, Bluey?

KENNETH: Nothing, nothing . . .

BETTY: Yeah, well, just keep your hands on the desk, that's all. For all I know you might be makin' obscene gestures under there.

KENNETH: I wasn't, I assure you.

BETTY: Oh. You some sort o' <u>prude</u>, or somethin'?

KENNETH: No, no. I was asking if you'd turned your hand to anything . . . I'll rephrase that! Have you got a job?

BETTY: Certainly I've got a job. I'm one o' them Temporary women.

KENNETH: I don't think I'll say anything.

BETTY: You know, shorthand typin' an' that. It's been a real eye-opener, I can tell you. These office pommies are all sex mad. One feller [came out with it, bold as brass . . .

KENNETH: Surely not?

BETTY: He certainly did . . . 'Come into my office' he said, 'I want you to take something down.' I swiped him with me tuckerbag! Another dirty devil] tried to get me into the duplicatin' room, and we all know what <u>that</u> means!

KENNETH: Well, they do expect a secretary to have an active role.

[BETTY: You're as bad as the rest, you foul-mouthed drongo!

KENNETH: If you're not happy as a typist, there must be other fields you

could go into.]

BETTY: There you go again! Keep away from me! You're all the same, you poms . . . [sex mad! That's all you think about.] Well, you're not gonna catch <u>me</u> that way! I've got it up here!

KENNETH: Yes, well, if you've got it up there, you should be pretty safe. Thank you, Miss Judy Coolibah . . .

*Orchestra: Play-off*

KENNETH: Like many a man of my age, I have a bit put by for a rainy day. Recently I saw an advertisement which said, 'Sound investment for shrewd business omi. New song-writing team wants backer for new musical. Apply Bona Trans World International Song Publisherettes.' So the next day I went round to their address in Chelsea. The sign on the door said 'Private, enter without knocking'. So I did –

*F/X: Door open*

KENNETH: Hello, is there anybody there?

HUGH: Oh, hello. I'm Julian and this is my friend Sandy.

KEN W: Oh, hello, it's Mr. Horne. What brings you trolling in here?

KENNETH: I'd like to invest in your enterprise.

KEN W: . . . Bold!

KENNETH: What sort of thing are you planning?

HUGH: We're involved in diverse spectacles.

KEN W: We've done several exciting things in the West End. But now we want to do something risky in Drury Lane.

KENNETH: Well, good luck. [If things go wrong you can always plead the headaches.]

KEN W: Oh, bold. No, Jule and I are going to do something we've always wanted to do –

HUGH: We're going to mount a musical.

KENNETH: A musical what?

HUGH: It's too early to tell. We've toyed with *The Three Musketeers* . . .

KEN W: And mooted *Midshipman Easy* . . .

HUGH: We haven't definitely settled on the book yet . . .

KEN W: We've been thinking along the lines of that one with Barbra Strident in it –

HUGH: You know, *Funny Palone*.

KEN W: The story of that what's-her-name Bryce –

KENNETH: Fanny?

HUGH: Maybe to you, but we was enthralled.

KEN W: We went together, didn't we, Jule. It was a magic evening.

HUGH: My lallies turned to water when she sung that song –

KEN W: He's sensitive, Mr. Horne. Touched, he gets – He gets easily touched – and moved. Touched and moved.

[HUGH: I can't help it. The tears well up. Everything is forgotten. I wilfully suspend my disbelief.]

KEN W: Every time he goes to the theatre he wilfully suspends his disbelief, Mr. Horne.

HUGH: Then I got touched and moved.

KENNETH: I can quite believe it.

KEN W: When he's in the theatre he's in another world. You offer him a chocolate – nante. He won't even accept a walnut whip and they're his favourites. [You like them, don't you, Jule?]

HUGH: Well, I've got a sweet tooth – but goodies are as of naught when I'm in the theatre. I'm transported to another place.

KENNETH: After you've been touched and moved.

KEN W: Yes – that's why we thought we'd do our own musical.

HUGH: We've already written a number of songs.

KENNETH: You write your own songs?

KEN W: Yes. We have a musical bent. We are what you might call a modern day Rodgers and Heartface.

HUGH: Or we have been described as another Loewe and Lerner.

KEN W: 'Cos we're both low and we're both learners.

HUGH & KEN W: *(Laugh heartily at this merry quip)*

KEN W: I've been compared with Frank Loesser.

KENNETH: Oh, I see. You're the lesser of two evils.

KEN W: Play him some of our numbers, Jule. He's a miracle of dexterity at the cottage upright.

HUGH: Right. Here goes. Here's a little song Sand and I wrote. We'd been to see *My Fair Palone* and we thought, why not adapt another of Bernard Shaw's works.

[KENNETH: Pardon?

HUGH: Bernard Shaw's works.

KENNETH: Not any more it doesn't.]

KEN W: Anyway, we thought we'd tackle *Back to Methuselah* and here's our title song.

*Max: Piano intro: Ken & Hugh sing to last bars of 'Oh, Oh, Antonio'*

Oh, oh, Methuselah
Oldest of all the Jews you are –
So fantabulusula
Methusu – luse – u – lah.

HUGH: Then we thought of doing his *St. Joan.*

*Ken and Hugh sing with piano acc. to tune of 'One Alone' from* The Desert Song

Oh St. Joan – be mine alone,
Be my palone, though you're just a
   farmer.
Ladvenu may love you too,
But I'll be true
So take off your armour.

HUGH: But it didn't work out –

KEN W: Neither did *Captain Brassbound's Conversion* –

HUGH: Or *Omi and Super Omi.*

KEN W: Then Jule had a blinding flash.

HUGH: It come over me in waves, Mr. Horne – I thought, why not do a musical based on the life of the grand old Omi himself.

KENNETH: You mean Bernard Shaw?

KEN W: Yes. We're going to call it *Bernie* – and it's all about Bernard Shaw's unrequited love for Patrick Campbell.

HUGH: Him that's Lord Dungravy now.

KENNETH: I think you're a bit mixed up. Surely you mean Mrs. Patrick Campbell?

KEN W: He's right. I always wondered what they saw in each other.

HUGH: Anyway, the big song comes when Mrs. Patrick Campbell sings to G.B.S. of her love for him.

KEN W: It's a song and dance number.

KENNETH: A sort of buck and wing Pinero.

KEN W: Right, Jule. After four –

*Max: Piano intro – Ken W and Hugh sing to the tune of 'Babyface'*

Bernard Shaw, I love you more and
   more and more and more,
Although you like to eat your carrots
   raw,
It's a bore,
On me you've put the mockers –
Crazy 'bout your knickerbockers.
G.B.S. – oh darling Bernie won't you
   please say, yes, yes, yes.
Don't let my spirits ebb –
To hell with Beatrice Webb –
Be my darling G.B.S.

*(Coda)* Although you may look weird,
Just love that ginger beard –
You're my darling G.B.S. – I don't
   mean Ibsen –
You're my darling G.B.S.

*Orchestra: Play-off*

KENNETH: In the end I decided not to invest in their musical. I thought I'd put my money in something much safer – so I bought several hundred shares in a building company planning to erect a synagogue in Cairo.

Cheerio – see you next week.

DOUGLAS: That was *Round the Horne*, starring Kenneth Horne, with Kenneth Williams, Hugh Paddick and Betty Marsden.

The music was supplied by the Max
Harris Group. The script was by Barry
Took, Johnnie Mortimer and Brian
Cooke, and the programme was
produced by John Simmonds.

*Orchestra: Sig. tune up and out*

*(Applause)*

*Orchestra: Play out*

*(Applause)*

# SERIES 4
# PROGRAMME 12

*FIRST BROADCAST* – Sunday 12 May 1968

## INTRODUCTION

Compare this script to one of the early episodes, and you may notice that the style has become a bit more fast-moving. The essential elements are all basically the same – daft gags, ancient puns, innuendoes both bold and sly, exuberant word play – but now it's all delivered in a more tightly edited, rapid-fire manner. In part, this must reflect the influence of the very quick American shows, such as Rowan and Martin's *Laugh-In*, which were by now just beginning to have an effect on British comedy.

Not that *Round the Horne* was ever, or ever tried to be, a particularly trendy show – as proven by its large audiences, and subsequent reputation as the last radio programme that the whole nation listened to. Less than a decade later, BBC radio comedies like *The Burkiss Way* would ignore, flout or ridicule most of the conventions of form that Took and his colleagues had been largely happy to work within. The Burkiss mob used false openings, false endings, and even (on one notoriously controversial occasion) a false announcement of the death of one of its performers.

*RTH*, on the other hand, was never especially interested in experimenting with the *shape* of radio comedy. For example, the instruction to the orchestra in this episode – 'Pay-off' – is the equivalent of Basil Brush's 'Boom-boom!', and just about as old-fashioned.

Good thing, too; experimental shows are essential to the health of the genre, but *RTH* is intelligent comedy for intelligent people, more concerned with content than form. We would not still be listening to it today, otherwise, as nothing dates faster than last year's fashions.

KEN W: *(Upper class)* Ladies and gentlemen, we continue the auction with Lot 22. A reclining nude in the Florentine manner, formerly belonging to the late Duke of MacFadgin. Now, can I say twenty thousand? Thank you, sir . . . twenty-five . . . Thirty thousand pounds. Sold to the gentleman at the back! Will you take this 'decorative' piece with you, sir?

BETTY: *(Coarse)* Gawd bless yer, guv, I'll see 'e doesn't regret it!

DOUGLAS: Ladies and gentlemen, it's *Round the Horne*!

*Orchestra: Signature tune*

KENNETH: Hello and welcome to the show. Now I've just been handed the result of the first race in the flat-racing season. It was won by 23a, Jubilee Mansions, Kilburn. Only three flats ran.

Yes. Well, I thought you might like to hear about some of the things I've been doing since we last met. As you know, I'm a bit of a bon viveur and on Tuesday I decided it was time I replenished my cellar, so I went out and bought a packet of salt. Wednesday I went for a run in my new car. Didn't really enjoy it, I banged my ankle on the handbrake every time I passed the dashboard.

Thursday I popped into the barber's, more out of nostalgia than anything else, Friday I took a book on horticulture into the garden and spent the afternoon weeding it . . . and Saturday I decided an old suite I'd had for years needed recovering, so I went out and bought a toffee paper. Well, that's more than enough of that. Now here's the only man with the less fattening centre, it's rich, chunky, pedigree Douglas Smith. Forward, Smith.

DOUGLAS: Sir. It's time for the *Round the Horne* Forum of the Air in which listeners phone in to air their views.

*F/X: Phone rings*

KENNETH: And here's the first call now.

*F/X: Phone up*

KENNETH: Hello?

KEN W: *(Distort) (Heavy breathing)*

KENNETH: Hello, Mr. Gruntfuttock.

KEN W: Hang on a minute, I have inserted sixpence and now I cannot get it out again. Never mind, I'll try later with a bit of wire.

KENNETH: Yes. What can I do for you this week?

KEN W: I wish to ventilate my spleen, Mr. Horne. The woman at the Labour Exchange has been unable to find me a suitable position in my chosen profession.

KENNETH: Which is?

KEN W: Window cleaner, specializing in bathroom windows.

KENNETH: You don't entirely surprise me. How exactly do you work?

KEN W: I stands on me ladder, rubbin' the pane with a damp chammy, I find it eases it somewhat. Yes, I frequently works for hours on a bathroom window, Mr. Horne. I tries to . . . er . . . I tries to . . . what's the phrase?

KENNETH: 'Keep it clean'.

KEN W: Oh, all right, I won't say it then.

KENNETH: Perhaps you're too specialized, I mean, many shops would be glad of a window cleaner. For instance, I have a butchers . . .

KEN W: So do I, but not as often as I used to.

KENNETH: No. Well, have you tried advertising under 'Household Services' in the local paper?

KEN W: Yes, I have, but they made a typographical error. They put me down as a 'Widow Cleaner'.

KENNETH: How unfortunate.

KEN W: Not really, I've got fifty of 'em round here now. You'll have to excuse me, the water's boilin'.

KENNETH: Thank you, Mr. Gruntfuttock.

[F/X: *Phone down: phone rings: phone up*

KENNETH: Hello?

HUGH: *(Distort: Smarmy)* Good afternoon, your name has been specially selected and you have won a free dancing lesson.

KENNETH: Splendid. What do I have to do?

HUGH: Well . . . hold the phone in your right hand and . . .

*Grams: (Distort) Victor Sylvester quick step: Keep under*

HUGH: *(Over music)* . . . left foot forward, side, together . . . right foot forward, side, together, slow, slow, quick, quick, slow . . .

KENNETH: I don't think I'll bother, thank you.]

*F/X: Phone down: Cutting off music*

*Phone rings: Phone up*

KENNETH: Hello, Horne here.

BETTY: *(Distort: Refined)* Are you the man who's been phoning me up at all hours of the night and making

improper suggestions?

KENNETH: Er . . . who is that?

BETTY: Mrs. Emily Bulstrode of 49 Coronation Buildings, Putney.

KENNETH: *(Relieved)* Forty-nine? No, in that case it's not me.

BETTY: Oh. Well, if you ever feel like it, my number's in the book.

KENNETH: Thank you.

*F/X: Phone down*

KENNETH: Well, that's all the phone calls we have time for. If you'd like us to give you a call, just write in. The names of the lucky listeners will be produced from an old hat. And speaking of old-hat productions brings me to our next item featuring Dame Celia Molestrangler and ageing juvenile, Binkie Huckaback. We bring you an excerpt from their least, but by no means last, film, *Brief Re-Encounter*.

*Grams: 'Lilli Marlene'*

*F/X: Door bell rings: Door opened*

BETTY: Yes?

HUGH: Fiona . . . Don't you remember me?

BETTY: Charles! It can't be!

HUGH: It is.

BETTY: But it can't be. It's impossible, incredible, inconceivable, unimaginable . . . and yet . . .

HUGH: Inevitable, Fiona?

BETTY: Yes.

HUGH: Yes. Fiona, you must give it to me.

BETTY: Give it to you? But what, Charles?

HUGH: You know what I've come for, Fiona. The money, Fiona.

BETTY: Money, Charles? How can you stand there in your old uniform and ask me for money?

HUGH: I must, Fiona. Standing here in my old uniform.

BETTY: But you've never asked me for money before. Why now – standing there in your old uniform and saluting in that peculiar way?

HUGH: Because this is bob-a-job week, Fiona!

*Orchestra: Play-off*

KENNETH: Now, many of you have written in with medical problems, in particular 'Lefty' of Potters Bar, and all I can say to him is, don't worry. It's quite common for one to be longer than the other. I suggest you consult an earlobe specialist. However, in view of these letters, we've persuaded Nurse Florence MacGanderpoke to come along and give us the benefit of her advice.

BETTY: *(Scots)* Thank you. First, I'd like to talk to you about old wives' tales. These can now be successfully operated on and any old wife who has one shouldn't worry too much. One listener has written to say that his stomach hangs out over his bathing trunks. Well, if I were him I would diet. Preferably the same colour as his trunks.

Some of you have asked me how to remove unsightly moles from the lower limbs. I myself find that a sharp blow with a rolled-up newspaper soon has them scurrying for their burrows. And finally, a piece of advice on how to avoid Macwhirter's disease. Keep away from Macwhirter.

KENNETH: Thank you, nurse. Next week she'll be giving you advice on your moulting toupee, and if you accept the advice, be it on your own head.

*(Lead in to song: 'Among My Souvenirs')*

KENNETH: *(Lead out of song: Link to Douglas)*

DOUGLAS: Sir. Horneographic Productions, in reluctant association with 'Rentathug' Debt Collectors Ltd., present the memoirs of a newspaper editor . . .

*Orchestra: Fanfare*

DOUGLAS: *I Showed Them In Fleet Street*!

*Orchestra: Intro. music*

KENNETH: My name is Hieronymous Newtgrasper. For many years I was editor of the *Daily Globe*. In fact, I've spent most of my life in one newspaper or another, I find they're cheaper than suits. As our story opens, I'm in conference with some of my staff. [I turned to my racing correspondent, Captain Putter, a stocky, square-set man in a green suit, with a potted plant on his head.

KEN W: *(Snide)* That's the filing cabinet, chief, I'm over here. Listen, chief, somebody's just slipped me a red-hot tip, 'Dancing Admiral' to win tomorrow's big race!

KENNETH: Oh, perhaps I'll put ten bob on the nose.

KEN W: Um, I prefer it each way, myself.

KENNETH: Yes, I think you might as well go back to your nap.] Now, Marge, as woman's editor, do you have anything to put forward?

BETTY: Yes, I must protest about the way our sub-editors use their blue pencils. Once they get their hands on my articles there's no stopping them.

KENNETH: I'll see what I can do, Marge. Now, let's hear from our society columnist, Peregrine de Vere Fitzaubergine.

HUGH: *(Thug)* Yeah, well. Last night the Duchess o' Kent was seen 'avin' a bit of a knees-up wiv the Duke at a charity nosh. 'E stayed an 'ad a little thing on a stick, but she scarpered abaht eleven on account of 'er plates o' meat was givin' 'er gyp.

KENNETH: Ah, how elegant it all sounds. I wish I could have been there.

HUGH: Yeah, well, you didn't go to Eton an' 'Arrow, like what I done.

KENNETH: Quite. I adjourned the meeting and [began to study the letters on my desk. Well, a man in my position ought to learn the alphabet.] Suddenly the door burst open . . .

*F/X: Door opens*

KEN W: *(Young, eager: Coming on)* I can do it, sir! I can! Give me a chance and I'll show you I can do it!

KENNETH: I'm sure you can, but what?

KEN W: I can be an ace reporter, sir. I used to work for the *Wapping and District Courier*.

KENNETH: Ah, yes. That folded, didn't it?

KEN W: Yes, sir. That way it was easier to push it through letter boxes.

KENNETH: Quite. Well, I'm not sure if I have an opening.

KEN W: Oh, you must have. I'm willing to work my way up, sir.

KENNETH: All right, I'll see what I can do. What's your name, young fellow?

KEN W: Arnold Creamtea, sir.

KENNETH: Not one of the Devonshire Creamteas, are you? No, I suppose not. Very well, you can start as a copy boy, but stay out of my hair.

KEN W: That won't be difficult.

*Orchestra: Brief link*

KENNETH: Arnold set to with a will . . . that was another young copy boy.

KEN W: Listen, Will, I'm not going to be a copy boy all my life. One day I'm going to make it big!

[HUGH: *(Cockney lad)* Here, Arnold, don't talk so loud. You gotta remember your place.

KEN W: I'm going to be up there before you know it!] I'm gonna be a great reporter. I'll be known as 'The Man They Can't . . .'

HUGH: Can't what?

KEN W: I haven't decided yet. I mean, you gotta keep your options open. Hang on, there's somebody coming. Is it the racing correspondent, Captain Putter?

HUGH: No, it's Marge Poops, the woman's editor. Can't you tell Marge from Putter?

BETTY: *(Woman's editor)* Come along, you boys, there's no paper in my office and I'm writing an article on lace panties.

KEN W: Sorry, Miss Poops, here's some paper. While you're here, Miss Poops, I've got a feature you might like to look at.

BETTY: Oh? Let's see . . . hmm . . . is it all your own?

KEN W: Yes.

BETTY: It's rather interesting. I might be able to use this. Perhaps it's a little wordy, you could shorten <u>that</u> sentence . . . and take that 'and' out of there . . .

KEN W: Anything you say, Miss Poops.

*Orchestra: Brief link*

KENNETH: After that Arnold often submitted items for Marge's column. Kitchen hints . . .

KEN W: Housewives who like their lettuces crisp should put their heads in cellophane bags and pop them in the refrigerator.

KENNETH: Fashion tips . . .

KEN W: The new look in dress is waisted . . . well, it's wasted on me, anyway.

KENNETH: Eventually I made him a cub reporter, but this didn't satisfy him.

KEN W: Sir, I'm fed up with being a cub reporter. They never make news! They just sit in a circle going 'Dib-dib-dib' all the time.

KENNETH: I see.

KEN W: I'm a hard worker, sir. I'm learning all the time. Every day I buy all the newspapers and study them.

KENNETH: Good, good, well, keep taking the tabloids. [Meanwhile, you can assist our top crime reporter, Pat O'Printersink.

HUGH: *(Laconic Irish)* I'll show ye how to catch the public's attention, lad. Now here's a story about a model aeroplane competition. The judge gave first prize to a vicar who entered an unpainted Spitfire. Now this vicar isn't likely to have worn a frock, is he? So what's your headline?

KEN W: Er . . . 'Unfrocked Vicar Beat Coloured Models, Says Judge'!

HUGH: Exactly, an' yer reader's eyeballs are bulgin' out like globe artichokes. Right, come with me, we'll do a story on bribery and corruption in the police force.

KEN W: How will we get the facts?

HUGH: We'll slip the superintendent a couple of quid for 'em.

*Orchestra: Link*

KENNETH: Arnold Creamtea's name became widely known. He had it changed by deed poll and who can blame him? I could see he was going to be a success in Fleet Street.]

DOUGLAS: Perhaps this is an opportune moment to mention that I, Douglas Smith, play Fleet Street. I've lined myself with newspapers for the occasion. I start off at Ludgate Circus, bend in the middle, and end up in the Law Courts. I am old and narrow . . .

KEN W: *(Self)* You can say that again.

DOUGLAS: . . . and yet visitors come for miles to see my bustle. So much traffic passes through me that sometimes I get rather choked.

KENNETH: Never mind, Smith, I think you're a nice street. You're surrounded by several rather quaint old squares.

DOUGLAS: I shall refrain from comment, sir.

KENNETH: You better had. Now, where were we? Oh, yes, Arnold had started to make his mark in Fleet Street, but the police made him scrub it out. I had my own problems, the proprietor of the newspaper, Lord Stoatstream, was worried about circulation.

HUGH: *(Crotchety old man)* Me feet are goin' numb, Newtgrasper!

KENNETH: Your suspenders are too tight, sir. Here, borrow mine.

HUGH: Ah, thank you. Yes, that's much better. Now, what's this I hear about our cookery columnist being sent to jail?

KENNETH: I'm afraid it's true, sir. She refused to reveal her sauces.

HUGH: Plucky little minx. Now look here, Newtgrasper, I've got a report on our potential readership. Here it is, thirteen million people broken down by age and sex . . .

KENNETH: Really?

HUGH: Yes, and it shows that our main appeal is to this under-twenty-five group.

KENNETH: Splendid.

HUGH: What? Only twenty-five out of thirteen million? It's not good enough! You've got to pull your socks up, man!

KENNETH: I can't, you've got my suspenders.

HUGH: Dammit, if you haven't doubled the circulation in six months you're sacked! Understand?

*Orchestra: Dramatic link*

KENNETH: I was worried. That night I tossed and turned and I confess I cried a little. The man on the next seat complained and they threw me off the bus. Next morning I called a meeting and asked the staff for suggestions.

BETTY: *(Woman's editor)* I've got a suggestion, handsome.

KENNETH: Later, later. What's important now is the future of the *Daily Globe*.

HUGH: *(Dentures)* Well, speaking as 'Stargazer', the staff astrologer, I foresee a massive surge in circulation. I say that in six or seven weeks we shall have super sales!

KENNETH: Oh, don't talk wet. Anybody else got an idea?

MAX HARRIS: I have one. Why not print it in invisible ink for people who haven't got time to read newspaper?

KEN W: *(Self)* Here, what's Max Harris doing in a sketch? Get back to your piano, you great cloth-eared clown!

KENNETH: Now, now, Williams.

KEN W: Well! He can't read <u>lines</u>. It takes him all his time to read those little dots with tails . . . any fool can do that. *(Off to Max)* Go on, get out of it!

KENNETH: Yes, well, back to the plot.

KEN W: It's a disgrace!

KENNETH: It was then that young Arnold stood up and spoke. He was pale and nervous, but he still gave a good account of himself.

KEN W: *(Arnold)* I'm five foot ten, dark wavy hair, incredibly handsome, good teeth . . .

KENNETH: Yes, yes, but what's your idea for improving circulation?

KEN W: Well, I can tell you what's <u>wrong</u> with the paper. We've got half-naked women showing their legs on every page! We should be aiming higher than that. Let's appeal to the intellectuals!

KENNETH: You mean we should have half-naked Oxford dons?

KEN W: Yes!

KENNETH: I put the idea up to the proprietor.

HUGH: *(Lord Stoatstream)* I like it! This young feller, Arnold Whatsisname has got something, or if he hasn't, he <u>looks</u> as if he has. I want you to promote him.

KENNETH: And so I promoted him. He came up with many more ideas.

KEN W: Let's put vinegar in the printing ink to appeal to the chip shops! Let's print on cellophane, so commuters can read it an' look at girls' legs at the same time!

KENNETH: These revolutionary ideas produced a dramatic change in the fortunes of the *Daily Globe*. We lost every single reader.

KEN W: I can't understand it! They don't seem to want transparent, vinegar-soaked pictures of half-naked Oxford dons!

KENNETH: Yes, well, some people are funny that way. Arnold and I lost our jobs, but we weren't out of work for long. With our reputations we soon got two of the most important positions in Fleet Street. I was under the clock and he was outside the pub. *(Calls)* Read all about it!

KEN W: *(Slightly off) (Calls)* 'Daily Globe Goes Bankrupt!' Read all about it!

KENNETH: Yes, read all about it in your *Daily Clarion*, read all about it!

*Orchestra: Pay-off*

KENNETH: So ends this week's production. Next week I'll personally introduce an extract from *Seven Brides for One Brother* and I think you'll agree that's bigamy.

KENNETH: And now we step into the Twilight Zone to meet Rambling Syd Rumpo.

KEN W: Hello, my dearios.

KENNETH: What many-splendoured thing have you brought for our delectation this week?

KEN W: Well, I feel I can truly say that the song that I'm about to fuddle your wits with is without doubt the most lacklustre piece of tawdry effluence with which I never ever strained my adenoids.

KENNETH: I see – one of your better efforts.

KEN W: Precisely. Its burden – and I use the word advisedly – is of a lugubrious nature and goes after this fashion, briskly and furtively.

*Ken W: Sings to the tune of 'Dashing Away With The Smoothing Iron' with guitar accompaniment*

'Twas on a Monday morning
Just as the day was dawning,
My sweetheart stood a-yawning
Beneath the Holly tree.
Her artifacts were woggling,
No wonder I stood goggling
As she whirdled away with her
    looming fork,
Grundled away with her groating cork
Until I spilled my tea.

'Twas on a Tuesday morning,
She stood beneath the awning,
Her possett she was pawning
For twenty-five and three.
Her cordwangle was chilly-oh,
(So) she huffed on it like Billy-oh,
As she traddled away at her fumble
    jug,
Nadgered away at her grumble mug
'Twas worth a trip to see.

'Twas on a Wednesday morning,
The landlord came a-fawning

Without a proper warning
To ask her for a fee.
It seems she had to pay a fine
For hanging moulies on the line,
And taddling oats on the Queen's
    highway,
Gathering groats on the first of May
Although she did it for free.

*(Applause)*

KENNETH: Thank you, Rambling Syd Rumpo.

A few days ago I started getting anonymous phone calls. At first I thought nothing of it . . . it was obviously the work of a crank . . . but the calls persisted. When I'd pick up the receiver a voice, heavily disguised, would make threats such as kidnapping my wife, or getting at the budgerigar by means of drugged cuttlefish, and of course I couldn't let that continue – I'm extremely fond of the budgie – so I thought I'd better get some protection, and as luck would have it, I saw an advert in my local paper. It read: 'Bona Private Detective Agency. Personal Protection Guaranteed.' So the next morning I paid them a visit.

*F/X: Door open*

KENNETH: Hello, anybody there?

HUGH: Oh, hello. I'm Julian and this is my friend, Sandy.

KEN W: Hello, Mr. Horne. What brings you trolling in?

KENNETH: Are you private detectives?

HUGH: Private and confidential. We specialize in delicate enquiries.

KEN W: You can put yourself in our hands unreservedly.

KENNETH: Are you qualified?

HUGH: Yes. I'm Ex-Cid.

KENNETH: Cid? Criminal Investigation Department?

HUGH: No, Syd Goatsbreath. That was my name. I changed it by deed poll. Now I'm Julian Lestrange.

KEN W: After that inspector in the Sherlock Holmes stories. He's modelled himself on him, haven't you, Jule? He loves Holmes. Don't you, Jule?

HUGH: I love Holmes, Mr. Horne. I've read all his tales.

KEN W: He loves Holmes' tales.

HUGH: I've read 'em all. 'The Yellow Eek', 'The Crooked Omi', 'The Red Riah League'.

KEN W: He sees hisself as the Sherlock of the over-sixties.

KENNETH: A sort of old people's Holmes –

KEN W: Oh, he's bold.

KENNETH: And what role do you play in the organisation?

KEN W: Well, I'm his Man Friday when he's in town.

KENNETH: I see – you're his Watson in London.

HUGH: You want protection, don't you?

KENNETH: How do you know that?

HUGH: After that last joke you <u>need</u> protection.

KENNETH: Well, it's true. I'm being threatened.

KEN W: We can give you all the protection you need. Fire, Theft, Flood. You name it.

KENNETH: Flood?

HUGH: We've got a small insurance business on the side. But to return to our moutons.

KEN W: That's your actual French – we give three grades of protection. There's the comprehensive at eighty guineas a week – that includes armed guards at your side day and night, a professional food taster and a ravenous Alsatian stationed outside your door.

HUGH: Or there's your partial cover – plain clothes man outside your window, telephone interception service and a wire-haired terrier on the landing. That's fifty guineas a week.

KENNETH: That's more than I planned on spending.

KEN W: Well, there is your four guinea ordinary.

KENNETH: How does that protect me from attack?

KEN W: Jule restrains himself.

KENNETH: Look, are you sure you're qualified?

HUGH: Yes – we've got certificates from the Home Office.

KEN W: I've got a double '0' number.

KENNETH: Licenced to kill? Like James Bond – 007?

HUGH: No – 0071. It's the phone number of the Marine Commando Club in Paddington. They'll take a message.

KEN W: But the law is in our blood. We met through the law, didn't we, Jule?

HUGH: Bow Street it was. We'd been demonstrating in Trafalgar Square.

KEN W: We had – protesting. He don't tell no lies. Who was it who'd been addressing us? Him with the collar – the vicar –

HUGH: Josie Collins?

KEN W: Josie? Canon Collins[1]. We'd all marched from Aldermaston –

HUGH: I joined the march in the Haymarket 'cos of my feet.

KEN W: Terrible feet he's got – he's a martyr to them. It's all them years dancing on point. He's got toes like a bunch of knotty bananas. Haven't you, Jule?

HUGH: It was for my art.

KEN W: He suffered for his art. He strained himself in the middle of Stravinsky's *Sacre du Printemps* and he had to give it up, the ballet. He was like thistledown, he was. Tell him what Dame Alice said to you.

HUGH: What, about keeping out of the girls' dressing rooms?

KEN W: No – about how light you were.

HUGH: She said I was light on my feet.

KEN W: Like a fairy he was. His lallies were his fortune till that fatal matinée. They say you could hear the click all over the theatre – and from that day to this he hasn't danced a step.

HUGH: Well, it's all liniment under the bridge now.

KEN W: But it's left his feet in no state for protest marches.

HUGH: So I joined them in the Haymarket.

KEN W: Anyway, to cut a long story short, there we was in Trafalgar

---

1. A leading figure in the Campaign for Nuclear Disarmament.

Square – singing 'We Shall Not Be Moved' – when all of a sudden we was – and before we knew it we was in the Black Maria, and off to Bow Street.

HUGH: But we were so impressed by the demeanour of the police . . . we decided to take the law into our own hands and become private eyes.

KEN W: So here we are – ready to give of our all, to help fight the crime wave. What's your actual problem?

KENNETH: Well, all it is really is that I've been getting these anonymous phone calls.

KEN W: Oh – the anonymous phone calls.

HUGH: Well, I'm sure we can help you there. If you pay us a retainer of ten pounds a week, we guarantee these phone calls will stop.

KENNETH: How can you be so sure?

KEN W: Easy, ducky. We'll stop making them.

*Orchestra: Play off*

KENNETH: Well, that's it for this week except for a late news item – the winner of this year's Miss Universe contest is an eighteen-year-old girl from Mars. Her vital statistics are 38 – 26 – 35 – 78 – 44 – 67 – 3. Thought you'd be interested. Cheerio – see you next week.

*Orchestra: Sig. tune – timp roll continues under credits*

DOUGLAS: That was *Round the Horne*, starring Kenneth Horne, with Kenneth Williams, Hugh Paddick and Betty Marsden. The music was supplied by the Max Harris Group, and the script was by Barry Took, Johnnie Mortimer and Brian Cooke. The programme was produced by John Simmonds.

*Orchestra: Sig. tune up and out*

*(Applause)*

*Orchestra: Play out*

*(Applause)*

# SERIES 4
# PROGRAMME 15

*FIRST BROADCAST* – Sunday 2 June 1968

## INTRODUCTION

The last script in our book, and the penultimate show in the final series. It wasn't supposed to be the final series; *Round the Horne* was still a popular hit, as fresh and funny as ever – who knows how long it might have run? But in February 1969, while hosting the BAFTA awards in London, Kenneth Horne suffered a massive and immediately fatal heart attack. He was aged just sixty-one. Took and Feldman were with Horne when he died; he'd just presented them with an award for writing the TV show *Marty*.

Horne's death, inevitably, meant the death of *RTH*. The BBC attempted to fill the gap with a Kenneth Williams vehicle, originally called *Stop Messing About*, but it soon became obvious that nothing and no-one could replace Kenneth Horne, and that an era of radio entertainment had come to a sudden end.

During a period of almost unprecedented social change, Horne's wry, avuncular good humour seemed to give millions of people, of different classes and generations, the confidence to laugh at things that might otherwise have worried and divided them. For all the jokes about his 'squareness', he came across in *RTH* as a man entirely at ease with himself, and with the times.

In fact, Kenneth Horne's private life was far from straightforward, but 'Kenneth Horne', the comic creation of Took and Feldman, was an unruffled, sanguine chap whose response to the revolutionary mood of the 1960s was a quiet chuckle, a raised eyebrow, and a generous love of life. The message seemed to be, 'There's nothing new under the sun – and here are the jokes to prove it.'

Far more important than all the above, of course, *Round the Horne* was funny. Sometimes subtly funny, sometimes screamingly funny, but always, in every single edition of every series, so funny that you wouldn't dream of missing it.

It still is. And to prove it, here comes . . . *Bona Prince Charlie.*

DOUGLAS: Advertising on the BBC? But how?

HUGH: Well, each ad would be designed to fit in with the programmes around it. Before *Listen With Mother* we'd advertise gripe water and teething rings – after Jimmy Young – indigestion powder. Here, listen to these . . .

KEN W: Getaway people use Senna pods.

*F/X: Splash splash of water in bath*

[BETTY: When I take a bath I always use Parkinsons Carbolic Soap, the soap that is used by nine out of ten Hollywood stars. Won't you join me?

HUGH: Righto – move over, gel.

*F/X: Splash*]

HUGH: Want to look twelve pounds lighter?

BETTY: Yes. How?

HUGH: Get your gear off.

[BETTY: Join the smoking revolution – our cigars are revolting.]

KEN W: And what programme could possibly follow dreadful advertisements like that?

DOUGLAS: There are no prizes for the answer – it's *Round the Horne*.

*Orchestra: Sig. tune*

KENNETH: Hello, and welcome to the show. First, an apology for a misprint in this week's *Radio Times*. In Sunday's Choral Recital, the singers should have been named as the Tredwyllin Male <u>Voice</u> Choir – and not the Male <u>Vice</u> Choir, who produce an entirely different sound.

Well, our friends the Over-Eighties Nudist Leapfrog Team are in the news

again. Apparently they're getting ready for the First Nudist Olympic Games, which will be held in Chile. Which is bad luck, really. There will be the usual events – the high hurdles, the hop, step and jump, the pole vaults and weightlifting. I understand there's a record entry for the marathon and I for one can't wait to see them come swinging into the stadium.

The disadvantages of Nudist Olympics are that in the opening parade it's hard to tell which country is which, and that even if you <u>do</u> win a medal there's nowhere to pin it. I'm sure you'll join me in wishing them good luck. Smith.

DOUGLAS: Sir –

KENNETH: Stop fiddling with your executive toy and announce the next item.

DOUGLAS: Yes, sir. And now, the *Round the Horne* Forum of the Air, where people phone in with their problems.

KENNETH: And I fail to cope with them.

*F/X: Phone rings*

KENNETH: Ah, there's the first call now.

*F/X: Phone up*

KENNETH: Hello – Horne here.

KEN W/HUGH: *(Both breathing heavily – Hugh continues throughout next lines)*

KENNETH: Hello – Gruntfuttock?

KEN W: Yes.

KENNETH: Are you alone?

KEN W: No. Hold on, there's someone on my extension. Get off – sling your hook. *(Hugh stops heavy breathing)*

KENNETH: Ah, that's better. Now, what's your problem?

KEN W: My private discourses are being interfered with.

KENNETH: It's hard to tell whether you're boasting or complaining.

KEN W: You do not grasp my meaning. I cannot put up with it any longer.

KENNETH: What's the matter?

KEN W: I'm being bugged.

KENNETH: Are you?

KEN W: Yes. People are listening in to my phone conversations – I'm being tapped. Tapped and bugged. And I'm at the end of my tether.

KENNETH: Is that your only problem?

KEN W: No, my main concern is to do with ancient lights.

KENNETH: Ancient lights?

KEN W: Yes. I want them modernized so as I can get a better view of the nurses' hostel.

F/X: *Phone down – phone rings – phone up*

KENNETH: Hello?

BETTY: Hello. I'm six.

KENNETH: *(Aside)* We'd never get away with this on television. So you're six. How nice. What's your problem?

BETTY: Well, I'm staying in a hotel and our room's on the top floor. Well, I get in the lifts and go up to the third floor, then I have to get out and walk up the rest of the way.

KENNETH: That's a long way for a little girl to walk. Why don't you take the lift right up to the top?

BETTY: I can't reach the button.

F/X: *Phone down*

KENNETH: Isn't that sweet.

KEN W: It's enough to turn your stomach over.

KENNETH: And now it's time for our weekly report from roving correspondent Gerald Monkshabit, and as usual I must apologize for the bad line. Come in Gerald Monkshabit.

HUGH: Hello. I'm speaking to you from one of Britain's atomic submarines in the mid-Atlantic. We've been at sea for two months now and the captain has only

*(Atmospherics)*

once in this whole period. By brilliant manoeuvring he managed to

*(Atmospherics)*

immediately under the North Pole and the crew took it in turns to

*(Atmospherics)*

through the periscope. Our next port of call was Iceland where the crew were allowed to

*(Atmospherics)*

together in batches of twelve. The chaps are in good heart and it is expected that on our return to port, the C.-in-C. Portsmouth will

*(Atmospherics)*

in our honour.

*(Applause)*

KENNETH: Thank you, Gerald Monkshabit. And now, with jumbuk akimbo and her billabong at a rakish angle, direct from the outback of Cromwell Road, here is Miss Judy Coolibah.

BETTY: Hello, cobber.

KENNETH: Good to have you back –

BETTY: What do you mean by that?

KENNETH: Nothing, just extending the hand of friendship.

BETTY: Yeah? With what purpose in mind, might I ask? I'll tell you – to lull me into a sense of false security so that you can work your evil desires upon me.

KENNETH: Nothing of the kind, I assure you.

BETTY: Oh, satiated, are you?

KENNETH: Not at all. Oh dear, it seems awfully hard to get through to you.

BETTY: Too right, sport. [You go the grope with me and you'll be in the casualty ward like a rat up a drainpipe. I'm drummin' ya.

KENNETH: I've no intention of – er, what you said – although to be honest I didn't understand a word.

BETTY: Don't come the raw prawn with me. You understood every word. Do you take me for a galah?

KENNETH: Gala?

BETTY: That means 'fool'.

KENNETH: I thought a gala was a sort of fête.

BETTY: Yes, and I know what sort of fate you have in mind for me. The sort that's worse than death.

KENNETH: Not at all.

BETTY: Well, you can slake your evil desires somewhere else. Because Mr. Right has entered my life.] Look at this – third finger, left hand – do you know what it is?

KENNETH: A hangnail?

BETTY: No, sport – an engagement ring. I met him on Anzac day. *(Suddenly soft and wistful)* It was love at first sight. Our eyes met across the crowded bar. He came over to me and straight away he put the hard word on – frankly I thought he was Adrian – 'cos he'd been knocking back the steam – but, Mr. Horne, my heart melted, my defences were down and I knew I was in love.

KENNETH: How charming.

BETTY: Would you like to meet him?

KENNETH: I'd love to.

BETTY: *(Shouts)* Oi – Herbert, you great pommy faggot, come out of the dunny – I want you to meet a friend –

*Orchestra: Aussie play-off*

KENNETH: If any of our Australian friends are listening, could we have some more phrases, please, as we're running a bit short.

*Intro. to song 'Hawking Me Greens About' (Kenneth Williams)*

KENNETH: Which brings us to our 'Movie-Go-Wrong' series. Forward, Smith!

DOUGLAS: Sir! Horneographic Productions, in association with Finnegan's Four Star Sump Oil, the aperitif of the smart set, present a story of the Young Prince who led the Jacobite rebellion . . . starring Kenneth Williams as –

*Orchestra: Fanfare*

KEN W: *Bona Prince Charlie*!

*Orchestra: Intro. music – Scottish overtones*

KENNETH: Seventeen forty-five . . . my name is Hamish McGropesporran. I'm a simple Scottish crofter. I breed bagpipes for a living . . . well, I <u>said</u> I was simple. I was eating my heather sandwiches in the field one day when a horse galloped up.

HUGH: *(Scots, breathless)* The Prince has landed in Scotland and is coming this way!

KENNETH: I was astonished by this. I'd never heard a horse talk before.

HUGH: It's not the horse, y'fool, it's me, on the back of it. D'ye not recognize the flaming red beard and the hairy legs?

KENNETH: Of course! How are you, Auntie?

HUGH: I'm fine. [Ye must look your best for the Prince, Hamish . . . on your knees. Brush it off before he sees it.]

KENNETH: Even as Auntie spoke, a lone, regal figure appeared over the hill. The hope of Scotland, leader of the clans, a man who struck fear into the heart of every Sassenach.

KEN W: *(Snide)* No, 'ere, don't be like that. I am the Young Pretender, Charlie. People call me Bonnie, on account of this long skirt, the beret and the machine gun. I have travelled far to seek the throne.

KENNETH: It's just across the yard and to the left. Have no fear, my Prince, every man in Scotland will follow you!

KEN W: I'd rather they didn't.

KENNETH: That night the Prince slept under my roof. Well, I wasn't having him in the bedroom. The following morning, I prepared a special treat for breakfast . . . Good morning, Sire. Would you like a little grouse?

KEN W: Yes, I would! I've had a shockin' night on that rafter. It's no fun up there with the wind whistlin' up your lum, I can tell you.

DOUGLAS: Translator's note: 'Lum' is the Scottish word for chimney.

KEN W: Nice!

Brrr. What I need is a drop of the hard stuff. Have you got any?

KENNETH: Certainly. I gave him a lump of frozen porridge.

KEN W: Thank you. [Today I want you to arrange a meeting of all the clans. The McDonalds, the McDucks, the McHobleys, the Stuarts . . .

KENNETH: We mustn't forget the MacIntoshes.

KEN W: Quite right. It <u>is</u> a bit cloudy.] The clans must all be told that I have arrived in Scotland. 'Ere, take this and spread it throughout the glens.

KENNETH: What is it? Is it your message of hope?

KEN W: No. It's your rotten lump of frozen porridge.

*Orchestra: Link*

KENNETH: The leaders of the clans came from far and wide. The meeting was to be held in the grand hall of the McWomen's Institute. The first to speak was Angus McSpray.

HUGH: *(Dentures)* Fellow Scotsmen, I speak sincerely when I say that Scotland's Prince should have our support in his struggle to seize the sovereignty of this island . . .

KENNETH: Strong men turned away as he spoke.

HUGH: . . . Shall we stand aside like mice, or shall we rise against the Sassenachs and restore a Stuart to the throne of his ancestors?

KENNETH: When he'd finished, there wasn't a dry eye in the hall. In fact, there wasn't a dry anything. Then leader after leader stood up to pledge his support. The McLeods, the McBawbees . . . every clan supported him. The Prince was visibly touched . . . but in that crowd there wasn't much he could do about it.

KEN W: Friends, I came to Scotland for only one reason. I got on the wrong boat. But now I have your support . . . to arms!

*Orchestra: Stirring link*

DOUGLAS: The scene shifts to some time later, in London. The Queen is in conference with her trusted advisor, the Duck of Cumberland.

HUGH: *(Duke)* 'Duke', not 'Duck'!

DOUGLAS: Sorry. It's a mistake anyone could make. Especially the way you walk.

HUGH: Swine!

BETTY: *(Sexy royalty)* Now look, Cumbie, the way I see it is this. Jacobitewise we've bought a lot of grief. Bonnie Charlie's campaign is going over big. North of the border he's topping the tam o'shanter ratings. It's gotta stop.

HUGH: What do you suggest, your Highness?

BETTY: I suggest you advance and stand against them.

HUGH: If you say so, Ma'am.

BETTY: Not me, you fool. The enemy. Oh, I don't know, though . . .

*Orchestra: Link*

KENNETH: Meanwhile, the Young Pretender had marched into England at the head of his army.

DOUGLAS: At this point it should be placed on record that I, Douglas Smith of *Ten O'Clock News* fame, play England. I am a precious jewel set in a silver sea. The Scottish border runs alongside of me, but he's wasting his time.

KENNETH: Good for you, Smith.

DOUGLAS: Thank you, sir. Many men have tried to conquer me, none have succeeded . . . with the exception of a certain Norman but that was long ago. Anyway, I certainly shan't surrender to the likes of Mr. Williams.

KEN W: We'll see about that. Forward, men! Into battle!

KENNETH: He won at Carlisle. He won at Manchester, but he could only manage a draw at Derby County, even after extra time. That was the start of the troubles. Sire! The men are beginning to grumble about the food . . . listen.

HUGH, DOUGLAS, KEN W: Rhubarb . . . rhubarb . . . rhubarb . . . rhubarb.

HUGH: . . . why can't we have porridge, instead?

KEN W: I dunno what they're complainin' about. Rhubarb is the best thing in the world for a regular army.

KENNETH: Possibly, but they're all deserting. Our ranks are thinning out.

KEN W: How many have we got left?

KENNETH: Well, counting the advance guard, the right flank, the left flank, the centre battalions, the rear guard and the auxiliaries, we've got two. You and me. Oh, and a few camp followers.

KEN W: And they're not much good to anybody. I am undone, Hamish, I am undone! What am I going to do?

KENNETH: That's what was worrying me. I hear the Duke of Cumberland is planning to march against us. There may be a battle and who knows what the outcome will be?

*Orchestra: Dramatic chords*

HUGH: *(Duke)* I yield! I yield! I have done my best and fought bravely for many hours, but now I give in to superior strength. I'll do anything you say.

BETTY: *(Sexy royalty)* That's more like it, Cumbie. [Remember, I am the queen here.] Now go! Rid England of this Pretender.

KENNETH: Meanwhile, Charlie was retreating north. He marched by way of Carlisle, crossed the border and stopped to invest Stirling. He took his profit in dollars and hired another army. The scene was set for the bloody battle at Culloden.

KEN W: *(John Arlott[1])* And it's a bright, sunny day here at Culloden. The Duke of Cumberland has won the toss and he's setting his field. Infantrymen at silly mid-on, Cannon in the slips, and Cavalry in the gully. And here come the Scots . . .

*Grams F/X: Sound of battle: Cries: Cannon: Explosions etc. Keep under, bringing up occasionally where appropriate*

KENNETH: It was an inspiring sight, five thousand kilted Scotsmen, rushing through the tall thistles, screaming.

KEN W: *(Snide: Proclaiming)* C'mon, men! Face the enemy and charge! If that doesn't work, turn your back and charge!

KENNETH: It was an old Scottish trick, reversing the charges . . . but this time it didn't work. Cumberland led his men forward . . . the smell of powder hung over the battlefield.

HUGH: *(Duke)* Well, I can't bear a shiny nose. Forward, men! Show no mercy! After this I shall be known as The Butcher of Culloden!

KEN W: *(Self)* Mmm, you'll have to play it a lot butcher than that.

KENNETH: It was obvious that the battle was lost. Men were falling wounded on all sides. I myself was shot in the gorse.

KEN W: Nasty! Come on, Hamish, don't just lie there. Tuck your skean-dhu into the top of your stocking and we'll run for it!

*Orchestra: Hurry link*

KEN W: *(Heavy breathing)*

KENNETH: Ah, hello, Mr. Gruntfuttock!

KEN W: *(Self)* Eh? I'm the Young Pretender, you fool! Pull yourself together. We're on the run from the English.

KENNETH: Sorry . . . yes. Er . . . Ah, Flora McHaggis will hide us! This is her cottage.

*F/X: Doorbell ringing: Door opened*

BETTY: *(Scots)* Ye rang?

KENNETH: No, it was the bell. *(Horne laugh)* Oh, dear, reversing the charges . . .

KEN W: *(Snide)* My friend is wounded and delirious, as you can tell from that last joke. Is there a doctor here?

BETTY: *(Scots)* Aye, I'll call him. *(Calls)* Doctor Cameron[2]!

---

1. The greatest of all cricket commentators.
2. Dr Finlay's aged mentor, in *Dr Finlay's Casebook*.

HUGH: *(Doctor Cameron)* Aye. Bide your time while I finish this bowl o' nourishing soup. Noo then, let's have a look at ye. Umm. Have ye kept up the ante-natal exercises?

KENNETH: No.

HUGH: Why not?

KENNETH: I'm not having a baby.

HUGH: That's no reason to disregard your health. Here, take these. I want ye to swallow one three times a day.

KENNETH: He handed me a pack of lies, then left. The loyal Flora hid us in her cottage for many days. Then came that fateful knock on the door.

*F/X: Door knocked*

HUGH: *(Off: Duke)* Open up in the name of King George!

BETTY: *(Stage whisper)* It's the redcoats! Not a sound, or they'll have us entering a knobbly knees contest or something. I'll open the door and divert their suspicions . . .

*F/X: Door opened*

BETTY: I haven't seen him! He isn't here! What makes you think he's here? He isn't, I tell you, I swear it . . . he isn't here, why should he be here . . . he positively is not here, definitely not, without a shadow of doubt he is not here!

HUGH: There's a reward of thirty thousand pounds.

BETTY: Come to think of it, he's in the kitchen.

HUGH: Right! In here, men!

*F/X: Door opening*

HUGH: Don't move! So, we meet again, Bonnie Prince Charlie . . . wait a minute! You're not Charles Stuart!

KEN W: 'Course I'm not. I never said I was. I'm Charlie Fennakapan, of Friern Barnet.

*Orchestra: Play-off*

KENNETH: And on that shattering anti-climax we end this week's production, thereby avoiding hordes of irate Scotsmen from descending upon the BBC and tearing up their radio licences – last year's, of course.

Well, things are never so bad that they can't get worse, and here to prove it is England's proud rebuttal to the accusation that we're a nation of second-class boglers. Rambling Syd Rumpo.

KEN W: Hello, me dearios. This week I have nurdled in my ganderbag –

KENNETH: I say – what bad luck –

KEN W: And I have come up with an old patriotic air that dates back to the time when the British Nadgers ruled the world.

KENNETH: Good heavens – the week before last.

KEN W: Precisely. It is a stirring strain that goes after this fashion – sturdily but with a whiff of grapeshot or wintergreen – 'tis optional.

*Sings to guitar accompaniment (to tune of 'Here's A Health Unto His Majesty')*

Here's a grunge unto your artifacts,
With a fa la la la la la la.
And a munge to your digestive tracts,
With a fa la la la la la la.
And those who would not grip their
     spong,
I wish them neither groat nor gong –
Nor yet a splod to hang it on,
With a fa la la la la la la la la la –
And I think I've bodged my
     cordwangle.

Confusion to your whirdling fork.
With a fa la la la la la la la.
And agonies from rancid pork,
With a fa la la la la la la la.
And he who nurks his moulies fine,
Will find no merrier turve than mine
When I'm trundling grussetts on the
   line,
With a fa la la la la la la la la la –
And I know I've bodged my
   cordwangle – oh!

*(Applause)*

KENNETH: Thank you, Rambling Syd –
I'm sure that in your song you were
expressing what we all feel. Acute
nausea. Quite recently – in fact as
recently as the beginning of this
programme – the subject of
advertising on the BBC has cropped
up again. In general I think advertising
is a jolly good thing, so when I was
approached recently by an agency to
make a TV commercial, I agreed, and
the following morning I turned up at
their studio in Chelsea. The sign on
the door said 'Bona Ads. Commercials
for the Trade. Don't knock – Enter.'
So I didn't, and did.

*F/X: Door opened*

KENNETH: Hello, is there anybody
there?

HUGH: Oh, hello. I'm Julian and this
is my friend Sandy.

KEN W: Hello – how bona to vada
your dolly old family-size new-
improved eek again. What brings you
trolling in here?

KENNETH: I've been sent up by the
agency.

KEN W: You don't surprise me.

HUGH: What ad are you doing?

KEN W: Well, it's obviously not hair
cream.

HUGH: Oh, I don't know. It could be
for that new riah restorer. What's it
called – Fuzzitop – you know, Before
and After.

KEN W: Before and after? He looks
more like 'Instead'.

[HUGH: Perhaps he's a voice-over.

KENNETH: I beg your pardon?

HUGH: Voice-over. We've got one of
them on our list for today – we've
made the film already.

KEN W: We make it, you see, and then
afterwards we fit your voice to the
action.

KENNETH: And what is the film?

KEN W: Well, there's these chimps,
you see, and they're dressed up as
beefeaters and they're all flinging
custard at each other.

HUGH: And your voice is heard
saying, 'Ramadan's Custard Surprise
is part of Britain's heritage'.

KEN W: It's your actual prestige
advertising.] No, hold on, it's not Mr.
Horne doing that . . .

KENNETH: I should rather hope not.

HUGH: No. 'Course it isn't him. How
silly of me. It's Sir Laurence Olivier.

KEN W: Sir Laurence? You great fool,
it's Laurie Oliver – friend of
Gordon's . . .

HUGH: So it is – for a moment I
thought we'd made the big time.

KEN W: Big time, yes. 'Course, we are
still a struggling concern.

HUGH: A two-man band, you might
say.

KENNETH: There's only the two of
you?

KEN W: Yes. I do the copy and struggling and Jule is the lay-out man.

HUGH: We started as models.

KEN W: And worked our way up. You may have seen some of our work. Jule was the symbol of inner cleanliness for Malpractices Tonic Fruit Salts, wasn't you, Jule?

HUGH: I was. I was dressed in a white cloak and a cloche hat, and I used to stand there with it fizzing in me hand and say 'I am Swiftie, the tonic fruit salts kit'.

[KEN W: And then a heavenly choir would sing 'Start the day right with Malpractices'.]

HUGH: It was considered quite artistic in its day.

KENNETH: And what did you do, Sand – he said, reminding the listeners that he was still there.

KEN W: Well, I used to specialise in cigarette adverts. I was never alone in the Strand[3].

HUGH: He wasn't. [They was round him like flies.]

KEN W: And then whatever the pleasure, I completed it. I used to sit on this horse in me polo neck all butch and dominating.

HUGH: Brilliant acting, it was.

KEN W: Then I'd take a puff and gallop off.

HUGH: Lovely he was – poetry in motion.

KEN W: But then come that fateful day.

HUGH: Tell him about it.

KEN W: I don't like to.

HUGH: *(Suddenly dominating)* Go on, purge yourself! *(Suddenly normal!)* Oh, I've been dying to say that for years. Go on –

KEN W: Then came that fateful day – the government made advertising cigarettes illegal. Yes, Mr. Horne – they banned fags from TV.

HUGH: It hit him hard, Mr. Horne.

KEN W: It did – my career was finished. I tried to adapt myself – I was the voice of a pork sausage for a bit, but I could never get into the part.

HUGH: Then for a time he advertised a new girdle that was enriched with marrowbone jelly.

KEN W: But I knew my day as a sex symbol was over.

HUGH: Over, it was, so we decided to team up and open our own little bijou studioette. [Of course, we'd learned enough about advertising to grasp the essentials.

KENNETH: And what are they?

KEN W: Well, if you study commercial TV you can see for yourself what the advertisers visualise as the typical consumer.

KENNETH: Who is?

HUGH: A fat, drunken, pet owner who never takes a bath.

KENNETH: Which describes so many of us.]

KEN W: Precisely. Now what did you come here for, heartface?

KENNETH: A commercial.

KEN W: Yes, but which one?

---

3. In advertising folklore, 'You're never alone with a Strand' was the most dramatically unsuccessful commercial slogan of all time.

KENNETH: I'm not sure.

KEN W: Jule – look up your appointments.

HUGH: I am doing. Hm. Well, he could be the ome with the falcon on his wrist, driving this palone along the Andalusian seashore in a convertible.

KEN W: He <u>could</u> be – but let's face it – he's more your Darby and Joan club outing to Bexhill.

HUGH: True. Or he could be in the one where he pongs a bit and his friend says have a bath so he does and wins the all-comers quickstep.

KEN W: No, that can't be right. And he can't be in the one that's set in this posh cellar and someone says 'Ginger's back in town'.

HUGH: No. That's Reynard La Spoon.

KEN W: Of course. [Is he the new cat food, 'Soppy Cat'?

HUGH: No. 'Bona Dog Food'?

KEN W: The one with the slogan, 'Give a dog-a bona'? No.]

HUGH: Well, there's only one ad left.

KEN W: Here, show us – here, that can't be Mr. Horne, can it?

HUGH: Must be.

KEN W: All right, Mr. Horne. Right, stand here. Now hold this basin in your hand –

HUGH: Stick the chef's hat on your head.

KEN W: Your words are on this board – just look into the camera and say 'em with sincerity. Right, lights.

KENNETH: What, just like that?

HUGH: Yes, go on – you're a trouper –

KEN W: This should make advertising history. Right – roll 'em. Action.

KENNETH:

'If you are a cook,
There's no need for a book –
For this product has nothing but good in.
Whether languid or pert,
You can't beat this dessert –
It's Feldman's Banana Puddin'.'

KEN W: Fantabulosa!

*Orchestra: Play-off*

KENNETH: So don't forget, look out for my pudding. It's coming your way. Cheerio – see you, for the last time in the present series – next week.

*Orchestra: Sig. tune: Timp roll continues under*

DOUGLAS: That was *Round the Horne*, starring Kenneth Horne, with Kenneth Williams, Hugh Paddick and Betty Marsden, and music by the Max Harris Group. The script was by Barry Took, Johnnie Mortimer and Brian Cooke, and the producer was John Simmonds.

*Orchestra: Sig. tune up and out*

*(Applause)*

*Orchestra: Play out*

*(Applause)*